San Diego Christian College
2100 Greenfield Drive
El Cajon, CA 92019

GOD AND THE ART OF HAPPINESS

God and the Art of Happiness

Ellen T. Charry

WILLIAM B. EERDMANS PUBLISHING COMPANY
GRAND RAPIDS, MICHIGAN / CAMBRIDGE, U.K.

Published 2010 by

Wm. B. Eerdmans Publishing Co.

2140 Oak Industrial Drive N.E., Grand Rapids, Michigan 49505 /

P.O. Box 163, Cambridge CB3 9PU U.K.

Printed in the United States of America

16 15 14 13 12 11 10   7 6 5 4 3 2 1

Library of Congress Cataloging-in-Publication Data

Charry, Ellen T.

God and the art of happiness / Ellen T. Charry.

p.   cm.

Includes bibliographical references (p.   ) and index.

ISBN 978-0-8028-6032-3 (pbk.: alk. paper)

1. Happiness — Religious aspects — Christianity — History of doctrines.

2. Obedience — Religious aspects — Christianity. I. Title.

BV4647.J68C43 2010

241′.4 — dc22

2010010184

www.eerdmans.com

Dana

1946-2003

Contents

With Thanks

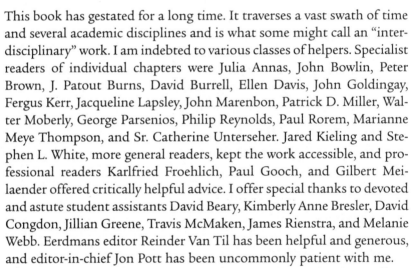

This book has gestated for a long time. It traverses a vast swath of time and several academic disciplines and is what some might call an "interdisciplinary" work. I am indebted to various classes of helpers. Specialist readers of individual chapters were Julia Annas, John Bowlin, Peter Brown, J. Patout Burns, David Burrell, Ellen Davis, John Goldingay, Fergus Kerr, Jacqueline Lapsley, John Marenbon, Patrick D. Miller, Walter Moberly, George Parsenios, Philip Reynolds, Paul Rorem, Marianne Meye Thompson, and Sr. Catherine Unterseher. Jared Kieling and Stephen L. White, more general readers, kept the work accessible, and professional readers Karlfried Froehlich, Paul Gooch, and Gilbert Meilaender offered critically helpful advice. I offer special thanks to devoted and astute student assistants David Beary, Kimberly Anne Bresler, David Congdon, Jillian Greene, Travis McMaken, James Rienstra, and Melanie Webb. Eerdmans editor Reinder Van Til has been helpful and generous, and editor-in-chief Jon Pott has been uncommonly patient with me.

I am grateful for having been awarded the Alan Richardson Fellowship at Durham University, as well as for a grant from the Evangelical Education Society of the Episcopal Church.

Beginnings of this book were delivered as the Stob Lectures at Calvin College, 2005.

This book is a contribution to an interdisciplinary project on the Pursuit of Happiness: Scientific, Theological, and Interdisciplinary Perspectives on the Love of God, Neighbor, and Self, which was established by the Center for the Study of Law and Religion at Emory University and supported by a grant from the John Templeton Foundation.

Introduction

This book is a sequel to *By the Renewing of Your Minds: The Pastoral Function of Christian Doctrine,* where I argue that classical doctrinal theology is pastorally motivated and that its end is human flourishing. At the outset of that book I note that "all the thinkers to be examined here held that knowing and loving God is the mechanism of choice for forming excellent character and promoting genuine happiness."[1] Having argued there for the pastoral function of Christian doctrine, here I review the history of the theological conversation about happiness and offer a constructive proposal for reopening it now.

My attention turned to happiness when my beloved husband and companion of forty years died an untimely and pointless death. The gap between eschatological happiness and temporal happiness needs to be addressed because people experience hardship and grief that sets them off balance, and they wonder whether they can ever be happy again in this life, or whether life amounts to no more than a vale of tears simply to be slogged through somehow in hopes of a heavenly reward.

That practical concern focused on the observation that Western Christian theology is skittish about temporal happiness, not because the tradition has not engaged the subject but because happiness has been primarily construed in terms of eschatology. If proper Christian interest is in one's ultimate destiny, attending to temporal happiness is at least beside the point, if not an affront to the Lord. Future eschatology, penned primarily by Augustine, was, of course, motivated by pas-

---

1. Ellen T. Charry, *By the Renewing of Your Minds: The Pastoral Function of Christian Doctrine* (New York: Oxford University Press, 1997), p. 18.

toral concerns, but it flourished at the expense of tending to thriving in this life.

In addition, the modern construal of truth, which was more interested in intellectual coherence than in goodness, gave rise to Protestant Scholasticism in order to systematize Protestant teaching and establish it as an academic discipline.[2] Attention turned from the formative effects of doctrines on those who professed them to how well or how poorly doctrines perform intellectually. Ultimately, this may also be to a pastoral end; but as the need for systematizing and academizing theology moved to the foreground in the seventeenth century, attention to the spiritual vocation of theology moved to the background.

Despite this shift in emphasis, the pastoral agenda of theology has not disappeared. It is quite evident in Schleiermacher and is present in Barth as well. Schleiermacher organized his *Glaubenslehre* to support piety. Barth's pastoral agenda is equally thoroughgoing, though a bit more subtle. His *Church Dogmatics* is a corrective to Calvin's *Institutes* — and behind him, Aquinas and Luther — structuring the law in a No-Yes order: first the law, then the gospel. With Calvin, the No resounded powerfully. Like Israel before him, who crossed his hands when he blessed his sons Manasseh and Ephraim to favor the younger Ephraim (Gen. 48:13-14), Barth also crossed his hands to argue for God's great Yes to humanity before the dreaded No. I am offering this book as a contribution to that important crossing of the hands — that is, for the sake of God's great Yes.

This study addresses the general concern for theology's emphasis on future eschatology at the expense of temporal happiness by proposing that happiness is a realizing eschatology with salvation centered in sanctification. Salvation is growing into the wisdom of divine love and enjoying oneself in the process. I address the concern for academic theology by asking how the doctrines shape a way of life that forms people for living their lives excellently.

The work is in two parts. Because it is not customary for theologians to speak of a Christian doctrine of happiness, the first half of the book reconstructs the main outline of the Western discussion, noting what it looked like and why and how it got lost. The second half proposes a biblical doctrine of happiness in which salvation is maturing in

2. For the development of Reformed dogmatics, see Richard A. Muller, *Prolegomena to Theology*, vol. 1, *Post-Reformation Dogmatics* (Grand Rapids: Baker, 1987), 1:63-97.

the wisdom of divine love, and concludes with examples of what that looks like in practice.

Part I, in six chapters, recovers the historical trajectory of the Western theological discussion of happiness. It begins with a review of ancient moral philosophy that is central to the theological tradition and then examines four Western theologians between the fourth and eighteenth centuries: Augustine, Boethius, Aquinas, and the Anglican divine Joseph Butler, pausing between Aquinas and Butler to account for what happened in the half millennium between them.[3] Those wishing to jump into the discussion as I carry it forward from that point may wish to begin at Part II.

Part II, in seven chapters, is the constructive proposal: asherism. It is inspired by the soteriology of Augustine's moral psychology, which he presents in the second half of his *De Trinitate*. Salvation is the healing of love that one may rest in God. Asherism works out that healing process in a life of reverent obedience to divine commands that shape character and bring moral-psychological flourishing and enhance societal well-being. Salvation is an excellent pattern of living that is personally rewarding because it advances God's intention for creation. It is a realizing eschatology.

Chapter 7 lays out asherism's theological and doctrinal foundations inspired by Augustine and drawing on the achievements of the theologians explored in Part I, particularly Aquinas and Butler. In examining selections from the Pentateuch, Psalms, and Proverbs, chapters 9 through 11 propose the biblical foundation of asherism: enjoyment of life through dynamic obedience to edifying divine commands that enable us to flourish that God may enjoy us and we enjoy God. The word "asherism" comes from the Hebrew word *asher,* frequently translated "happy" or "blessed." Its first canonical appearance is in Genesis 30:13, which records Leah's joy at the birth of a second son to her through her sexual surrogate Zilpah: "And Leah said, 'I am happy! For the women call me fortunate'; so she named him Asher" (my translation). The word appears frequently in Psalms and Proverbs.

Chapter 12 carries the conversation into the Younger Testament by

---

3. There are other, more prominent eighteenth-century figures whom I might have discussed, notably Jonathan Edwards and John Wesley. Butler, though a dark horse in this race, offers a distinctive view of happiness that will be important in constructing this particular theory of happiness.

examining happiness in the Gospel of John, which portrays it as eternal life brought by Jesus, who is sent by his Father on this dangerous mission to enlighten the world — that it may thrive. Chapter 13 treats asherist soteriology christologically: for Christians, happiness is being healed by Jesus with and for the wisdom of love. The church equips people to pursue eternal life that God may celebrate the work of his hands.

Some readers may ask why I wish to retrieve the Christian doctrine of happiness now. With affection for pieties and theologies espousing self-denial, the redemptiveness of suffering and a towering fear of hell are out of favor; Christianity is in an upbeat mood, and Christians reassure one another that God loves and encourages them in their struggles. While this book is written to address older weaknesses in Christian theology, it addresses them in order to reclaim Christianity's offering of happiness from secular captivity.

Untethered from God, there is little call to locate happiness in a spiritual-moral framework. Christian doctrine has not adequately linked piety to pleasure, thus leaving a theological gap between goodness and happiness. Happiness unlinked from goodness and linked to excitement instead has moved in to fill the space. My hope in reopening the theological discussion is to reconnect pleasure to goodness so that happiness may regain its soteriological calling, not only for Christians who may have ceded the term to the marketplace but also for those who seek spiritual flourishing. This treatment of happiness agrees with most classical ones that, while all want to be happy, many are looking in the wrong place. While all seek happiness, this offering carries a special burden for those traumatized by life's adversities — that they may be comforted and encouraged.

PART I

The State of the Question
of a Christian Doctrine of Happiness

CHAPTER 1

The Western Philosophical Heritage

The Bible provides direction for — but does not formulate — a doctrine of happiness that theologians worked from. Rather, they integrated classical moral philosophy with Christian doctrine and Scripture. Part I of this work recovers the main trajectory of the history that authorizes rethinking a Christian doctrine of happiness. Saint Augustine of Hippo (354-430) was the first major Christian thinker to reflect on happiness. Although he quotes Scripture and relies on doctrines at every turn, the orientation and important themes of Augustine's teaching on happiness are influenced by the Greco-Roman philosophical heritage in which he was trained. I will review that heritage here because it is central for most of the figures in part I.

Although the differences among them are significant, all the various ancient philosophical pathways with which Christianity competed affirmed that life ought to be lived purposefully. One should strive for the highest good that life offers: *eudaemonia* (variously translated as "well-being," "flourishing," or "happiness"). The schools disagreed about the content of what a flourishing life looks like and about how to achieve it, but they agreed that a principled life is best. A casual or haphazard life is not likely to be as successful or enjoyable as a well-crafted one. Ancient philosophies of happiness are teleological: life reaches toward an achievable goal.

In her retrieval of happiness for classical philosophy, Julia Annas makes an important distinction between the ancients and ourselves that illuminates both the classical heritage and Augustine's Christian reshaping of it. In contrast to happiness as sustained external pleasure, the ancients agreed that happiness is enjoying oneself in living morally and productively, and it is an external judgment on how one is faring at life. It is a judgment on how one orders one's life as a whole, and it is the enjoyment of that life's positive results. Both the enjoyment and the judgment are inspired by a pattern that identifies a life that is going well enough to be called a fine life — we might even say, a beautiful life. Overall, well-being comes from using oneself consistently, intentionally, and effectively, and hence it is a moral undertaking. Flourishing reflects the moral quality of one's ultimate purpose or organizing principle.[1]

Although the ancient philosophical schools agreed that a well-crafted life is better and more enjoyable than a haphazard one, they then went in different directions. Of these, Epicureanism, Stoicism, and Neo-Platonism are the most important for Augustine.[2] They influenced Lactantius, who in turn influenced Augustine, Boethius, and through them many others in the great chain of transmission.

By writing on happiness, Augustine presented Christianity as another school among the contemporary philosophies that suggested how best to live. To argue that the Christian view was the best one being offered meant that Augustine had to refute the competitors. Lactantius had previously discussed happiness, putting it on the Christian intellectual docket, so to speak. Augustine quotes and refers to representatives of the three philosophical schools (Lucretius the Epicurean, Seneca the Stoic, and Plotinus the Neo-Platonist), so we can see some of what he read in addition to what he tells us he read. Some of his knowledge of Epicureanism and Stoicism, however, was second-hand through Varro (116-27 BCE) and Cicero (106-43 BCE). He read Plotinus in translation.

In his important treatise on hermeneutics, Augustine advised Christians to plunder the Egyptians, that is, to use the liberal arts and moral philosophy as needed to establish themselves intellectually and morally.[3] He used philosophy eclectically, avoiding what was incompatible with Christian teaching and adapting what could help Christian teaching as it displaced both popular and philosophical paganism.

1. Julia Annas, *The Morality of Happiness* (Oxford: Oxford University Press, 1993), pp. 38-44.

2. For a comprehensive view of the philosophical struggle with happiness, see Nicholas White, *A Brief History of Happiness* (Oxford: Blackwell Publishing, 2006).

3. Augustine, *Teaching Christianity* ed. John E. Rotelle, trans. Edmund Hill, O.P., part I, vol. II, *The Works of St. Augustine* (Hyde Park, NY: New City Press, 1996), 2.40 (pp. 60-61).

Here is a taste of what Augustine plundered from these sources. He agreed with the Epicureans that a flourishing life must be a judgment about the whole of a life, both psychological and physical. Obversely, he thought that complete well-being is never assured: against the Epicurean denial of divine providence and judgment he asserted a strongly eschatological teaching that happiness is not completely realizable given the vicissitudes of life. He agreed with the Stoics that a happy life is a consistently virtuous one, but he disapproved of their disdain for the emotions and, like the Epicureans, disagreed that material well-being is not valuable as a good in its own right, even if it is not the highest good. From Plotinus he took the idea that happiness is a form of self-realization: realizing that our true identity lies in God and our likeness to God. Of course, Augustine meant the God of Israel, not of Plato. Again, he disagreed with Plotinus that care of the body is irrelevant to that realization, though he did not spell out how physical and spiritual well-being hold together.[4] Augustine patterned one of his most important works — *City of God* — after Lactantius's *Divine Institutes,* leaned on the latter's eschatology, and followed some of his criticisms of the Epicureans and Stoics.

Epicureanism

The teaching of Epicurus (341-270 BCE) survives partly through his own writings, but it was transmitted to the Roman world largely through the poet Lucretius (c. 94-c. 50 BCE) and Cicero (106-43 BCE). It is the most this-worldly of all the schools, and it is closest to the modern secular view. The world "is an accidental and transient product of complex atomic collisions, with no purposive origin or structure, no controlling deity."[5] It is not ordered by divinity, reason, or any overarching conception of nature. Human beings create their own life on their own terms in freedom and with self-direction.

The goal of life is to enjoy it through simple pleasures and friend-

---

4. It was only when Aristotle's ethics became known in Latin that Thomas Aquinas could attempt to explicate the relationship between physical and spiritual well-being.

5. A. A. Long and D. N. Sedley, *The Hellenistic Philosophers* (Cambridge: Cambridge University Press, 1987), p. 6.

ship. Augustine, along with most ancient philosophers, also valued friendship highly, but with Lactantius, he found Epicureanism incompatible with Christianity. He portrays two types of pleasure: kinetic pleasure that arises from movement and that we get from the body, and katastematic pleasure, which is rooted in a state of mental tranquility *(ataraxia)* and provides freedom from psychological distress, our larger and final goal. Happiness comes primarily through freedom from disturbance of the soul but also through freedom from disturbances of the body. Our basic objective in all that we do is to rid ourselves of these pains in order to achieve pleasure. This supports delayed gratification and the toleration of short-term or limited pain for a better outcome.[6]

Enjoying life's simple pleasures is often interrupted or impeded, however, by physical pain and psychological distress. We should seek to avoid these. Epicurus analyzed psychological distress, especially what arises from injustice in the world, and viewed it as stemming largely from fear of divine wrath and, when conceived as the threat of divine punishment, fear of death. But his theology did not support the rationality of such fear. He held that the divine nature is at rest, not actively watching over and involved in what occurs on earth. While Epicurus insists that the gods exist, they have at best a semisubstantial existence and are not involved with the world; thus there is no reason to fear punishment from them.

Epicureanism was not a theological system, but it did threaten Christianity, which promoted moral accountability. Because it held that the gods are not interested in us and do not respond to what we do, it appeared to undermine the moral life. Emotions were suspect in the ancient world, especially by the Stoics, and divinity was understood to be beyond emotionality. If divinity has no emotions and the gods are uninvolved in human affairs, they do not get angry, become displeased by specific forms of human behavior, or stand in moral judgment over them. Humans have nothing to fear from them; living in fear of divine punishment is simply a superstitious waste of energy. This philosophy hoped to liberate us to enjoy life's short-term sensual pleasures without anxiety or remorse. Christians, on the other hand, believed that, without a commanding voice from beyond, a voice that

---

6. Long and Sedley, *The Hellenistic Philosophers*, p. 114, citing Epicurus's *Letter to Menoeceus*.

imposes standards for the moral life, society would devolve into moral confusion.

The rejection of fear of divine punishment goes hand in hand with Epicurus's attempt to undermine another source of psychological distress: the fear of death. Epicurus thought that, although fearing a violent or painful death is quite appropriate, fearing being dead is a waste of time. If one no longer exists, death cannot be a state vulnerable to being judged. In that case, there is no need to fear divine punishment. Thus did he deny divine judgment, a position that — beginning with Lactantius — Christians would oppose. Pain and suffering from illness or torture by one's enemies will be short-lived, says Epicurus, compared with an eternity of nothing, where there will be release and peace. At death we simply cease to be, and suffering ends. Epicurus denies the immortality of the soul, reincarnation, and resurrection. Death will be for us as it was before we were born, and this is not to be feared.[7] If the gods do not entertain anger or mercy, there is no hell, no heaven, and therefore nothing to worry about. In book 3 of *On the Nature of Things*, Lucretius, by contrast, argues for the morality of the soul and that fear of death is based on a conceptual blunder, or perhaps the vain indulgence of despairing of one's own dissolution. Death ends suffering; it does not inaugurate it.[8]

Epicureanism provoked criticism, and not only from Christians. Cicero's *The Nature of the Gods* argues that Epicurus was a covert atheist because he denied divine judgment. Cicero cites this Epicurean dictum: "What is blessed and immortal neither is troubled itself, nor causes trouble to its neighbour; thus it is gripped by neither anger nor partiality, for all such attitudes are a mark of weakness."[9] Cicero says that this position is impious and socially problematic because it opens the door to moral indifference.

Nor did Epicurus's cavalier attitude sit well with Christians. The Christian apologist Lactantius (250-325 CE) had more at stake in refuting Epicurus than did Cicero. Lactantius is understandably exercised by Epicurus and responds, holding to his belief in reward and punishment for a holy or a wicked life: "[D]eath must be measured by the pre-

---

7. Lucretius in Long and Sedley, *The Hellenistic Philosophers*, p. 151.

8. Long and Sedley, *The Hellenistic Philosophers*, pp. 151-52.

9. Marcus Tullius Cicero, *The Nature of the Gods*, trans. P. G. Walsh (Oxford: Clarendon Press, 1997), 1.45 (p. 19).

ceding acts of the life."[10] The usual Christian view is that complete happiness is possible only eschatologically: heaven is God's reward for righteous living. To Lactantius, Epicurus's denial of divine providence is a direct threat to religion altogether — not only the Christian teaching on happiness, but also Christianity's doctrine of creation and its argument for moral living.[11] Lactantius responds to Epicurus's denial of divine judgment in two places. In his *Divine Institutes,* he confronts Epicurus's denial of judgment with the orderliness of the world as God's creation.[12] In *On the Anger of God,* he notes that although Epicurus says that the gods exist and are worthy of veneration, his "deist" view that they do not intervene in human affairs is incompatible with the Christian view that God genuinely cares about the world.[13] Epicurus had to be combated. Lactantius agreed with the Stoics that anger discloses an embarrassing loss of self-control. If that behavior is unbecoming for humans, how much more so is it for God! Once he eliminated anger as a divine possibility, Epicurus saw that other emotions were equally problematic and thus denied them all, taking refuge in an inert God who is totally at rest. This, Lactantius says, amounts to the conclusion that God does nothing because no actions based on emotions can be admitted of him. He insists that proper piety depends on there being both kindness and anger in God. Using Cicero's argument, he asks: If God does not reward and punish, what will restrain wickedness? Unless we believe that God sees our actions, knows our thoughts, and judges them, we will not restrain ourselves, and society will fall apart.[14] "It is therefore the fear of God alone which guards the mutual society of men, by which life itself is sustained, protected, and governed. But that fear is taken away if man is persuaded that God is

10. Lactantius, *Divine Institutes,* trans. Anthony Bowen and Peter Garnsey (Liverpool: Liverpool University Press, 2003), 3.19 (p. 206).

11. Marcia Colish questions why Lactantius spends so much time refuting Epicurus rather than Porphyry, whose thought was at the time an opponent of Christianity. Lactantius's insistence on combating Epicurus may be due to the centrality of reward and punishment in Lactantius's theology. Marcia L. Colish, *Stoicism in Christian Latin Thought through the Sixth Century,* 2 vols., *The Stoic Tradition from Antiquity to the Early Middle Ages* (New York: E. J. Brill, 1990), 2:47.

12. Lactantius, *Divine Institutes,* 3.17.1-27 (pp. 198-201).

13. Lactantius, "A Treatise on the Anger of God," in *Fathers of the Third and Fourth Centuries,* ed. A. Cleveland Coxe, Ante-Nicene Fathers (hereafter ANF) (Peabody, MA: Hendrickson, 1994), p. 262.

14. Lactantius, "Anger," p. 264.

without anger. . . ."[15] Christians would long rely on the fear of God as an instrument of social control.

Lactantius takes issue with the Epicurean view that the basic cause of unhappiness in life is fear and thus is to be eliminated. Fear has positive work to do. He might have distinguished fear of God from fear of misfortune: it would have weakened his doctrine of providence slightly, but it would have responded in part to the Epicureans' concern to eliminate what they took to be an irrational impediment to happiness. Instead, as a Christian, Lactantius argues that fear of God's anger is necessary because it suppresses vice and instills confidence that God is just and will avenge the weak. Divine anger expresses love, and thus it is both comforting and motivating. Lactantius is already operating with a high doctrine of providence that was lacking in the philosophers. This would not be lost on Augustine.

In sum, the Epicurean prescription for a happy life is to eradicate irrational fear of things that cannot really cause pain or distress in order to be free to enjoy the pleasures of life that reward one's efforts. The key is to avoid a transcendent framework in which one is morally scrutinized by God and to remember that, for the most part, physical pain will be short-lived and in death there will be no distress or suffering. Stoics and Christians found this position impious and dangerous because they were convinced that, without a deterrent to aggressive and untoward behavior, society would collapse. Stoicism offers a clear response.

Stoicism

Stoicism, especially in the later Roman form that Lactantius and Augustine received it, differs considerably from Epicureanism. It is far more theological and is morally rigorous, and thus closer to Christianity. In Stoicism the goal of life is also to flourish, which is understood as maintaining one's dignity and grace whatever may happen.

Roman Stoicism saw the universe as rational and good, designed and presided over by the divine, which it understood more personally than did early Greek Stoicism. God was "intelligent, a designing fire and a breath pervading the whole world which takes on different names owing to the alternations of the matter through which it

15. Lactantius, "Anger," p. 269.

passes."[16] God was not clearly identified, but was "an immanent, providential, rational active principle imbuing all matter," identified with nature or fate or sometimes with the world and its elements or with the traditional Greek gods interpreted symbolically.[17] The cosmos was united by the divine breath, the materialistic Stoic world-soul; it was "co-extensive with the grosser matter which forms the world's body."[18] This cosmic, unifying providence imposed a moral obligation on humans to live in accord with the basic moral structure of the universe. In this philosophy, life was oriented toward concord with the natural order.

Stoicism and Happiness

Stoicism has a prescription for happiness, but it is concerned only with spiritual or moral well-being and not with physical well-being. The Stoic sage is an ideal person, so in control of her impulses and bodily needs that she can remain unperturbed whatever may befall her. Nothing more is desired in life but consistency with one's own nature or highest calling: to flourish morally by behaving appropriately in every circumstance. If this is being happy, no external circumstance or condition whatsoever can perturb the peace of mind that results. There is no way that happiness can be misconstrued in this system as transient external pleasure. Stoic happiness lies in a principled virtuous life, and the evidence of that is *apatheia*. If virtuous living produces pleasurable feelings of self-satisfaction, so be it. However, these pleasurable feelings are not what humans seek, because happiness is the enjoyment of self that comes from the conviction that one is living a principled life of the highest integrity.

Stoicism is a rationalist cognitive therapy. Along with most of the Greek philosophical tradition, it holds that knowing the virtuous thing to do suffices for humans to be able to do it because reason is powerful enough to control the impulsive or irrational aspects of the soul. There is no inner conflict between an irrational part of the soul

---

16. Aetius in Long and Sedley, *The Hellenistic Philosophers*, p. 275.

17. Long and Sedley, *The Hellenistic Philosophers*, p. 331.

18. Long and Sedley, *The Hellenistic Philosophers*, p. 319. This may have been the source of Augustine's materialist notion of God, which plagued him until his interaction with Neo-Platonism provided resources for moving past it.

and a rational part, such as what Paul emphasizes in Romans 7 and what Lactantius and Augustine also emphasize, as we shall see. For Stoics, bad decisions come from people being ignorant of or confused about what is best for them. If we are thinking rightly, why would we act to our own detriment?[19]

The Stoic position on happiness is a formal principle of moral virtue that is in itself devoid of content. Being virtuous is happiness with living virtuously; it is enjoyment of inner beauty that comes from using oneself well based on directing one's desires rightly.

Seneca

Of special interest to this project is the treatise "On the Happy Life" *(De Beata Vita)*, by the Roman Stoic philosopher and dramatist Seneca the Younger (c. 4 BCE–65 CE), which he wrote far in advance of any Christian treatment of the subject.[20] It treats Roman Stoic ethics after Cicero generally, and the Stoic teaching on happiness specifically. One of ten ethical treatises that Seneca wrote (c. 58/9), it defends the Stoic insistence that happiness depends on virtue alone.

We do not know whether Augustine read this treatise.[21] However, he does mention Seneca approvingly several times and cites his *Against Superstitions* at length and favorably.[22] Because Seneca was popular and represented Roman Stoicism, it is likely that his thoughts on this subject would have been in the philosophical air that Augustine breathed, and would have been, if not a foil for what he wrote on the subject, at least part of the philosophical heritage behind it.

In Seneca's view, only the virtuous are happy, and these are very few — himself not included. In contrast to Lady Wisdom's indiscriminate

---

19. For an excellent presentation of Stoic ethics, see Terence H. Irwin, "Socratic Paradox and Stoic Theory," in *Companions to Ancient Thought*, vol. 4, *Ethics*, ed. Stephen Everson (New York: Cambridge University Press, 1998), pp. 151-92.

20. Lucius Annaeus Seneca, "On the Happy Life," in *Moral Essays*, ed. T. E. Page (Cambridge, MA: Harvard University Press, 1958), pp. 98-179.

21. As we anticipate later developments, it is important to note that Seneca had a clear and direct influence on John Calvin. Indeed, the first book that Calvin published was a commentary on Seneca's *On Mercy (De Clementia)*, which appeared in 1532.

22. Augustine, *City of God*, trans. Henry Bettenson (Harmondsworth, UK: Penguin Books, 1984), 6.10 (pp. 248-51).

invitation in the biblical Proverbs to all to come and eat at her table (Prov. 9), wisdom in Seneca is a rigorous intellectual and moral discipline limited to accomplished moral athletes. Serious inquirers will need to put on their moral hiking boots, because happiness is a strenuous undertaking. Seneca understands happiness to be the effect of having one's life flow well as a result of consistent moral living. The happy person is an ideal personality type who is not anxious about the future and thus is without ambition because, with virtue intact, there is nothing more to strive for. Such a one can love others without thought for reciprocity, for no one has anything to give that the sage does not already have. Thus indifferent to fortune, the morally competent are always decorous and of sound mind and judgment. Just as there is no suggestion that happiness is a feeling, there is no possibility that it is adventitious, for it is a judgment. There may be pleasure in this, but that is not the Stoic point.

While some moderns may appeal at this point to congenital personality types — some more sanguine, others more phlegmatic, and others more volatile or high-strung — the Stoics did not differentiate among the temperamental factors that one works within. Happiness is the quality of principled integrity that can be cultivated through education and discipline, and especially through control of one's vices and emotions. Wisdom is the art of indefatigable gracefulness, in season and out. Once acquired, it is a person's possession forever. One cannot later fall, lest it be discovered that one was not morally accomplished after all. The morally accomplished are highly regarded because they are generous and solicitous of others. They do not disrupt social or political life. They know better than to offer advice to others or to depend on them. Yet the sage cultivates friendships that she carries off with gentle charm.

Augustine and Christians long after him drank deeply from this well of wisdom. Personal integrity is the standard of the Christian life. Christian one-pointedness, whether it be to integrity or to humility, follows the precedent set by Stoicism.

After presenting these Stoic commonplaces in the first half of his treatise, Seneca engages the Epicurean position and its criticisms of his own position with honesty. He acknowledges that, practically speaking, the difference between Epicurean and Stoic conceptions of happiness is smaller than is often assumed. Epicurus, he says, has been distorted by those who use his philosophy to justify their lusts: "The teachings of

Epicurus are upright and holy and, if you consider them closely, austere; for his famous doctrine of pleasure is reduced to small and narrow proportions, and the rule that we lay down for virtue, this same rule he lays down for pleasure — he bids that it obey Nature."[23]

Seneca's real complaint against Epicurus is that, by allowing any direct role at all for valuing the well-being of the body — apart from its being an unintended by-product of the practice of virtue — the Epicurean view of happiness permits the unrefined to ignore the importance of virtue while claiming to follow the philosopher. Therefore, Epicurus insists on virtue, and Seneca acknowledges pleasure as a side effect of virtue, making room for genuine engagement with the issues. Posturing and polemic give way to candid reflection.

Helpful conversation begins when Seneca admits that he looks like a hypocrite to his Epicurean interlocutor. He talks about virtue alone but is a wealthy man enjoying an affluent lifestyle.[24] At this point, he admits that he is not the sage he is portraying, exclaiming a bit petulantly: "You have no right to require me to live up to my own standard. Just now I am still fashioning myself to the height of a lofty ideal; when I shall have accomplished all that I have set before me, then require me to make my actions accord with my words!"[25]

Seneca realizes the strenuousness of the Stoic ideal, but says that it is good to have goals for which to strive. He then blurts out his real opinion about the difference between the Stoic and the Epicurean: "In my [Stoic] case, if riches slip away, they will take from me nothing but themselves, while if they leave you, you will be dumbfounded, and you will feel that you have been robbed of your real self; in my eyes riches have a certain place; in yours they have the highest; in fine, I own my riches, yours own you."[26] Boethius, as we shall see later, returns to the Stoic view as he faces execution, having given himself over to valuing the gifts of fortune for much of his adult life.

At the same time, Seneca justifies his wealth from a Stoic perspec-

---

23. Seneca, "Happy Life," 13.1 (p. 131).

24. Stoicism admits an appreciation of appropriate material things, such as health and wealth, but it does not think that they contribute to our flourishing because their definition of flourishing has excluded such things. Still, the position looks strange because it renders an affluent lifestyle compatible with the belief that such things do not finally matter.

25. Seneca, "Happy Life," 24.4 (p. 163).

26. Seneca, "Happy Life," 22.5 (p. 157).

tive. Wealth is to be preferred to poverty because it makes life more comfortable, but it does not make people more virtuous and thus not happier. This expresses the tenet of Stoic ethics that goods such as health, wealth, status, and a fine reputation are to be preferred to their opposites because they make life more pleasant. However, they do not constitute happiness, for that lies in virtue alone. Wealth requires the cultivation of virtue in a way that poverty does not. Seneca does not extol poverty as good for the soul or claim that it trains the soul in virtue, as some Christians would, though he does acknowledge that poverty requires endurance. Rather, different material circumstances call for different forms of moral strength. The wealthy must show liberality, moderation, and kindness in distinguishing which requests from all sorts of charities to entertain, while they protect themselves from abuse and betrayal. The poor, on the other hand, require perseverance, patience, and fortitude simply to survive their situation. As Seneca puts it, perhaps somewhat tongue-in-cheek, "I prefer to temper my joys, rather than to stifle my sorrows."[27] Would that everyone had such an opportunity!

At this point, Seneca's account does look a bit odd. It is perhaps easy to hold, from a position of wealth and leisure, that the goods of fortune are morally neutral. Yet, without them or in the event of their loss, temptation to meanness of spirit, envy, despair, depression, or aggression may well be strong. Deprivation can be both morally and physically damaging, and Seneca does not sufficiently appreciate this. It may well be that wealth and poverty pose different moral challenges, but the stamina required to decide who will be the object of one's philanthropic gesture is quite different from what is needed to hold up psychologically when one has children to feed on an inadequate income or one's home is lost to flood, war, or some other disaster.

From Augustine's perspective, Stoicism fails on at least two points. One is that it cannot acknowledge genuine misery in this life, believing that one can be happy by one's own effort. Christianity recognizes that, given the changes and chances of this life, worldly things can't make us happy — only God can. Christianity counsels endurance of suffering with the promise of bliss in the next life.[28] The other problem with Stoicism is that it fails to acknowledge sin and its strength. Augustine will

27. Seneca, "Happy Life," 25.3 (p. 167).
28. Augustine, *City of God,* 19.1-4 (pp. 843-57).

later insist that sin is more powerful than virtue; we lack the will power to overcome it. Again, divine assistance is needed.

Contemporaneous Criticism of Stoicism

As a statesman devoted to the Roman republic, the urbane and well-educated Cicero was deeply interested in ethics. He was more sympathetic to the Stoics than to the Epicureans, though not unreservedly so. He treats the Stoic concept of happiness in the last book of the *Tusculan Disputations* and again in the third book of *On Moral Ends*.[29] The last question of the *Tusculan Disputations* is whether virtue alone suffices for happiness. Cicero's Stoic interlocutor, Marcus Brutus, holds that it does. While Cicero is sympathetic to this claim, his personal experience of the collapse of his public career in defending the republic and the death of his beloved daughter make it difficult for him to hold that happiness requires virtue alone. Happiness is more complex than that. Fear and sorrow encourage people to blame events and circumstances for their misery rather than their moral failings.

In *On Moral Ends,* Cato the Younger (95-46 BCE) speaks for the Stoics. Cicero distinguishes the Stoic position from that of the Aristotelians, who, like Epicurus, find happiness more complex a matter than virtue alone. The presentation here is more nuanced than that in the *Tusculan Disputations.* Cicero himself responds to Cato's exposition immediately. The part of Cicero's criticism that comes from personal experience is that Stoicism operates with a faulty definition of human nature. It is unrealistic to think of a person's ultimate purpose as having to do only with the well-being of the soul and not also with that of the body. In this objection Cicero shows sympathy for the Aristotelian and Epicurean perspectives: a human being's ultimate good must address the whole person — body and soul. Stoicism's category of "preferables" (health, freedom from pain, wealth, and so on), which are not "goods" strictly speaking because virtue is the only good, appears disingenuous since these preferables actually are admitted as desirable. This is why Seneca appears to be a hypocrite to his Epicurean interlocutor, and this is a common criticism — or perhaps misunderstanding — of the Stoic position. Yet Cicero is making a point not about how it works out in practice but about the formal principle on which the philosophy stands. He takes issue with the Stoic definition of happiness: his criticism is that Stoicism has defined well-being too narrowly by limiting it to virtue; living well should surely also include material well-being.

Despite these criticisms, Stoicism has the advantage of liberating happiness from dependence on fortune and shrewdness. It defines people as morally able to the extent that they know where to seek and how to define flourishing. While the Stoics turned away from Epicurus's interest in pleasure, they did not discount enjoyment of a virtuous life.

The importance of knowing where to seek happiness was not lost on early Christian theologians. They realized that many things distract us from what we ought to be about, namely, fulfilling the purpose of our life as God's creatures. Stoics gave us the idea that living consistently with who one really is at the deepest level is happiness. That deeply impressed Christian theology, in which happiness is found only in being who one is called to be by God. In the meantime, another philosophical school also took this point most seriously.

Neo-Platonism

While Stoicism left a clear imprint on Christian ethics, as we shall see with Boethius, the impact of the late antique interpretation of Plato that moderns dubbed "Neo-Platonism" was probably more significant. By the time Lactantius and Augustine were writing, Neo-Platonism was more important than the earlier philosophical schools we have examined. Plotinus (205-270 CE) writes about happiness, locating it in the context of three of his teachings that relate to the other philosophical schools we are considering.[30] (1) Plotinus defines people exclusively as souls, not as embodied souls or ensouled bodies: a "person" is immaterial and immortal like God, so that genuine communion between them is possible. This definition rejects both Aristotelian and Epicurean philosophy, which view "persons" as soul and body and claim that happi-

---

30. Paul Henry, "The Place of Plotinus in the History of Thought," in *Plotinus: The Enneads* (London: Faber & Faber, 1962).

ness pertains to both, and it follows the Stoic view that flourishing pertains to the soul alone. (2) According to Plotinus, God, like the soul, is absolutely transcendent, immaterial, and immortal. This theology combines "the Good" spelled out in Plato's *Republic* with "the One" of Parmenides: the cosmic order that ontologically connects all things. It contrasts with Stoicism's materialistic view of deity as diffused throughout the cosmos.[31] (3) Happiness or — perhaps more appropriately here — "salvation" is the soul's consciousness of its inner nature (beyond the practice of virtue) as identity with true being, that is, with God. The supreme aim of human life is "imitation of God or assimilation to the divine and to the incorporeal."[32] This rather fresh teaching rejects Stoic "salvation" as the accomplishment of virtue itself.

Plotinus wrote his most important work, *The Enneads,* during the last seven or eight years of his life. His clearest teaching on happiness is in tractates four and five of the first *Ennead*.[33] They represent a radicalized Stoic doctrine of happiness.

The first two chapters of *Ennead* 1.4 restrict happiness to humans. Plotinus bows to Aristotle and Epicurus, but his goal is to fortify the Stoic teaching on happiness on one point: while the Stoics correctly realize that happiness resides in virtue, which reason alone provides, they could not (or at least did not) identify the source of that reason.[34] The source is the absolute good at the core of the soul: "transcendent intelligible reality" is one's best and truest self.[35] As Pierre Hadot puts it, for Plotinus the "spiritual world was nothing other than the self at its deepest level. It could be reached immediately, by returning within oneself."[36] Plotinus's theology is one of self-realization: because everyone

---

31. Augustine's introduction to philosophy, through Cicero, was probably to this materialist view of God; reading Plotinus gave him an immaterialist conception of the deity that sustained his Christian thought. See Augustine, *Confessions,* trans. Henry Chadwick (Oxford: Oxford University Press, 1991), bk. 7.

32. Maria Luisa Gatti, "Plotinus: The Platonic Tradition and the Foundation of Neoplatonism," in *The Cambridge Companion to Plotinus,* ed. Lloyd P. Gerson (Cambridge: Cambridge University Press, 1999), p. 16.

33. Plotinus, *The Enneads,* ed. Paul Henry and Hans-Rudolf Schwyzer, trans. A. H. Armstrong, Loeb Classical Library (Cambridge, MA: Harvard University Press, 1966), pp. 40-55. Tractate 5 is chronologically, though not canonically, prior to tractate 4.

34. Plotinus, *Enneads,* 1.4.2 (pp. 177-79).

35. Plotinus, *Enneads,* 1.4.3 (p. 181).

36. Pierre Hadot, *Plotinus, or, the Simplicity of Vision* (Chicago: University of Chicago Press, 1993), p. 25.

has psychological access to herself or himself, those who do not achieve this self-realization are less mature.

Plotinus's transcendentalizing of the Stoic insistence on living in accordance with nature is the seat of his spirituality. Our reason is universal reason that undergirds and orders reality. The ordering principle of the cosmos is incarnate in us. We have all that we need to be happy, and if we do not actualize it, we are simply immature or ignorant of this truth; we are deceived by appearances that we ought to penetrate. Spiritual maturity is the realization that the good life is not defined by health or freedom from pain. Rather, it is defined by possessing the true and transcendent good that we not only understand but are. The transcendent is immanent. The wise go inside themselves to find ultimate goodness and actualize it. The sage's character is so secure that she is virtuous even when asleep or otherwise unconscious.[37] Enlightenment, for Plotinus, is the recognition that the soul is one with God.

Against the Aristotelians (who insisted on the importance of the goods of fortune for happiness), the Epicureans (who honored both bodily and mental pleasures), and even the Stoics (who conceded that health and freedom from pain are preferable to their opposites, though morally neutral), Plotinus utterly discounts the body: the person is spiritually constituted.[38] To define the body as an intrinsic part of the person would mandate care for it, making the body a proper focus of philosophical consideration, as do Aristotle and Epicurus. Instead, the Plotinian sage must take care of her body because it happens to accompany the soul, not because it is valuable or helpful. Plotinus advises whoever would be happy: "If he has any care for his true life, the tyranny of the body he will lay aside. While he will safeguard his bodily health, he will not wish to be wholly untried in sickness, still less never to feel pain. . . . If he should meet with pain he will pit against it the powers he holds to meet it; but pleasure and health and ease of life will not mean any increase of happiness to him nor will

---

37. Plotinus, *Enneads,* 1.4.9 (pp. 195-97).

38. Augustine appears to depart from this spiritualized anthropology when, in *The Happy Life,* he begins with the assumption that a person is both body and soul, and that the soul needs food just as the body does. Augustine, "The Happy Life," in *Augustine of Hippo: Selected Writings,* ed. Mary T. Clark, Classics of Western Spirituality (New York: Paulist Press, 1984), pp. 171-72. However, Augustine is not expressly refuting Plotinus in this early work; this balanced view is one that Augustine sustains throughout his career.

their contraries destroy or lessen it."[39] Although the Stoics agreed that there are not degrees of happiness, but that health, wealth, and status are preferable to their opposites, Plotinus held, to the contrary, that these things are not even to be preferred. Happiness resides in a person's realization that she is one with divinity, though she only realizes or experiences this in flashing moments. Happiness is living into this awareness of one's unity with eternity. It has nothing at all to do with embodied life.

Ennead 1.5 addresses a question that Cicero discusses but that I have not mentioned earlier. Can happiness increase or decrease? Plotinus is quite clear that happiness is an unchanging state of mind, not an emotion. It cannot increase by being remembered in the past or anticipated for the future.[40] In this he agrees with the Stoics. Even if some people grasp wisdom all at once while others grow into it, happiness itself is a stable all-or-nothing affair because it is about understanding who and what one is *sub specie aeternitatis*. It is about one's nature and living in accord with it. The Stoics agreed, but they did not identify that nature with eternity.

Plotinus is well aware that chronic illness can be emotionally as well as physically debilitating, but happiness — again, "salvation" is perhaps a better word here — is unaffected by that because it is of a far more stable order. Indeed, it is eternal and neither increases nor decreases but constitutes human being: the happy person participates in eternity. Stable happiness derives from the stability of eternity itself.

This proposition completes the Plotinian correction of the Stoics: they grasp that happiness is a function of virtue, but they fail to understand that to actualize our nature and truly flourish is to participate in eternity, not simply to be virtuous. The Stoics have too local an outlook. The source that they are missing is the One.

It is perhaps at this very point that Plotinus captivated Augustine, yet the latter adapted Plotinus to Christian purpose. Augustine, too, longed to rest in eternity, but he could not set aside the genuine suffering of this life, as Plotinus and the Stoics did. He sides with Epicurus, Aristotle, and Cicero in affirming that physical well-being does matter. We cannot disregard "grievous evils" such as war: "A man who experiences such evils, or even thinks about them, without heartfelt grief, is

---

39. Plotinus, *Enneads*, 1.4.14 (p. 51).
40. Augustine will also disagree with Plotinus on this point.

assuredly in a far more pitiable condition, if he thinks himself happy simply because he has lost all human feeling."[41]

Clearly, however, the fact of instinctive reactions to possibly dangerous circumstances — like a nearby falling building — indicates a natural response of fear that subsequent reasoning works to eliminate. Denying that these are emotions simply because they are short-lived and not rationally assented to seems to define away their reality. The Stoic sage is to be immune to fear and grief, but cannot necessarily prevent *unreflective* reactions. The sage can at best be immune to fear at the level of conscious reflection, not at the level of mere experience. In the above passage, Augustine insists on the importance of "heartfelt grief," indicating that he does not consider it a fleeting reaction that will quickly be held in check through rational deliberation. It is precisely the kind of enduring emotional response that the Stoics considered vicious.

Permanent well-being will finally exist only after this life. Again, we see that Plotinus, like the Stoics and even the Epicureans (but for different reasons), drive Augustine to eschatology. The latter permits and even authorizes the sage to grieve and weep at life's tragedies. Temporal suffering may be temporary, but should it turn out that one is not among the elect, it is only the beginning of one's troubles.

Plotinus's teaching on happiness is a radically otherworldly form of Stoic teaching. By discounting the body as essential to human personhood, he does away with Stoicism's tolerance for material well-being. Here there is not pleasure in the self as we saw with the Stoics and as implied in Kant. Pleasure is participation in eternity. This is quite a fresh direction in the ancient world. Happiness requires going inside oneself and discovering the divine there. It is a process of self-discovery, not the effect of transient events or hard work. This transcendental spirituality gives us a fresh angle on why Plotinus rejected the Stoic doctrine of preferences — preferring the condition of health and wealth, even if these do not define happiness. Attending to material goods at all would distract from enjoying one's identity with eternity.

---

41. Augustine, *City of God,* 19.7 (p. 862). T. H. Irwin argues that this is not an effective argument against the Stoics because they accept nonrational (emotional) responses to events that arise before one has the opportunity to think about and adopt an appropriate response, and they do not admit that these initial responses are passions. Even the sage may be caught off guard before regaining composure. Terence H. Irwin, "Augustine's Criticisms of the Stoic Theory of Passions," *Faith and Philosophy* 20, no. 4 (2003): 441.

Lactantius

Lactantius, the first Christian in this narrative, dwells in Augustine's shadow. We have already met him, but here we consider him for his own contribution to the conversation on happiness, not merely as representative of another philosophical school. He did his writing in Roman North Africa, as did Augustine, amidst the persecution of Christians under the Roman Emperors Diocletian and Galerius (303-305 CE), some fifty years before Augustine's birth.

Although Lactantius lived into the Constantinian age, his writings reflect the earlier period of Christian distress that stimulated his radical plea for religious toleration and his eloquent and passionate attack on pagan philosophy and religion — especially pagan moral philosophy.[42] Lactantius is especially interesting for us because the last book of his *Divine Institutes* is entitled "The Happy Life" *(De Beata Vita)*, though he mentions the subject much earlier in that work, and each step of his argument builds toward this finale. In addition, his *Divine Institutes* is a significant predecessor to Augustine's treatment of the doctrine of happiness in his *City of God*, as I have noted above. Here I explicate what Lactantius does with the various elements of Christian teaching as he carves out the first Christian position on happiness.

Lactantius's Christian presuppositions include the following. Against the Epicureans, he held to a strong doctrine of divine anger and judgment: God is actively involved with human beings, administering justice and mercy personally. Against the Stoics, he argued that virtue alone cannot make us happy; it is only a means to that end. Against the Epicureans — and with Plotinus — Lactantius claims that the soul is immortal.

Lactantius's teaching on happiness presupposes that, though the spirit is from God, the person is comprised of good and bad elements. Plato and Aristotle both recognized that we have nonrational desires that can direct behavior away from what we know to be the best course of action, and Saint Paul agrees. This recognizes the possibility of moral struggle that is foreign to Stoic or Plotinian psychology. The purpose of moral striving is to bring the sinful side of ourselves under the control of our nobler side. If our dark side is in control and we live this life in death and darkness, God will punish us forever in the next

---

42. Lactantius, *Divine Institutes*, bks. 1-3.

life. We fight against our sinful side by learning peaceable wisdom that will shape us and bring us on the course toward happiness, our supreme good.

Wisdom is knowledge that trains us in virtue, which is not our chief good but aims at it. God is our chief good. Virtue does not eliminate lust but enables us to tame it so that "our souls return pure and victorious to God who is their origin."[43] We have previously seen that Lactantius argues for both the immortality of the soul and the importance of divine anger in order to maintain that we face moral judgment by God at death. His teaching on happiness is correspondingly eschatological: bliss is the eternal reward for nourishing and exercising the soul well in this life. Through Augustine, this teaching has sustained millions of Christians.

The major difference between the Stoics and Lactantius is that, for the philosophers, happiness is virtue that resides in the soul while, for the Christian apologist, pain cannot be avoided in this life and even virtue is not enough to undermine its power. We cannot bring about our own happiness, no matter how hard we try and no matter how skillfully or admirably we act. Rather, happiness is finally the gift of eternal life with God.

Augustine's Debt to the Classical Heritage

Augustine inherited the ripple effects of Epicureanism, and he read Stoic and Neo-Platonic works offering philosophies that claim to promote flourishing. I have considered them in roughly chronological order, but that also turns out to be in order from the most worldly to the least worldly. Here I wish to explore their influence on Augustine and through him on Western Christianity.

The Epicurean view is that well-being is the enjoyment of embodied life and is impeded by the fear of physical suffering. Epicurus located the source of much of that fear in theology — belief in the power and wrath of god(s), the view that death is evil, that pain and suffering last, and so on — and he sought to undermine it by dismantling various theological tenets. Death is no more frightening than our state before birth, and temporal suffering passes quickly into eternal freedom from suffering at death.

---

43. Lactantius, *Divine Institutes*, 3.12.25 (p. 188).

Epicureanism points out the role of beliefs for psychological well-being. This was not lost on Augustine, who concluded that Christian beliefs in the afterlife and in the inability to overcome sin by effort alone were more pastorally useful than other beliefs offered by Stoicism, for example. However, he rejected Epicurus's slide toward atheism because eliminating the fear of divine wrath jeopardizes moral accountability.

The Stoic suggestion is to locate happiness not in the simple pleasures of daily life but in the satisfaction with self and the admiration of others that virtuous living brings. While the Stoic is of a higher mind than to be distressed by misfortune, some misfortunes — such as illness and pain — are undesirable even though it is not strictly necessary to avoid them in order to be happy. Similarly, goods like health and wealth are preferred, though unnecessary for happiness. Happiness is a moral matter, not related to material circumstances. Stoic preferences have been criticized as a kind of legal fiction to get around the strict tenets of their basic doctrine, thus rendering the Stoics hypocrites, though they are quite consistent within the structure of Stoic ethics.

Augustine absorbed some elements of Stoicism and rejected others. He embraced the philosophical task as articulated by Cicero: "the cultivation of the soul is philosophy; this pulls out vices by the roots and makes souls fit for the reception of seed, and commits to the soul and, as we may say, sows in it seed of a kind to bear the richest fruit when fully grown."[44] He took from Cicero the idea that the mind is the center of the soul and is spiritually superior to the body. His epistemology is essentially Stoic, and he used it early in his theological career in a treatise against the skeptics (or academics), who held that true knowledge is not available to the mind.[45] Augustine has confidence in the intellect. Certain knowledge is possible, he argues, because the senses take in data experienced by them and the intellect processes it and renders judgments on it.[46]

On the other hand, he rejects the Stoic doctrine of unperturbedness as being both impossible and undesirable, and he rejects Stoic approval of rational suicide. Moreover, against the Stoics, Augustine argues that although happiness requires virtue, virtue is not itself happiness.

---

44. Cicero, *Tusculan Disputations*, trans. J. E. King (Cambridge, MA: Harvard University Press, 1950), 2.5.13 (pp. 159-60).

45. Augustine, *Against the Academicians; The Teacher* (Indianapolis: Hackett, 1995).

46. Colish, *Stoicism*, p. 237.

Neo-Platonism is the most spiritual of the three ancient philosophical schools, and it influenced Augustine deeply. For the Neo-Platonist, the goal of life is spiritual depth. Salvation is the realization that one's true nature partakes of the divine. Other philosophies are looking in the wrong place. Epicurus, the Stoics, and the skeptics all consider temporal life in either its material or spiritual dimension to be significant. Plotinus thinks they are missing the point. He alone wants to transcend daily life in order to dwell with God.

Plotinian mysticism gave Augustine a cosmic framework of universal harmonious beauty within which to locate human striving. The Christian master wants to move people beyond self-preoccupation, not simply to the grandeur of the universe but to the grandeur of the God of Israel. He argues that true blessedness requires the emotional stability that comes only with enjoying God, and he agrees with Plotinus that cultivating virtue is a strategy for sharing in that stability during this life. Yet he Christianizes the Plotinian notion that happiness is the eternal vision of God by insisting on the immortality of the soul.[47]

Plotinian spiritual transformation is wrought by the soul's return to the One. Its doctrine of the spiritual life centers on ecstatic experience that yields true self-knowledge. Conversely, Aristotle and the Stoics have a strongly social dimension to their philosophies that perhaps is not clear in Plotinus. However, seeing one's life in cosmic perspective unites each life to every other ontologically and unites things at the deepest level. Augustine, too, was criticized for being too inwardly directed and insufficiently social. But that is a hasty judgment. Augustine knows that social harmony depends on morally healthy individuals. He drank deeply from the Platonist well but finally could not be satisfied there because the incarnate Christ brought God down from heaven to earth.

In conclusion, Augustine used the intellectual currents of the day selectively as he crafted a spiritually compelling Christian philosophy that was intelligible, grounded in the God of Israel, and concretized in Jesus Christ. He deftly shaped postbiblical Western Christian thought, and we will now consider his writings on happiness.

---

47. Augustine, "Letter 147: On Seeing God," in *Letters 100-155*, ed. Boniface Ramsey, *The Works of Saint Augustine: A Translation for the 21st Century* (Hyde Park, NY: New City Press, Augustinian Heritage Institute, 2003), pp. 317-49.

CHAPTER 2

Saint Augustine of Hippo

Augustine is important at the very least because he lived long enough to write more than anyone before him ever had. Late in life, he wrote a book annotating his major publications because he knew that they would shape Western civilization as Roman civilization faded.[1] As for his teaching on happiness, he warms to the philosophically standard idea that everyone wants to be happy, and he offers Christians a pathway to happiness in God because he believes that God wants us to be happy by living righteously. In order to reclaim a Christian doctrine of happiness, we must carefully consider Augustine's treatment of the theme.

Happiness is examined far less than many other themes in Augustine's work, though it threads through his massive corpus like blood vessels through the body.[2] The theme recurs in many of his works over the course of his forty-year episcopal career. We will follow his development of our theme in eight of his works spanning his entire career: *The Happy Life* (*De Beata Vita*, 386),[3] *Soliloquies* (*Soliloquia*,

1. Augustine, *The Retractations*, The Fathers of the Church, vol. 60 (Washington, DC: Catholic University of America Press, 1968).

2. Commentators include Werner Beierwaltes, *Regio Beatitudinis: Augustine's Concept of Happiness*, Saint Augustine Lecture Series: Saint Augustine and the Augustinian Tradition (Villanova, PA: Villanova University Press, 1981); Carol Harrison, *Augustine: Christian Truth and Fractured Humanity*, Christian Theology in Context (Oxford: Oxford University Press, 2000); Margaret R. Miles, "Happiness in Motion: Desire and Delight," in *In Pursuit of Happiness*, ed. Leroy S. Rouner (Notre Dame, IN: University of Notre Dame Press, 1995), pp. 38-56; Eugene TeSelle, *Augustine, the Theologian* (New York: Herder and Herder, 1970), pp. 61-73.

3. Augustine, "The Happy Life," in *Augustine of Hippo: Selected Writings*, ed. Mary T. Clark, *Classics of Western Spirituality* (New York: Paulist Press, 1984), pp. 165-93.

387),[4] *The Catholic Way of Life* (*De Moribus Ecclesiae Catholicae*, 388),[5] *On Free Will* (*De Libero Arbitrio*, 395),[6] *On Christian Teaching* (*De Doctrina Christiana*, 396, 426/7),[7] Sermon 368,[8] *Confessions* (*Confessiones*, 397-401),[9] *The Trinity* (*De Trinitate*, c. 413-15),[10] and, finally, *City of God* (*De Civitate Dei*, 427), where the theme appears in its fullest eschatological form.[11]

Shorter Works

Wisdom of God, Happiness, and Purpose in *The Happy Life*

One of Augustine's earliest works is a dialogue patterned after the classical Latin dialogues that he had studied in his youth. It forms part of a group of dialogues from his time at Cassiciacum, a retreat outside Milan, where he spent the fall of 386 while preparing for baptism the following Easter. *De Beata Vita* is his only work specifically dedicated to happiness.[12] In it he struggles through the transition from pagan philosophy to Christianity by arguing that only God makes us happy.

The Happy Life records a discussion among eight people, including Augustine, that he undertook on his thirty-second birthday (November 13, 354) and the two following days. The participants are his mother,

4. Augustine, "Soliloquies," in *Augustine: The Earlier Writings*, Library of Christian Classics (Philadelphia: Westminster, 1958), pp. 23-63.

5. Augustine, *The Catholic Way of Life*, trans. Donald Arthur Gallagher and Idella J. Gallagher, The Fathers of the Church (Washington, DC: Catholic University of America Press, 1966).

6. Augustine, "On Free Will," in *Augustine: The Earlier Writings*, pp. 102-217.

7. Augustine, *On Christian Teaching*, World's Classics (Oxford: Oxford University Press, 1997).

8. Augustine, "Sermon 368: Whoever Loves His Soul Will Lose It," in *Sermons 341-400*, ed. John E. Rotelle, *The Works of Saint Augustine: A Translation for the 21st Century* (Hyde Park, NY: New City Press, 1995), pp. 229-303.

9. Augustine, *Confessions*, trans. Henry Chadwick (Oxford: Oxford University Press, 1991).

10. Augustine, *The Trinity*, trans. Edmund Hill, *The Works of Saint Augustine: A Translation for the 21st Century* (Brooklyn, NY: New City Press, 1991).

11. Augustine, *City of God*, trans. Henry Bettenson (Harmondsworth, UK: Penguin Books, 1984).

12. Augustine scholar Etienne Gilson recognizes the centrality of this theme for Augustine's oeuvre; see Gilson, *The Christian Philosophy of Saint Augustine*, The Random House Lifetime Library (New York: Random House, 1960).

his brother, his son, two cousins, two students, and his good friend, Alypius. It reads like a set of classes, with Augustine as the teacher who asks questions of the others and offers answers in the form of speeches or lectures; he also offers encouragement for the students, and they carry the discussion where he wants it to go. The brightest member of the class is Augustine's mother, Monica. Her comments regularly turn and refocus the class in important directions.[13] Even at this early stage of Augustine's writing career, we find several themes that were to inform his teaching on happiness over the years, with tantalizing hints of ideas that would become major themes. His fecund mind worked tirelessly over decades to render important questions more precise and clear. Issues raised obliquely here — election or predestination, grace, and eschatology — would dominate his thinking down the line. But his main concern here is wisdom. In his retrospective of his life's work he tells us the point of this piece: "that the happy life is nothing else than a perfect knowledge of God."[14] All people want to be happy, and God has made this possible.

The work develops by arguing against some aspects of pagan philosophies that look for happiness in the wrong places (§§1-3). More elaborate statements of these criticisms appear at the end of his life in *City of God*, but they do not change substantially. He agrees with the Stoics and Plotinus (though he does not name them) against the Epicureans that happiness is a spiritual matter (§§7-8). Against Plotinus, he defines personhood as both spiritual and physical. Happiness comes with nourishing the soul through virtue that stabilizes the person who enjoys the consistency of self-use that comes by living righteously, not via passing sensual pleasures. Significantly, Augustine does not begrudge humans physical well-being, though he holds the intellect to be spiritually superior to the body. Bodily well-being is important because material and emotional sufferings impede happiness. Against Plotinus, Augustine defines the person as both soul and body — sustaining the Christian commitment to the goodness of creation — and he says that the former requires nourishment as the latter requires physical nourishment (§8). One does not trump the other; rather, they facilitate one another. Mate-

---

13. For a wonderful rehabilitation of Monica, see Catherine Conybeare, *The Irrational Augustine,* Oxford Early Christian Studies (Oxford: Oxford University Press, 2006), pp. 61-138.

14. Augustine, *Retractations,* p. 12.

rial goods are not bad but of only limited value because they will pass away; however, the fear of losing them is disturbing and impedes happiness (§§10-11). Wealth, for example, is often mistaken to be a primary way to happiness (§§26-27); but that sentiment is foolish and exposes a dearth of wisdom. Indeed, wisdom is what is truly wanted, and that wisdom is the wisdom of God and not the wisdom offered by any pagan philosophical school (§§28-35).

Human life is purposeful. True happiness is stable and enduring, not evanescent. Happiness lies in having something that cannot be lost or taken away (§27). The only thing that abides forever, and thus can grant a stable, happy life, is the wisdom of God made known through the Son of God (§§33-34). The eschatological focus here is not overt, though it lies just below the surface. It may be possible to enjoy God largely in this life, but that enjoyment is always limited by changing circumstances and our own moral and intellectual instability. It is simply impossible to avoid misery and suffering in this world.

The first step toward enduring happiness lies in realizing that there is a difference between a valuable and a worthless life.[15] Living fruitlessly, that is, foolishly, is a character flaw, that is, a sin.[16] At Monica's suggestion (§11), the dialogue's interlocutors identify lack of wisdom as a need — a moral defect — that they restate as a form of poverty. They search for a word to designate the opposite of such poverty, and they come up with "fullness" *(plenitudo)* (§31). Augustine works toward conceptualizing a virtuous life as abundant in good spiritual things: to be happy is to be spiritually filled with good things. This is the secret of wisdom that countermands a foolish life.

Wisdom is the key to a happy life. Heretofore, the theological themes that later would become central Augustinian concerns have been hypothetical. The christological content of wisdom surfaces in the last three sections. A short homily (§34) identifies the "supreme measure" of the wisdom of God as the Son of God (alluding to 1 Cor. 1:24). Here Augustine formulates the classic Christian doctrine of hap-

---

15. The background for virtue ethics is Aristotle's "golden mean": the notion that virtue is an intermediate measure of the soul between two extremes, both of which are vices. Augustine seems aware of this tradition but does not explicitly mention it. The idea of a mean that avoids extremes connects with the idea of stability: stable happiness is balanced between opposite extremes.

16. Note that here sin does not consist of wrong acts, but of failing to live productively — a far more dynamic category.

piness: "But what should be called wisdom except the wisdom of God? Moreover . . . that the Son of God is none other than the wisdom of God, and the Son of God is truly God. Therefore, whoever possesses God is happy. . ." (§34).

Wisdom (the Son) is begotten of the supreme measure of truth (the Father) and "to know precisely and perfectly Him through whom you are led into the truth [the Son], the nature of the truth you enjoy, and the bond [the Holy Spirit] that connects you with the Supreme Measure [the Father] . . . is unmistakably the happy life, a life which is perfect, toward which it must be presumed that, hastening, we can be led by a well-founded faith, joyful hope, and ardent love" (§35). Here, obscurely stated, is the great Trinitarian theology that would blossom in Augustine's mature work *The Trinity*. Possessing the triune God is happiness itself.

To know and possess God is to enjoy oneself. This is the most central theme of Augustine's great corpus. Enjoyment of God is the light of life. Holding fast to it is the challenge. This he realizes even at the moment of his happiest discovery, and so he concludes on a cautious note that becomes the *basso continuo* of his mature works: eschatological hope. "[A]s long as we seek and are not yet satisfied by the source itself — and to use that word, by fullness *(plenitudo)* — let us confess that we have not yet attained our measure and therefore, although we already have God's help, nevertheless we are not yet wise and happy" (§35). Although we understand all that he has led us through, and even though we already have God's help, we are not yet there. Happiness is perfectly knowing and enjoying God, who leads us into truth and connects us with himself. We can hasten toward this culmination through faith, hope, and love, Monica wisely adds, but cannot finally arrive there in this life. On that ambiguous note, the interlocutors bid one another adieu with thanks and blessing.

Here is the foundation of Augustine's doctrine of happiness, indeed, his theology *in nuce*. Happiness is knowing, loving, and enjoying God securely. For that, one must both seek and find God, and this seeking proceeds by cultivating wisdom. It is the highest end of human life. Wisdom requires virtue but is not itself virtue, for wisdom resides in God revealed in Christ. Only those who know or have God and are filled with him experience spiritual joy. All who lack knowledge and wisdom of God are foolish and unhappy by definition. Only Christians can be happy because only they lack nothing by having Christ, the wisdom of God. Augustine will develop this teaching on happiness over time, and his fundamental convictions will not change. What we will see is that the cautionary eschatological note at the end sounds louder and louder as Augustine moves through his career. Happiness is complete only in the eschaton. What happiness *is* never changes for the master, but it recedes further into the future as he ages.

This very early work has accomplished the following: all people want to be happy, and God has made this possible; humans are defined as both body and soul, implying (against the Stoics and Plotinus) that the well-being of the body is important. Further, human life is purposeful: to become wise and filled by enjoying God as much as possible in this life is to achieve our purpose, knowing that here we will never be completely safe from suffering and distress. Only those who know or have God to the fullest experience this spiritual joy. Yet, as well as we may know, love, and enjoy God in this life, happiness will never be complete until fulfilled in the *eschaton*. While being filled with the wisdom of God surfaces here early on as central to Augustine's teaching on happiness, it will eventually be eclipsed by love.

Faith and Hope in the *Soliloquies*

Augustine wrote the *Soliloquies* during the same year and at the same location that he wrote *The Happy Life*. Its two books portray a conversation Augustine conducted with himself about his intellectual and moral quest to know God and the soul. We have already seen that knowing God is happiness, and this treatise follows the same inquiry. He mentions happiness *(beatitudo)* in the extended prayer of invocation in which he addresses God as the "father of truth, father of wisdom, father of true and perfect life, father of happiness, father of goodness and beauty, father of intelligible light, father of awakening and of our illumination, father of the sign by which we are admonished to return to you."[17] This expansive vision of God that concludes with an allusion to Christ sets up the framework not only for this work, but also for his theology in general.

The *Soliloquies* add two notes to what we have seen — faith and

---

17. This author's translation of "Soliloquies," 1.2, lines 5/2-5, "Corpus Augustinianum Gissense," ed. Cornelius Mayer (Makrolog GmbH, 2000).

hope. Happiness, Augustine tells us, is the spiritual vision of God.[18] Life's sufferings realistically help us to hope for perfect happiness only in the next life, when happiness will be perfect, even if we are illuminated somewhat by the vision of God in this life.[19] The eschatological framework of happiness, associated primarily with Augustine's later work, is already in place. Until the *eschaton*, temporal life carries a limited but genuine blessedness of its own that comes from knowing the good and choosing well.[20] Although many scholars attribute the impetus of the strong eschatological drive that seems to take over Augustine's thought to his accumulated experiences as a bishop, we see it here already before he was baptized. The eschatological horizon relocates the hope for happiness to the next life, in appreciation of the real obstacles to happiness in this one.

Love and the Four Cardinal Virtues in *On the Catholic Way of Life* (388 CE)

This treatise is designed to cure the Manichees of their erroneous interpretation of the Older Testament by showing them that the two Testaments fundamentally agree. At this stage, Christianity is more an existential submission to a way of life *(mores)* than intellectual assent to a carefully worked out set of ideas, and Scripture is central to that construal. The practical import is great. Since Augustine himself had previously adopted the Manichaean way of life and belief that he now rejects, this work has autobiographical resonances. Again, the theme of the need for divine guidance appears, now with Augustine guiding people to the Catholic faith that can carry them from error into truth.

This work on Christian wisdom introduces the third great Pauline virtue, love, into Augustine's doctrine of happiness and his theology more broadly. Love in this life and the hope for the next life would fi-

---

18. Augustine, "Soliloquies," 1.6.12-3 (p. 30). Augustine wrote a full treatise on this topic in a letter to a woman named Paulina. Augustine, "Letter 147: On Seeing God," in *Letters 100-155,* ed. Boniface Ramsey, *The Works of Saint Augustine: A Translation for the 21st Century* (Hyde Park, NY: New City Press, Augustinian Heritage Institute, 2003). This basically establishes the doctrine of the vision of God as a major plank of standard Christian eschatology until the sixteenth century.

19. Augustine, "Soliloquies," 1.7.14 (pp. 31-32).

20. Augustine develops this theme in *City of God,* 19.13.

nally become the most powerful of the virtues for him. Happiness characterizes God-lovers, and loving well is the key to happiness. Augustine's distinctive elaboration of the connection between happiness and love breaks decisively with the pagan schools. It receives further refinement in book 1 of *On Christian Teaching*, which he wrote some six years later. Discussions of love and happiness often coincide. Here the obstacle to happiness is not that we do not know what brings true happiness; rather, we fail to attain what we rightly love. We flourish when we enjoy our chief good, the end for which we are made — enjoyment of God.

According to Augustine, our chief good must both stretch and satisfy us. It stretches us if it is better than we are; it satisfies us if it is something we can be confident we will not lose involuntarily, lest our happiness be undermined by worrying about its loss. Such a good is spiritually helpful by stretching us in ways that draw us closer to fulfilling our God-given end — actually improving and even perfecting us. "Better" here means greater conformity to the destiny for which God created us. In Christian terms this is greater conformity to the image of God in Christ. To become better is to become wiser. Wise teachers and models help us in this endeavor, but they will die (or be lost some other way) and we fear losing them. The only teacher, indeed, the only wisdom, that can perfect us and that we cannot lose involuntarily is God, whom we lose only by abandoning him. Therefore, ultimate happiness is becoming wiser and better by loving God.

Lacking direct knowledge of God, we must rely on Scripture and the experience of its interpreter, the church — especially its depiction of Christ, who is the Christian way to fulfill the command of Deuteronomy 6.5: "You will love the Lord your God with all your heart, with all your soul, and with all your strength." The church leads Christians to this true Teacher, who conveys to us the wisdom that is the way to perfect happiness. To love God is to follow others whom God has drawn near. Loving God means approaching him, seeking contact with him. Indeed, we want to be near those we love, for being there makes us happy. Augustine concludes: "For the better and more widely God is proclaimed, the more fervently he is loved and esteemed. And when this comes about, the human race cannot but advance surely and steadfastly toward the life of perfect happiness" (*Catholic Way of Life*, 1.14.24 [p. 22]).

Toward achieving perfect happiness, Augustine Christianizes the four cardinal virtues — self-control, courage, righteousness, prudence — as ways of stabilizing our love of God and enabling us to cling steadfastly to the truth that is God, which spiritually renews us. Spiritual strengthening enables us to let go of lesser visible goods as we become more attached to loving the highest and best good, which is invisible. We use material goods only as "needed for the necessities of life," not "as desirable for their own sake." We must use them, that is, "in the measure that [our] life and duties require with the moderation of a use rather than the passion of a lover" (1.20-21.37-39 [pp. 32-34]).

While we should use material things cautiously, we should be generous in helping our neighbors meet their material needs, because a person is defined in terms of both soul and body. Happiness requires cultivation of virtues beyond spiritual self-care because God enjoins love of neighbors, and we cannot be happy until we practice that love. Concern for bodily well-being was hinted at in *The Happy Life*, but it becomes explicit here. Love of neighbor is not only care for his or her spiritual well-being through instruction in Christian discipleship and by setting an example of righteous living; it is also care for his or her body with "food and drink, clothing and shelter, and all those things that protect the body against external blows or mishaps. For hunger and thirst, cold and heat, and every injury inflicted from without threaten the bodily health that we are now considering" (1.27.52 [pp. 41-42]).

Physical well-being is important, but Augustine does not equate it with spiritual well-being. He does not explicitly say that bad physical circumstances impede enjoyment of God by embittering the soul, for example, but neither does he espouse the position of the Stoics and Plotinus that material circumstances are irrelevant to happiness.

Confusion, Conflict, and Maturity in *On Free Will*[21]

In *The Happy Life*, Augustine argues that acquiring the wisdom of God is a key to happiness. In *Soliloquies*, he introduces the love and vision of God as attaching us to a happiness completed only after death. In *The Catholic Way of Life*, he connects loving and happiness in a distinctive

21. Augustine wrote book 1 of this work in 388; he completed books 2 and 3 in 395, by which time he was deeply concerned about sin. Hereafter, references to this work will appear in parentheses in the text.

way. Happiness is high-quality loving by means of which one extracts the best that life has to offer.

The question of happiness arises in a different context in *On Free Will*. As with *The Catholic Way of Life*, Augustine wrote it against the Manichaean view that radically separates good from evil as two competing cosmic principles. Augustine addresses happiness while discussing evil and gives us a rather different picture of the connection between love and happiness than we saw previously.

He agrees with Aristotle that everyone wants to be happy, though clearly not everyone is happy. *The Happy Life* argues that the wise locate themselves in eternal truth and thus are happy, while the foolish distance themselves from eternal truth and thus are unhappy. They lack what it takes to be happy, and this is a spiritual failing. Even though everyone wants to be happy, only those who draw near to God through Christ can be happy. Living virtuously and wisely is rewarding: it brings happiness. In this work Augustine says that to live wisely is to "rejoice in good things that are both true and certain" (1.13.29 [p. 130]). To be good is to love in a manner consistent with one's God-given nature. Living wisely is living virtuously — that is, in obedience to the self God created us to be. This is related to but not identical with the Stoic position that to be virtuous is to be aligned with "nature." Augustine, perhaps following Plotinus, treats "nature" in theological context, though he grounds his position in the doctrine of creation, a significant difference.

As opposed to the Manichees, Catholic Christianity teaches that there is only one cosmic principle: the Creator. God cannot be the author of evil because he is wholly good: "In him there is no darkness at all" (1 John 1:5). Of all the good things that God creates, human beings top the list because we alone of all the visible creatures were given the ability to love God consciously and freely. This natural endowment should enable us to avoid sin through the right exercise of our will. Here Augustine elaborates happiness in terms of loving a good will and exercising it well by willing and doing only good things (1.13.28 [p. 129]). This description seems to take a step back from the view — in *The Catholic Way of Life* — that the love in question involves loving God, not loving our own good will, when controlled by reason. "This very joy which comes from attaining this good [will], especially when it keeps the mind calm and tranquil and stable, is what we call the happy life. . ." (1.13.29 [p. 130]). On these terms, the unhappiness people experience must be voluntary: "Their wills are in such a state that unhappiness

34

must follow even against their will. So it is not inconsistent with our previous reasoning that men wish to be happy but cannot be; for all do not wish to live aright, and it is that wish that merits the happy life" (1.14.30 [p. 130]). In short, while all people say they want to be happy, their actions belie their words, for they are looking for happiness in the wrong place, as Augustine has argued before. People are confused because they mistakenly expect happiness to lie in external pleasure and ignore the deeper lasting pleasure of a life of integrity and dwelling in the goodness of God.

The point is not that people do not know what is good for them. Rather, they are conflicted, saying they want what is good while being pulled in the opposite direction. Augustine lifts up the power of sin and the role of psychological conflict in determining action noted in the previous chapter. Disobedient people are not willing to bend their wills to the unbounded good that makes us everlastingly happy, enjoying ourselves in willing the good and conforming to our God-given identity.

Book 2 of *On Free Will* elaborates the theme of *The Happy Life* — that people look for happiness in the wrong place — when Augustine introduces what will become a major concern of his mature thought: sin. Moral freedom makes sin possible by making us will badly: turning away from the self God created us to be. Thus book 2 picks up where *The Happy Life* concludes. Wisdom is a conjunction of truth and happiness, and now Augustine uses that connection to explain how people go wrong. Even though people do not agree on what wisdom is, they all seek its key components: truth and happiness. Augustine thinks that this is self-evident. Although all people seek truth and happiness, they mistakenly believe that their chief good lies in various things rather than solely in the truth that alone is the wisdom of God. They pursue different goods because they value different things, and all at some time value the wrong things. Such conduct reflects bad judgment and signals a lack of wisdom and mature knowledge of the chief good: God. This is the foolishness of the wealthy that he pointed to previously. One may want to be happy and know that living wisely is key to it, but lack the skills of wise living, chief of which is directing oneself toward God, the Father of eternal wisdom, and Christ, its earthly manifestation. "For as the soul is the whole life of the body, so is God the happy life of the soul" (2.16.41 [p. 161]). Although encouraging, Augustine again intones the eschatological emphasis of his later writing on happiness. Even though "these true and certain blessings . . . glimmer for us even now, on our still darkly shadowed way" of earthly life, we inevitably fall from eternal truth, distracted by worldly exigencies (2.26.41 [p. 161]).[22]

The third and last book of *On Free Will* tackles the difficult question of divine foreknowledge and freedom of the human will, asking whether God makes us happy or whether we make ourselves happy. Augustine wants to maintain the force of both positions, and he ultimately argues that even if God knows that one will be happy a year hence, this does not rob one of the will to happiness now. This may not be a very satisfactory answer, and Augustine later struggles with it against both Pelagius and John Cassian. He teeters on a trembling fence, fearing that any concession of power to us would undermine God's power, but also knowing that denying all power to humans would destroy moral responsibility. It is not clear that Augustine ever resolves this tension.[23] It recurs at *City of God* 19.13. It could be, however, that he used rhetorical exaggeration to encourage morality while at the same time denying all human responsibility for our eternal fate. Because the danger of human vanity is so great, we speak as though God does everything, knowing full well that we make important choices along the way.[24]

Love, Self-love, and Loving God in *On Christian Teaching*, Book 1

Book 1 of *On Christian Teaching* highlights the teleological nature of Augustine's ethics and the place of love in it. It is already clear from his works heretofore examined that we are to love God because he is the greatest good. Augustine here presses this further with respect to love

---

22. The continuities between books 2 and 3 of this work, written in 395, and *The Happy Life* suggest that there is not a sharp turn on the question of whether happiness in this life is possible or not, as suggested by Carol Harrison, *Augustine: Christian Truth and Fractured Humanity*, Christian Theology in Context (Oxford: Oxford University Press, 2000), pp. 85-86.

23. Eleonore Stump, recognizing that Augustine did not adequately resolve this problem, offers an alternative that she calls "moderate libertarianism." Stump, "Augustine on Free Will," in *The Cambridge Companion to Augustine*, ed. Eleonore Stump and Norman Kretzmann (Cambridge: Cambridge University Press, 2001), pp. 124-47.

24. I am grateful here for a comment from Kimberly Anne Bresler to this effect. See also Augustine's letter 188.7-8 in Augustine, *Letters 156-210*, ed. Boniface Ramsey, *Works of Saint Augustine: A Translation for the 21st Century* (Hyde Park, NY: New City Press, 2004), 2.3.255-56.

of self and others, where we are to love not only because we are commanded to love our neighbor as ourselves but also because our happiness lies in fulfilling our God-given destiny to rest in him. Augustine assumes that we naturally love ourselves because Scripture assumes it (Lev. 19:18; Matt. 19:19; Mark 12:31; Luke 10:27). It must be good when done properly. A problem with self-love only arises when we pursue it outside our theological identity as God's creatures whose home is him.[25] Any perceived tension among these three loves is resolved by ordering them properly.

At the outset of *On Christian Teaching*, Augustine addresses the tension between loving God with all that we are — which he read Neo-Platonically as above all things — and loving the neighbor. He distinguishes things we are to enjoy (the three persons of the Trinity) from things that we are to use for the sake of that enjoyment (everything else). We are to enjoy only God while we are to use all other things to that end (1.7-10 [pp. 9-10]).[26] Only God truly makes us happy and is enjoyable in himself and not to any further purpose. Such enjoyment of God fulfills the purpose of life. When Augustine distinguishes use from enjoyment, he is clear that things "which are to be enjoyed *[frui]* make us happy, [while] those which are to be used *[uti]* assist us and give us a boost, so to speak, as we press on toward our happiness, so that we may reach and hold fast to the things which make us happy" (1.7 [p. 9]). Happiness is having what you love when that object of love is worthy of such devotion, and only God is so worthy.

On the face of it, the distinction between enjoyment and use is offensive from the biblical perspective that calls us to love the neighbor. It also appears exploitative, as Kant implies. Oliver O'Donovan traces Augustine's evoking of the use-enjoyment distinction to argue that, though the distinction appears consistently, over time the meaning of *uti* changes until love of neighbor is a form of enjoyment of God. He identifies stages of its expansion even within this work. First, it does not rule out love of neighbor, albeit the way we love others is inferior to the way we love God. O'Donovan also notes Augustine's increasing fo-

---

25. We saw this explicitly at the end of *The Happy Life* and implicitly at the end of the prayer of invocation in *Soliloquies*.

26. For the background and meaning of the distinction between *uti* and *frui* that Augustine uses, see Oliver O'Donovan, *The Problem of Self-Love in St. Augustine* (New Haven, CT: Yale University Press, 1980); see also O'Donovan, "Usus and Fruitio in Augustine, De Doctrina Christiana I," *Journal of Theological Studies* 33 (1982): 361-97.

cus on eschatology, where all things find their end in God, suggesting that he intends to distinguish temporal from eternal things. Conceived as use for God's sake, *usus* becomes a form of love for the sake of the other's ultimate well-being, that is, for its end in God. "Our 'use' of others is *brought into the project of our need*. It serves our 'utility' in that its reference is not simply to God's goodness as such, but to our enjoyment of God's goodness." Finally, O'Donovan argues, Augustine holds that we are to love the neighbor for God's sake. In effect, over time he withdrew the manipulative categories to argue that neighbor-love is a form of enjoyment, though never without instrumental overtones.[27]

"Whoever Loves His Soul Will Lose It": Sermon 368

Amid the singular tensions now besetting Augustinian ethics, it behooves us to examine his insistence on godly self-love precisely because it sits in the gap between agapism and moral self-definition. To find a place in that awkward space, we leave *On Christian Teaching* and consider a sermon that Augustine preached to some clergy on self-love.[28] He distinguishes proper from improper self-love and urges his readers not to fear talking about proper and improper self-hatred either. The sermon is a précis of his teaching on self-love, which is an important component of his ethics.

Augustine begins with the arresting text of John 12:25: "Whoever loves his soul *(animam suam)* will lose it"; he contrasts that with Ephesians 5:29: "Nobody ever hated his own flesh *(carnem suam)*." The first text suggests to him that it is blameworthy to love oneself, while the second affirms that self-love is natural, following Leviticus 19:18 (". . . you shall love your neighbor as yourself"). If we are to hate our souls in order to live longer, as John 12.25 seems literally to advise, we must necessarily hate the body; however, Ephesians says that we do not do that.

Augustine realizes that the Johannine verse is preposterous when taken at face value, for we all love ourselves — soul and body. This verse in John, then, must be God's way of teaching us to love ourselves well. For Augustine, however, the issue is not whether we should love ourselves in order to flourish, but rather how adeptly we manage to love

---

27. O'Donovan, "Usus and Fruitio," pp. 379-83, 386, 389 (italics in original).
28. Augustine, "Sermon 368: Whoever Loves His Soul Will Lose It," pp. 229-303.

ourselves. Some attempts at self-love are only *apparently* genuine: that is, they are self-hatred disguised as self-love. Augustine grants that self-love is natural, since Scripture assumes it. If we do that badly, we destroy our life ("lose it," in John's terms). If we hate ourselves properly, we will thrive and reach eternal life. Therefore, both loving and hating ourselves well are key to flourishing.

What does this mean? Some loves are harmful while others are helpful; when we pursue helpful ones and let them push out harmful ones, better self-love will prevail. Therefore, one way to grasp the healing of the soul is to see it as learning to love oneself well. This is not in any way individualistic, antisocial, or prideful, because, for Augustine, self-love exists always in the context of comprehensive Christian identity — in relationship with God and others. There is no independent self-determined basis for self-love in Augustine. This is a point that moderns steeped in Kant's insistence on self-definition tend to forget when they read Augustine. Again, he had no notion of self-determined self-love, but only what was tempered by being a creature of God.

Augustine's sermon goes on to explain growth in good self-love to those who want to progress in their journey into God. At the lowest level, we love ourselves automatically. Even animals love themselves, which we can perceive by watching them fight for their lives and take care of themselves and their young. In this lower self-love, we are properly in solidarity with them. Yet we diverge from other animals because we also love other things. Matters become ambiguous at this point, because some of the other things we love are beneath our dignity. Loving money, for example, is fine because gold and silver are creatures of God, just as we are. We need to use them. The challenge is to love money well, thus not using it for nefarious purposes or being tormented when we lose it. Loving money inordinately is undignified, and using money unwisely is spiritually degrading. Augustine challenges us to become attached to things that are or can be used, as he puts it, at or above our own moral level. In this way, love for things as they are related to God pulls us up and heals the soul.

Scriptural support for this approach is found in the double love command of God and neighbor (Mark 12:30-31 and parallels), and Augustine assumes self-love based on Leviticus 19:18. Once he sets the order correctly — love of God, self, and neighbor in God — we can discipline love properly. Here he is not pitting self-love against love of neighbor, as happens "when [people] snatch other people's property, when they get drunk, when they make themselves the slaves of lust, when, by a variety of false slurs, they make unjust profits."[29] Loving iniquity in either self or neighbor is self-hatred; hating iniquity is proper self-love. What he does not help us understand is how we learn to love God, self, and neighbor, and how being loved helps us hone the skill of loving well.

The sermon ends with an exhortation to love well: acting justly and mercifully, shunning self-indulgence, loving friends and enemies. This is the ascent into perfect love and true happiness, in which the craving for novelty, wealth, or fame can assume a healthy rather than a pathological place.

Summary

According to Augustine, the soul is intended to enjoy God but is unstable. There is no isolated or individual soul; there is only the related one that suffers from disordered love, but that can be healed by enjoying God and others in God. Paradoxically, the instability of the soul comes from its chief strength. Love is its most powerful faculty, yet it is ambiguous: it is the means to both salvation and perdition. Augustine's account of the soul is reminiscent of Plato's famous chariot allegory in the *Phaedrus* (246a-254e); but for Augustine the charioteer is love, not reason, as it is for Plato.[30] This emphasis on love should help dispel any residual idea that Augustine is a rationalist. It is not reason that directs Augustine's horses, but love. The problem Augustine identifies is that love can be unstable, so that people are conflicted. While each person benefits from the help of friends, teachers, and ministers — and we are bidden both to seek and to offer such help — the unstable aspect of love is never brought under the full control of healthy love. That is why the self is constantly playing proper self-love and proper self-hatred against one another.

This instability of love is the greatest impediment to the training of love unto salvation. Vanity and greed are distorted forms of love that create psychological and spiritual dysfunction. Augustine realizes that the specific form this dysfunction takes depends on individual differ-

---

29. Augustine, "Sermon 368: Whoever Loves His Soul Will Lose It," p. 302.
30. Augustine, *The Trinity*, 3.1 (p. 127).

ences, but the conflicted self is a universal human experience essential to Augustine's theological psychology. Finally, he argues, divine grace is the only way that the divided soul can truly be healed. However, our ultimate reliance on God for this healing does not absolve us of the responsibility to be guided and to guide others in loving as best we can here and now.

Major Works

On Loving What We Know in *Confessions,* Book 10

The tone of the *Confessions* differs from that of Augustine's other works. It is both a philosophical exploration and a monumental prayer-drenched meditation that probes human psychology, with himself as the primary subject. He exposes good intentions as well as self-serving and self-contradictory speech and actions that inhibit well-being. He honors personal integrity where it is due and exposes foolishness in its turn. Immaturity and thoughtlessness impede the relentless quest for the truth that is God. Augustine's style here is straightforwardly philosophical yet unreservedly personal. The effect is that he draws readers into his meditation, catching them up in his personal quest, for he believes that his personal struggle to find God is paradigmatic. All want God. He has found a way forward and offers it to others.

As I have noted above, beginning with *The Catholic Way of Life,* love began replacing wisdom as the way to God and happiness in God. Book 10 of *Confessions* dramatizes that shift. Augustine's great twist on the philosophical outlook was to identify the triune God as the truth and wisdom that the philosophers sought, and to say that the way to God is through love rather than insight alone. Well-ordered love enables one to dwell in the fineness of things, their rightness and goodness, their beauty and excellence. Augustine's famous meditation on his love for God is an exemplary expression of the relationship between love and dwelling in the wisdom that is God:

> But when I love you, what do I love? It is not physical beauty or temporal glory or the brightness of light dear to earthly eyes, or the sweet melodies of all kinds of songs, or the gentle odor of flowers

and ointments and perfumes, or manna or honey, or limbs welcoming the embraces of the flesh; it is not these I love when I love my God. Yet there is a light I love, and a food, and a kind of embrace when I love my God — a light, voice, odor, food, embrace of my inner[ness], where my soul is floodlit by light which space cannot contain, where there is sound that time cannot seize, where there is a perfume which no breeze disperses, where there is a taste for food no amount of eating can lessen, and where there is a bond of union that no satiety can part. That is what I love when I love my God.[31]

Love now becomes the primary form of happiness. It is not blind love but love based on knowledge. Augustine still assumes that the search for happiness is ultimately the search for God but that search is now a quest for the ability to love deeply. His questions recognize that: Is happiness a memory so utterly forgotten as to be unrecoverable? Is it discovered by remembering something we once had, or is it a new life still unknown to us? Happiness, he concludes — as he did in *The Happy Life* — remains a form of knowledge. "My inquiry is whether this knowing is in the memory because, if it is there, we had happiness once."[32] Yet knowledge of God is not bare; it is tied to love.

As I have noted, Augustine assumes that because everyone wants to be happy, everyone must already know about it intuitively. Even desiring happiness implies some apprehension of it. Augustine believes that one can imagine states of being that one may never experience. Even if an Inuit may never experience heatstroke, he could understand what it is. Augustine believes that we can want what we have never experienced directly by imagining beauty, goodness, justice, and wisdom regardless of explicit models. He firmly believes that though we want God who escapes our grasp, God would not leave us destitute of access to him. Augustine reasons here as he did when considering loving God. Since we cannot love what we do not know, we must have some prearticulate intuitive awareness of God.[33] So it is with happiness. We

---

31. Augustine, *Confessions*, 10.6.8 (p. 183).

32. Augustine, *Confessions*, 10.20.29 (p. 196).

33. This is a major theme in Augustine's struggle to know God. The quandary comes from Plato: see Plato, "Meno," in *The Dialogues of Plato* (New York: Bantam Books, 1986). For a contemporary example of attention given to the intuitive aspect of human knowledge, see Michael Polanyi, *Personal Knowledge: Towards a Post-Critical Philosophy* (New York: Harper and Row, 1958).

cannot love what we are unacquainted with; but we do object to being unhappy, and that implies envisioning another state in which we would be happy.

Imagination includes remembering enjoyable experiences that have passed and that we long to recapture, relive, or protect from diminution or loss. We may experience enjoyment in different things, but happiness is also a function of remembering what has been. Such memories orient hope and expectation.

Augustine persistently hammers away at the theme that only enjoyment of God is true and proper joy. Only this joy is complete and everlasting. This reinforces what we have seen in earlier texts. Even if one has never tasted happiness, one can imagine it even if it is only the lifting of misery. Escape from misery suffices; no further end is expected or needed to enjoy God. For Augustine, since everyone's true identity is in God, enjoying others as they are in God is loving them for who they truly are. He has brought Plotinian thought together with enjoying the God of Israel and Jesus Christ.

Augustine concludes by returning to his insistence that, although all people say they want to be happy, not all really do: some lack the strength of character needed to admit that God alone is the only true and lasting happiness. People say that they want to be happy; they say that they want the truth and do not want to be deceived by falsehood. But they are unwilling to be convicted by the truth when it criticizes their distorted love. We saw this in *On Free Will*, but here he declares it more strongly. Augustine complains that he finds himself criticized when he preaches the truth: instead of rejoicing over it and embracing it, people love truth only when it confirms and supports them. They hate it when it accuses them because they do not want to admit that they may have followed a wrong path: "They love the truth for the light it sheds but hate it when it shows them up as being wrong."[34] People are genuinely ambivalent about it: the truth may set us free, but it is often hard to hear. This is a psychological reason why some people are unhappy. Psychological defenses guarding their way of life cannot admit a need for change. Perhaps only individuals emotionally strong enough to risk change and engage self-criticism can be open enough to new ways to make their way to a happy life. *Confessions*, then, sustains Augustine's baseline that happiness is rejoicing in lov-

---

34. Augustine, *Confessions*, 10.23.34 (p. 200).

ing God, while it adds that we intuitively recognize happiness when we experience it. This experience is stored in memory and gives hope for the future.[35]

Knowledge Serving Wisdom in *The Trinity*

Augustine worked on his great treatise on the Trinity for twenty years. In 414, the first twelve books were pirated and published by eager friends. It took him an additional five years to complete all fifteen books of this massive and intense work. Oliver O'Donovan has shown the pervasiveness of the theme of love, especially self-love, in the second half of this work; this is also where we find Augustine's most extensive moral psychology. It is a treatise on the soul's healing journey into its identity as the image of the Trinity. It elaborates the point of book 1 of *On Christian Teaching* that enjoying Father, Son, and Holy Spirit is bliss. It is a journey away from self-estrangement into the healing of the soul through the realization of its identity and destiny in God, which is accomplished by seeking the image of God in the soul that is its union with God. O'Donovan puts it sharply: "The whole enterprise takes on the lineaments of the doctrine of redemption, which, for Augustine, means the Plotinian ascent refashioned in the light of faith in Christ." The journey into God is a healing journey into one's soul, for each step deeper into God heals and strengthens love. In this journey, love of material goods loses its power as the soul is perfected in the love of God, which is perfect self-love.[36]

The particular contribution to Augustine's teaching on happiness in this work is the development of the role of faith, introduced in the *Soliloquies* and elaborated here with reference to the importance of faith in the immortality of the soul as the source of hope. All but two references to happiness occur in the second half of this work. One of these references sustains the claim made in *On Christian Teaching*, book 1, and is set in the Trinitarian terms of *On Free Will*: "[T]he fullness of our happiness, beyond which there is nothing else, is this: to enjoy God the three in

---

35. This is a clear departure from the steady-state view of Plotinus that happiness never increases or decreases. It markedly distinguishes the ancient view of happiness as grounded in virtue from the modern view grounded in evanescent feelings.

36. O'Donovan, *Self-Love*, pp. 75-92, esp. pp. 75, 82.

whose image we were made."[37] The other reference exhorts the reader: "Man ought to follow no one but God in his search for bliss, and yet he was made to perceive God . . . that we may be refashioned to the image of God; for we follow the Son by living wisely. Though we must not forget that the Father too is wisdom, just as he is light and God" (7.5 [p. 223]). This reference states the major theme that we have been following since *The Happy Life*: happiness lies in enjoying God and, as *On Christian Teaching* added, other things as they are in God. Happiness is not only christological, but fully Trinitarian.

Book 11 of *The Trinity* returns to the matter of the good will that dominated *On Free Will*. Happiness is the result of a good will, and that requires loving well.

> I am not talking about the will of man as such, which has no other final end but happiness. . . . All such wishes or willing as these have their own proper ends which are referred to the end of that wish or will by which we wish to live happily and to come to that life which is not to be referred to anything else but will be all-sufficient to the lover in itself. . . . Thus a sequence of straight wishes or wills is a ladder for those who would climb to happiness, to be negotiated by definite steps; but a skein of bent and twisted wishes or wills is a rope to bind anyone who acts so, and have him *cast into outer darkness* (Matt. 8:12). Happy then are they who in their deeds and behavior sing the *song of steps.* (11.10 [pp. 311-12])[38]

Willing is not simply a rational decision to take a certain attitude or course of action on some issue or object, as it might have seemed in *On Free Will*. In *The Trinity*, Augustine associates will with wishes and desire, and thus includes love. Augustine's ethics of desire is drenched in love; the desire for happiness is the desire for God.

Aside from these passing comments in *The Trinity*, Augustine mounts an important discussion of happiness in sections 6-12 of book 13 [pp. 347-64]. This is the second of a pair of books treating knowledge

---

37. Augustine, *The Trinity*, 1.18 (p. 77). Hereafter, references to this work will appear in parentheses in the text.

38. The "song of the steps" refers to the Psalms of ascent (120-34), so called because of their superscript that signifies going up to Jerusalem or ascending the steps of the temple. Here Augustine uses the term metaphorically to designate the soul's ascent to God, alluding to the distinction between things used for a good life in this world and God, whom alone we enjoy for his own sake and who is our eternal destiny in the next life.

and wisdom respectively, the two definitive functions of the mind. Wisdom is the higher function through which we know and reflect on God, while knowledge pertains to those parts of the mind required for managing daily life. Knowledge serves wisdom, that is, the healing of love by and in the Trinity. Indeed, the whole first part of this massive work addresses the dogmatic knowledge about the Trinity that serves the second part, Augustine's moral psychology, where wisdom and happiness come to fulfillment. This distinction harks back to Augustine's earlier insistence that worldly things are to be used in the service of eternal things, which are to be enjoyed. Because wisdom is so closely associated with happiness in his thought, this discussion is almost to be expected. The section we consider here is a classic statement of Augustine's doctrine of happiness in comparison with the positions taken by various philosophical schools that have no role for love in wisdom. The foils for Augustine here are Zeno (the founder of Stoicism), Cicero, and Epicurus; he proceeds to dispatch both Stoicism and Epicureanism in turn, elaborating on his work in *The Happy Life*.

Although all desire happiness, not all know what it is. The philosophical schools are divided. Stoics think it lies in virtue, while Epicureans see it in enjoyment of material goods. Still others (whom Augustine does not treat) locate happiness in both of these or in other things altogether. Asking whether happiness lies in virtue or in material goods suggests that happiness is an object, whereas the *Confessions* present it as a form of knowledge of God stored in memory.

The Stoics maintain that living virtuously is living happily, and they seem to think that that is relatively easy to do. It is for them a matter of knowing and willing. But Augustine has a deeper grasp of human psychology: happiness is spiritual growth, and it does advance through powers of the soul; but the four cardinal virtues, while perhaps necessary, are insufficient. Without love, that is, the ability to love well — or, rather, to love God well — the divided soul will never heal.

On the other hand, though Augustine sees moral growth as possible and desirable, his gradually strengthening doctrine of grace, which grew out of his dark reflections on sin and its social consequences, rejects the Stoic doctrine that virtue is happiness. Although doubts about achieving happiness in this life sound in his earliest work, in his mature works he plays the need for divine grace in fortissimo. The perfect *visio dei* in the next life is not only perfect understanding of God but it is perfect love of God.

A person who does not recognize his or her need for that healing, does not want it, and does not take instruction (from the church) on how to do it will never have it. For it is the church that offers the faith, hope, and love that are essential for enduring life's miseries with dignity and grace. Augustine concludes that very few people want to live happily (13.7 [p. 348]). This is a reprise of the anti-Stoic position he took in *On Free Will*. The crucial point is that the Stoics recognize only the ignorant soul and not the divided soul. They are rationalists who hold that ignorance about what is good for one is the only impediment to happiness. According to this view, it should suffice for us to explain to one another where happiness lies. Augustine is far more sophisticated, recognizing that this is a faulty psychology. He understands the power of defense mechanisms that entrench us in patterns of thought and behavior and that resist insight and change.

Next, Augustine tackles Epicureanism. He follows Cicero's argument against the Epicurean view that happiness is living in ways that one enjoys — ways that provide a maximum of personal pleasure (and a minimum of pain). Yet this course may lead to a morally bankrupt life devoid of virtue.[39] Anyone not organized around the highest good cannot be happy.

Augustine concludes that only those who have everything they want — and want nothing wrongly — can be happy (13.8 [p. 349]). The best thing to want in this life is a will to love well and desire good things in proportion to their goodness, the getting of which will make the seeker as happy as possible for as long as possible. A good will that aspires to God can bring a person near to complete happiness, but Augustine holds tenaciously to the view that life is so challenging that true happiness eludes us. Temporal happiness, then, is wanting and having what is good — righteous love of self, neighbor, material things, and all these in God — in proportion to their goodness. This requires spiritual training. "If [one] pursues such good things as are possible in this unhappy life with a sagacious, moderate, courageous, and just

---

39. It is interesting to speculate that Augustine's insistence that pleasure is only properly enjoyment of God is posed against Epicurus's idea that pleasure is also or even primarily from enjoyment of worldly pleasures such as freedom from fear of punishment. Against previous commentators who hold that the use-enjoyment distinction is of Stoic origin, O'Donovan holds that this framework is Augustine's own. O'Donovan, "Usus and Fruitio," p. 368. This view would not preclude its being an anti-Epicurean move, but there is no evidence to support the view that it is.

mind, and takes possession of them as they come his way, then even in evil circumstances he will be good, and when all evil circumstances have come to an end and all good ones have been completed he will be happy" (13.9 [p. 349]).

Life is stressful, and even the good things that we experience here are less than perfect because they are transient. Hope for good things in the next life is our only promise of secure comfort. "God is the only source of good things that will make a man happy. . . . And only when a man passes from this life to the happy life, will there really and truly be what now cannot possibly be, namely that a man lives as he would" (13.10 [p. 350]). So happiness is not a reward for trying hard in this life. Rather, the removal of spatial and temporal constraints enables perfection of the soul — one's ability to love exquisitely.

Meanwhile, the "philosophers" (here he means Stoics) think that they can construct happiness now by living as they want and avoiding what they do not want. Many people bravely fight their way to abiding high-mindedness through transitory evils, and they are happy in sustaining their integrity. Augustine dismisses this as a path merely to bravery, not to true happiness, which is the perfection of loving. The Stoic waiting patiently for happiness offers no hope. Stoicism can produce brave people, but not genuinely happy ones whose joy enriches them because, without a belief in the immortality of the soul where loving will be perfected, they have not hope, but endurance. The Stoics have nothing to hope for after life's hardships end. Those who are not presently living virtuously cannot be "happy." Finally, even virtue does not equip us to will only as we wish, for that would include avoiding the decay of the body, and no one has control over that.

Augustine thus repudiates what he thinks is the Stoic claim that happiness lies in the skill of bearing patiently what one does not want to have happen. Happiness, he argues, is not courage writ large (13.10 [p. 350]). It is ascending to or growing into God through loving him and his creatures.

It is not clear, however, that Augustine has understood Stoicism well. It is not hoping for hope when all shall be well. Its happiness is contentment with integrity for its own sake. It looks for no vindication, rest, or moral improvement that would bring satisfaction at some future time. The virtue of endurance is its own reward, so that the promise of immortality that would vindicate endurance is beside the point.

Hope for eternal enjoyment of God, and enjoyment of oneself in that enjoyment, is the bridge that Augustine claims moves one from bravery, or perhaps satisfaction with bare integrity, to a genuine anticipation of happiness in living as one would hereafter. As long as one despairs of immortality, one will seek happiness in faulty places. No one can be happy who dies against his will, and Augustine takes that to be most of us. Everyone loves life. Fearing being deprived of it, no one can live happily. This brute fact is the foundation of our craving for eternal bliss with God. And if a person does not die against his will, he cannot have been happy either. Rational suicide proclaims unhappiness, not dignity (13.11 [pp. 351-52]). Augustine concludes that it is altogether impossible for one to be genuinely happy unless that happiness is invested in wanting to remain alive in some sense. This requires faith in the immortality of the soul; here is Augustine's eschatology at full tilt.

In the concluding book 13, Augustine summarizes his discussion of happiness. Although everyone wants to be happy, not all have the faith in immortality that can purify the heart needed to attain happiness. On the contrary, only by way of something that not everybody wants — sharing in the immortality of God — can we proceed toward something that everybody does want, namely, happiness. For "many despair of ever being immortal, though no one can be happy without this. By failing to believe that they could be [immortal], they fail to live so that they can be. So faith [in immortality] is necessary if we are to obtain happiness . . . of body and soul" (13.25 [p. 364]).

The climax of this seminal work is its final book. There, toward the end of his career, Augustine returns to his starting point, the happy life promised to us in contemplation of eternal things, that is, God, "the best and happiest spirit of all" (15.6 [p. 399]). Recognizing the manifold divine attributes that are the divine life, he contains them within twelve: eternal, immortal, incorruptible, unchangeable, living, wise, powerful, beautiful, just, good, happy, and spirit. These, in turn, he reduces to three: eternal, wise, and happy; and these, again, he reduces to one: wisdom. For Augustine, all the attributes are various ways of groping toward the same truth. In concluding this work, I will come back to the attributes that characterize the divine life: goodness, beauty, happiness, and wisdom.

Capturing the verve of the divine life is essential for grasping the soteriological import of Augustine's moral psychology and is the foundation of the constructive proposal offered here. The implicit teaching on happiness in *The Trinity* is soteriological. Salvation is the healing of the soul through the slow and painful recovery of the shattered and lost image of God that we are intrinsically by the grace of creation.

Working our way incrementally through false and misleading understandings of who we are, phrased as what it means to be in the divine image, is a recovery of our spiritual homogeneity to God. It is the healing of love, of the divided self. Augustine, the therapist, brings his readers into wholeness by leading them into God. Dogmatic knowledge of God *(scientia)* moves toward spiritual knowledge of who we are in God *(sapientia).* Knowledge moves toward wisdom. He says that part 2 of *The Trinity* recapitulates part 1 psychologically, and he has been criticized for an inner-directed spirituality that lacks a social dimension. However, that is a literalist reading. While his therapy moves toward arriving at correct self-knowledge, that knowledge is also knowledge of everyone else. It is personal and public and the basis on which we genuinely help one another on the journey into God.

Oliver O'Donovan points out the pervasiveness of the theme of love, especially self-love, in the second half of *The Trinity,* where we also find Augustine's most extensive moral psychology. It is a treatise on the soul's healing journey into its self-definition as the image of the Trinity. It elaborates the point of book 1 of *On Christian Teaching* that enjoying Father, Son, and Holy Spirit is bliss. It is a journey away from self-estrangement into the healing of the soul through the realization of its identity and destiny in God, accomplished by seeking the image of God in the soul that is its union with God. O'Donovan puts it well: "The whole enterprise takes on the lineaments of the doctrine of redemption, which, for Augustine, means the Plotinian ascent refashioned in the light of faith in Christ." The journey into God is a healing journey into self, for each step deeper into God heals and strengthens love. In this journey, love of material goods loses its power as one is healed in, by, and for the love of God, which is, at the same time, perfect self-love.

The healing of love is the salvation we seek in longing to rest in God. While the moral psychology of *The Trinity* is the healing of the image and is, in its own way, a journey into sanctification, there is a sense in which the recovery of the image is the precondition for the Christian life. As in *De Beata Vita,* with its ship tossed at sea scanning the horizon for a safe harbor, the repair of the image is the end of Christian novicehood and the beginning of Christian maturity. Yet who is so foolish as to claim to have left the novitiate of this school? Augustine's therapeutic soteriology is the primary handhold for the current effort

40. O'Donovan, *Self-Love,* pp. 75-92, esp. pp. 75, 82.

to reclaim a Christian doctrine of happiness. He did not state his soteriology in terms of happiness, though for him life's goal is to enjoy God utterly. The complete healing of love may not be possible in this life, and so the proposal we make here is for a realizing eschatology in which healing is real and powerful despite its incompleteness in this life.

Augustine's therapeutic soteriology is, of course, grounded in Genesis 1:26. Ironically, he is often regarded as the theologian who set Western theology on the ground of Genesis 3. He does indeed expatiate on sin and connect it to the Fall, based on his reading of Romans 5. Yet the books of *The Trinity* that I am considering here are writings of his maturity, and they are not polemically driven, as were so many of his works. He did not ask himself whether he was a Genesis 1 theologian or a Genesis 3 theologian, and perhaps neither should we. However, it is possible to suggest that, as serious as sin is, it is located and handled within the knowledge that we are created in the divine image. Genesis 3 never impugns that most fundamental divine gift.

Ending Wretchedness in *City of God*

Book 19 of the *City of God* is Augustine's most comprehensive statement on political theory, but it is also a treatise on happiness. Indeed, the whole massive work is Augustine's final statement on the subject, and he states it in strong eschatological language that finally casts all that he has said previously about temporal happiness in a darker light. Throughout this work Augustine develops the idea of the two cities — one temporal, the other eternal. He has been hinting at this distinction since his division between what we use and what we enjoy in *On Christian Teaching*, and it recurs in other works. The terrestrial city is trying, and life is distracted from pure enjoyment of God by material needs. Hope of living without this distraction lies beyond our reach. Though we cannot enjoy God utterly and uninterruptedly, we can anticipate that we will. What makes people happy is the chief good that is enjoyable in itself alone. The chief evil is that for which other things are shunned and is shunned itself. So far, we are in territory carved out in earlier works, but Augustine adds a dire note: the supreme good leads to heaven, while the supreme evil carries us to hell's perpetual torment. This he spells out in book 21.

People philosophize because they want to know how to be happy. To this the master offers his sustained reply that only the chief good brings happiness, and that only in eternity. The philosophical schools offer false pathways, as he has said all along. Augustine follows Marcus Terentius Varro (116-27 BCE), who conveyed the three life pursuits of the ancient world: philosophy, business, and a balanced combination of these two. These are to be sought for the sake of virtue, according to Varro, and virtue is to be sought for their sake.[41] The relationship is circular.

Varro, like Augustine, defines a "person" as both body and soul.[42] The soul is more important because it partakes of eternal goods. People can be happy by cultivating the soul, but since human nature includes both soul and body, genuine happiness must involve bodily well-being also. Natural blessings care for it, but the art of conducting one's life uses these blessings as well. If one uses natural blessings badly, they become useless — even detrimental. Happy is the one who enjoys virtue together with other concrete and spiritual goods. Furthermore, the happiest person is the one who conducts life wisely. Learning wise conduct through the teaching of others can enhance happiness (19.3 [pp. 850-51]).

Still, moral effort is insufficient because even the wise do not escape bodily suffering. Augustine rejects what he takes to be the Stoic position: that virtue alone enables the wise to endure the pain of life's normal hardships with equanimity. Like Cicero, Augustine breaks with what he believes is the basic Stoic counsel of "mind over matter." Physical suffering is simply too powerful to be overcome by the joy of virtue. Augustine is affronted that the Stoics could imagine that the mentally ill and physically debilitated attain happiness in this life by their own mental effort (19.4 [p. 855]). He holds that matter matters. He recalls Cato, the Stoic who took his own life: if a "happy" life can be overtaken by evil to the point of suicide, that life is miserable, not happy, despite whatever dignity and aplomb may attend the deed (1.23 [p. 34]).[43]

---

41. Augustine, *City of God*, 9.2 (p. 847). Hereafter, references to this work will appear in parentheses in the text.

42. This may seem unremarkable, but we have seen that Plotinus would later define the person as soul only. Both Varro and Plotinus were strong influences on Augustine. On this point Augustine follows Varro, though he does pointedly say that he departs from Plotinus.

43. For a full discussion, see John M. Cooper, "Greek Philosophers on Euthanasia and Suicide," in *Reason and Emotion: Essays on Ancient Moral Psychology and Ethical Theory*, ed. John M. Cooper (Princeton, NJ: Princeton University Press, 1999), pp. 515-41.

Augustine judges rational suicide to be intolerable. The Stoics may look on it as a dignified exit when it is well timed, but Augustine sees it quite differently. Endorsement of rational suicide refuses to accept the truth that human happiness is not merely a matter of maintaining one's public reputation; ultimately, it is a hubristic refusal to embrace the reality and limitations (with all their goodness) of human life. The resolution of the problem of suffering in temporal life is not bravery; rather, it is taking pleasure in life's genuine beauty and, beyond that, hoping for uninterrupted enjoyment of eternal life with God.

Nevertheless, comfort amidst life's distress comes only by hoping for lasting future happiness won for us by Christ. Hope — not our taking refuge in the goodness of our virtue — brings comfort. We await salvation from misery and the sufferings of life born of our own and others' sinfulness. "We are beset by evils, and we have to endure them steadfastly until we reach those goods that will supply us with delight beyond the telling, and there will be nothing any longer that we are bound to endure. Such is the salvation which in the world to come will be ultimate bliss" (19.4 [p. 856]). Augustine thinks that because Stoicism lacks a doctrine of immortality, it must fall back on virtue and envision a delusory temporal happiness. His argument is that, while Stoicism commends hard moral work, Christianity offers real hope along with genuine pleasure in the beauty of the world and the blessings of God throughout life (22.24 [pp. 1070-76]). This criticism of Stoicism is revealing. Augustine is substituting the Pauline virtue of hope in eschatological bliss for the self-control and endurance that Stoics rely on.

Yet Augustine may misread Stoicism, which relies on what T. H. Irwin describes as moral "preconceptions," to which consistent adherence will result in opposing conventional intuitions.[44] These preconceptions are standards for assessing conventional ethical beliefs that lead Stoics to hold positions that seem to violate common sense. Citing Epictetus, Irwin identifies these standards: "[T]he good is beneficial and choiceworthy and . . . we must seek and pursue it in every circumstance."[45]

---

44. Terence H. Irwin, "Socratic Paradox and Stoic Theory," in *Companions to Ancient Thought,* vol. 4, *Ethics,* ed. Stephen Everson (New York: Cambridge University Press, 1998), pp. 157-59.

45. Irwin, "Stoic Theory," p. 157.

Augustine might well agree with the Stoic point of view if it is put this way; nonetheless, he is making a Christian — not a philosophical — response to Stoicism. Stoic preconceptions celebrate the truth that the mind can discern the good so that it informs one's priorities and attitudes. The theological virtues, by contrast, place faith and hope in God rather than in preconceived standards. Shift from trust in reason to trust in God is a regular Augustinian — and subsequently Christian — move. He will not abandon the classical virtues, but neither will he define happiness through them, because enjoying God is true happiness. This is a properly Christian response to Stoicism. The point is not finally that Stoicism does not work because it cultivates false bravery, but that it trusts in reason rather than in the mercy of God, which inspires hope.

Augustine offers a modest tempering of suffering from the vicissitudes of temporal life — both circumstantial and the result of sin — through the Pauline virtues. These do not bring complete temporal relief, for death is our only escape from suffering. The locus of hope here is Christ, by whom the faithful walk.[46] This anti-Stoic stance explains his rationale for emphasizing hope in immortality, the walking by faith that will be replaced by the sight of God. Faith in, hope for, and love of God provides better protection from life's vicissitudes than anything the philosophers offer.

While Augustine's understanding of sin as a relentless foe against which we are helpless is salient, the material from *City of God* that we have been exploring here sheds additional light on the great bishop's view of it. There is no body-spirit dualism here; rather, there is a realistic appraisal of the challenges with which life confronts us and the moral limits within which we are constrained. Augustine follows this discussion with a long and vivid account of life's troubles: false peace from friends who later turn against us; corrupt or inept judicial systems where the innocent are tortured and punished; language barriers that inhibit friendship; international and civil wars; loss of loved ones; spiritual death by becoming corrupt oneself; or losing all human feeling by becoming numb to it all (19.5-9 [pp. 858-64]). For Augustine, "the wretched condition of humanity in this life is the punishment for sin, and we praise God's justice in that punishment" (22.24 [p. 1070]). Tem-

46. This expands on his vision of God. See Augustine, "Letter 147: On Seeing God," pp. 317-49.

poral suffering traces back to the fount of sin, disordered love, as does eternal suffering to divine judgment.

At the same time, Augustine does not lose sight of the joy and gladness of the life graced with blessings: reproduction, the arts, agriculture, navigation, medicine, and so forth, even though these are still condemned under the guilt of sin. Virtue makes good use of these, but sin is finally stronger. Only death ends the lifelong struggle to sustain a blessed life. Heaven is utter peace in the metaphorical Jerusalem — finally. Augustine adverts to Romans 6.22: "But now that you have been freed from sin and enslaved to God, the advantage you get is sanctification. The end is eternal life" (19.11 [p. 865]). As servants of God, the saints in the celestial city are free from sin and enjoy holiness and everlasting life. Death ends suffering from the changes and chances of life, as Epicurus pointed out. Heaven completes the journey into the vision of God.

In the meantime, peace in the earthly city must be tended to, even if it cannot be perfectly achieved. Earthly life strives for internal harmony in all its parts and for emotional peace with others and God. God has given us what we need for this peace, which "consists in bodily health and soundness and in fellowship with one's kind and everything necessary to safeguard or recover this peace." If we use them well and as they were intended, "light, speech, air to breathe, water to drink, and whatever is suitable for the feeding and clothing of the body, for the care of the body and the adornment of the person" serve the penultimate goal of peace on earth (19.13 [p. 872]). Note that Augustine does not call this a "happy" life; that term is now reserved for eschatological perfection.[47] Still, a well-ordered body and mind that uses things well is a step in the right direction.

City of God 19.13 concludes with a "just deserts" exhortation. Those who use temporal goods to serve the common good "shall receive goods greater in degree and superior in kind, namely, the peace of immortality, and the glory and honour appropriate to it in a life that is eternal for the enjoyment of God and of one's neighbour in God, whereas he who wrongly uses those mortal goods shall lose them, and

47. Thomas Aquinas was to name Augustine's vision of happiness as perfect happiness. What Augustine called temporal peace, Aquinas called imperfect happiness. Augustine's rhetoric may be confusing, because in some passages he focuses on the miseries that can befall us in life, while in others he acknowledges that a pleasant life of peace and fellowship is also possible.

shall not receive the blessings of eternal life" (19.13 [p. 872]). This exhortation to human effort with the promise of eternal reward sits awkwardly with Augustine's doctrines of grace and predestination, which place all the power on God's side.[48]

Finally, we see that both the heavenly and the earthly cities are guided by love, although these end up being of different orders. Despite his sporadic defense of self-love, Augustine qualifies his support for it by noting that in the earthly city it can be degraded to the point of "contempt for God" (14.28 [p. 593]). This does not deny that self-love might not appear in a degraded form in the terrestrial city. Terrestrial harmony — both within and beyond the family — requires a well-cultivated love of God, self, and neighbor that entails the ability to use oneself artfully. Be at peace with everyone by practicing good habits: harm no one, love everyone equally, help everyone whenever possible, accept help when needed.[49] Augustine does not disjoin earthly from heavenly love but underscores the pain of life and love that he learned from experience. The city of God is also guided by love, but here love is liberated from self-centered temptations. That Augustine entertains the binary opposition between contempt for God and for self in such a facile manner perhaps contributed to the rigid monastic opposition between love of self and love of God that has haunted Western Christian thought ever since. Nevertheless, even though the form of love differs radically depending on the perspective, it remains the glue that cements life in both the terrestrial and the celestial city.

The two cities come together in *City of God* 19.17. The heavenly city, reached by pilgrimage through the earthly city, refers earthly peace to the heavenly peace that death cannot end, "for this peace is the perfectly ordered and completely harmonious fellowship in the enjoyment of God, and of each other in God" (19.17 [pp. 877-79]). Anticipation of

---

48. Augustine's doctrine of grace is usually interpreted as ruling out the freedom of the will presupposed by this paragraph. In addition to Eleonore Stump (see n. 23), see James Wetzel, "Snares of Truth: Augustine on Free Will and Predestination," in *Augustine and His Critics*, ed. Robert Dodoro and George Lawless (New York: Routledge, 2000), pp. 124-41, and Wetzel, "Predestination, Pelagianism, and Foreknowledge," in *The Cambridge Companion to Augustine*, ed. Eleonore Stump and Norman Kretzmann (Cambridge: Cambridge University Press, 2001), pp. 49-58. In addition to the passage in "On Free Will" noted above (p. 36), this paragraph confirms that Augustine moved back and forth between two positions.

49. Augustine, *Christian Teaching*, 19-24.

perfect celestial social harmony inspires the earthly pilgrimage. It is inspiring to envision heaven, where perfect love sidelines righteousness, wisdom, endurance, and self-control. Social well-being requires these virtues that Augustine had long before reinterpreted as aspects of the love of God in *The Catholic Way of Life*. The Pauline virtues prepare us for eternal bliss. In the heavenly city, the strain of cultivating faith and hope will cease, and perfect love, even though it may entail contempt for self, will prevail. Peace is the foundation of a good life here and now, and of perpetual bliss hereafter.

Until we reach the heavenly city, the most we can hope for is that God will "rule an obedient [earthly] city according to his grace, forbidding sacrifice to any . . . save himself alone; and where in consequence, the soul rules the body in all who belong to this city and obey God, where righteous people live on the basis of faith active in love" (19.23 [p. 890]). Eventually, though, earthly peace will be transcended by the longed-for eternal, heavenly peace, that ultimate peace where there will be no distorted love and where faith and hope will be unnecessary. Our nature will be healed for immortality and incorruption; it will have no perverted elements. We will then love perfectly. "There, for each and every one, this state will be eternal, and its eternity will be assured; and for that reason the peace of this blessedness, or the blessedness of this peace, will be the Supreme Good" (19.27 [p. 893]).

Assessing the Augustinian Foundation

For Augustine, happiness is the spiritual benefit of knowing, loving, and enjoying God, and loving self and others in pursuit of that goal. It is being at rest in God, as he so famously said: "Our hearts are restless until they rest in you."[50] This sentence is a window into the therapeutic soteriology he develops in the moral psychology of the second half of *De Trinitate*. It is a soteriology of ascent of sorts, but it is perhaps more accurately described as a soteriology of penetration. He calls his readers to penetrate God and themselves until they recover the unbroken image of God that they seek to return to, because God has created them for that exalted identity and the beautiful life that expresses it.

50. Augustine, *Confessions*, 3.

Augustine maintained this view, but by the end of his life he concluded that the enjoyment of life that comes with such a spiritual breakthrough is impossible to sustain — or perhaps even achieve. He backed off from the hope that happiness is sustainable in this life. The graphic portrait of the final judgment and hell at the end of *City of God* introduces the theistic sanction as the primary "stick" that presses people into virtuous living. For the constructive purpose of my proposal in this book, however, Augustine's belief in a therapeutic soteriology that heals the broken image of God in us holds promise. It has not been often discussed, though it deserves to be heard. So I will give voice to it here.

In *The Happy Life,* Augustine embraced an optimistic Christian Platonism, with a soteriology of ascent that discovers oneself in God and is healed by that discovery. *De Trinitate* does not abandon that hope but tempers it in the face of the changes and chances of life and the reality of death. Augustine becomes more eschatological in order to avoid offering false hope of temporal happiness.

The bookends of the materials examined here suggest that Augustine was sympathetic both to an ascent soteriology and to the eschatological vision of God as the only enduring happiness. For him, "we can" and "we can't" integrated a cautiously hopeful soteriology of healing ascent with an enthusiastic hope for complete happiness through the vision of God by and by. The two positions are not finally in tension.

In Augustine's earliest work, the Plotinian soteriology of ascent comes to the fore. Happiness lies in discerning the wisdom of God that seems to be available through Christian philosophizing in *The Happy Life.* He is teaching us how to seek God, and he is really doing that for and with us.[51] We can find happiness by looking in the right place. Even at the end of this dialogue, however, the Plotinian thrust is considerably qualified at several points. First, Augustine acknowledges that God is christologically qualified, so that we cannot reach the full measure of divine wisdom except through Christ, the wisdom of God (§34). In the next section (§35) he urges us to seek and thirst after God "with recently opened eyes" that have now been turned to the light — an allusion to Plato's analogy of the cave — to "find every perfection in

---

51. He uses the same technique in *Confessions,* in the second half of *The Trinity,* and in other shorter works.

its entirety." So, even though it is christologically qualified, ascent soteriology is still firmly in place. We can find happiness if we look in the right place. Then comes the "but":

> But as long as we seek and are not yet satisfied by the source itself — and to use that word, by fullness — let us confess that we have not yet attained our measure and therefore, although we already have God's help, nevertheless we are not yet wise and happy. This, therefore, is the complete satisfaction of souls, that is, the happy life: to know precisely and perfectly him through whom you are led into the truth, the nature of the truth you enjoy, and the bond that connects you with the supreme measure.[52]

Although he urges us to seek the source of the perfect measure of divine wisdom through Christ, "we seek and are not yet satisfied." His emphasis on grace, which seems to stop ascent soteriology dead in its tracks, is already in place: "we already have God's help. . . ." Then comes the clincher: "[N]evertheless we are not yet wise and happy," and we will not be until we have perfect knowledge of Christ. Since we already know Christ, the source of happiness in this life, the implication is that we will know him perfectly only in the next life. The soteriology is one of ascent, but ascent through knowing Christ enabled by divine grace. Even that knowledge is at best only partially possible in this life, if not finally theoretical altogether, for the *visio dei* is only perfect in the celestial city.

In the last four books of his last work, *City of God,* Augustine's eschatology is fully unfurled in the final judgment, where the saved experience precisely the bliss suggested at the end of *The Happy Life,* and the lost suffer eternal punishment in hell. Even at the end of his life he affirms the soteriology of ascent offered cryptically in *The Happy Life.* The explanation is worth quoting in full:

> For "God knows those who belong to him" (2 Tim. 2:19), and "all those who are led by God's Spirit are the sons of God" (Rom. 8:14)

---

52. Augustine, *The Happy Life,* p. 193. The rhetorical use of this triplet — know the source (Christ) perfectly, the nature of this truth, and the bond that connects you to Christ — is precisely the way he will develop the doctrine of the Trinity where the bond is the Holy Spirit, who is the love that binds the Father and the Son together. In *The Trinity,* Augustine's soteriology revolves around our being in the image of God. Since that is adumbrated here, it is reasonable to suggest that the "bond" of the end of *The Happy Life* is our thirsting love for God.

but they are sons by grace, not by nature; for God's only Son by nature was made the Son of Man for us by compassion, so that we who by nature are sons of men might become sons of God through him by grace. He, as we know, while continuing changeless, took our nature to himself from us so that in that nature he might take us to himself; and while retaining his divinity he became partaker of our weakness. His purpose was that we should be changed for the better, and by participation in his immortality and his righteousness should lose our condition of sinfulness and mortality, and should retain the good that he did while in our nature, perfected by the supreme good in the goodness of his nature. For just as we have descended to this evil state through one man who sinned, so through one man (who is also God) who justifies us we shall ascend to that height of goodness. And yet no one should be confident that he has passed over from the one state to the other, until he has arrived where there will be no more temptation — until he has achieved that peace which is his aim in the many varied struggles of this present warfare, in which "the desires of the body oppose the spirit, and the spirit fights against the body's desires" (Gal. 5:17). (21.15 [pp. 992-93])

Salvation reconstructs the happiness that existed before the Fall, and that again will be in heaven, where the temptation to sin — that struggle of the self against itself — will end and we will achieve perfect rest in God. To ascend is to transcend this inner struggle and find peace in God.

The consistency of vision between these two passages suggests that Augustine's understanding of happiness — indeed, his soteriology — did not change significantly over time, though he nuanced it in various ways and emphasized different themes. From the previous passage, the note of caution in the early work may be read in a strong sense suggesting that, as persuasive as the dialogue may be, it is constructing a theoretical vision of happiness that is only experienced after terrestrial life is done. In other words, he was cautious about terrestrial happiness all along. He did not take that to mean that we cannot be healed, as if the most that we might hope for is relief from the fear that God truly hates us on account of sin. His doctrine of happiness remains hopeful that we can have and enjoy what we seek and be healed by that enjoyment. It is cautious in that it discourages high expectations of persistent flourishing as life proceeds.

Perhaps the most distinctive feature of Augustine's doctrine of happiness is that it heals the soul. It is a christologically grounded eschatological theory of happiness that is salvific. To be healed is to be happy. If we cannot be happy in this life, it is because we cannot be *fully* healed here — not that we cannot be healed here at all. The soul's rest in God is its healing. Augustine experienced that rest and was inebriated by it. Yet he was unable to luxuriate in it continually, and thus he hoped for the time when he would be able to do so.

At the same time, Augustine believes that the incarnation is an instrument of healing. In becoming human, God takes us into his healing goodness. Salvation is completely the work of God in Christ through grace, and we are genuinely healed of the defect. Or, as Augustine puts it, God changes us back to what or how he intended us to be from the beginning: at peace with ourselves, others, God — and perhaps today we can add, the earth — perfected by his goodness, wisdom, and truth. It seems that the incarnation is itself a source of genuine healing in this life. For if it were not, it would be at best an announcement of salvation that cannot be had. Augustine seems to suggest that happiness is not just that we enjoy seeking God, but that his goodness, wisdom, and beauty actually do heal us to the extent that we know, love, and enjoy him. So he encourages us sotto voce and discourages us aloud. Perhaps this is at least part of the reason why Augustine is still so fascinating to read 1500 years after his entrance into perfect happiness, when he stopped worrying abut the spiritual well-being of the church.

Augustine's eschatological word on happiness has been more strongly heard by the theological tradition than has his cautious acknowledgment of temporal happiness. The hope of eternal happiness sustains us as we endure the miseries of life. The strongly noetic character of his final word, combined with its clearly eschatological emphasis, discouraged the later tradition from thinking about actual terrestrial happiness. This is the gap that asherism seeks to close.

At the same time, the moral psychology of *De Trinitate* is a theological framework for reclaiming happiness as the journey into God that heals the broken image that makes one whole. That ascent is made possible by the triune God, in whose image we are made and who makes himself known in the incarnation of Christ and the descent of the Holy Spirit, the economy of salvation.

While Augustine grounds the main thrust of Western theology, his work on happiness was not influential until the high Middle Ages. Between him and Thomas Aquinas comes Boethius, a tragic character best known for his *Consolation of Philosophy*. From a modern perspective, this sixth-century work is philosophical rather than theological, though the distinction is anachronistic. It is the next building block in the pursuit of Christian doctrines of happiness.

CHAPTER 3

Anicius Manlius Severinus Boethius

From the magisterial Augustine we turn to a tragic contributor to Christian thought. The philosophy of Anicius Manlius Severinus Boethius (c. 482–c. 525) formed a transition in the West from late antiquity into the Middle Ages. His most important work, *The Consolation of Philosophy,* is a poignant philosophical theodicy that he wrote in prison while he was awaiting execution.

Consolation's authority comes from its setting. There is no strong reason to suspect that it is a literary fiction. It agrees with Augustine that God is happiness and that, in locating happiness in divine goodness, one is able to achieve one's "homeland," where negative conditions cannot harm us. The word "homeland," for Boethius, does not refer to the life after this one; rather, it means philosophical clarity. His theodicy, unlike Augustine's, is not primarily eschatological; however, also unlike Augustine, he makes his argument in purely philosophical terms without reference to Christ or the Trinity. Philosophy is an urgent, practical matter: its message is that happiness is divine goodness from which we come and to which, philosophy reminds us, we are to return. It is a soteriology of ascent that rests in — that is, becomes — God, the good itself. This is similar to Augustine, but it does not rely on revelation, because philosophy suffices. People suffering unjustly are sad because they are confused about happiness.

A biographical note is in order. Boethius was a gifted and well-trained intellectual, himself of noble birth, and he married into a most noble and virtuous Roman family of the day. Then, by his own account, he was imprisoned for treason. He tells us in *Consolation* how, inspired by Plato and Cicero, he served his country as best he could.[1] He had served Emperor Theodoric as sole consul, a prestigious though not a powerful position, and later as master of offices in the Ravenna court, which was a powerful position. His two sons were named consuls at a young age, indicating the honor and respect his family was accorded.

In 523-524, the Roman senator Albinus was accused of having written insultingly of King Theodoric to the Emperor of Constantinople (Albinus was informed on by Theodoric's private secretary), and the king charged Albinus with treason. Boethius believed Albinus to be innocent and spoke on his behalf. Theodoric took this amiss, believing that Boethius and the senate were conspiring to overthrow him. He had Boethius arrested along with Albinus, imprisoned, and condemned to death — without the right of being able to testify in his own defense. His execution can be dated to about 525.

Boethius wrote *The Consolation of Philosophy* from his prison cell in Pavia, some thirty-five miles south of Milan. In this dialogue between the Prisoner and Philosophy, Boethius portrays himself. He invites us to watch him, condemned to death for a political offense he did not commit, teaching himself to regain his composure about what is happening to him.

This work is shocking to liberal sensibilities that urge acting aggressively on behalf of those who suffer injustice. The author has a completely different agenda: to bring us to God, the only safe haven in adversity. We know what true happiness is when it is conceived within this stronger framework, and when we accept our circumstances. The argument is Stoic when it argues that virtue is its own reward, but is ultimately Neo-Platonic, because it argues that true happiness is recognizing our true nature in the divine goodness. *Consolation* takes the form of a Platonic dialogue between the author's projected prison persona and Philosophy, who is portrayed as a feisty woman. A biblically attuned reader may see in her an aggressive version of the Lady Wisdom in Proverbs, who draws the condemned prisoner out of self-pity and into spiritual composure through her interrogation and prodding.

As is standard in ancient literature, *Consolation* argues that the happiness that we all want escapes our grasp because we often seek it in the wrong things. This is anti-Epicurean: happiness is not found in any

---

1. Boethius, *Consolation of Philosophy*, trans. P. G. Walsh (Oxford: Clarendon Press, 1999), 9-11; 1.4.

worldly goods. One commentator denies that *Consolation* is an ethical treatise, suggesting instead that it is designed simply to console the unfortunate.[2] It may not formally constitute a system of ethics in the modern sense, but it is moral exhortation urging that God is the source of our true identity and happiness. It offers an alternative value structure for thinking about how one's life is going.

The *consolatio* genre of literature is not always as confrontational as Boethius's is; usually they were moral exhortations that took the form of letters written to an individual on the occasion of some grievous event that has occurred in the person's life.[3] They were not designed to comfort, lest they countenance self-pity.[4] They urge the person to get on with life. All of the exhortations chastised people who were indulging their grief rather than appreciating what they had and still have to move forward with life.

Boethius's *Consolation* is unusual in that the author exhorts himself! It stings modern readers because it offers no comfort, only challenge. Its treatment of happiness chastises the prisoner's desire for comfort as well as the rage for justice. Ancient moralists were bold and had high standards.

Literary Concerns

Boethius's *Consolation* is a multilayered, multiform work that is fascinating in its ambiguities and intriguing in its agenda.[5] It is not typical

2. Wendy Raudenbush Olmsted, "Philosophical Inquiry and Religious Transformation in Boethius's *Consolation of Philosophy* and Augustine's *Confessions*," *Journal of Religion* 69, no. 1 (1989): 29.

3. Seneca wrote three *consolatios*: to Marcia on the death of her son, to Polybius on the death of his brother, and to Helvia, his mother, on the event of his own exile. Lucius Annaeus Seneca, in *Seneca: Moral Essays II*, ed. John William Basore, Loeb Classical Library (London: William Heinemann, 1932), pp. 2-97, 356-415, 416-89. Chrysostom wrote two *consolatios* to his friend Theodore when the latter left the monastic life to take up worldly interests, a move that Chrysostom saw as calamitous. John Chrysostom, "Letters to Theodore after His Fall," in *Chrysostom*, ed. Philip Schaff, *NPNF* (Peabody, MA: Hendrickson, 1994), pp. 91-116.

4. Perhaps this is why John Chrysostom graciously waited some time before sending his *consolatio* to a young widow exhorting her to desist from grief. "Letter to a Young Widow," in Schaff, *Chrysostom*, p. 121.

5. Much scholarship on this work focuses on its formal aspects and their derivation from or imitation of earlier authors. Scholarship over the last 25 years has sought to

of philosophy, but rather a literary experiment that combines styles, genres, and points of view not often brought together.[6] But, it is frustrating in that it does not answer all the questions it raises.[7] It is staged as a dialogue between the prisoner, Boethius, and the figure of Philosophy. Her long prose speeches are interspersed with the prisoner's comments or answers to her questions. The speeches are interspersed with poetry, written in various meters and of varying lengths, which either restate the message of the prose section or offer some spicy tidbit to top it off. Many of them use Greek mythology to illustrate the philosophical point metaphorically. Much has been written about this unusual blend of literary forms.[8]

Until his arrest, Boethius's plan had been to harmonize Plato and Aristotle. Perhaps in the *Consolation* he was harmonizing philosophy, which had a bad reputation in some quarters, with poetry, which had a bad reputation in others, since the latter was often a bawdy form of crass entertainment and mythology that was criticized for lacking moral depth. By writing refined, philosophically sophisticated poetry, Boethius showed that poetry could assist philosophy in a moral pursuit.[9] Philosophy, he seems to be saying, need not be dull and tedious, titillating only effete minds. It is medicine for the wicked and hope for the suffering.

Consolation has elements that parallel Augustine's *Confessions* in its autobiographical — though not first-person — form and some aspects of its style.[10] It also resonates with other ancient consolatory literature,

---

combat an earlier view that the *Consolation* was little more than a pastiche garnered from Boethius's erudition, but showing little ingenuity. Currently there is more interest in what Boethius is doing in this work — rhetorically, linguistically, and philosophically.

6. For more on the blend of forms that Boethius uses, see John Marenbon, *Boethius*, Great Medieval Thinkers (Oxford: Oxford University Press, 2003), 97-99.

7. Joel C. Relihan and William Earnshaw Heise, *The Prisoner's Philosophy: Life and Death in Boethius's Consolation* (Notre Dame, IN: University of Notre Dame Press, 2007), p. 129. Relihan is persuaded that *Consolation* is a form of Menippean Satire, an ancient style of rhapsodic prose satire used by Lucian, Varro, and Seneca. Relihan sees *Consolation* as a Christian argument on the limits of pagan philosophy. Joel C. Relihan, *Ancient Menippean Satire* (Baltimore: Johns Hopkins University Press, 1993).

8. See, esp., Anna Crabbe, "Literary Design in the *De Consolatione Philosophiae*," in *Boethius*, ed. Margaret Gibson (Oxford: Basil Blackwell, 1981), pp. 251-56.

9. Crabbe, "Literary Design," pp. 256-57.

10. See John R. Fortin, "The Nature of Consolation in 'The Consolation of Philosophy,'" *American Catholic Philosophical Quarterly* 78, no. 2 (2004): 305-7.

as I have noted, though here the drama is heightened because the author is consoling himself over his own downfall and anticipated execution, following Plato's view that philosophy is preparation for death.

There is also scholarly debate as to whether the *Consolation* actually consoles. Anna Crabbe has noted that Boethius is not as emotionally gripping a writer as Augustine is, and the treatise shifts from being biographically fascinating to being an abstract work of professional philosophy.[11] Not much emotional consolation there. John Fortin suggests that Philosophy and the prisoner console each other, she by admitting that he has a right to reject her advice by the end, he by wanting to learn from her — even though the prisoner ultimately rejects her invitation to forsake public life for the contemplation of God.[12] Does *consolatio* mean to console in the modern sense of offering sympathy? If it is rather moral exhortation, and consolation is to help the addressee adjust to her circumstance, and even to chide her, the criticism is off-point.

While the work has occasioned scholarly speculation about how best to interpret it, most writers agree with Henry Chadwick and Anna Crabbe that, all things considered, it is a Neo-Platonic exhortation, an exhortation to embrace God as the means to overcome sentimental self-pity — that is, the way from grief to happiness. By extension, it is written at least as much to encourage his readers as to encourage the author himself. For what could be a more compelling sight, then or now, than talking about happiness while awaiting unjust execution? It is Boethius's biographical setting that focuses the reader's attention on his philosophy.

As an exhortation to embrace God, the source of all goodness, the *Consolation* is clearly a Neo-Platonic work, but it is not as clearly a Christian work.[13] The absence of explicit biblical references and doctrinal al-

11. Crabbe, "Literary Design," pp. 256-57.

12. Fortin, "Nature of Consolation," pp. 293-307. John Marenbon agrees with Relihan that the work satirizes philosophy itself, for the character Philosophy fails to console, even though she remains a highly respected figure throughout. Marenbon concludes that the parts of the work do not fit together well or resolve the theodicy that it purportedly raises. He also agrees with Relihan that it should rather be read as a work patterned after Menippean Satire. Marenbon, *Boethius,* pp. 160-63. See also Edmund Reiss, *Boethius,* Twayne's World Authors Series (Boston: Twayne, 1982), p. 143. However, if *consolatio* does not intend to comfort but to inspire, to exhort, and even chastise, the judgment on philosophy's failure is inappropriate.

13. Henry Chadwick observes that, although it is not an explicitly Christian work, it rests on Christian assumptions. See Henry Chadwick, *Boethius: The Consolations of Music,*

lusions makes it clearly a work of natural theology, quite apart from revelation — a point he advertises in the last chapter of book 3, where he summarizes Philosophy's teaching on happiness.[14] The prisoner points out that Philosophy has made all these arguments "without adducing any external authority; rather you drew on the internal proofs proper to our discipline [philosophy]." She responds: "You need not be surprised if we have mounted arguments not adduced from outside, but set within the boundaries of our subject, for you have learnt from Plato's prescription that the language we use must be germane to the species [discipline] under discussion."[15] Whatever the strictures of disciplinary purity, Boethius's failure to mention revelation or to cite Scripture is nevertheless odd to biblically attuned ears. Perhaps he had lost his faith. Or perhaps he was writing for those remaining pagans who had resisted the Christian gospel. We do not know. Several interests are evident here. One is the justice of God seen in light of the injustice in the world; this implies the personal God of Jews and Christians, which neither the Stoic nor the Neo-Platonist pagans have. Another interest is in the issue of human freedom, which also concerned Augustine. A third, which overlaps with Augustine's concern in the second half of the *De Trinitate,* is to enable us to realize our true self in God, the source of true happiness.[16]

Logic, Theology, and Philosophy (Oxford: Clarendon Press, 1981), pp. 251-52. Boethius's explicitly Christian theological writings are in several tractates on the Trinity and the incarnation and a summary of the Catholic faith. Boethius, *The Theological Tractates and the Consolation of Philosophy,* trans. E. K. Rand, H. F. Stewart, and S. J. Tester (Cambridge, MA: Harvard University Press, 1973), pp. 2-129. Etienne Gilson, cited by Edmund Reiss, notes the similarity of Boethius's theology to Augustine's and comments that, even when Boethius speaks only as a philosopher, he thinks as a Christian. Reiss, *Boethius,* p. 149.

14. It is noteworthy that his theological tractates do not cite Scripture either.

15. Boethius, *Consolation,* 3.12.25 (pp. 68-69). Hereafter, references to this work will appear in parentheses in the text.

16. Relihan, noting the obscurity of the author's motives for writing the piece, proposes "a genuine religious honesty." Relihan and Heise, *Prisoner's Philosophy,* p. 130. He sees Boethius rejecting philosophy and retreating to the prayer that the divine will be done on earth as in heaven. Yet Philosophy herself is the first to offer prayer in the work, so there is no clear bifurcation between religion and philosophy.

Dramatis Personae

Philosophy is the protagonist in the work. She appears suddenly in the prisoner's cell as a goddess who has "come gliding down from the pole of heaven" (1.3.7 [p. 7]). She is a tattered goddess: her dress is torn, but it bears in its damaged gossamer folds the key to wisdom. At the bottom of her dress, the Greek letter *pi* is appliquéd, while at the top is a *theta*; a ladder connects the two letters (1.1.4 [p. 4]). The symbolism is regularly interpreted as an invitation to move from practical to theoretical (philosophical) concerns, as the work itself does from books 1-3 to books 4 and 5. Because there was not an appeals process in the Roman judicial system, philosophical reflection is Boethius's only way to rise above the indignity of his circumstances. But the *theta* may stand not only for *theoria* but also for *theos*. The ladder connecting the two letters, echoing as far back as the biblical patriarch Jacob, calls the maligned to rise to heaven and find comfort there. The ambiguous *theta* makes the work all the more intriguing.

Though she has been tattered by misuse from bad philosophers, Philosophy is a feisty goddess.[17] She presents herself as a physician or therapist with medicines and tonics that the prisoner must swallow. At no point in the dialogue does she offer him a single word of sympathy. She is relentlessly confrontational. She and the prisoner get into quarrels in which the stakes are high: she is arguing for the prisoner to turn to God as the only true and lasting happiness, while he is holding his miserable ground, lamenting his demise.

The author is an amazing yet hazy character. At certain points he carries us into a dense and unsatisfying philosophical conversation; at other times he obstructs conversation. Yet he seems always ready to learn from the woman who has taught him what he knows to be valuable. He is by turns spirited and passive, finally allowing himself to be pulled out of self-pity into a deep reverence for God before retreating into prayer. Boethius models a conversion from puerile vanity to moral and spiritual adulthood. Ultimately, he is also a kenotic character, will-

---

17. Philosophy complains that "Epicureans, Stoics, and the other schools each did their best to plunder [Plato's] inheritance. As part of their loot they dragged me off, in spite of my protestations and resistance; they ripped apart the gown that I had woven with my own hands and they departed bearing the ragged pieces which they had torn from me" (1.3.7 [p. 7]).

ing to empty himself emotionally for what he is persuaded will be true consolation and hope at the last.

Boethius portrays himself as both a prisoner of the king and a patient of the physician Philosophy.[18] His role as patient grows as he struggles against and then succumbs to Philosophy's invitation to clear up his confusion. As appropriate, I will refer to him as prisoner and patient.

In addition to the prisoner and Philosophy, there is a third character in the dialogue: Fortune, whom Philosophy calls "that monstrous lady" (2.1.1 [p. 19]). Although Fortune cuts a powerful figure, she never actually appears. Philosophy speaks both about and for her. Even though many trust her, Fortune readily confesses her basic fickleness. She and Philosophy jolt the prisoner out of his confused self-pity and toward a stronger understanding of happiness than he had when his life was rolling merrily along. The work pays particular attention to the flippancy of Fortune, who smiles one minute and frowns the next. Realizing her utter capriciousness proves to be a turning point for our prisoner. Perhaps he had previously understood his blessed life as the result of his own cleverness or of his virtue, and not as the gifts of Fortune. Perhaps only ill fortune will capture our attention so that we can focus on the source of true happiness. Shifting reliance from fortune to God is the wake-up call of the work. And it is no cavalier call. The author realizes that even when God is recognized as true happiness, philosophical problems remain. He treats these in the second part of the work. Even if he did not provide satisfying answers to these problems, the author, Boethius, was courageous enough not to sweep them under the proverbial rug.

Although there are loose ends at the conclusion of the work, Boethius seems to wish to leave us with the thought that he (or his portrayal of himself) has made the turn from relying on Fortune to adhering to God, the source of true and lasting happiness.[19] The three char-

---

18. The notion of being a prisoner also has a double entendre. Our protagonist is not only a prisoner of the state; he is also a prisoner of bad thinking and bad attitudes.

19. Marenbon and Fortin are keen to point out ways in which *Consolation* fails to answer the bedeviling philosophical problems it raises. Marenbon points out that it fails to resolve the theodicy problem and is rather a satirical attack on philosophy. Marenbon, *Boethius*, pp. 160-62. Fortin suggests that the work may remain unfinished, pointing to the absence of a concluding poem. Fortin, "Nature of Consolation," p. 304.

acters coalesce to offer us a way from self-defeating anger and self-pity to divinity. It is a long, hard, and counterintuitive journey.

From Self-Pity to Happiness

Beginning Treatment

The work opens with the prisoner mired in self-pity. Encouraged by the muses, he is writing a lament for his lost possessions, reputation, and freedom. Philosophy enters suddenly and routs these harlot-muses, putting a stop to this literary foolishness (1.1.7 [p. 4]), which moderns often take to be consolation. Interrupting Boethius's grief, she turns him in a different direction and to a quite different writing project. She will bring him her own high-caliber muses to replace the tawdry companions who comfort with self-pity (1.1.11 [p. 4]).

The exhortation begins at the very outset. Lament is an indulgent act of self-absorption that must be exorcised and replaced with a more dignified approach. The prisoner must step back from complaining and take a broader view that will call forth his best. Indeed, his misfortune itself provides the opportunity for him to turn from his preoccupation with himself to the spiritual life through philosophical theology. As it turns out, this is the soul's journey into God. In short, this misfortune is, paradoxically, good fortune. As Fortune herself puts it when she admits that she did withdraw her favor from him, "This fickleness of mine gives you just cause to anticipate a better future" (2.2.14 [p. 22]).[20] Philosophy's job is to wake up the stronger part of her patient's character and mind, calling him back to his best self so that he can become one with God.

Philosophy begins this therapeutic process by telling Boethius in no uncertain terms that bemoaning his losses is dysfunctional and unseemly; it simply will not do. She will diagnose his illness and cure him by retraining him in her methods and the theology that guided him ear-

---

20. P. G. Walsh thinks that this "better future" suggests the possibility of a reprieve. Walsh, "Introduction," in *Boethius: The Consolation of Philosophy*, ed. P. G. Walsh (Oxford: Clarendon Press, 1999), p. xviii. Still, given that no reprieve is ever mentioned and that such a turn of events would entail a return to a reliance on Fortune that the whole treatise is meant to undermine, it is more likely that it refers to the *theosis* that is commended as the way to happiness in book 3.10.

lier in life (1.6.2 [p. 16]).²¹ Her dual diagnosis is that he is suffering from memory loss and is confused about what he does remember. They are connected. The first problem is that he has forgotten the wisdom he had previously gained, which taught him who he really is. With this loss of self-knowledge, he has also lost his true dignity, turning into something of a beast, lacking self-awareness and language.²² Because he has forgotten his true identity, he has mistaken Fortune for happiness, wasting energy, anger, and grief on something unworthy of devotion.

At first, the patient receives Philosophy's pastoral care as an insult rather than an invitation. He becomes defensive and is filled with rationalizing self-justification. He tries to persuade her that he does not deserve this treatment, further adding that she has betrayed him. He studied her ways as a young man and embraced her advice by becoming a philosopher-guardian of the state (an allusion to Plato's *Republic*), as she expected of him (1.4.2-9 [pp. 8-9]). In public life, he spoke truth to power when it threatened injustice: "No man has ever dragged me away from the path of justice to commit injustice" (1.4.11 [p. 9]). He rose high in Theodoric's administration and prided himself on his virtue in doing so.

However, the system turned on him precisely when he stood up for justice. It was that passion for justice — taught to him by Philosophy herself — that finally laid him low (1.4.14ff. [pp. 9-10]). He complains bitterly: "Instead of being rewarded for genuine virtue, I am punished for a crime that I did not commit" (1.4.34 [p. 11]). Summing up his venting in a more philosophical tone, Boethius introduces the theodicy question. He sees the wicked prospering, "while good men are prostrate with fear as they survey my danger" (1.4.46 [p. 13]). The lesson people will reap from what has happened to him is that acting justly does not pay. How does that advance the cause of justice that Philosophy teaches?

21. This could be read as a retreat from Catholic Christianity and a turn to pagan moral philosophy, but it was not read that way by later Christians, on whom this work was deeply influential. Further, his later references to God as "source of all things" and "father" imply his Christian convictions (3.9-10 [pp. 53-61]).

22. Just what he means by saying that humans can lose their nature and become beasts is discussed in M. V. Dougherty, "The Problem Of *Humana Natura* in the *Consolatio Philosophiae* of Boethius," *American Catholic Philosophical Quarterly* 78, no. 2 (2004). On the loss of language, see Seth Lerer, *Boethius and Dialogue: Literary Method in the Consolation of Philosophy* (Princeton, NJ: Princeton University Press, 1985).

Here he interjects a poem that poses the problem sharply. It is a hymn to God the Creator that recognizes divine governance over the natural world; yet its author is frustrated with God. "But human acts you do not school; You justly spurn to wield your rule" (1.5.27-28 [p. 13]). As Philosophy paraphrases it, "You prayed that the peace which prevails in the heavens might also govern the earth" (1.5.10 [p. 14]). It does not seem to. Our patient's faith in divine justice is shaken.

Philosophy does not immediately respond to the question the prisoner poses; instead, she blames him for his plight! He complains of his exile from Rome, but she retorts that he has not been exiled from home and stripped of his possessions, as he thinks. Boethius has exiled himself by straying from his spiritual identity, the theology with which he will be able to answer his problem. She is tough. He thinks on the material level, but she keeps pulling him to the spiritual level. The remainder of this opening book portrays Philosophy's gradual unfolding of the answer: acknowledge "one lord and one king" and obey his commands (1.5.1 [p. 14]). But with this theological tip-off to the reader, she is already getting ahead of herself. Her patient has not yet caught on. She is leading him back to — or more deeply into — God.[23]

Philosophy points out that she has not betrayed Boethius as he thinks. On the contrary, he has abandoned her by trusting Fortune, whom he thinks should reward him for being just. Herein lies the confusion, and a common one at that. Philosophy must battle not only her patient's confused hope in Fortune, but also his pride in his own virtue. Philosophy strips him naked; but she does so not by scolding him to snap out of it, but by helping him unravel the confusion that is causing his grief. The Stoic urging him to regain his composure is only a side issue on the way to a deeper recognition of who he really is and how he is to think about things in order to rise above his plight and ascend to God, who is true happiness.

Next, Philosophy conducts a thorough examination to reveal just how entrenched the prisoner's confusion is, and, in so doing, she begins to carry him out of it. She ascertains that he believes in God the Creator, but has forgotten that the God who is the source of all is also the goal of all. That he does acknowledge God is the seed of health in

---

23. Christians did not doubt that both the God of Abraham and the God of Plotinus (and company) were the one Creator God.

him that she can cultivate. The problem is that he has forgotten the *reditus* pole of the *exitus-reditus* structure of Neo-Platonic thought, which is so powerfully present in Christian theology. At the heart of Boethius's problem is the fact that he has forgotten that the goal of life is to return to God. His true identity is one who is still going to God, not only having come from God (1.6.12 [p. 17]). This psychological confusion is the reason he is upset at his plight (1.6.17-20 [p. 17]). Thus, book 1 not only establishes the terms of his cure but begins applying it right from the start.

Fickle Fortune

Part of the prisoner's confusion is that he thinks he is angry at Philosophy, but he is really angry at Fortune for being herself. There are clearly no grounds for this bitterness. Book 2 brings Fortune into the conversation so that the prisoner can see the mistake he has made in entrusting himself to her — or perhaps in mistaking her for Philosophy! If the first step in his therapy is to identify his illness as forgetfulness, the second is to sort out his confusion. As a student of Philosophy, he should have realized all along that Fortune is fickle and that to trust her is foolish (2.1.18-19 [p. 20]). The wheel of Fortune sports with human life; it does not represent justice. Boethius's anger at Philosophy is unjustified. She has not abandoned him, for he never truly understood her to begin with. From his earlier study of Plato, he learned only that pursuing justice is an honorable way of life. This much is true. However, philosophy has much more to teach.

At this point, Philosophy and Fortune (who may be monstrous but is at least honest) join forces to effect the patient's cure. Philosophy speaks in Fortune's words: "You owe me a debt of gratitude for having enjoyed possessions not your own; you have no right to complain as if you have lost what was indisputably yours" (2.2.5 [p. 21]). Here the Christian understanding of creation peeps out: all creation is God's; our enjoyment of it is an act of pure grace; we may be the stewards of created goods, but never their owners. Further, the patient's desire for God to exert the same degree of control over human affairs that he does in ordering nature is shortsighted and naïve. It is shortsighted because it ignores the inconstancy even in nature; it is naïve because "nothing that comes to be remains unchanged" (2.3.18 [p. 25]). The only constant in created existence is change, the women remind him. It is foolish to expect life to be stable. Together, Philosophy and Fortune trump the patient's complaint at every turn.

Even after all this, the patient is still complaining, showing that he has not yet gotten their point. "The unhappiest aspect of misfortune," he opines, "is to have known happiness." Here the arrow finds its mark. Boethius is still confused about what happiness is. He still expects the goods of fortune that he once enjoyed to provide it. The remainder of book 2 is Philosophy's systematic deconstruction of his longing for and trusting in the material benefits that he enjoyed in the past. She derisively calls this confusion his "hollow claim to unsubstantial happiness" (2.4.3 [p. 25]). She strikes to the quick: what these possessions were really doing was flattering him. Losing them is a blow to his vanity. Toward the end of this book, Philosophy retorts: "My opinion in fact is that adverse Fortune benefits people more than good, for whereas when good Fortune seems to fawn on us, she invariably deceives us with the appearance of happiness, adverse Fortune is always truthful, and shows by her mutability that she is inconstant" (2.8.3 [pp. 37-38]). Ill fortune is a blessing in disguise. In addition to helping us see ourselves more clearly, it enables us better to distinguish true from false sources of happiness by stripping us of pride in our own cleverness and virtue (2.8.6-7 [p. 38]).[24]

The prisoner's vanity is thick and deep; he continues to resist. To pierce his entrenched defenses, Philosophy states plainly a pastoral commonplace. Boethius is looking for happiness in the wrong place: in external goods that are granted by Fortune. These are not wrought by his own cleverness, as he is vain enough to think, but by Fortune. Instead, Philosophy teaches that true happiness lies in self-mastery, key to all the virtues. Fortune has no control over that (2.4.23 [p. 27]). She returns to this point in the poem that concludes book 3.5. Following the moral of the "Three Little Pigs" story, Boethius must build his house solidly. All possessions are lost at death, if not sooner, but virtue truly belongs to us and cannot be destroyed. Boethius's reputation may be destroyed by slander, but his virtue is untouched. His virtue is a life raft, but it will prove to provide only temporary refuge.

Without pausing for breath, Philosophy details the spiritual dan-

---

24. Fortin also notes this, saying that bad fortune has the advantage of "giving a truer account of a person's virtues and vices." Fortin, "Nature of Consolation," p. 296.

gers of relying on material goods for happiness. Wealth breeds avarice, political ambition engages in the shameful practice of controlling others instead of self, and international fame "is not just trifling but wholly non-existent" (2.7.18 [p. 36]). In book 3, she elaborates these and even discusses more.

On the Mend

Book 3 is both the center and the centerpiece of the work. Philosophy has finally pierced her patient's self-righteousness. He no longer resists her treatment, and she stops chastising him; she finally discloses where true happiness lies.

Having told her patient where not to look — or, rather, where to stop looking — for happiness, she now moves ahead, agreeing with Aristotle that everyone wants to be happy. "Happiness is the state of perfection achieved by the concentration of all goods within it" (3.2.3 [p. 41]). The search for wealth, high public office, or other forms of power and renown is really a search for a complete and total good in disguise. People mistakenly think that the delights they derive from these and other particular goods that give pleasure — like family, the perfect body, and good health — are happiness. Basically, however, people have the right idea. They seek the good, but they look for it in "[material] self-sufficiency, respect, power, renown, and joy" (3.2.19 [p. 43]). The problem is that this is a misguided intuition about where happiness is to be found.

Augustine, too, believed that unhappiness is caused by confusion, but not only that: his austere doctrine of predestination held that some of us simply cannot look in the right place. Boethius is more encouraging. He is always urging us to look up to find our proper identity.[25] To be sure that her patient is fully on board, Philosophy again reviews the false sources of happiness that bring confusion: wealth that requires constant protecting; public office with its invitation to sycophancy that thinly disguises hatred and promotes corruption; military power that must be protected with bodyguards; and international re-

25. Along this line, a great deal has been written about the poem on the Orpheus myth that appears at the end of book 3. See Fortin, "Nature of Consolation," p. 297; see also Lerer, *Boethius and Dialogue*, pp. 156-62, 227ff.

nown, where mass popularity "is not even worthy of mention" (3.6.6 [p. 51]). She adds noble birth, which is a theological lie because "all men on earth from one source take their rise: One Father of the world all things supplies" (3.6.1-2 [p. 50]).

As in the previous book, these false goods are contrasted with the virtue that arouses true respect as well as diminishes fear of retribution and the need for self-protection. A problem with the direction of Philosophy's answer here is that, as previously noted, this is precisely the tack that Boethius had charted for himself all along — and it failed. That his virtue is intact should console him, but it does not. She will have to do better.

Philosophy returns to explaining the true happiness that lies in God. The dialogue takes the form of Socratic interrogation about why each of the avenues previously discussed will fail. "The explanation is readily accessible. What in nature is simple and undivided is split by human error" (3.9.3-4 [p. 53]). True happiness is the realization that only one "substance" is self-sufficient, powerful, honorable, famous, and even pleasurable. The good that people seek piecemeal in so many different temporal goods is, it turns out, one simple "substance": goodness itself. Those who seek happiness in wealth, office, reputation, and bodily pleasure are grasping at pieces of goodness, for wanting them is to desire the good. Seeking the good in objects rather than in activities is misplaced. Happiness can never be attained in this way because it is not to be had when enjoying any of these goods. The seeker who looks there confuses the pleasure these objects bring with genuine happiness that is enjoying goodness itself even when that brings no external reward and even misfortune.

According to Boethius, happiness is not found in trying to sustain external pleasure, or in accumulating wealth, health, power, or renown. A new car, the perfect mate, another child, a better job, and being clever at securing them — even in the aggregate — are not what is truly valuable and so to be desired. "So there is no way in which happiness is to be found in those pursuits which were believed individually to bestow desirable things" (3.9.23 [p. 55]). The issue is that we do not know what true happiness is because we do not know what is truly worth wanting. We want things that are not worthy of our attention.

Now the patient is sitting up and taking nourishment. He realizes that he has been thinking about happiness improperly. It is not wealth, political power, fawning admirers, and physical pleasure that give happiness, but the reverse. And here is the better answer to the previous partial answer offered by hope in virtue: "If I am not mistaken, true and perfect happiness is what makes a person self-sufficient, powerful, venerable, famous, and joyful" (3.9.26 [p. 55]). Not only had he been looking toward the wrong objects, he was facing in the wrong direction! No object is worth the effort compared to wanting God. With Philosophy's prodding, Boethius adds that the happiness he seeks cannot be found in any transient things. At last he is getting the point. Happiness lies not in acquiring various goods and honors, or even in the pride of virtue, which is sustained and rewarded in a just world. Rather, goodness itself bestows bliss.[26] This requires massive rethinking.

Now that he is on the mend, Boethius must "recognize the source from which you can seek the true happiness" (3.9.31 [p. 55]). Here Stoic reliance on virtue gives way to a Neo-Platonic and Christian resolution of the search for happiness. We reach the climax of the work in Philosophy's hymn-prayer to the Creator of earth and sky, the supreme good. While the patient/prisoner had early on recognized God as the Creator of all things, this hymn prays for the soul to rise to the Father, who is the goal of all. The hymn is patterned on the *Timaeus* of Plato, one of the most widely known of Plato's works in late antiquity.[27] I quote it here in full.

> [Creator] of earth and sky, You steer the world
> By reason everlasting. You bid time
> Progress from all eternity. Yourself
> Unshifting, You impel all things to move.
> No cause outside Yourself made You give shape
> To fluid matter, for in You was set
> The form of the ungrudging highest good.
> From heavenly patterns You derive all things.
> Yourself most beautiful, You likewise bear

26. In this Neo-Platonic view, Boethius follows Augustine. "[Y]ou can perceive good itself by participating in [ways in] which these other things are good — and you understand it together with them when you hear a good this or that — if then you can put them aside and perceive good itself, you will perceive God. And if you cling to him in love, you will straightaway enter into bliss." Augustine, *The Trinity*, trans. Edmund Hill, *The Works of Saint Augustine: A Translation for the 21st Century* (Brooklyn, NY: New City Press, 1991), 8.2 (pp. 244-45).

27. For a discussion of this poem, see Gerard J. P. O'Daly, *The Poetry of Boethius* (Chapel Hill: University of North Carolina Press, 1991), pp. 163-65.

In mind a world of beauty, and You shape
Our world in like appearance. You command
Its perfect parts, to form a perfect world.

Its elements You bind in harmony.
Dry cold with fluid flames closely conspires,
So rarefied fire may not fly out above,
Nor earth be dragged by weight to depths below.
The soul which stirs all things You intertwine
In threefold nature as its middle part;
You distribute it through harmonious limbs.
The soul, thus split, then concentrates its course
Within two orbits, as it journeys back
Upon itself, encircling the mind
That lies deep down. The soul turns round the heavens,
Which mirror in this way its very self.

Through causes of like nature You send forth
Both human souls and those with lesser lives.
Installing them aloft in weightless cars,
You plant them through the heavens and on the earth.
Your genial law prompts them to turn to You,
To journey back when guided by their fire.

Let my mind rise to Your august abode,
And there, dear Lord, survey the source of good.
Then grant that, once I have attained the light,
My inward eye I may direct on You.
Disperse the fog and the encumbering weight
Of this earth's bulk, and shine forth, clear and bright;
For in the eyes of all devoted men,
You are calm brightness and the rest of peace.
Men aim to see You as their starting-point,
Their guide, conductor, way, and final end. (3.9 [pp. 56-57])

The poem falls into four parts. Its first stanza describes an eternal,
immutable, unmoved mover, who created the world, governs it in perfectly ordered harmony, and is beautiful. He is the self-sufficient and
perfect good. Positing such a God implies that pursuing wealth, power,
fame, and pleasure as ways toward self-sufficiency is imperfect at best,

for self-sufficiency is a good higher than these things possess themselves and thus cannot provide. The perfect good that they imperfectly exhibit is a unified singular good that people blindly try to grasp without realizing precisely what it is or why they should want it.

The second stanza is obscure. It praises the divine sustainer of the world with "the soul which stirs all things"; it "turns round the heavens, which mirror in this way its very self." The third stanza identifies God as the source of angelic, human, and animal souls, and introduces the *reditus* theme that Philosophy had diagnosed as missing in Boethius on her first interrogation. Here she calls her patient to "journey back" to his homeland, the goodness from which he came.

The final stanza invites the reader to abandon managed efforts toward happiness and to look instead to the source of good that enlightens life by the divine calm, brightness, and peace. Finally, Philosophy's now pliant patient finds a way to escape his vanity by transcending its imperfect confines and turning to the source and destination of good.

In book 3, chapter 10, the prisoner posits that a single intelligence must guide everything. To this, Philosophy adds that all things willingly submit to that highest good. Even if they tried to resist, they would still be constrained to do so. The universe arises from a single source that is intact and fully developed. If people mistakenly seek imperfect happiness in brittle things that can be lost, they will not find it. Only perfect goodness is perfect happiness, and that goodness is God.[28] True happiness is God himself. To have happiness is to have God; to be happy is to be God, that is, the goodness that is God. There cannot be two highest goods that differ from one another. If true happiness is the highest good, and God is the highest good, then God must be perfect happiness (3.9.18-20 [p. 54]).

He draws the following corollary: "Since men become happy by achieving happiness and happiness is itself divinity, clearly they become happy by attaining divinity. Now just as men become just by acquiring justice, and wise by acquiring wisdom, so by the same argument they must become gods once they have acquired divinity. Hence every happy person is God; God is by nature one only, but nothing prevents the greatest possible number from sharing in that divinity"

---

28. Aquinas makes significant use of Boethius's distinction between perfect and imperfect happiness. See Thomas Aquinas, *Summa Theologiae*, 60 vols. (New York: Blackfriars, 1964), 1.2.2-5.

(3.10.23-24 [p. 59]). This is the Plotinian doctrine of ascent that leaves material pleasure behind, not because it is evil but because it is insufficient. Our true self is the basic intelligent, creative principle of the universe: "God," that is, harmony, order, peace, and contentment. Realizing this brings "the highest self-sufficiency, the highest power, the highest respect, and renown and pleasure" (3.10.30 [p. 60]). That is, when we realize that we partake of the ordered beauty and goodness that is God, enjoying that goodness becomes the basis on which we enjoy the world and find the power, riches, and wealth that we were looking for in their material expressions.[29] This possession of goodness and power can carry us through misfortune, for having realized our identity in God, we no longer mistake penultimate for ultimate goods. In short, happiness is a spiritual, not a material matter. Here is the consolation. Happiness is realizing that we partake of goodness — God — the unified principle that "causes created things to remain in being and in motion that I call God" (3.12.8 [p. 66]).

Philosophy then cements her consolation by arguing that this divine destiny of experiencing the unity of all things in goodness is our human destiny, just as fire rises and earth falls to the ground. Her patient is cured and shamefacedly confesses: "Now at last I am ashamed of the stupidity which has inflicted such wounds on me" (3.12.23 [p. 67]). The book closes with a warning poem not to turn back — as did Orpheus once he had rescued his wife, Eurydice, from Hades — or all would be lost.[30] And it was.

Securing Happiness

The first three books of *Consolation* whip the prisoner out of his self-pitying confusion. He has made great progress and learned his lesson, but theodicy still needs to be addressed. Boethius is working with a privative doctrine of good and evil, as was Augustine. That notion is no longer current, so his answer to the problem of evil will not satisfy many readers today. Indeed, throughout book 3 the prisoner protests

29. Acceptance of human participation in divinity was commonplace in the ancient world. Here humans becoming God is mentioned twice (3.10.24-5 [p. 59] and 3.12.33 [p. 68]).

30. For a full discussion of this and other mythology in the work, see Lerer, *Boethius and Dialogue,* chaps. 3 and 4.

to Philosophy that her answer to the problem of evil is so counter-intuitive that not many will find it comforting.

The privative doctrine of evil was then and remains today difficult to appreciate because, to casual observers, evil seems both real and powerful. To Philosophy it is neither: evil has no existence and thus cannot have power. Boethius's misery, she says, is from his confusion in thinking that evil has overpowered him, when, in fact, evil has no power at all. The only power it has over him is what he allows it to have because he is seeking to experience happiness as pleasure, rather than recognizing that it is a moral construct. Teaching him to readjust his thinking will take him away from the alien territory in which he currently dwells to his "homeland," in the safety of God. Philosophy's response to the problem of evil is a high doctrine of divine providence based on the omnipotence and goodness of the God of classical theism.

The previous argument established divine providence. God governs the world by ordering its disparate parts into a harmonious whole. That unity is itself good and self-sufficient. God's perfect goodness is happiness itself, and it is both necessary and sufficient for happiness for us as participants in the goodness of the whole. In book 4, Philosophy will develop this starting point to argue that dwelling in goodness, that is, God, is happiness and that anything beyond that is irrelevant.

In this serene intimacy that binds God, the world, and humans in the unity of goodness, evil is destructive. When good people suffer and the wicked go unpunished, the peaceful harmony of goodness is disrupted. Philosophy sets this commonplace view on its head. The good are morally strong and powerful, and the bad are humbled and weak. The path to happiness is to realize that "vices never go unpunished, nor virtues unrewarded; that the good always achieve success, and the wicked suffer misfortune" (4.1.7 [p. 71]).

Her point is that all are happy by virtue of participating in the goodness of God. Since happiness is the goodness of God, no more, no less, those who act badly are abandoning themselves, their power, and their happiness. Being wicked is losing the power of goodness and being overcome by nothing. It is to relinquish one's freedom. Such people renounce their humanity and become powerless. They are unable to achieve the happiness they desire. To be good is to be strong and happy; to be bad is to be weak and miserable. "Thus by resorting to wickedness they have lost their human nature as well. Since goodness alone can raise a person above the rank of human it must follow that wickedness deservedly imposes subhuman status on those whom it has dislodged from the human condition" (4.3.15-16 [p. 79]). The wicked are feral, and the more wickedness they pursue, the less human they become.

The core of the answer to the theodicy question comes in chapter 6, where Philosophy argues that, though the world looks topsy-turvy — with the wicked in control and the good marginalized and harmed — this is not the case. Divine providence is in control. Here Boethius offers a fresh response to the problem: Philosophy separates providence from fate to argue that God is in complete control of events. Providence is God's thoughtful plan for all events; fate, while it may control individual things, is not ultimately autonomous. Providence, the simple unchanging web of divinely ordered goodness, encompasses fate within its purview.

Thinking of ourselves as victims of fate rather than as beneficiaries of divine providence, as Boethius was wont to do, is to take the wrong vantage point. Both are playing their part in the divine plan for the well-being of the cosmos, because both move toward medicinal ends. The suffering of the just enables us to discover our strengths and to exercise virtue. They give others examples to follow, and unjust death brings posthumous renown. The wicked, for their part, provide counterexamples: by looking foolish and subhuman, they act as a deterrent. When they are punished, their just suffering is an opportunity to review themselves in light of their foolishness and to repent. Of course, this last point skirts Boethius's complaint that justice is turned upside down when the wicked go scot-free and seem to be winning. He adverts to the pedagogical power of ultimate eternal punishment that is Christianity's main answer to the theodicy problem, but he declines to discuss it (4.4.23 [p. 82]). The argument remains unsatisfying.

The thrust of the argument is that the prisoner has been feeling sorry for himself because he considers himself to have lost happiness, ending his life humiliated by evil men. This is quite inappropriate, Philosophy tells him. His righteousness is his stanchion, and leaning on it is his strength and power. He had known this from studying Philosophy in his younger years, but adversity overcame his knowledge. Philosophy is taking him home to the truth by reminding him that he is happy because he has clung to the goodness of God. And he would be happy if only he were to consider his situation properly.

Book 5 sews up loose ends of the argument to complete the case for a spiritual doctrine of happiness. By separating fate from providence,

Boethius denies us the comfort of simply being the victims of random events, for providence rules out chance. If chance is no comfort, the prisoner, still struggling to hold onto a shred of hope for the efficacy of human behavior, asks about free will. Philosophy admits that there is freedom of choice for those who act completely from divine goodness, but freedom diminishes and finally becomes enslavement to those trapped in wickedness. It, too, is precarious.

With no chance and precarious freedom, the prisoner, yet unbowed before Philosophy's tough stance, charges against the implication of this doctrine of providence yet one last time, for it renders hope and prayer pointless. This calls forth a defense of divine foreknowledge. Philosophy maintains that, just as there is a sense in which free will is sustained, so there is a sense in which contingency is also real if understood properly, that is, from the perspective of divine intelligence, not human reason, imagination, or sensory experience. Those who penetrate reality to its core of divine intelligence, seeing beyond all human capacities, will see as God sees, in the "simplicity of highest knowledge confined by no bounds" (5.5.12 [p. 109]). This is to experience eternal life, where all human limitation is scaled and temporal considerations no longer matter. Happiness is a matter of seeing as God sees, where events are foreseen "as knowledge of the unceasingly present moment" (5.6.17 [p. 112]).

Boethius's Contribution

Happiness is commonly thought of experientially; Boethius rejects that notion because experience is unreliable. Stoicism and Neo-Platonism, set in a theistic framework, offer a doctrine of happiness that is invulnerable to events. It is emotionally safer, Boethius argues, to hold that happiness is purely noetic than to believe that it is in anything that might or might not happen to us. Happiness is an outlook arising from a staunch commitment to divine omnipotence and goodness in the face of contradictory experience. Like Augustine, Boethius wants to turn us from the material to the spiritual realm, but he does so far more rigorously. He offers a cognitive-behavioral therapy to lead those who look for happiness through events from that false hope to a nonexperiential definition of happiness. Happiness requires looking away from the events of life and toward the idea that happiness is dwelling in the eternal mind of God. Aquinas would come to a comparable conclusion, but he would hold that this is not possible in this life, though lesser forms of happiness are attainable.

Since experiential happiness is unreliable, we do better to rely on our own dignity, which is the ability to see as God sees. Happiness requires penetration of the divine mind, where, with Augustine, the soul transcends experiential disappointment in life because it sees all events *sub specie eternitatis*. Believing that one's misfortunes are part of a larger invisible divine plan for the well-ordered functioning of the cosmos should enable the sufferer to be content that his suffering is not pointless or that it damages the divine reputation. Rather, one's suffering is somehow part of the divine plan that shows forth divine goodness and the goodness of the cosmos. The suffering of the just does not escape divine governance on the view that evil, fate, or fortune is powerful, because all that befalls us is within the purview of divine intention. Ultimately, happiness is participating in divine intelligence wherein all makes sense.

This is a hard teaching. Happiness is enjoying being part of the divine plan. While there is nothing in Boethius's presentation that departs from Christian theism — indeed, Calvin's position on providence is sympathetic to it — the redemptive dimension of Christian theology that gives hope is missing. His notion of happiness is tinged with despair about the need to be ever striving for intellectual perfection and vigilant against feelings of dejection, anger, and defeat. Finally, Boethius offers only the power of unremitting strength, unqualified by relaxed joy. He has the tool for luxuriating in God, but he does not use it.

Boethius's doctrine of happiness is theological, noetic, and temporal. Because Augustine compassionately gave credence to suffering, he could not take the hard line that Boethius did. Augustine's future eschatology offers hope of reward while counseling endurance now. Boethius offers a realized eschatology, at the expense of succor for the suffering in this life. That being said, Boethius does believe he is succoring sufferers, only not in the way they might hope. Succor is the strength not to be brought low by experience but to rise above it and to exercise one's dignity by doing so.

CHAPTER 4

Saint Thomas Aquinas

Early in his theological career, Augustine famously said that he wanted to know only God and the soul.[1] We see the intimacy of these two desires in his use of erotic female imagery:

> How shall I call upon my God, my God and Lord? Surely when I call on him, I am calling on him to come into me. But what place is there in me where my God can enter into me? . . . Why do I request you to come to me when, unless you were within me, I would have no being at all? . . . I would have no being, I would not have any existence, unless you were in me. Or rather, I would have no being if I were not in you.[2]

Augustine's desire to know God assumes a less erotic but no less intense tone in his faithful disciple Thomas Aquinas (1225-1274), who believed that thinking is the greatest human ability. He sought to know God utterly, and he did find a way for God to come into him — into his mind to illuminate it with divine glory. Thomas's scholastic rationalism should not dissuade us from appreciating the passion behind the elegance and complexity of his arguments.

---

1. Augustine, "Soliloquies," in *Augustine: Earlier Writings*, Library of Christian Classics (Philadelphia: Westminster Press, 1958), 1.2.7 (p. 26).

2. Augustine, *Confessions*, trans. Henry Chadwick (Oxford: Oxford University Press, 1991), 1.2.2 (pp. 3-4).

The Context

Aquinas received Aristotle as fresh Latin translations of Aristotle's Greek texts became available. It is not surprising that, in a philosophically sophisticated environment, happiness was of general interest, since it was such a prominent theme in ancient philosophy. Abelard (1079-1142) and Lombard (1100-1160) both discussed the subject. The translation of the complete text of Aristotle's *Nicomachean Ethics (NE)* in the mid-thirteenth century intensified interest in the subject because the first and last books are on happiness, suggesting that the moral life and happiness are inseparable.[3] That message was not lost on Aquinas.

The Setting

Aquinas wrote as a Dominican fighting the Albigensian heresy that had been spreading throughout southern France for over 200 years by his day. The sect was Manichaean and therefore strongly dualistic; its most advanced devotees vowed to be celibate, not to swear oaths, own property, go to war, or eat food that resulted from sex. It fell to Thomas to combat the heresy intellectually, and he did so by founding his philosophical theology on the goodness of creation. Having Aristotle, of course, strengthened his hand.

Intellectual Sources

Aquinas used non-Christian sources that supported his effort because for him all truth is of God. He set Aristotle's naturalistic approach to the material world within the classic *exitus-reditus* framework of Neo-

---

3. Georg Wieland has chronicled the widespread interest in this subject by theologians and philosophers in that age of sympathetic reception of — and lively debate over — Aristotle. See Georg Wieland, "Happiness: The Perfection of Man," in *The Cambridge History of Later Medieval Philosophy*, ed. Norman Kretzmann et al. (Cambridge: Cambridge University Press, 1982), pp. 673-86. Wieland surveys William of Auxerre, Robert Kilwardby, Boethius of Dacia, Siger of Brabant, John Buridan, and several anonymous commentaries. See also P. S. Eardley, "Conceptions of Happiness and Human Destiny in the Late Thirteenth Century," *Vivarium* 44, no. 2/3 (2006): 276-304.

Platonism used by Augustine and Boethius.[4] In this way, he transformed both Aristotelian and Platonic sources.[5] For example, Thomas based happiness on Augustine's formulation of the vision of God (beatific vision) as the eschatological goal and hope of heavenly glory. Yet, by distinguishing imperfect from perfect happiness, and paying special attention to the physical well-being needed for the former, Aquinas integrated Aristotle's appreciation of material good into the larger teleological whole.

It will be helpful to review Aristotle's teaching on happiness and Aquinas's interaction with it. *NE* is ensconced in a discussion of happiness as the highest good of life that guides our moral efforts. Goodness is the only way to true happiness.[6] Putting happiness at the head of NE signals the practicality of philosophy on which all the ancients agreed. Aristotle's interest is not in theorizing about the good life but in helping us live it. This means becoming excellent persons through the cultivation of virtue. This is standard for ancient moral philosophy. The highest good is valuable in itself alone and is desired for its own sake, not as a means to some further good.[7] Christian theology followed Aristotle in this.

In defining our chief good as happiness, Aristotle says that the common assumption that happiness lies in acquiring external goods

4. Fergus Kerr has challenged the overall Platonic interpretation, suggesting that Thomas instead had the biblical structure of creation-resurrection in mind. Fergus Kerr, "Thomas Aquinas," in *Medieval Theologians* (Oxford: Blackwell Publishers, 2001), pp. 201-20. Perhaps for many theologians, philosophical frameworks articulated the Christian worldview so well that the various pagan sources could point to the one truth of God that informs them. Despite the diversity of discourse, all truth is of God. For example, the fourth Gospel has an *exitus-reditus* framework, since Jesus comes from the Father in heaven, returns to him, and even promises to have his friends eventually join him there.

5. Paul Mercken identified four ways in which Thomas transforms Aristotle's moral philosophy, but he did not note that at least two of them — the addition of perfect happiness as the vision of God and the introduction of the role of will — come from Augustine. Paul Mercken, "Transformations of the Ethics of Aristotle in the Moral Philosophy of Thomas Aquinas," in *Agire Morale* (Naples: Edizioni Domenicane Italiane, 1977), pp. 151-62.

6. Thomas follows Aristotle by putting his treatise on happiness at the head of the massive ethics of the *Secundae* of the *Summa Theologiae*. See Thomas Aquinas, *Summa Theologiae*, 60 vols. (New York: Blackfriars, 1964), 1a2ae. q. 1-5. He also discusses it at the head of the entire work at 1a. q. 12.

7. On this point, see Aristotle, *Nicomachean Ethics*, ed. Sarah Broadie, trans. Christopher Rowe (New York: Oxford University Press, 2002), p. 9.

(he mentions wealth, honor, health, and physical pleasure) is mistaken. Happiness is an activity, a way of doing things. It is living one's life well, "through the active engagement of individuals themselves," as Sarah Broadie puts it.[8] Happiness is not a matter of acquiring something outside us, but of adopting a particular way of life.

At this point, Aristotle makes a significant methodological move. To distinguish his position from Plato's, he says that he will work inductively, beginning with what is knowable to us from experience, as opposed to working from first principles, as did Plato. And Thomas follows Aristotle in this, working from effects to cause.

Aristotle leaves an opening for the Christian teaching that happiness is found in God when, in the opening book of the *NE,* he muses that happiness may be a gift of the gods. Even if learning and practice help us acquire it, there is something godlike and blessed about it. The path to happiness is unflinchingly social, not private, because it takes place in the context of interpersonal and public relationships and behaviors.[9] One must know what behaviors to cultivate, and this knowledge comes from a good upbringing that inculcates moral discipline and good priorities, as well as from a keen intellect that practices good judgment.

Happiness is being an excellent person, and that is demanding; learning to "do" one's life excellently takes time. Aristotle's theory implies that we become happier as we become better able to handle a wide range of experiences, settings, and relationships. It requires using ourselves well. Learning to live happily (morally) is not an exact science that can be calculated, but an art to be cultivated.[10] Aristotle emphasizes that the skill of living excellently requires the right use of self. Both Augustine and Aquinas concur in this, even if they did not believe that it could be done — or at least done perfectly — in this life. Moral and intellectual acumen require deliberation and practice.

In defining happiness, Aristotle argues that it is not only desirable in itself, but also complete in itself, and thus is unable to be improved on. It is self-sufficient. He is, of course, speaking of temporal happi-

8. Aristotle, *Nicomachean Ethics,* p. 11.

9. Augustine's eschatology is also deeply social. Heaven, after all, is a city. True happiness is in a harmonious community where peace pervades all relationships.

10. For a recent critique of the calculation model for arriving at happiness in favor of the idea of searching for happiness, see Stephen Theron, "Happiness and Transcendent Happiness," *Religious Studies* 21 (1985): 349-67.

ness. Augustine and Aquinas would disagree, because for them complete happiness is possible only after this life, when physical distractions are gone and we can know and love God intellectually, perfectly, and uninterruptedly. Since we are unable to do this on our own either in this life or the next, Augustine and Aquinas shy away from the notion that happiness in this life can be self-sufficient or perfect.

Aristotle returns to the criteria of completeness and self-sufficiency for true happiness in the last book of the *NE*. He exalts the advantages of the philosophical life of study over the active life of politics, military achievement, and business, which lack time for reflection and are wearying. Reflective activity is the most pleasant because it is the most refined. Here is a two-tiered account of happiness. As an intellectual, Aristotle not surprisingly values reflective over political activity for the insights and self-examination it offers. However, he also acknowledges that politics requires a virtuous life that is enjoyable, satisfying, and productive.

I have noted that as he begins *NE*, Aristotle muses that happiness may be a gift of the gods. He returns to this thought at the end of the work, where he argues that the delight of intellectual activity is an awareness of divine things. Suggesting that perhaps the intellect itself is "something divine, or the divinest of the things in us," he reasons that, "[i]f, then, intelligence is something divine as compared to a human activity, so too a life lived in accordance with this will be divine as compared to a human life."[11] Aquinas picks this up and likens the happiness of reflective activity to the activity of a god: "For the life of gods is blessedly happy throughout, while that of some human beings is so to the extent that there belongs to it some kind of semblance of this sort of activity."[12] Therefore, some people have a godly life, and since this has been a treatise on ethics, it seems that a godly life is a morally excellent one.

Aquinas presses further. Happiness is not analogous to the delight that the Olympian gods enjoy, but knowing the mind of the God of Scripture. While Aquinas agrees with Aristotle that practicing moral goodness is happy and godlike, learning to do that or becoming such a person is the result of knowing, loving, and enjoying God by focusing directly on him. Aristotle cannot reach this conclusion because he does not have a detailed account of God's actions and characteristics on

---

11. Aristotle, *Nicomachean Ethics,* 10.8 (pp. 250-51).
12. Aristotle, *Nicomachean Ethics,* 10.8 (p. 253).

which to focus. Thomas has Scripture and the theological tradition that richly elaborate the Christian understanding of the Creator/Redeemer.

Aquinas's Treatments of Happiness

Following the ancients, Aquinas holds that happiness is everyone's goal. He discusses happiness in various writings, but discerning a pattern among them is difficult because he does not always name the various kinds of happiness as he considers them, nor is his word usage consistent. Therefore, this review is tentative. Formally speaking, "happiness . . . means actively possessing the ultimate end" (1.2. q. 1, art. 8).[13] Materially, he follows Augustine in saying that happiness is knowing and loving God. Thomas is especially interested in knowing God, and, though he does not always call it happiness, life's goal is to know God perfectly. Perfect knowledge is the eschatological intellectual activity of the blessed in heaven, though inklings of it are possible in this life. It is possible only by divine grace and can be called supernatural happiness. Knowledge from the unaided or natural mind is possible, but it is limited to sensory knowledge for the most part. Perfect knowledge of God is perfect happiness for Aquinas. It is not limited to enjoying the moral life itself, though that is central to it. Parsing his discussions is complicated because sometimes he talks about knowing without mentioning happiness *(felicitas* and *beatitudo)* when that saving knowledge is the subject of the discussion. His teaching is that salvation is comprehensive knowledge of God, which is happiness.

Aquinas is unique among theologians in that mixed in with his eschatological vision is a temporal construal of happiness that is experiential. He is the first Christian theologian to embrace temporal flourishing in this life by enjoying material goods — though it is a minor theme, one inspired by Aristotle.

An element of Aquinas's theology with unrecognized potential for a doctrine of temporal flourishing is his doctrine of secondary agency. Its moral and psychological implications for happiness have not been appreciated, and I will explore those implications when I discuss *Summa Contra Gentiles* and again in chapter 7 below.

---

13. Thomas Aquinas, *Purpose and Happiness*, ed. and trans. Thomas Gilby, vol. 16, *Summa Theologiae* (Cambridge: Blackfriars, 1969).

In chronological order, Thomas's discussions of happiness appear in: (1) his *Commentary on the Sentences of Peter Lombard (CS)*, written when he was a Bachelor of the Sentences in Paris (c. 1252-1254); (2) *Summa Contra Gentiles (SCG)*,[14] written when he was in Italy·(1258/9-1264/5); and (3) *Summa Theologiae (ST)*.[15]

Commentary on the Sentences of Peter Lombard

Happiness appears in most of the books of the *CS*, which follows Lombard's four-part structure.[16] *The Commentary* introduces three basic themes: first, there is more than one type of happiness; second, happiness is teleological (that is, we achieve it when we aim at the proper goal of our existence); third, perfect happiness is spiritual: it is knowing (seeing) God.

In 1.1.1, on "Whether another teaching beside the natural sciences is necessary for Humans," Aquinas agrees with Aristotle that philosophy is a natural science (because it is done using the mind unaided by grace) that can bring contemplative happiness *(felicitatem contemplativam)*. It is a lower form of happiness because, though it can help us understand the world, it does not offer knowledge of God, which requires divine grace. Theology is knowing God, and that is a supernatural discipline and thus higher than philosophy, which is a natural discipline. "There is another contemplation of God whereby God appears directly by his essence; and this contemplation is perfect, because it will be in the fatherland (heaven) and is possible to man according to the supposition of faith."[17] But it is perfect only in heaven, "insofar as man is led by the hand to this contemplation while still in the state of the

---

14. Thomas Aquinas, "Summa Contra Gentiles, Book III," in *Basic Writings of Thomas Aquinas*, ed. Anton C. Pegis (New York: Random House, 1945), 3.25-40, 46-63.

15. Aquinas, *Summa Theologiae*, Ia. q. 12; q. 62, a. 1; Ia2ae. qq. 1-5.

16. Lombard's *Quattuor libri Sententiarum* (c. 1150) offers a systematization of Christian doctrine that integrates Scripture with the church fathers (mostly Augustine) and later writers, including John Damascene and the Victorines. It was the theology textbook of the universities until the sixteenth century. To become a doctor of theology, one had to lecture on it for two years. Saint Thomas's commentary on it was the foundation of his *Summa Theologiae*.

17. Thomas Aquinas, "Selections from Thomas's 'Commentary on the Sentences of Peter Lombard,'" in *Saint Thomas Aquinas*, ed. Hugh McDonald (http://www.hyoomik .com), q. 1. a. 1.

way (in this earthly life) by a knowledge that is not derived from creatures but inspired directly by the divine light [*ex divino lumine inspiratam*]. This is theological teaching."[18] Theology is superior to philosophy by virtue of its divine source, "by which our understanding is perfected with respect to infused knowledge, and our character is perfected with respect to a love that is produced by grace."[19]

In this passage, supernatural happiness (knowledge of God) seems to be possible in this life by infused grace, which enhances understanding and the supernatural virtues of faith, hope, and love, which also require infused grace. In this early work of Thomas, the intellect seems to be capable of both natural and supernatural activity in this life.

In concluding his *CS*, Thomas emphasizes that happiness — even that of the active life — is knowledge and not physical well-being. It is an intellectual activity that is completed by delight in loving what we desire.[20] This definition pulses through his entire treatment of the Christian life: happiness as the complete achievement of the blissful vision of God. Desire for it is imprinted on us by God, and that leads us to want to know him as he knows himself.

Summa Contra Gentiles

Aquinas's second discussion of happiness elaborates what he has already said in the *CS*, and it maps what was to come later in the *ST*.[21] It has all the features of his most mature treatment of our subject, and adds two more. From Augustine he takes the idea that divine illumination is the means to know God; but he goes beyond Augustine when he adds that illumination *is* union with the divine mind. The other addi-

---

18. Aquinas, "Selections from Thomas's CS," q. 1. a. 1.
19. Aquinas, "Selections from Thomas's CS," q. 1. a. 1.
20. Servais Pinckaers, "La Voie Spirituelle du Bonheur selon Saint Thomas," in *Ordo Sapientiae et Amoris* (Fribourg, Switzerland: Universitätsverlag Freiburg Schweiz, 1993), p. 270.
21. This appears in three segments in Book 3 of the *Summa Contra Gentiles*, trans. Roberto Busa, SJ, *Corpus Thomisticum* (Pampilonae: Fundación Tomás de Aquino, 1961): (1) chapters 1-2 and 16-25 argue that all human behavior is purposeful; (2) chapters 26-40 define happiness as the knowledge of God, which is the purpose of all human activity; and (3) chapters 46-63 explain that ultimate happiness is the vision of God. Hereafter, this work will be cited as *SCG*, and references will appear in parentheses in the text.

tion that is relevant to retrieving a Christian doctrine of happiness is the notion of secondary agency, though he does not make specific use of it with respect to happiness.

The introduction of secondary agency comes in the course of his doctrine of providence, which reasserts that all behavior is purposeful and that its purpose is to seek goodness. Even evil deeds intend some good, thwarted and twisted though they be.[22] The good most worth seeking is the highest good: God. All of life's activities aim at this.

Thomas follows Aristotle and Boethius by eliminating false definitions first, because happiness is not the possession of material items but spiritual joy, even though material conditions are also necessary for it. He begins using the adjective *ultima* to modify the heretofore unmodified *felicitas,* suggesting that what we previously may have thought were completely false materialist definitions of happiness are not completely false, but only imperfect or partial (beginning at *SCG,* 3.34).[23] Indeed, this is the argument from continuity that he employs in the *ST,* using the imperfect-perfect distinction to separate a genuine but inferior form of happiness from its perfect form. While sensual pleasures are wholesome, they are not spiritual, as is the intellect (*SCG,* 3.27).[24] Ultimate happiness is a spiritual activity: it is seeking our ultimate good, which is, of course, God.

Complete happiness is knowing God utterly. "By this operation man is united to [spiritual] beings above him, by becoming like them. . . . Man's ultimate happiness consists in wisdom, based on the consideration of divine things" (*SCG,* 3.37). Here Aristotle's musing that there is something vaguely godlike in the philosophical life becomes a Christian theology of happiness as spiritual union with God, which means becoming like God. While Aquinas stayed with the *visio*

22. Here we see his anti-Albigensian program at work.

23. The confusing failure to clearly distinguish false from imperfect happiness comes from Boethius (*Consolation,* 9.4). Thomas did not clear this up, as I have noted in discussing the *CS.* This ongoing confusion — about whether there are two types of happiness where both are possible in this life, or where one is possible in this life and one in the next — has also contributed to the debate about continuity or discontinuity and compatibility between philosophy and theology. It could be that Thomas would want to say that bodily happiness is temporal but spiritual happiness can begin in this life with divine illumination, continue, and be perfected in the next. However, he never makes this explicit.

24. This contrasts with Augustine's argument that the problem with material goods is that they do not last.

dei as a soteriological goal, he had no notion of seeing/knowing/understanding God as a purely cognitive activity. For him there is no such thing as a purely cognitive activity that does not involve the whole soul. Cognition and affect — "head" and "heart" — were separated only centuries later. Seeing God satisfies the heart's longing to rest in God. This is beyond the reach of bare cognition. Aquinas relies on the divinely illumined intellect. Happiness is "that knowledge of God the possession of which leaves no knowledge to be desired of anything knowable" (*SCG*, 3.39). Knowing God is not information about God but an intimacy with divinity itself (the divine mind, essence, or nature) that satisfies the soul's deepest desire; it is simultaneously intellectual and emotional joy, in which love infuses knowledge.

Divine Illumination

Since happiness is knowing the divine mind, we are hamstrung using our mind alone because our little minds cannot grasp the divine mind. They need help. For help on getting help, Aquinas turns to Augustine and his idea that God illuminates the mind and enables it to know him.[25] Whether divine illumination is possible in this life is unclear; even if that does happen, illumined minds cannot know God as they would wish. The full effect of God's power, the extent of what he wills, and the full effects of what he does still escape us. In this life we can never understand God as well as he understands himself, and this is precisely what Aquinas craves (*SCG*, 3.56). He wants to share divine goodness. This is eternal life (3.61), and it is the ultimate goal of life (3.59).

Thomas seems to have what we would call a growth-oriented psychology. Although he does not have that modern concept, dramatic jumps or advances from one level of knowing to another are nowhere in evidence. Deepening understanding makes one wiser and morally stronger; intellectual and moral improvement are one and the same. Happiness happens in doing. As one "does" better, one becomes more morally effective and as a result enjoys knowing God more. This growth into goodness is theological self-realization for those blessed

---

25. Augustine never brought his thoughts on divine illumination together in a single work. Minor discussions are in *Soliloquies*, 1.1.3, 1.8.15; *Letters* 144.1 and 166.4.9; *Sermon* 23; *City of God*, 8.7, 10.2; *Confessions*, 7.9.13; *Homilies on 1 John*, Homily 4.

with illumination to the degree that this happens in this world. By becoming spiritually adept, one becomes emotionally secure and less needful of external sources of gratification.[26] This benefit is lost on those who miss the signs of God in this world that would enable them to understand the true source of goodness.

In order not to miss the signs of divine goodness, one needs extra help in knowing God (*SCG*, 3.52). Realizing this, the divine mind joins itself to our minds, illuminating them. In this life we can know God "as [one] sees the divine essence itself, that is, by means of itself; so a vision of the divine essence is both what is seen and the means of seeing it" (*SCG*, 3.51).[27] Divine illumination is the foundation of Aquinas's doctrine of happiness: God is both the means and the object of human happiness.

Divine illumination enhances the intellect to know God immediately and everything else perfectly.[28] It is the light of glory that unites the mind with God (*SCG*, 3.55).[29] Those so empowered know him directly, though the comprehensiveness of their understanding of God varies with the degree of illumination they have been granted. Aquinas develops this further in the *ST*.

Secondary Agency

While knowing God requires divine illumination, other kinds of knowing and being creative are ours by virtue of natural God-given intellect. The concept of secondary agency elaborates the power of that original

26. Aquinas uses "sufficient" *(ad hanc etiam operationem sibi homo magis est sufficiens)* to describe moving away from less exalted notions of happiness (*SCG*, 3.37, n6). This word is rather misleading in modern English because, quite contrary to Thomas's intention, it denotes independence from the source that bestows the knowledge that is ultimate happiness. Beyond this, however, it is altogether ambiguous when transferred from a naturalistic Aristotelian to a Christian theistic setting, where only God is sufficient unto himself. See John D. Jones, "Natural Happiness: Perfect Because Self-Sufficient?" *Gregorianum* 83, no. 3 (2002): 529-44.

27. See comparable discussions in Aquinas, *Summa Theologiae*, 1a. q. 12, a. 4-5, Aquinas, "Supplement, qq. 1-99," in *Summa Theologica* (New York: Benziger Brother, 1948), 92.1.

28. The "else" refers to angels and "separated substances," those that are without a body (*SCG*, 3.59).

29. For a fine article on Aquinas's mystical theology, see A. N. Williams, "Mystical Theology Redux: The Pattern of Aquinas' Summa Theologia," *Modern Theology* 13 (1997): 53-74.

divine gift. It is one of Aquinas's most important theological contributions. He discusses it in *SCG*, book 3, and in the treatise on divine government in the *ST* (*SCG*, 3.64-83; *ST*, 1a. qq. 103-9). Here we examine its moral and psychological implications.

Aquinas needed to account for human creativity within his doctrine of providence.[30] God is the ultimate cause of everything, yet we make things happen, too. Understanding ourselves as instruments of divine providence comes from belief in the good and loving Creator. "God loves His creature, and so much the more as it has a greater share of His goodness, which is the first and chief object of His love. Hence He wills the desires of the rational creature to be fulfilled, since of all creatures it participates most perfectly in the divine goodness" (*SCG*, 3.95). God supports us in our desire to flourish because we share in divine goodness.

Although God causes all that is and happens, things are like God in that they can be the creative agents of other things. We are like God in causing and maintaining the flourishing of creation for its own goodness and well-being, just as God causes and supports us for our well-being. Since all things seek their own perfection, as they tend toward a good, they tend toward the likeness of God. All things are "theotropic," as befits their particular nature. Their common goal is to be perfect, and that is to be like God (3.24).

The agent of a thing is not its own end. A builder builds a house, but the purpose of the house is to be a dwelling: the thing produced is the purpose of the agent. The builder's goal is to build houses and when he does — especially when he does it well — he is meeting his own end and advancing his own perfection. Likewise, God creates us to ensure the flourishing of creation just as the shipbuilder ensures the means of travel and commerce by building a ship. The excellent artisan and the excellent person both express human perfection as they more attentively perform and delight in their abilities (*SCG*, 3.26). Delight in doing and making things well and tending them carefully fulfills our nature and purpose. Since all things are purposeful, the better we advance other things to their proper purpose — the more godly we are — and the happier we become as the persons we are and are becoming

30. The idea comes originally from the anonymous ancient *Liber de Causis*, on which Thomas wrote a commentary. Aquinas, *Commentary on the Book of Causes*, trans. Vincent A. Guagliardo, Charles R. Hess, and Richard C. Taylor, Thomas Aquinas in Translation (Washington, DC: Catholic University of America Press, 1996).

(3.64-70). The good bestowed by anyone on something else becomes shared property, binding the agent and the recipient together in goodness: "The good of one becomes common to many if it flows from the one to the others, and this can be only when the one, by its own action, communicates it to them. . . . Accordingly, God communicated His goodness to His creatures in such wise that one thing can communicate to another the good it has received" (3.69).

Thomas wants to be absolutely clear that our limited participation in God by virtue of our God-given creativity, intelligence, and goodness suffices to bring other things to their own flourishing. He adds: "[It is not] necessary that whatever has a form by way of participation [in God] receive it from that which is a form essentially [God]; for [whatever has a form] may receive [that form] immediately from something having a like form in a like manner [human intellectual creativity], namely, by participation [in that] . . . and thus like agent produces like effect" (3.69). In other words, human intelligence conveys divine intelligence to the things it authors and shapes. By enhancing the well-being of creation's materials, both inert and living, we transmit God's creative goodness to the things on which we act for their gainful use. That use is in turn transmitted to those who will use and enjoy them. We do not have to be exceptionally good, creative, wise, or beautiful to transmit these traits to other things; we only have to be intentional about using our moral and intellectual endowment felicitously.

We can summarize human providential agency as follows. (1) Each creature is an agent of divine providence with greater or lesser powers. (2) Each creature is created by God with a potential that is to be enacted for it to reach its zenith, just as the acorn is potentially an oak. (3) The more perfectly each creature fulfills its God-given purpose, the more perfectly it is an agent of divine providence. (4) Thus, fulfilling our nature is fulfilling God's will both for us and for creation more broadly. (5) Human nature includes the capacity for conscious and rational participation in God's plans for creation. (6) Conscious and rational participation in God's plans for creation improves through participation in the mind or life of God. (7) Therefore, people are better agents of divine providence the more they participate in the divine economy of salvation. Self-realization is living as an agent of the divine will.

The implication of this doctrine of secondary agency for a Christian understanding of happiness is direct and stellar. As we tend toward God, we actualize ourselves. That tending is a deeply social and outward-pressing activity that communicates and transmits divine goodness to all that we touch. Acting on things for their good advances their purpose, and as this happens we are also improving: enhancing the flourishing of others enhances our own. This is enjoying ourselves and being happy in this life.

While this is a philosophical construal of happiness, it has emotional traction. We experience deep and lasting pleasure from accomplishing practical and artistic tasks, furthering relationships, and caring for material objects. In addition to being godlike, living excellently is simply pleasurable.

Summa Theologiae

Although the *Summa Theologiae* was to strike a blow against the Albigensians, it was written in a more specific setting.[31] Much of it was probably written in Rome when Thomas had the opportunity to create his own theological curriculum for beginning theology students. His goal was to embed practical pastoral and moral instruction in a doctrinal context. There are two treatises on happiness in the *ST,* one in the *Prima Pars* and another in the *Prima Secundae,* though only the second is so identified. The *ST* remains incomplete because Aquinas died just shy of his fiftieth year, but its outline is preserved in notes for the completion of the *Tertium Pars,* which would have concluded the massive work with a final account of heavenly bliss.[32]

31. Here I follow Leonard Boyle, "The Setting of the *Summa Theologiae* of St. Thomas — Revisited," in *Ethics of Aquinas,* ed. Stephen J. Pope (Washington, DC: Georgetown University Press, 2002), pp. 1-16.

32. Thomas Aquinas, "Supplement, qq. 1-99." It may be ill-advised to turn to this *Supplement,* which was compiled posthumously under the direction of his friend Fra Rainaldo da Piperno, who used book 4 of Thomas's commentary on Lombard's *Sentences,* written some twenty years earlier. One difference between this commentary and the *ST* is that the earlier one has many more objections — and frequently more contradictions to the objections — from classical sources. This suggests that Aquinas was streamlining rather than expanding in the later work. Thus, in using the *Supplement,* we may have more than we would have had if Thomas had lived longer. This, together with his great consistency of thought, encourages us cautiously to consider the *Supplement.* Despite this limitation, Thomas did write the material in the *Supplement,* so it is a legitimate source for understanding his eschatology, even if it may not reflect his final thoughts on the matter.

Graced Happiness

The *Prima Pars* does the heavy doctrinal lifting for the whole work. Question 12 is on knowing God. Article 1 states the content of happiness previously sounded in *SCG*: "When [God] is revealed, we will be like him, for we will see him as he is" (1 John 3:2).[33] Here Aquinas reads the verse eschatologically. The same article also makes clear that the subject of question 12 is the knowledge that is ultimate happiness: "The ultimate happiness of man consists in his highest activity, which is the exercise of his mind. If therefore the created mind were never able to see the essence of God, either it would never attain happiness or its happiness would consist in something other than God."[34] This sets the subject matter of the whole question. Ultimate happiness is knowing the divine essence.

Question 12 is an epistemological treatise on how the created mind can comprehend God. This happens when God enlightens a human mind with the light of divine glory *(lumen divinae gloriae),* conforming it to himself. The light of glory is God participating in us for our happiness. Those so blessed begin to know God directly.

Different people know God and become like him differently, depending on how God illumines them; this, in turn, depends on how much *caritas* a person has. "Those share more in the light of glory; because a greater charity implies a greater desire, and this itself in some way predisposes a man and fits him to receive what he desires. So that he who has greater charity will see God more perfectly, and will be more blessed" (*ST,* 1a. q. 12, a. 6). They will see and understand him better, be more of his mind, and be happier. It will emerge in Aquinas's treatment of the theological virtues that *caritas,* too, is a gift — an infused virtue — but there is no indication of that here (*ST,* 1a2ae. q. 62, a. 3; q. 63, a. 3).

Articles 1-10 seem to be talking about happiness in general, but articles 11-13 take back much of what precedes them by severely restricting what can be known of God in this life. Even the graced person can at best know God only partially. It must be possible to a limited degree because Scripture notes prophetic experiences, miracles, dreams, and ec-

33. Aquinas, *Summa Theologiae,* 1a. q. 12. Hereafter, references to this work will appear in parentheses in the text.

34. Thomas Aquinas, *Knowing and Naming God,* ed. Thomas Gilby, trans. Herbert McCabe OP, vol. 3, *Summa Theologiae* (London: Blackfriars, 1964), 1.1.2 q. 12, art. 1.

stasies in which some people do learn of God. Further, the light of grace (i.e., the light of glory) strengthens the intellect, helping it understand the revelations of God described in Scripture. Divine illumination must occur in this life; otherwise, Scripture would be wrong. Denis Bradley argues that there is a deep paradox in Thomas's treatment of this subject: on the one hand, Thomas argues that we all naturally want to see God; on the other, we are unable to do so without grace, which belongs to divine election. This conflict violates the principle that it is impossible for a natural desire to be in vain. It is a conflict that Thomas never seems to resolve or even face directly.[35]

Imperfect Happiness

At the beginning of the *Prima Secundae,* Thomas has another go at happiness. Standing at the head of his ethics, which occupies the lion's share of the *ST,* the treatise on happiness appears to be about temporal happiness that prepares humans for celestial happiness, but he never makes this explicit. He always considers temporal happiness in relationship to happiness more broadly construed, but this treatise seems to embrace both perfect and imperfect happiness. Still, it has a shape of its own and is quite different from the happiness depicted in *Prima Pars,* question 12. This treatise is unique in Christian literature in that it deliberately considers mundane happiness as valuable in itself. Its placement at the head of the ethics, following Aristotle's lead, indicates that Aquinas understood, along with Aristotle, that happiness and moral life are inseparable.

Scholars debate whether natural and graced happiness are mutually exclusive but simultaneous in this life, each used in a different sphere, whether they are continuous so that happiness in the next life completes happiness in this life, or whether terrestrial and celestial happiness are of different kinds and thus discontinuous. Anton Pegis espouses the discontinuity between natural and graced happiness; he is opposed by Oscar J. P. Brown.[36] Denis Bradley argues that it is impossible to extract a purely philosophical ethics from Thomas (of which the

35. Bradley, *Aquinas on the Twofold Human Good: Reason and Human Happiness in Aquinas's Moral Science* (Washington, DC: Catholic University of America Press, 1997), pp. 424-81.

36. Anton Pegis, *Introduction to Saint Thomas Aquinas* (New York: Random House, 1948); Oscar James Patrick Brown, "St. Thomas, the Philosophers and Felicity," *Laval Théologique et Philosophique* 37 (1981): 69-92.

teaching on happiness is the foundation). Bradley is, in turn, opposed by John Finnis, who sees in Thomas a discontinuity between worldly and heavenly happiness.[37] More recently, Jean Porter has sought to end this unproductive debate by arguing that Thomas's moral theory is both philosophical and theological, though she sympathizes with the theological side of his moral theory.[38]

This treatise on happiness (*ST,* 1a2ae. qq. 2-5) is preceded by an argument that human life is meaningful and that human activity is to a single principled purpose. Despite differing delights, the ultimate human purpose must be absolutely good, and that is God. Humanity's purpose is happiness in God. The next four questions hone in on what happiness is, beginning with what it is not (qq. 2-5).

The discussion begins with the traditional ruling out of wealth, honor, fame, power, health, and material pleasure as constituting happiness. No created good can fit the bill, for happiness is a spiritual pleasure (q. 2). Question 3 argues that happiness is the *visio dei,* which is a reprise of happiness from *Prima Pars.* In this life, imperfect happiness is through the senses, but in the life to come the senses will not be needed, for enjoying God will be a purely intellectual activity.

Part of question 4 treats imperfect, temporal happiness. While question 2 agrees with Boethius that happiness does not consist of the goods of fortune, some of these return as necessary for temporal happiness. Question 4, with eight articles, begins with the Augustinian view that life is enjoyable when we have what we desire (art. 1). Resting in, enjoying, or having a desired object, however, does not exhaust happiness.

---

37. Bradley, *Aquinas on the Twofold Human Good;* John Finnis, *Aquinas: Moral, Political, and Legal Theory,* Founders of Modern Political and Social Thought (Oxford: Oxford University Press, 1998). L. Hamain and Kevin M. Staley argue for discontinuity between natural happiness and the happiness of grace, while Rollen E. Houser and Edouard-Henri Wéber see ultimate happiness in heaven as completing the happiness possible in this life. L. Hamain, "'Beatitudo Imperfecta' et Théologie des Réalités Terrestres," *Ephemerides theologicae Lovanienses* 36 (1960): 685-93; Rollen E. Houser, "The De Virtutibus Cardinalibus and Aquinas' Doctrine of Happiness," in *Atti del IX Congresso Tomistico Internazionale,* 3 (Vatican City: Libreria Editrice Vaticana, 1991), pp. 250-59; Kevin M. Staley, "Happiness: The Natural End of Man?" *Thomist* 53 (1989): 215-34; Edouard-Henri Wéber, "Le Bonheur dès Présent, Fondement de L'Éthique selon Thomas d'Aquin," *Revue des sciences philosophiques et théologiques* 78 (1994): 389-413.

38. Jean Porter, "Right Reason and the Love of God: The Parameters of Aquinas' Moral Theology," in *The Theology of Thomas Aquinas* (Notre Dame, IN: University of Notre Dame Press, 2005), pp. 167-91.

Enjoyment is actively loving and resting in the thing desired, at which point the desire for the object ceases because the object is possessed. However, following Aristotle, as we have seen, Aquinas defines happiness as an activity, so it cannot have ceased. Therefore, enjoying what we want, while it is an important component in happiness, does not exhaust it. Equally important is "the activity in which the will finds rest, and not the actual resting because of it" (art. 2). In this way, Aquinas comes to the conclusion that enjoying an object includes desiring it or having it incompletely. Augustine explicitly rejected this idea, because enjoyment cannot be not having what we want but having it. It is ceasing to want something because we have what we have desired. This may sound odd, but it is essential to the argument that imperfect, temporal happiness is genuine but can only be complete in the next life, when what we desire we fully possess, and the desire for it is completely stilled. It justifies temporal happiness because, even if we cannot completely have what we want, we nevertheless genuinely enjoy loving desired objects even though desire for complete possession is not extinguished (art. 3). The satisfaction of desiring requires virtue (rightly oriented desire) in order to achieve its aims (art. 4).

Although all of question 4 implies temporal happiness, its second half turns specifically to temporal happiness. It is not a purely noetic activity, because it embraces experience. Virtue is necessary but not sufficient for temporal happiness. This is a deep break with Christian Stoicism and Neo-Platonism. Even if it is an intellectual pleasure, enjoyment is embodied and the body contributes to happiness (art. 5). Happiness needs a healthy body because poor health can impede virtue and thus impede the correct orientation or will toward selecting appropriate desires. At the same time, "happiness of soul overflows into body which drinks of the fullness of soul" (art. 5). Physical and spiritual pleasures work together because soul and body are an indivisible unity. Aquinas here takes issue with Augustine, who wants to sever happiness from everything corporeal. "How odd this is. For since it is natural for the soul to be united to the body how is it credible that the perfection of the one should exclude the perfection of the other?" (*ST,* ia2ae. q. 4. art. 6). Not only does happiness include physical enjoyment, because a person is the union of body and spirit, but physical well-being is necessary for it (art. 6). Happiness requires adequate nourishment and wealth that are the "tools to serve happiness which lies, says Aristotle, in the activity of virtue" (art. 7). Finally, happiness is a social activity.

One needs a community of friends who experience one's care, and one enjoys seeing them flourish (art. 8).

The final question of the treatise on happiness asks whether and how happiness is obtained (q. 5, with eight articles). We can, of course, be happy because we are intellectually outfitted to apprehend perfect goodness — God — even if not naturally (art. 1). There is hope despite limitation. Happiness in knowing God is the same for everyone since we are all similarly endowed, but we are differentially happy depending on how well disposed we are to enjoying God (art. 2). We can be happy in this life, but not perfectly so (art. 3). Imperfect happiness can be lost because it is dependent on virtue and circumstance, but perfect happiness cannot be lost (art. 4). We can be happy in this life by our own strength, but perfect knowledge of God is by grace (art. 5). Angels cannot make us perfectly happy; only God can (art. 6). Righteousness is necessary for happiness, and that is not possible except by Christ's merits and membership in Christ through baptism (art. 7). Everyone wants to have what he or she wants, and so everyone wants to be happy, but not everyone knows how to be happy.

In conclusion, the treatise on happiness spans both terrestrial and celestial happiness. These share some components and requirements but are quite distinct. Temporal happiness is a psychological activity that requires virtue, physical well-being, and friends (*ST,* 1a2ae. q. 4). It seems to be possible without divine illumination but seems also to prepare us for celestial happiness by letting us sample delight. Enjoying life carries over to perfect happiness because it teaches us what enjoyment truly is. We taste it here, knowing that it can be lost, and we anticipate it all the more there, where it cannot be lost. Enjoying life prepares us for enjoying God.[39]

On the other hand, turning away from material goods can also prepare one for the beatific vision. Thomas thinks of external and spiritual goods in inverse proportion to one another. The more we are conformed to God, the less we need external rewards (the reverse is also true). Curiously, however, he also implies that food, drink, and wealth enable our conformation to God, for they give us a taste for ultimate happiness and the dignity by which we are raised to union with him. The last condition for mundane happiness — namely, friends — is standard throughout

---

39. Although he was a member of a mendicant order, Aquinas's commitment to the goodness of creation prevented him from disparaging prosperity.

classical philosophical literature. In cultures that do not have companionate marriage, friends enable one to delight in helping and caring for them. They, in turn, help one's spiritual journey. Even in heaven, friends "add a well-being to happiness" (*ST,* 1a2ae. q. 4, a. 8).[40]

In sum, honoring material happiness, even to the quite limited degree that Aquinas does, is an innovation in Christian theology. Augustine and Boethius and the great weight of the theological tradition often contrasted spiritual with material well-being. Augustine concluded that happiness is not sustainable in this precarious life, while Boethius disparaged the goods of fortune. Thomas bows to Augustine in highlighting the precariousness of mundane happiness (quoting *City of God,* p. 19), but views celestial and temporal happiness as of a piece, though just how they work together remains ambiguous. Nevertheless, by appearing at the head of the ethics, the moral life controls temporal happiness. They come together in a fresh way for Christian theology.

Happiness through the moral life prepares us for eternal bliss. A quality life develops the right attitudes and skills needed to enjoy God hereafter. Thomas's embrace of material well-being expresses his firm belief in the goodness of creation. Heaven is not an escape from this vale of tears but the culmination of an ethically strong life. Imperfect happiness here serves perfect happiness there. Mundane happiness uses the faculties we have, and God illumines some for spiritual happiness with his grace.

Now we are in a better position to return to a question raised earlier by those who set mundane happiness under the rubric of philosophy and celestial happiness under the rubric of theology, positing discontinuity between them. Thomas does insist that, although mundane happiness is possible, celestial happiness — even if we prepare for it by living virtuously — is the province of the blessed. However, this distinction does not presuppose a strong discontinuity between the two orders of happiness. Thomas argued that a well-ordered will is needed for happiness in this life and in the next. One must want God in order to be as happy as possible in this life, though the desire is completely realized only in the next. The desire itself is a gift from God as Augustine had insisted. In this respect, mundane happiness is a foretaste of what will become perfect for the blessed in heaven and after the general resurrection.

---

40. This is the social high point of Thomas's teaching on happiness. It is, however, still more Stoic than Augustine's account of heaven as a city.

Further, in both cases, happiness is an intellectual activity, and Thomas is clear that the same mind enjoys God both on earth and in heaven. Therefore, while there is a distinction in happiness because bodily well-being is necessary in this world but not the next, there is also strong continuity between mundane and celestial happiness — the same person is happy in both cases — and virtue glues them together.[41]

Here we conclude Thomas's construal of happiness that is traditionally eschatological yet makes space for temporal happiness without competition. It could have taken Christian piety in a fresh direction, but it was too weak. L. Hamain has argued that Thomas's construal of mundane happiness loses its force because it is presented as relative — and relatively inferior — to perfect happiness in heaven. It remains partial, inchoate, and vague.[42]

The imperfect knowledge of God possible in this life is ultimately unsatisfying for Aquinas, who craves complete knowledge of everything. His intellectual passion leads him to suppose that everyone wants to know everything about everything, to understand every agent from the effects that we experience.[43] Since God is the best "thing" to know, we want to understand him utterly and thereby share his own enjoyment of himself. Therefore, we press on.

Aquinas says that God *is* what he does; his existing is his acting. He has no desire or need to act in order to become happy, as we do, for he is perfect happiness itself. Being God is being happy. Since God is perfect, his happiness is also perfect. This claim is a twist on the Aristotelian premise of the divine as the unmoved mover, first agent, or thought thinking itself, which informs the Thomistic vision of ultimate bliss. To grasp the full scope of his teaching, we need to explore one further aspect of Thomas's work, though we have met it already: the beatific vision.

---

41. The continuity is explicit. See Aquinas, *Summa Theologiae*, 1a2ae. q. 3, a.2-3. A happy culmination of life is "the full development of what has begun to live [in us]" (art. 2). The difference between happiness in this life and in the next is the degree of constancy by which we can gaze on God (art. 3).

42. Hamain, "'Beatitudo Imperfecta' et Théologie des Réalités Terrestres," pp. 685-93.

43. I have earlier noted female sexual imagery in Augustine's desire to have God come into him. Here the overtones are male: Thomas wants to use his mind to penetrate the very being of God and possess it.

Eschatology

Thomas portrays perfect happiness as the sublime bliss of contemplating God in heaven. He believes that everyone longs to see God just as he does. The inspiration for this view may be partly Aristotelian, but it is primarily biblical: from Genesis 32:30 (Jacob, after wrestling with the angel of God, exclaims, "I have seen God face to face") and especially, as Aquinas points out, from 1 John 3:2: "Beloved, we are God's children now; what we will be has not yet been revealed. What we do know is this: when he is revealed, we will be like him, for we will see him as he is." Thomas tells us what he thinks this will be like and what we need for it. The heavenly vision presupposes the immortality of the mind. This premise is so accepted by his readers that he does not need to mention it. The disembodied mind in heaven awaiting resurrection will experience complete delight in gazing on God because it has found what it seeks, and it can finally rest from its search and enjoy its fruits.

According to him — and Christian eschatology generally — disembodied minds, awaiting resurrection and reunion with their spiritualized bodies, are alive in some sense. Saintly and divinely illumined minds fly straight to heaven and "see" God face to face. There they become completely absorbed in enjoying the presence of the one longed for and loved throughout life, for they have found their heart's desire.

The beatific vision is central in a much larger drama. Augustine paints hell and the resurrection life vividly at the end of the *City of God*. Thomas fills in this picture of heaven, using the Augustinian eschatology that was transmitted to his age.[44] Medieval eschatology is vivid and speculative, and Thomas's scholastic treatment is picturesque. It generally follows Augustine's classic outline in *City of God*, books 19-22, which is largely based on Revelation 21-22 and hints at the future life of the blessed in texts such as 1 Corinthians 12 and 1 John 3:2.

The "Supplement" to *ST* discusses life in heaven before the general resurrection. The saintly soul is now pure intellect, devoid of sense experience but retaining some kind of memory and self-awareness. Emotions become acts of the will (desires) of the disembodied mind. These minds enjoy the perfect vision of God that has been the object of their

---

44. Important figures in the transmission history of Christian eschatology after Augustine are Gregory the Great (d. 604), Ivo of Chartres (d. 1116), Honorius of Autun (d. 1151), and Peter Lombard (d. c. 1160). See Marcia L. Colish, *Peter Lombard*, 2 vols., Medieval Theologians (Oxford: Blackwell Publishers, 2001), 1:698-710.

deepest desires and the focus of their pious devotion throughout life. Not only do they gaze on the face of God, but they are freed from the fear of sin because they are no longer able to sin. They can no longer become separated from God. Yet they all await the Lord's coming in glory to judge the living and the dead, when the created world will be cleansed of sin by fire. Christ's return will be accompanied by a general resurrection and the final judgment. Although the saints will not be judged (they are already in heaven), they eagerly anticipate reunion with their bodies, whose loss they have grieved in the interim. This reunion inaugurates eternal happiness for them.

Perfect Happiness

Augustine portrayed heaven as perfect inner, interpersonal, and human-divine peace; he emphasized the sociality of heaven with the imagery of a city. Aquinas, the intellectual's intellectual, asks whether the saintly mind can grasp the divine core. The glory that is the goal of resurrected life becomes the fullest grasp of the divine glory in the glorified body of Christ, known also through the glorified bodies of the saints, who "see" by means of them ("Supplement," q. 92.2). In heaven, the blessed soul can never fall away from God or tire of gazing on him. The saints grow in this understanding of glory and help one another grow in understanding God (friends are still important) until the last judgment, when they are reunited with their spiritualized body (q. 92.3). With the general resurrection, however, growth stops, for the blessed know God as he knows himself.

Even in heaven, however, differences among the saints remain, depending on the degree of perfection each mind attains, which in turn depends on how deeply one desires and loves God (q. 93.3).[45] Love increases understanding of things known, including God. Therefore, finally, love is the key to happiness for Thomas. Good loving makes for good knowing. Perhaps Thomas agrees with Augustine that knowing and loving are mutually enriching.

---

45. See Aquinas, *Summa Theologiae,* Ia. q. 12, a. 6.

Assessing Thomas's Contribution

Following Augustine, Aquinas believed that happiness is enjoying God, but he articulated it primarily as knowing or seeing God. Happiness is possible in this life in a limited but significant way, for it requires God to illuminate the human mind by uniting it to his own. This advances beyond Augustine, who was quite cautious about terrestrial happiness because it is so fleeting; perhaps he never fully overcame Manichaeism. On the other hand, Thomas was never attracted to Manichaeism. Seeing God requires divine illumination, and that is related to how much *caritas* one has. Yet *caritas* itself is a gift of divine grace; it is an infused supernatural virtue. It seems that Aquinas's position is that happiness depends on divine illumination, which, in turn, depends on the supernatural gift of love.

The ultimate delight that Thomas seeks is eschatological because it must be unloseable. Although disembodied minds may fly straight to heaven — or may get there by a more circuitous route — the ultimate hope of all but the damned is to be reunited with their spiritualized bodies at the final judgment that follows the general resurrection.

Thomas made two contributions to the development of the Christian doctrine of happiness. First, he integrated Augustine's notion of happiness residing in the enjoyment of God with divine illumination, the beatific vision, and immortal life. These were all Augustinian themes, but the bishop did not unify them. Aquinas incorporated Aristotle's valorizing of personal well-being into Augustinian theology to create a genuine if limited Christian doctrine of terrestrial happiness while sustaining central interest in eschatological happiness.

His second contribution is that he recognized that terrestrial happiness prepares one for eternal bliss. Augustine did not emphasize the continuity between material and spiritual happiness, which Aquinas appreciated more. For his part, Boethius tried to wean us from relying on good fortune and the ability to accumulate wealth, power, fame, and reputation; Aquinas, by contrast, valued mundane happiness because he saw continuity between temporal and eternal bliss: temporal happiness is a foretaste of the heavenly banquet, and enables us to anticipate and yearn for eschatological fulfillment even more. To the degree that achieving this goal requires good attitudes, a well-disposed mind and body, and friends, divine grace enables us to be happy in this life. Thomas viewed the great river of time and space that we occupy as the arena in which the desire to celebrate our life in the goodness of God's creation, however imperfectly, enables us to develop knowledge of God and hope for eternal bliss.

A frustrating vagueness remains in Thomas's presentation, however, because he does not always say which matters pertain to this life and which to the next. Are imperfect and perfect happiness qualitatively different things, the former relying on purely human abilities and the latter requiring divine illumination? Or, as the terms "imperfect" and "perfect" suggest, are these continuous? Does the divine illumination that enables at least some to see God imperfectly in this life give them a taste of and for heaven, or are the blessed so designated wordlessly and sightlessly and thus have no idea of what awaits them in heaven? From this examination, it appears that Aquinas intends continuity — rather than discontinuity — between temporal and eschatological happiness. First, Thomas never says that the light of divine glory occurs only after this life. Knowledge of God is not possible to the naked mind but is only possible by divine gift. Second, those who fly straight to heaven at death do so not only because they have the correct sacramental status, but also because they already know God by virtue of the degree of divine illumination they have received. As Antoine de Saint-Exupéry said in *Le Petit Prince,* anticipating the arrival of the beloved is essential for knowing what love is. If craving the fulfillment of the *visio dei* does not begin in this life, what role could love play in heaven? Experiencing the light of divine glory must happen during earthly life, for without it no one would be oriented toward the eschatological *visio dei.*

Therefore, some people experience the light of divine glory more than do others. Illumination is the gift of loving and wanting to know God utterly; it gives unifying purpose to life. Thomas's painstaking detail in working through Christian belief is the tapestry of a realizing eschatology. While it may have been occasioned by the need for a school textbook, existentially he was motivated by his own longing for intimacy with God — into which he invites his students.

CHAPTER 5

The Modern Fate of the Doctrine of Happiness

With Aquinas, the Christian teaching on happiness reached its zenith. After John Buridan in the fourteenth century, Christian interest in happiness waned, until Anglicans responding to secularizing currents in their own day picked it up again in the eighteenth century.[1] As we move into modernity, it will be helpful to review briefly the fate of happiness between Aquinas and Anglican bishop Joseph Butler (1692-1752), both for the sake of the historical arc that we are tracing and to identify influences on Butler. Butler combatted moral cynicism with a theological doctrine of the commanding voice of God within.

The Sixteenth Century: Reformers

Protestants were wary of Aristotle and scholasticism — and therefore of Aquinas. Happiness was of little interest to them. While Aquinas thought from creation, Protestants thought from the Fall. Starting with Martin Luther's search for a gracious God, Protestants became preoccupied with finding a solution to the paralyzing fear produced by their belief in God's justifiable wrath about human sinfulness. Although Protestants did not talk much about happiness, it implicitly became relief from anxiety before God. Having rejected the penitential system, Protestants turned to Christology in a search for absolution.

---

1. Georg Wieland, "Happiness: The Perfection of Man," in *The Cambridge History of Later Medieval Philosophy,* ed. Norman Kretzmann et al. (Cambridge: Cambridge University Press, 1982), p. 686.

The search for peace of mind is a fresh form of Augustine's resting in God, though they do not use the language of felicity.

Martin Luther

Martin Luther (1483-1546), who was a monk for almost twenty years, refers to joyous moments in the Christian's experience, but he does not attend to happiness in a concerted manner. Paul Althaus notes that, on the eschatological side, "Luther . . . says nothing about souls without their bodies enjoying true life and blessedness before the resurrection," but they do enjoy a deep and dreamless sleep in "the peace of Christ" while awaiting the Last Day.[2] Protestant eschatology defends the rationale of bodily resurrection and moves away from the elaboration of immortality in heavenly abodes.[3] Dreamless sleep in the bosom of Christ while awaiting final judgment is a quiet time; it is not the enjoyment of the perfect vision of God that Thomas Aquinas imagined.

On the terrestrial side, Luther's theology stems from his preoccupation with divine wrath mediated through his encounter with the devil. When he thought, instead, of God's mercy in Jesus Christ, he found relief from his psychological torment and urged others to do the same. If God is merciful, then we can enjoy life fearlessly. This mercy-oriented posture allows for enjoying life more here and now. Luther's embrace of family life also fits with the turn toward daily life fostered by Renaissance humanism that spurred interest in this world. This may account, in part, for the decline of interest in eternal bliss.

Although he had the doctrinal foundation for it, Luther does not elaborate on well-being in this life; but he worries about human sinfulness. Embracing marriage and family left Lutheranism and Protestantism more generally with a paradoxical heritage, given the monastic skittishness about the body.[4] Even after his turn from divine wrath to divine mercy, Luther continued to swing back and forth between periods of what Julian of Norwich (1342–c. 1423) had earlier called "desola-

2. Paul Althaus, *The Theology of Martin Luther* (Philadelphia: Fortress, 1963), pp. 414-15.

3. Luther, however, does sustain the teaching that the saints fly straight to heaven upon death. See Althaus, *The Theology of Martin Luther,* p. 416.

4. Darrin M. McMahon, *Happiness: A History* (New York: Atlantic Monthly Press, 2006), pp. 167-72.

tion" and "consolation."[5] Depressive seasons that come when we doubt God's mercy toward us are the work of the devil, Luther says. Therefore, a distrust of God's mercy caused by continued focus on divine wrath becomes the chief sin for Luther.

Luther's vision of Christian freedom constitutes his theology of happiness to the extent that he has one. Freedom from fear of divine wrath means living into the righteousness of Christ, which is our justification. It is the assurance of salvation: freedom from servile fear is the joy of release from fear into the energy to live heartily and even to "sin boldly" in the assurance of divine mercy. Happiness here stems from fervent trust that divine mercy will overwhelm divine justice on judgment day. It is the quintessential Lutheran form of happiness: enjoying gospel freedom from "the law."

Luther's freedom is a noetic theory that offers a belief system that brings freedom from fear of divine wrath. The idea is that trusting in God's mercy will drive out fear of divine wrath. The fear does not arise from a judgment about the quality of one's life; rather, the feeling of deep vulnerability is about one's ultimate destiny. Relief is available for those who can continuously focus on divine mercy rather than justice. A sense of security about eternity comes from hope in the strength of divine mercy. Luther is emphatic that Christians are actually not doing well at all: all remain damnable sinners. Even the justified remain sinners. Luther extols the unfathomable mercy of God in Christ, who brings mercy to us with the promise of imputed righteousness for those who put their trust in him. Luther's view of happiness is the elimination of anxiety and trepidation before God that we experience via the justification that calms the emotions.

Luther's vision of the Christian life is based on this freedom from fear of God. Trusting in divine mercy, the justified are confident because they need not worry that every step they take may be calamitous for their eternal salvation. Sin and the bondage of the will may still be in place, but belief that God looks away from them makes that fact moot.

5. Julian of Norwich, *Showings,* trans. Edmund Colledge and James Walsh, The Classics of Western Spirituality (New York: Paulist Press, 1978).

John Calvin

John Calvin (1509-1564) was not a monk as Luther was, but a Renaissance humanist trained in law and philosophy. He brought a strong dose of Stoicism to his theology, having done his first piece of writing on Seneca's *De Clementia*. Although Calvin did not develop a discrete teaching on happiness, his thoughts on the subject are implied in his doctrine of providence that elevates absolute divine sovereignty.

Despite his humanist commitments, Calvin was perhaps more forceful about the ravages of sin and the bondage of the will than was Luther. His psychology begins with the vast divide between God and humanity. He sharply contrasts the goodness of God with the fallenness of humanity, and his piety revolves around the notion that utter humility before God is the only spiritually acceptable posture. This view led him to embrace a strong doctrine of divine sovereignty and providence in order to affirm that every event is the express will of God. One should be joyful and delight in God's goodness even when terrible things happen, for each event is what God intends.[6] Not to be joyful under every circumstance insults God, whose wisdom, goodness, and justice are at work in everything that happens. The command "Rejoice in the Lord always" (Phil. 4:4) provides scriptural warrant for this attitude. In fact, ingratitude or a lack of joy may be the cardinal sin for Calvin. Here, even being sad at bad circumstances is an act of disobedience. This orientation is a bit different from that of Luther, who taught that being afraid of divine wrath is the great sin because it betrays a lack of faith in divine mercy. Yet both agree that the chief sin is to second-guess God. Happiness for Calvin is being able to graciously accept whatever happens to us.

Calvin's high doctrine of providence provoked charges that he was

---

6. An important distinction between Calvin and Augustine arises at this point. For Augustine, God actively wills some aspects of creaturely existence while merely allowing others. Calvin, on the other hand, rejects such a notion of God's permissive will so that God's providential sovereignty actively determines all aspects of creaturely existence. See Augustine, *The Augustine Catechism: The Enchiridion on Faith, Hope, and Love*, ed. John E. Rotelle, trans. Bruce Harbert, The Augustine Series: Selected Writings from "The Works of Saint Augustine — a Translation for the 21st Century" (Hyde Park, NY: New City Press, 1999), pp. 111-12, §96; John Calvin, *Institutes of the Christian Religion*, ed. John T. McNeill, trans. Ford Lewis Battles, 2 vols. (Philadelphia: Westminster, 1960), 3.23.8 (pp. 955-56).

merely baptizing Stoic determinism. Recent scholarship has discussed this charge, generally concluding that Calvin was deeply influenced by Stoicism but critical of it at the same time. He especially departed from it by positing that God's will is not simply impersonal fate but an expression of his personal decision of loving care for his creatures. However, this ambivalence may not exonerate Calvin of the charge, because accepting one's suffering as the result of an impersonal fate may be emotionally easier than considering it to be an act of love from a good and powerful God.[7]

One might expect a civic passivity to have flowed from Calvin's commendation of resignation before the divine will. In fact, the opposite was the case. Seventeenth-century Calvinism spawned a strenuous work ethic and energetic interest in the liberal arts, education, and politics that influenced England, decisively shaped America, and powerfully influenced the Netherlands as well. Calvin's fatalism stems from his study of Stoicism, and it translated into a high doctrine of divine sovereignty that attributed all events to the divine will. However, his activist spirit also pervades his thought. It comes from his embrace of natural law, the idea that God has implanted knowledge of good and evil in the mind. It is an idea that he shares with Augustine and Aquinas. By the grace of God, that innate knowledge can be set to good use for the benefit of creation by those who are united to Christ by the power of the Holy Spirit.

There are two things to note about Calvin's psychology along this line. Although he often sounds pessimistic about human nature, at other times he is more positive. Heiko Oberman highlighted this more optimistic side: "Calvin is convinced that, since the fall, man has be-

7. See Egil Grislis, "Seneca and Cicero as Possible Sources of John Calvin's View of Double Predestination: An Inquiry in the History of Ideas," in *In Honor of John Calvin, 1509-64* (Montreal: McGill University Press, 1987), pp. 28-63; Patrick Henry Reardon, "Calvin on Providence: The Development of an Insight," *Scottish Journal of Theology* 28, no. 6 (1975): 517-33. Kyle Fedler points out that Calvin disagreed with the Stoics particularly on *apatheia*, arguing that emotions are part of our God-created identity and thus cannot be evil. Fedler, "Calvin's Burning Heart: Calvin and the Stoics on the Emotions," *Journal of the Society of Christian Ethics* 22 (2002): 133-62. Peter J. Leithart concludes that Calvin was a moderate Stoic. Leithart, "Stoic Elements in Calvin's Doctrine of the Christian Life," *Westminster Theological Journal* 56, no. 1 (1994): 59-85. W. J. Torrance Kirby, on the other hand, argues that he was a hyper-Stoic. Kirby, "Stoic and Epicurean? Calvin's Dialectical Account of Providence in the Institutes," *International Journal of Systematic Theology* 5, no. 3 (2003): 309-22.

come blind and deaf to all transcendental reality beyond the domain of the arts and sciences."[8] Yet, within that domain, Calvin so transformed the interpretations of the Fall and of the *imago Dei* that he created a notion of human dignity that could survive on its own once God receded into heaven and secular utilitarianism took shape. Oberman is convinced that Calvin, though he did not treat the theme directly and despite his adherence to Luther's insistence on the bondage of the will, opened a path to the more hopeful expectation that, through providence, humanity is destined to grow toward an enjoyment of life in this world that would surpass that of Adam in paradise. Indeed, Calvinists did make a vigorous showing in the temporal arts of social life. Calvin's energy to motivate hard work in this life, however, lacks a spirit of enjoyment and celebration that would make it inviting.

Calvin mentions happiness in passing in book 3 of the final Latin edition of his *Institutes* (1559), where union with Christ is the basis for hope and energy.[9] It remains an eschatological hope in the kingdom of God that "will be filled with splendor, joy, happiness, and glory" (3.25.10 [p. 1004]). However, Calvin warns that one should not even be too optimistic about that. He advises his readers to "keep sobriety, lest forgetful of our limitations we should soar aloft with the greater boldness, and be overcome by the brightness of the heavenly glory. We also feel how we are titillated by an immoderate desire to know more than is lawful" (3.25.10 [p. 1005]). Precisely here is the pessimistic note in Calvin's psychology. In contrast to Aquinas, who encouraged readers to believe that eventually the blessed will know God utterly, Calvin warns against even that. Hard work in mundane matters and sobriety in spiritual ones remained the emphasis of Calvinism, and they certainly inspired a great deal of energetic activity.

Mortification of self and vivification in Christ is a central spiritual dynamic in Calvin's theology, and self-denial is an important Calvinist virtue. This theme is strong in book 3 of the *Institutes*. For example, "we will never have enough confidence in [God] unless we become deeply distrustful of ourselves; we will never lift up our hearts enough in him unless they be previously cast down in us; we will never have consola-

8. Heiko A. Oberman, "The Pursuit of Happiness: Calvin Between Humanism and Reformation," in *Humanity and Divinity in Renaissance and Reformation* (Leiden: Brill, 1993), p. 257.

9. Calvin, *Institutes*, 3.25.2 (pp. 988-89). Hereafter, references to this work will appear in parentheses in the text.

tion enough in him unless we have already experienced desolation in ourselves" (3.13.8 [p. 762]). Valorizing self-despair should not be surprising: it follows from presupposing a vast canyon between us and humility. Still, it is important to note that Calvin does not attach physical practices to his admonition. Monastic practices had fallen out of favor. Instead, mortification became a psychological matter, a "sorrow of soul and dread conceived from the recognition of sin and the awareness of divine judgment" (3.3.3 [p. 595]). Nor does Calvin intend to condemn human endeavor altogether. Still, he is ever watchful for the slightest whiff of vanity. Peter J. Leithart sums it up: "Suffering is a means for renewing and strengthening our fellowship with Christ, a token of the genuineness of our sonship, and one of the Spirit's tools to perfect us. Suffering forces us to abandon all hope in ourselves and to depend on and hope in God."[10]

The antipode of mortification is vivification. Death of sin yields a spiritual life of righteousness enacted in both baptism and the Lord's Supper (4.15.5 [p. 1307]).

Renewed life is referred to as regeneration. While vivification is the goal, Calvin highly values psychological suffering to motivate spiritual renewal. He might be nervous about discussions of happiness lest they downplay the importance of suffering and render vivification too accessible.

The Rise of Psychological Egoism

The seventeenth century birthed political theory and the moral psychology on which it was based. As we trace the theological history of happiness, it is particularly important to investigate the rise of psychological egoism, which is the simple observation that human beings are thoroughly selfish and navigate through life at odds with all others to their own advantage. Pleasure is obtained at the expense of others. In short, the idea arose that self-love or self-interest is the natural human state, perhaps covered over with courtesies or virtues that are basically a mask for one's true feelings. Western Christians may gently nod in agreement and perhaps smile, knowing that Augustine had based his theology on something similar that he called "original sin." The mod-

---

10. Leithart, "Stoic Elements in Calvin," p. 84.

ern moral psychologists were not particularly religious, as it turns out, but even so, Christian sensibilities were in the air that non-church-goers also breathed. An important difference between them and the theologians is that the theologians found rescue from this dire realization in salvation through Christ, while the nonbelieving moral psychologists either seemed to be moral cynics or suggested political and economic arrangements to manage the problem.

Thomas Hobbes

Thomas Hobbes (1588-1679) is generally understood to have proposed psychological egoism in *Leviathan* (1651). People seek their own advantage by gaining power over another: "[I]f any two men desire the same thing, which nevertheless they cannot both enjoy, they become enemies; and . . . [they] endeavour to destroy or subdue one another." Life is a condition of "war of every man against every other," in a continuous cycle of adversarial relationships and interactions in which each person jockeys for power.[11] Starkly formulated, it can be expressed this way: "No person is ever motivated by any passions other than those that have benefit to their own self as an object."[12]

The key question here is whether all our actions are irreducibly selfish, including those that appear benevolent. Hobbes argues that we single-mindedly pursue self-interest in an effort to achieve what we lack: enduring happiness in this life. Therefore, it is not clear whether pleasure is in enjoying what one has wrested from one's opponent or whether the wresting itself is the keener enjoyment. Just a few years later, Pascal would observe that what we love is the chase.

Life is either a naked or disguised power struggle in which no one and nothing is secure. The Christian fear of divine wrath, which finds refuge in humility, becomes fear of one another, which finds security in power. In the "state of nature," people resort to force in an effort to perpetuate sensual pleasure, and this leads to further instability and conflict. In this competitive melee, others are perceived as enemies to be subdued or feared as potential masters. This fear breeds defensiveness,

11. Thomas Hobbes, *Leviathan,* ed. Richard Tuck, Cambridge Texts in the History of Political Thought (Cambridge: Cambridge University Press, 1996), p. 75.

12. Cited by Bernard Gert, "Hobbes's Psychology," in *The Cambridge Companion to Hobbes,* ed. Tom Sorell (Cambridge: Cambridge University Press, 1996), p. 167.

servility, tyranny, and pretension. Ironically, the turn from heaven to science reveals both the ugliness of the heart and the ingenuity of the mind.

Hobbes recognizes the disastrous implications of what he finds deep within us for society if it is unrestrained. Education and strong central government are the best deterrents. If the theistic sanction no longer has the force that it supposedly once did, political sanctions must take up the slack. Hobbes is a psychological moralist who sees a problem and poses public policy to tend to it. Others would be cynical.

François de La Rochefoucauld

Across the channel, a Parisian nobleman who had watched courtly behavior published a collection of over six hundred *Réflexions ou sentences et maxims morales* (first authorized edition, 1665) culled from his observations.[13] He came to Hobbes's conclusion, but he put it more pointedly. The standard text begins: "Our virtues are, most often, only vices disguised." Because he did not offer an antidote to the ugliness he found within us, he looked like a moral cynic. He set the arena in which Joseph Butler would later protect his parishioners from cynicism with his reflections on *amour-propre* or *l'amour de soi-même.*

In a collection of pithy epigrams, many of which are on self-love or self-interest, La Rochefoucauld's much longer reflection on self-love cries for attention. It opened the original publication of *Réflexions,* but was withdrawn in the next edition.[14] In this reflection, self-love is an all-consuming, uncontrollable monster:

> One cannot probe its depth, nor pierce the darkness of its abyss. There it is hidden from the most penetrating eyes; it makes a thousand imperceptible twists and turns. There it is often invisible to itself; there it conceives, there it nourishes, and there it raises — without knowing it — a great number of affections and hatreds; there it forms some that are so monstrous that, when it brings them into the light, it fails to recognize them as its own, or it cannot bring itself to

13. François de La Rochefoucauld, *Maxims,* trans. Stuart D. Warner and Stéphane Douard (South Bend, IN: St. Augustine's Press, 2001).

14. W. G. Moore thinks that its absence in the second edition is a result of "chiseling" to refine the maxims to their pithiest rather than a recantation. Will Grayburn Moore, *La Rochefoucauld: His Mind and Art* (Oxford: Clarendon Press, 1969), pp. 19-20.

acknowledge them as its own. . . . Indeed, in the greatest matters of self-interest, and in its most important affairs, where the violence of its wishes calls for its complete attention, it sees, it feels, it hears, it imagines, it suspects, it penetrates, it divines everything — so that one is tempted to believe that each of its passions has a kind of magic which is proper to it.[15]

Freud may have popularized the unconscious, but La Rochefoucauld called it out centuries earlier. Self-deception is our default setting.[16] Joseph Butler picked up this point but tried to combat it; La Rochefoucauld simply folded before its power. He seems to endorse moral cynicism by providing no way forward beyond the pursuit of short-term self-interest, as Hobbes did and as Freud's superego would later. Virtue — even love — are self-deceptions. They are masks through which self-love speaks. Hobbes, on the other hand, holds that enlightened self-interest should generate sufficient trust to overcome the urge for domination. La Rochefoucauld leaves us to ourselves. Perhaps he thought that we have enough moral strength to reform once he exposes us to ourselves.

Like Hobbes's reflections on self-centeredness, La Rochefoucauld's psychological egoism is not out of line with aspects of Calvinism and Jansenism. However, Calvin, Hobbes, and the Jansenists had sanctions to help us out of the morass of self. La Rochefoucauld, by contrast, offers no salvation from selfishness. The only hope he recognizes for genuine love and friendship lies in rigorous self-analysis and honesty about the self. However, he does not elaborate on how we might achieve that.[17]

Bernard Mandeville

Hobbes worried that the private little wars we entertain against one another would lead to societal ruin unless capped by state power. La Rochefoucauld may not offer an antidote to selfishness, but neither does he valorize it. With Bernard Mandeville (1670-1733), we turn a corner.

15. Moore, *La Rochefoucauld*, pp. 103-4.

16. For a discussion of this, see Theodore Dalrymple, "Discovering La Rochefoucauld," *New Criterion* 19, no. 8 (2001): 28-31.

17. Joseph Epstein, "La Rochefoucauld: Maximum Maximist," *New Criterion* 14, no. 10 (1996): 14-23.

His witty satirical poem *Fable of the Bees* (1705) hews to the now familiar line that human beings are naturally selfish, but it puts that in terms of financial greed.[18] Fifty years after the appearance of *Leviathan* — and though the industrial revolution was still a long way off — England was modern and humming. Contra Hobbes, Mandeville thought of selfishness in economic terms, and his vision was quite the opposite of Hobbes's. If Hobbes was a political psychologist, Mandeville was an economic psychologist. England's economy thrived on mercantilism; unrestrained mercantilism may create extremes of wealth and poverty and be nourished by corruption and greed; but a rising tide lifts all boats, he argued.

A staunch advocate of free trade and the production of the luxury items that support it, Mandeville argued that humans' gratifying their desires for material goods is economically productive.[19] Consumer excess and catering to the effete desires of the wealthy, though considered extravagant and therefore vicious, actually stimulate trade and create jobs for attorneys, justices, the army, and day laborers — even physicians and the clergy. Greed, deceit, fraud, theft, war, and natural disasters are socially valuable since they generate economic demand. Consumerism and corporate greed may still be morally frowned on, but they are economically beneficial. Perhaps, apropos of La Rochefoucauld's insistence on self-deception, even those who scowl at capitalist excess rely on it for their retirement. The *Fable* argues that those who scowled at ease and luxury in late-seventeenth-century England would suffer financial setbacks should virtue and moderate living undermine the productive power of greed.[20]

Mandeville is a hedonistic psychological egoist for the sake of economic growth. Politicians responsible for the "happiness of society under their care" gain personal satisfaction from the glory they win. The motivation is self-liking:

> Man is never better pleas'd than when he is employ'd in procuring ease and Pleasure, in thinking on his own Worth, and mending his Condition upon Earth. Whether this is laid on the Evil or our At-

18. Bernard Mandeville, *The Fable of the Bees or Private Vices, Publick Benefits,* ed. F. B. Kaye, 2 vols., collected facsimiles (Indianapolis: Liberty Classics, 1988).

19. At the time, luxury items in England were subject to high sumptuary taxes, so that government profited as well.

20. Mandeville, *Fable of the Bees.*

tachment to the World, it is plain to me, that it flows from Man's Nature, always to mind to Flatter, Love, and take Delight in himself; and that he cares as little as possible ever to be interrupted in this grand Employment.[21]

Hobbes, La Rochefoucauld, and Mandeville equated self-love with selfishness *tout court*. By turns, they feared, tolerated, and embraced self-liking, but none of them doubted its ubiquitous power. Whether for weal or woe, however, they agreed that self-love is the way to happiness. Valorization of greed and self-interest were center stage. Social chaos threatened. Post-Christian and Christian philosophers alike were aroused to address their blessing of potential moral chaos. Moral society had to be possible.

Moral Sense Theorists

While it recognized that the power of vice (sin) in human motivation resonated with Christian sensibilities, Mandeville's valorization of greed struck a raw nerve. Christianity may have been slipping away rapidly in Britain, but there was enough moral feeling left to call forth a backlash against moral cynicism from both deists and those who held a bit more tightly to Christianity. They argued that benevolence is better for society than avarice, and they worked toward a moral psychology — actually, a theological moral psychology — to reclaim compassion and neighbor-love as hard-wired in us. Dramatically inverting Augustinian pessimism, they offered a strength-based account of the "state of nature."

The Cambridge Platonists, beginning with Ralph Cudworth (1617-1688), began responding to moral skepticism by promoting a rational intuitionism that returned to the Platonic idea that reality is good, true, and beautiful. Nathaniel Culverwell called this the "candle of the Lord."[22] Sidney Carter's song about George Fox, the feisty founder of the Religious Society of Friends, put it this way:

---

21. From *Female Tatler*, cited by Malcolm Jack, *The Social and Political Thought of Bernard Mandeville*, Political Theory and Political Philosophy (New York: Garland, 1987), p. 74.

22. Nathaniel Culverwell, "Light of Reason Is Calm and Peaceable," in *Cambridge Platonist Spirituality*, ed. Charles Taliaferro and Alison J. Teply (New York: Paulist Press, 2004), p. 137.

There's a light that is shining in the heart of a man,
It's the light that was shining when the world began.
There's a light that is shining in the Turk and the Jew
And a light that is shining, friend, in me and in you.

CHORUS:
Walk in the light, wherever you may be,
Walk in the light, wherever you may be!
"In my old leather breeches and my shaggy, shaggy locks,
I am walking in the glory of the light," said Fox.

It is a shocking reversal of Western moral psychology, yet to the same end of saving moral society. The first significant retort to Hobbes that influenced Butler was from Lord Shaftesbury, who put forward the idea of natural moral and aesthetic intuitions as foundational to human psychology. Francis Hutcheson followed him, convinced that loving is part of our natural endowment and that we learn to use it by being loved by God. In both cases, however, the theological element is undeveloped, leaving it close to rational intuitionism. Shaftesbury influenced Butler more than Hutcheson did, and Butler would address the theological weakness in both. He was more willing to articulate the theological underpinnings of their thought by naming the moral sense as conscience implanted in us by God.

Lord Shaftesbury

Anthony Ashley Cooper was the third Earl of Shaftesbury (1671-1713). He published a compilation of his works in 1711, entitled *Characteristics of Men, Manners, Opinions, Times.*[23] In this work he seeks to counter Hobbes's claim that short-term self-interest motivates all human behavior with the idea of an innate moral sensibility. He argues that we are not irredeemably selfish, but are a complex system of desires, beliefs, and urges. Although he does not use the term much, he insists that we all possess a moral and aesthetic sensibility: we instinctively

23. Anthony Ashley Cooper Shaftesbury, *Characteristics of Men, Manners, Opinions, Times*, ed. Lawrence E. Klein, Cambridge Texts in the History of Philosophy (Cambridge: Cambridge University Press, 1999). Hereafter, references to this work will appear in parentheses in the text.

recognize goodness and beauty when we come upon them (Augustine had argued this as well).

> It is impossible to suppose a mere sensible creature originally so ill-constituted and unnatural as that, from the moment he comes to be tried by sensible objects, he should have no one good passion towards his kind, no foundation either of pity, love, kindness or social affection. It is full as impossible to conceive that a rational creature, coming first to be tried by rational objects and receiving into his mind the images or representations of justice, generosity, gratitude or other virtue, should have no liking of these or dislike of their contraries, but be found absolutely indifferent towards whatsoever is presented to him of this sort. (*Characteristics,* p. 178)

We can shape mental pleasures to promote virtuous living in accord with benevolent feelings. Shaftesbury's point against psychological egoism is twofold. Not only is our basic nature socially endowed with natural affection and what he calls a "communicative or social principle" (p. 193), but the pursuit of proper self-interest is not selfish. "For though the habit of selfishness and the multiplicity of interested views are of little improvement to real merit or virtue, yet there is a necessity for the preservation of virtue, that it should be thought to have no quarrel with true interest and self-enjoyment" (p. 188). Similarly, Shaftesbury argues for aesthetics: there is an independent, universal standard of the beautiful that we can grasp and enjoy instinctively. Our natural desire is to partake of that goodness and beauty by ordering our lives in their likeness. The *imago dei* may linger in the background here, but taking pleasure in the good and the beautiful does not call for gratitude and worship, for human nature now stands on its own terms.

There are virtuous persons because there is genuine goodness and people can recognize it. Affections and emotions are more than a jumble of conflicting impulses because reason can bring them into a harmonious whole. Some impulses are power-seeking, but others tend to the good. Reason enables one to hold these in proportional balance.

Butler was to retheologize "the moral sense" by insisting that it is conscience built into our very nature by God, as attested by Paul in Romans 2:14. Conscience makes the moral life "natural" (in the sense of according to our true and proper nature as designed by God) when we are true to ourselves. Butler's insistence that conscience is "the voice of

God within us" responds to John Locke's rejection of innate ideas and to Hobbes's psychological egoism, which called for education to take up the slack for natural moral strength. Perhaps Butler thought that, on the one hand, Hobbes and Locke provided an excuse for those lacking moral education to shirk their moral responsibilities, while, on the other hand, Shaftesbury insufficiently appreciated the divine authority of conscience before which "our whole conduct" is to be judged.[24]

Francis Hutcheson

Following Shaftesbury, Francis Hutcheson (1694-1746) joined the opposition to psychological egoism, arguing that being virtuous brings happiness.[25] Hutcheson wrests the reins from Hobbes by elevating the profundity of internal pleasure over the grasping urge for external pleasure that occupies Hobbes's attention. Hutcheson argues that benevolent love is part of our natural endowment and that expressing it should be recognized as part of attending to self-interest.

Hutcheson proposes that we are endowed with a moral sensibility by which we spontaneously approve and disapprove of things that we judge morally praiseworthy and things that we judge morally blameworthy. In contrast to the psychological egoists, these virtue theorists hold that moral approval cannot be reduced to self-interest. It is genuine. We do care about the well-being of others, as is evident from parental and filial concern. Further, we respond to benevolent feelings from others correspondingly, enhancing the benevolent sphere of relationships. Hutcheson's point is that we enjoy morally approving of the fine behavior and moral success of others, and that is our happiness. He does not deny that we also have selfish emotions and feelings; his point against the psychological egoists is only that not all emotions are so. Vice may be real, but virtue is, too.

24. Joseph Butler, *Fifteen Sermons Preached at the Rolls Chapel and a Dissertation Upon the Nature of Virtue* (London: Bell, 1949), pp. 102, 14.

25. Francis Hutcheson's primary works are the following: *An Inquiry into the Origin of Our Ideas of Beauty and Virtue: In Two Treatises,* ed. Wolfgang Leidhold (Indianapolis, IN: Liberty Fund, 2004); *An Essay on the Nature and Conduct of the Passions and Affections: With Illustrations on the Moral Sense,* ed. Aaron Garrett (Indianapolis, IN: Liberty Fund, 2002). Here I rely on Schneewind's reading: see J. B. Schneewind, *The Invention of Autonomy* (Cambridge: Cambridge University Press, 1998), pp. 333-42.

While Hutcheson is now considered a philosopher rather than a theologian — the two fields had not yet, by his time, decisively separated — there is a decidedly theological element in his thought (as there is in almost all seventeenth- and eighteenth-century thinkers). Schneewind, himself not partial to the theological view, points to the effect that Hutcheson, who was moving past theism yet still bearing traces of Calvinism, believed divine benevolence has on us in calling forth gratitude. We naturally respond positively to those who are kind to us, and God calls for obedience from us precisely because he has acted so graciously toward us. We love because we experience ourselves as loved.

In the war over selfishness, Joseph Butler enlisted on the side of the moral-sense theorists. If we set those theorists to the left of Butler, when we look to the right we find another tacit interlocutor who grasped the point of psychological egoism but took it in a different direction.

Blaise Pascal

Blaise Pascal was, by all measures, a genius. He was a brilliant mathematician, scientist, philosopher, and Christian apologist — a Renaissance-style feat that few could accomplish even then. It is fitting that one of the earliest computer programs is named for him, since he designed the first attempt at a computer. He reached for the truth in many directions. Unfortunately, this radiant prodigy, who gave us so much, died before his fortieth birthday.

Our interest here is in his Christian apologetic, which illustrates the hyper-Augustinianism of Jansenism. He left his apologetic in the form of almost a thousand maxims grouped into thirteen sections, together with an appendix that defended the Christian faith against modern criticisms. His concern to defend classical Christianity — in a Jansenist voice — against Enlightenment criticisms earned him the title of "the first modern Christian."[26] He was the first modern scientist to write Christian apologetics: that is, he was the first Christian to realize that holding science and religion together is now a necessity.

Like the Protestant Reformers before him, Pascal did not dwell on happiness. We will glean what we can from his writings. His apologia

26. Edward T. Oakes, "Pascal: The First Modern Christian," in *The Second One Thousand Years*, ed. Richard John Neuhaus (Grand Rapids: Eerdmans, 2001).

begins with the observation that people seek false happiness in this life. Science does not address human self-deception: despite its many benefits, it cannot bring wisdom. The vastness of the cosmos, compared to a human being, leaves the thoughtful observer filled with awe at our ignorance, not satisfied at having conquered its heights. Science depends on observations and knowledge gained through the senses; but these, Pascal notes, function only within narrow human limitations and thus can be deceptive. Given these limitations, he turns to another source for less precarious knowledge.

Since human error cannot be eliminated, we should be rather miserable when we realize that we can never reach the fullness of truth through the senses. However, dejection at realizing human imperfection is spiritually helpful: that is, the awareness of our limitations yields genuine self-knowledge. Pascal was psychologically astute. Normally we hate to be told hidden truths about ourselves, but scientific knowledge comes impersonally, so we avoid public embarrassment. Normally we like to be flattered by those we call friends but who really seek to ingratiate themselves to us for their own advantage. We want to be loved, but we settle for being flattered. We think that this makes us happy, but we deceive ourselves when we think so.[27]

This conclusion leads Pascal to a discussion of unhappiness, which he attributes to boredom. It is a prescient observation that was already made by Mandeville. Pascal takes it in a different direction. People are not content with homely pleasures; they seek self-forgetfulness as they hunt for some object, but the chase is better than the possession. We enjoy that Hobbesian war of each against all. The capture itself offers an opportunity to brag to "friends," who are then suitably awed. Pascal exclaims: "How hollow and full of ribaldry is the heart of man!" (§143 [p. 44]). The observation that the distractions of entertainment are self-deceptive paves the way for Pascal's Christian sentiment that such small-minded diversions keep people from the sober self-reflection that could save them from spiritual ruin. All this misguided preoccupation is sinful, he declares, a source only of false happiness.

Pascal adopts standard Western eschatology. Happiness is in the next life. His famous wager is that, if infinite happiness and infinite misery are the two possibilities, it is wiser to believe — perhaps even to

---

27. Blaise Pascal, *Pensées,* trans. William Finlayson Trotter (London: Dent, 1954), §109 (p. 35). Hereafter, references to this work will appear in parentheses in the text.

train ourselves to believe — that God exists than to scoff at God and religion. The result of believing is that

> . . . you will be faithful, honest, humble, grateful, generous, a sincere friend, truthful. Certainly you will not have those poisonous pleasures, glory and luxury; but will you not have others? I will tell you that you will thereby gain in this life, and that, at each step you take on this road, you will see so great certainty of gain, so much nothingness in what you risk, that you will at last recognize that you have wagered for something certain and infinite, for which you have given nothing. (§233 [p. 68])

He assumes that belief in God cultivates virtues, and that it is at the expense of "poisonous pleasures" that nonbelievers apparently enjoy because they lack the virtues that Christian practice cultivates. His pressure to accept the wager is because forgoing temporal happiness is well worth the price for the sake of infinite happiness. Yet there is temporal enjoyment in the certitude of having made the right decision.

True happiness is found in service to God, Pascal declares, and failure to live in God is foolish and produces only unhappiness. Here we have the sermon of the *Pensées*. The most concentrated comments on happiness are in Section 7, the section on morality and doctrine. Here he admits that all seek happiness but find only misery (§437 [p. 123]). Christian faith in God is the only way out of this muddle. He argues, with Augustine, that only the immutable God can satisfy human longing. Abandoning God because of affection for something else is sin. With that turn, everything becomes its own end instead of finding its end in the supreme good, as Augustine taught. This, Pascal says, is the path to unhappiness, because using things for the enjoyment they give and not for the ultimate end they should seek opens the door to condoning lust, and giving free rein to lust can root human identity in the brutish side of human nature.

Pascal defends Christianity on moral grounds. Sin is social misery, and its cure is Christ. He echoes Hobbes's claim that people innately distrust each other. "All men naturally hate one another. They employ lust as far as possible in the service of the public weal. But this is only a [pretense] and a false image of love; for at bottom it is only hate" (§451 [p. 127]). Pascal saw what the egoists saw, but he perceived its antidote to be in Jansen's refuge in Christ. In light of human fallenness, God's uniting himself to us in the incarnation makes us capable of knowing him. In the original state of grace, humanity was "raised above all nature, made like unto God and sharing in His divinity" (§434 [p. 122]). With the Fall, however, we fell prey to the lust of the flesh, the eyes, and the will (pride). Only divine grace can repair these defects of fallen nature by raising the elect back to the capacity for participation in God.

Pascal contrasts his theological position with that of "the philosophers" (perhaps this reference is to the deists). Although his opening defense of the existence of God is the argument from design, the wager bypasses philosophical arguments for the existence of God because the God of the incarnation — not the god of the philosophers — gives true wisdom. It is here that his attitude toward happiness comes to the fore.

Although "the philosophers" have a doctrine of God, it is Christless. If they believe in God, they approve of themselves for doing so in yet another act of self-flattery. But since they are unsympathetic to God and desire instead to establish a good reputation for themselves by being civic-minded and generous, they devote themselves to having other people love and flatter them. According to Pascal, both options are "horrible" (§463 [p. 129]). The Christian path is morally superior because it teaches people to "hate themselves" and then to seek a truly lovable Being who is their precise opposite (§468 [p. 130]). Jansenism taught Pascal that true religion consists in annihilating a wholly sinful self — which can do nothing good and deserves nothing good from God, only his displeasure — before a perfectly good God (§470 [p. 131]). Finally, "we must love God only and hate self only" (§476 [p. 132]). Pascal read psychological egoism as a basically Christian insight and put it in a hyper-Augustinian cage to contain it.

Christian virtue requires hating oneself because of inescapable lust, in order to cultivate utter humility and mortification before God, though it is not clear precisely what mortification is.[28] Anything less (or more!) than pure self-hatred amounts to spiritual blindness. Christianity thus teaches the greatness of God and the misery of man. Pascal agrees that all people seek happiness, but he puts himself in the odd position of claiming that happiness resides in self-hatred, for that is

---

28. "Mortification" is a word that Calvin frequently uses, but he did not recommend ascetic practices, so its import remains unclear there as it does here. Perhaps he means it psychologically rather than physically.

the logical result of what he sees as true self-knowledge: knowledge of our iniquitous wretchedness (§546 [p. 146]).

Unless this rhetoric is hyperbolic — and hence for homiletical purposes only — Pascal's thought marks a decisive turn in Christian teaching on happiness. It may be a radicalization of Calvin, and it certainly is an unbalanced view of Augustine. With Jansen, Pascal may have hoped to follow Augustine, but, as I have previously observed, Augustine distinguished *proper* from *improper* self-love and self-hatred: proper self-hatred is hatred of sin, not of self. Pascal's definition of "happiness," on the other hand, is a kind of "anti-happiness," in its older meaning as the perfection of the self God has created humans to be. Pascal inserts an absolute division between Christian *self-love* (interpreted exclusively as selfishness) and *love of God* (interpreted as utter selflessness, accompanied by strenuous self-denial).[29] It is of a piece with the quietism of Miguel de Molinos (1628-1696), the self-annihilation motif in Jeanne Guyon's spirituality (1648-1717), and the cross-inspired spirituality of François Fénelon (1651-1715).[30]

For the Jansenist genius Pascal, preaching self-hatred is the antidote to the psychological egoism's apparent license. Repudiating self-love and becoming self-hating (assuming that is possible) becomes central to Christian happiness, while self-love is utter spiritual misery. Perhaps Pascal thought that God approves of us more if we hate ourselves because that reflects better self-knowledge and the just judgment of God about us. Indeed, if Pascal is the "first modern Christian," it is not difficult to see why and how less religious souls turned away from a "Christian" vision of happiness to embrace a secular hedonist interpretation of happiness as immediate, short-term pleasure detached from the love of God. Pascal's vision is based on a theological psychology that emphasizes defect alone, as far as our relationship with God is concerned.

29. For an accessible review of the development of the piety of self-denial as a move away from Augustinian eudaimonism, see Stephen Garrard Post, *Christian Love and Self-Denial: An Historical and Normative Study of Jonathan Edwards, Samuel Hopkins, and American Theological Ethics* (Lanham, MD: University Press of America, 1987), pp. 1-13.

30. All three were investigated by the Inquisition, and Guyon and Fénelon came under fire from the Jesuit Jacques-Benigne Bossuet. Molinos, Guyon, and Fénelon were all condemned, by Popes Innocent XI and XII, as a result of several papal investigations into their writings. As a result of these investigations, Molinos and Guyon were both imprisoned, and Fénelon was banished from the court.

As a fillip to the defect-based piety of Pascal's kind, it is worth noting one of its later Anglican advocates. In the early twentieth century, Bishop Kenneth Kirk attempted to revive the mordant vision of God, reverting to self-denying piety in his highly influential Bampton Lectures of 1928.[31] In an idiosyncratic interpretation of the vision of God filtered through seventeenth-century piety based on self-denial, Kirk ends with approbation for Fénelon and Guyon against their opponent, the Jesuit Bossuet: they reasoned that, despite its acknowledged dangers, "disinterestedness [in worldly matters] can be and must be achieved by a process of willed, reflective, or conscious self-annihilation" (p. 191). The spiritual disinterestedness in material goods that Kirk advocates is a selflessness achieved only in the context of Christian worship, whose goal is "spiritual illumination, of inbreathing of grace" in a mystical vision of God, domesticated for daily consumption and accessible to all (pp. 193-94). He concludes that the moral rigorism of "renunciation, detachment, [and] self-denial must have their permanent place in every Christian life, however much at the same time we set ourselves to live in the joyous fellowship of human society" (p. 200). He advocates the renunciation of joys and liberties that are legitimate enough, in favor of opportunities to meditate on Jesus and strive for the psychological otherworldliness that God sets before us. It is confusing to try to embrace a psychology that urges us to enjoy human fellowship while believing that we need to strive for self-denial because of our worthlessness before God.

31. Kenneth E. Kirk, *The Vision of God: The Christian Doctrine of the Summum Bonum*, 2nd ed., Bampton Lectures (London: Longmans, 1932). Hereafter, references to this work will appear in parentheses in the text.

CHAPTER 6

Joseph Butler

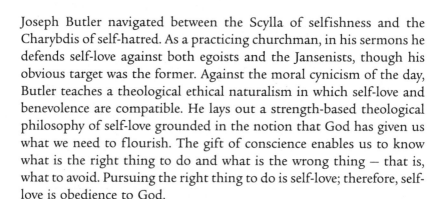

Joseph Butler navigated between the Scylla of selfishness and the Charybdis of self-hatred. As a practicing churchman, in his sermons he defends self-love against both egoists and the Jansenists, though his obvious target was the former. Against the moral cynicism of the day, Butler teaches a theological ethical naturalism in which self-love and benevolence are compatible. He lays out a strength-based theological philosophy of self-love grounded in the notion that God has given us what we need to flourish. The gift of conscience enables us to know what is the right thing to do and what is the wrong thing — that is, what to avoid. Pursuing the right thing to do is self-love; therefore, self-love is obedience to God.

This unusual starting point is the unifying theme of the *Fifteen Sermons,* published in 1726, which were drawn from his eight years of preaching at Rolls Chapel, London. In response to charges that this work was obscure, he republished the sermons in 1729 with an explanatory preface.[1] The purpose of some of the sermons is not to construct a Christian doctrine of happiness but to combat moral cynicism. Butler is important for the Christian conversation about happiness because he finds pleasure in the enjoyment of things we want to be Christianly toward.

---

1. Joseph Butler, *Fifteen Sermons Preached at the Rolls Chapel and a Dissertation Upon the Nature of Virtue* (London: Bell, 1949). Hereafter, references to this work will appear in parentheses in the text.

Butler's Project

Butler mentions the work of Hobbes and La Rochefoucauld's *Maximes* as two among a "whole set of writers" who fall into "the confusion of calling actions interested which are done in contradiction to the most manifest known interest, merely for the gratification of a present passion" (*Sermons*, pp. 20-21). Here is the key to his rebuttal of egoism. Wanting something is not to be interested in it: that is, it is not to believe that it is in one's best interest to have it. One may desire fine chocolate, but that does not mean that one is interested in it; that is, it does not mean that having these chocolates is in one's best interest. Wanting it is simply to gratify a desire. It is a repudiation of La Rochfoucauld's *amour-propre.*

Butler does not mention Mandeville, but he agrees with the latter's emphasis on self-deception, though he takes the unmasking of it in a different direction.[2] He enters the lists with his own moral psychology, beginning with a treatise on "human nature" in the first three sermons of the collection. He argues resolutely and quite independently that following our nature (as he redefines it) is obedience to the divine command and that self-love is an expression of that obedience. Without saying so, he relies on the *imago dei* that animated Augustine and the tradition following him.

Anglicans themselves had helped the church slip into a congenial deism in keeping with the Age of Reason. Butler's parishioners were precisely the people Mandeville's *Fable of the Bees* had in mind: educated, sophisticated, and wealthy.[3] There were among them many barristers, who come in for special attention in the *Fable*. With the authority of Scripture in decline, Butler could not appeal to it alone; thus, in order to provide a basis for benevolence and civil society with Scripture illustrating it, he presents a more positive moral psychology than was the case in either egoism or Jansenism. The word "more" in the previous sentence is important: the sermons take on various sins, though Butler does not develop a doctrine of sin as such. Rather, it is implied

---

2. For an extended discussion of the debate between Mandeville and Butler, see E. J. Hundert, *The Enlightenment's Fable: Bernard Mandeville and the Discovery of Society,* Ideas in Context (Cambridge: Cambridge University Press, 1994), pp. 126-39.

3. The original poem appeared in 1705 under the title "The Grumbling Hive: or, Knaves Turn'd Honest," but the version that attracted widespread attention was the 1723 edition, published three years before Butler's *Fifteen Sermons* appeared.

by his recognition that we can either obey or disobey the moral strength God implanted in us. In short, Butler is generally read as a philosopher; but he is a theological moral philosopher, if not a philosophical theologian.

Butler was cultivating a religious sensibility that framed reason theologically. He wanted his sophisticated audience to recognize themselves as guardians of a moral society that they must lead by example. He summarizes his project nicely: "That mankind is a community, that we all stand in a relation to each other, that there is a public end and interest of society which each particular is obliged to promote, is the sum of morals."[4] The text of the first sermon is Romans 12:4-5: "For as we have many members in one body, and all members have not the same office; so we, being many, are one body in Christ, and every one members one of another" (KJV) (*Sermons,* p. 31).

Butler was bold in abandoning fear as the primary instrument of moral compliance. Christians had always relied on it through the theistic sanction, but its power was wearing thin.[5] Hobbes and Mandeville also relied on fear, but not the theistic sanction.[6] Butler does not argue against the motivating power of fear; rather, he offers an alternative. God endows us with a moral plumb line to which we can adhere. Acting on it advances our well-being and society's well-being.

Recognizing that the fear of hell had been losing traction in England, Butler did not shout louder; he remained calm and responded thoughtfully.[7] Speaking from a Christian perspective, there is nothing remarkable in pointing to human selfishness. In his sermons Butler does not deny the power of sin; but unlike the bulk of the tradition — including Mandeville! — he does not construe it as pride (or, as it was

4. Quoted in James Downey, *The Eighteenth Century Pulpit: A Study of the Sermons of Butler, Berkeley, Secker, Sterne, Whitefield and Wesley* (Oxford: Clarendon Press, 1969), p. 54.

5. Seventy-five years earlier, Thomas Hobbes had pronounced eternal felicity promised in heaven "incomprehensible," and the beatific vision of the scholastics "unintelligible." Hobbes, *Leviathan,* ed. Richard Tuck, Cambridge Texts in the History of Political Thought (Cambridge: Cambridge University Press, 1996), p. 35. On the theological utilitarians, see Graham Cole, "Theological Utilitarianism and the Eclipse of the Theistic Sanction," *Tyndale Bulletin* 42, no. 2 (1991): 26-44; see also Ron Roizen, "God and the English Utilitarians," http://www.roizen.com/ron/bentham.htm.

6. For a discussion of the differences between Hobbes and Mandeville on governmental sanctions, see Hundert, *Enlightenment's Fable,* pp. 66-68.

7. D. P. Walker, *The Decline of Hell: Seventeenth-Century Discussions of Eternal Torment* (London: Routledge & Kegan Paul, 1964).

in current parlance, self-love). He does not scold, but, by preaching that they have what they need to live at their best, he calls on people to do so. God has equipped us to live rightly by giving us a conscience. However, being equipped is not being hard-wired; the gap between who we are and how we live is still great. Preaching can help bridge that gap.

Since he believed that we are properly equipped, Butler holds to Augustine's view that self-love is not vicious when rightly understood and targeted. Acting according to our theological nature — that is, heeding the voice of conscience — is self-love. In this radical move, self-love is no longer a monster to be feared but a love to be embraced. Psychological egoism pressed Christians to think through psychology carefully; Butler did so by reclaiming self-love as a proper theological category that distinguished self-interest from self-gratification. Self-interest both is virtuous and does not impede benevolence. Mistaking self-gratification for selfishness was the basic mistake of psychological egoism, and Butler corrected it.

Butler's Synthesis

Butler expresses the counterintuitive insight that self-interest or self-love is the moral way. Acting via conscience is acting in our self-interest and has nothing to do with pleasure from enjoying desired objects. Self-love, by contrast, is an exalted aspect of human nature that expresses our godly nature. Here is a radical inversion of the common-sense notion that self-interest is selfish. Instead, it is obedience to God. It is perhaps ironic that the psychological egoists believed that they were breaking with Christianity by relocating external sanction from heaven to earth. Butler, seeking to retain the authority of God and Scripture for the moral life, genuinely broke with the Christian impulse to identify self-love with sin. Like Aquinas and the Cambridge Platonists, he used the goodness of God and the goodness of creation to forge both a strength-based moral psychology and an anti-Stoic position, defending the goodness of human nature and the social utility of emotion.[8]

Butler's moral psychology comes from Genesis 1:26: we embody the

8. His remarks on resentment in "Sermon Thirteen" are quite interesting in this regard.

divine image, and moral strength is indestructible. Some theologians believe that moral strength is utterly inoperable after the Fall, but no one argues that God actively rescinded the *imago dei*. Rather, the undying Christian hope has been to see the divine image restored. Butler believes that we have access to it by means of prodding through scriptural preaching. In order to challenge moral skepticism, Butler begins with our godly identity rather than our fallen identity, which seemed to justify psychological egoism. Self-love is acting as befits our God-given nature, the *Sermons* argue, while betraying it leads to ruin.

Not only does Butler's moral psychology respond to psychological egoism; but again, ironically, it relies on precisely the love of flattery that La Rochefoucauld and Mandeville denounce. Butler flatters his listeners into believing that they were morally strong and capable of living ethically. The others, refusing to abide by their own findings, refuse to flatter and end up reproaching. Perhaps Butler got their point even better than they did!

Butler's Argument

Butler's *Fifteen Sermons* offer not a moral theory so much as a practical guide to the Christian life based on his theological psychology. The good life is advanced by "following nature," assuming that what that requires is not crushed under self-deception. A question is whether we can get beyond that (p. 51). Ethics, he says, may be approached either deductively or inductively. "One [way] begins from inquiring into the abstract relations of things" (pp. 6-7). Kant would choose this way. Butler proceeds by examining "what the particular nature of man is, its several parts, their economy or constitution" (pp. 6-7).[9] Data for that examination comes from both common experience and from the Bible.

The "nature" of a thing is diverse. A complete nature can best be understood by looking at how its parts form a coherent system, as with a watch (p. 10). In both the mechanical and the psychological cases, the whole has a purpose built into it by its creator. In the human case, the integrating psychological principle is a natural propensity toward the

---

9. W. H. S. Monck criticizes Butler for failing to come through on the first method, but Butler never claims to have followed this method at all. Monck, "Butler's Ethical System," *Mind* 3, no. 11 (1878): 366-67.

good. It organizes all aspects of our nature that separate us from lower animals — friendship, compassion, gratitude, abhorrence of what is base, and admiration for what is fair and just (p. 13). Human nature inclines toward goodness, and that inclination bends unstable appetites to a higher end. It is remarkable that he argues, on theological grounds, that human nature is to obey God.

God gave us both conscience and emotions. Sometimes they work together well, but sometimes not. When they do not work together well, it betrays our true nature, which tends toward goodness. Butler dismisses Stoicism's passion for imperturbability as unnatural. God created us with emotions and affections, and even those that can become unruly, like anger, can and should be used for good in accordance with our godly nature.

In the *Sermons*, compassion, forgiveness, and benevolence (neighbor-love, fairness, and temperance) are desirable — especially the last, which leads to love for God. Foibles to be avoided include loquaciousness, self-deceit, resentment, and retaliation. While the list of commendables is notably Christian, one can imagine the list of foibles arising from personal acquaintance. Still, he illustrates all of them with biblical texts, stories, and characters.

Butler identifies the ostensibly commendable and noncommendable emotions, attitudes, and affections; but he does not see these as categories, because all can be used both well and poorly. He opposes organizing the goal of life around certain emotions at the expense of others. The goal is not to transcend emotion and involvement in the material world but to use emotions productively. Attitudes and actions that further us toward that end are natural; those that carry us from that end are not. Emotions are neither selfish nor unselfish. Some are disinterested (i.e., impartial) and some are interested in their object, which is not ourselves. This is the core of his retort to psychological egoism. When emotions obey conscience, they advance self-interest; when they disobey, they act against our self-interest. Butler was a rationalist and thus believed that emotional self-control was within everyone's reach.

From the foregoing it becomes clear that self-deception is the primary sin in Butler's view, because it impedes acting according to conscience: it mistakes self-interest for immediate self-gratification. It is singular failure to act naturally. He argues that we love ourselves when we follow our un-self-deceived conscience. Human nature is not set over against revelation and grace, but is graced to be obedient to Scripture's moral teachings. In "Sermon 2" he says: "If by following nature were meant only acting as we please, it would indeed be ridiculous to speak of nature as any guide in morals" (p. 51). Conscience is certainly not the only psychological component of human beings, but it is the highest. In pointing out that shallow self-indulgence counters self-love — indeed, is perhaps self-harm — self-love guides a theologically good life. Discerning, strengthening, and following that moral center is the Christian life.

"Sermon 7" explores Balaam's inability to curse Israel on Balak's orders (Num. 23), and "Sermon 10" discusses Nathan's confronting of King David (2 Sam. 12). Together, those narratives illustrate the point that self-deception is conscience's nemesis. The sermon on Balaam shows that, though he wanted to curse Israel, his conscience would not allow it. The Bible supports the notion that the voice of God within is accessible to us.

The sermon on David makes the same point in reverse. By showing how self-deceived David is about his own actions until he is confronted by Nathan, the story shows how David is Balaam's opposite. When Balaam finally "follows his nature" — the created voice of conscience inside him — he is being both true to himself and obedient to God. This dual obedience to self and to God yields psychological self-consistency and peace of mind. Butler concludes that people want to be virtuous: "How much soever men differ in the course of life they prefer, and in their ways of palliating and excusing their vices to themselves; yet all agree in the one thing, desiring to *die the death of the righteous.* . . . There is no man but would choose, after having had the pleasure of advantage of a vicious action, to be free of the guilt of it, to be in the state of an innocent man" (p. 118; italics in original).

On the other hand, in his self-deceived suppression of his conscience's chastisement for having committed adultery and murder, David opposes his own nature. He has a conscience, but it is so weak that he has no access to it without Nathan's help. Nathan is the preacher par excellence. Yet Butler bemoans how readily people disregard good preaching: "Hence arises in men a disregard of reproof and instruction, rules of conduct and moral discipline, which occasionally come . . . their way: a disregard . . . [for] what may be of service to them in particular towards mending their own hearts and tempers, and making them better" (p. 152).

Human nature is caught between conscience and self-deceit. Yet, even if one's conscience is as moribund as David's was, it can be vivified. "[T]he very constitution of our nature requires, that we bring our whole conduct before this superior faculty; wait its determination; enforce upon ourselves its authority, and make it the business of our lives, as it is absolutely the whole business of a moral agent, to conform ourselves to it" (pp. 14-15).

For Butler, the highest human impulse leads "up" not "down": it is godly, not feral. Self-deception is unnatural. On this basis, Butler argues, "man is a law unto himself." The phrasing is odd, at best, to contemporary Christian ears. It comes from Romans 2:14: "For when the Gentiles, which have not the law, do by nature the things contained in the law, these, having not the law, are a law unto themselves" (KJV). That is, God has endowed humans with knowledge of the moral law apart from Scripture, so that even non-Christians can obey God. This natural strength is the source of moral freedom. We judge whether something is right or wrong so long as we are not mired in the sickness of self-deceit. Yet conscience is larger than immediate instinct. Even when the voice of God in us is operational, it may not be sufficiently strong for good decision-making in the social and interpersonal arena. Fine preaching may stimulate self-examination, as the sermons on Balaam and David suggest.

Butler elaborates his doctrine of human nature through Romans 2:14 in "Sermons 2 and 3." When obedient to one's moral nature, all "contribute to the happiness of society" (p. 49). Insisting that the well-ordered conscience can both avoid doing evil and bend toward the good inevitably downplays the necessity for revelation, even though his warrant for insisting on moral autonomy is scriptural. This surely was not Butler's intent, but it did contribute to the very decline of Christian authority that Butler himself bemoaned, preparing the way for its replacement with the idea of moral autonomy fully elaborated by Kant.[10]

At the same time, preaching does not suffice for all. Butler recognizes that some people are morally ill. What has been called "sociopathy" or "psychopathy" is now often called a "dissocial" or "antisocial" personality disorder.[11] While many will find Butler's optimism

10. Schneewind grants Butler an honorable place in the tale of the "invention of autonomy," despite the latter's lingering theological sensibilities. J. B. Schneewind, *The Invention of Autonomy* (Cambridge: Cambridge University Press, 1998), p. 347.

11. Its main symptoms are disregard for the feelings of others, deceitfulness, angry

naïve, society still agrees with Butler that healthy people have a sufficiently strong conscience to be able to restrain destructive impulses and be productive members of society. Criminal and violent behaviors are deviant perhaps because they lack what Freud called a "superego" and Butler called "conscience." Behavioral health is not simply a matter of prudent calculation in response to social policy and social convention. It is a moral issue and — from a theological perspective — a spiritual one. As Robert Hare puts it, "Lacking in conscience and in feelings for others, [psychopaths] cold-bloodedly take what they want and do as they please, violating social norms and expectations without the slightest guilt or remorse."[12] They lack the conscience that Butler believes God has given everyone. Failing to exhibit conscience is a sign of abnormality. Thus Butler sees David's behavior in the Bathsheba-Uriah episode as self-contradictory. To commit adultery and arrange for the cuckolded husband's death is unnatural. David was out of control and in the jaws of a confused search for moral self-destruction. Such people are truly miserable, no matter how long they enjoy the fruits of their exploits.

Butler looks naïve to those who believe that we live from our unconscious unruly desires to which the psychological egoists reduce us. Butler had a more nuanced view: he preached on both Balaam and David, though his case might have been more compelling had he argued that we all may be both Balaam and David. The question he poses is: Are we transparent to ourselves or opaque to ourselves? The moral egoists taught that we are so self-deceived that we are opaque to ourselves yet transparent to others. Butler teaches that, with the help of a fine preacher, we have a choice.

With human nature morally bent toward goodness, Butler has taken Christian moral psychology in a strikingly positive direction. Rather than telling his parishioners that they are trapped in sin and must throw themselves on divine mercy to avoid punishment, he tells them that God has equipped them to avoid moral shame. He wanted to persuade his sophisticated parishioners that God encourages them toward moral integrity.

---

outbursts, and poor impulse control. See Daniel Allen, "Building on Positive Relationships," *Mental Health Practice* 12, no. 7 (2009): 6-7.

12. Robert D. Hare, "Psychopaths: New Trends in Research," *Harvard Mental Health Letter* 12, no. 3 (1995): 4.

Butler knows how weak conscience can be, and he does appeal to the external theistic sanction, albeit rarely.[13] There are a few reminders for his parishioners to consider their long-term future as a stimulus for present virtuous behavior, but these are infrequent.[14] He prefers not to frighten his audience. Rather, his primary strategy is to encourage:

> There must be some movements of mind and heart which correspond to [God's] perfections, or of which those perfections are the natural object. And that when we are commanded to *love the Lord our God with all our heart, and with all our mind, and with all our soul:* somewhat more must be meant than merely that we live in hope of rewards or fear of punishments from Him; somewhat more than this must be intended: though these regards themselves are most just and reasonable, and absolutely necessary to be often recollected in such a world as this. (p. 27, italics in original)

That "somewhat more" is conscience, as the stories about Balaam and David explain. Destroying self-deceit liberates true self-love. This is true happiness. "Happiness or satisfaction consists only in the enjoyment of those objects, which are by nature suited to our several particular appetites, passions, and affections" (p. 170).[15] Conscience enables the proper ordering of love for those objects that we are rightfully interested in to the degree that they advance our genuine well-being. The operative phrase here is "by nature suited" to us. To be happy is to be emotionally gratified when self-love prevails, guided by sober assessment of right and wrong that requires preserving one's strengths for the output of energy. It applies to discerning what constitutes adequate neighbor-love as well. People flourish when they understand that only those who are "self-honest" act out of self-love. It and benevolence cooperate when humans make judgments about aiding others prudently and do not simply follow the desires of the moment. Providential reasoning is not problematic for Butler, as it would be for Kant; indeed, prudence is the way to a win-win situation for everyone.

Butler's is not a trenchant analysis of self-deception. He misses Augustine's point about the divided self. The moral egoists perhaps also

---

13. Butler mentions civil and criminal sanctions only in passing. Butler, *Sermons,* p. 17.

14. See Butler, *Sermons,* 3.8, p. 67; 7.13, p. 116; and 9.28, p. 48.

15. Space constraints prevent me from tracing the theme from self-love and neighbor-love to love of God, but it is very clear in Butler's texts.

lacked an adequate analysis, albeit from the other side. However, they both agreed that deep and clear self-knowledge is the way forward. What helps us get there is still open to debate.

Self-Love

Of the fifteen sermons, "Sermons 11 and 12," on love of neighbor, examine Romans 13:9, and "Sermons 13 and 14," on love of God, examine Matthew 22:37. Although Butler courageously rehabilitated self-love, he did not give any sermon that title. "Sermon 11," "Upon the Love of Our Neighbor," is his most arresting contribution to Christian ethics. Augustine had noted that there is proper self-love and that God intends us to love ourselves, but he had not developed the idea. Because "Sermon 11" is so significant and dense, Butler took pains to explain it in the preface he appended to the second edition.

The preface begins by arguing that self-love and benevolence are both universal human traits and are not necessarily at odds (p. 20). Benevolence does not defeat self-love; in fact, they may not even be in conflict. The assumption that they do conflict arises from a misunderstanding of self-love as necessarily being "distinguished from all particular movements towards particular external objects: the appetites of sense — resentment, compassion, curiosity, ambition and the rest" (p. 21). Self-love is not, however, directed toward external but internal goods. To clarify what self-love is, Butler distinguishes it from the egoist's broad generalization that all actions are motivated by the desire to take advantage of the other in order to gain advantage for oneself. He uses the word "selfishness" that is not helpful from our vantage point, but we can discern his intent. He distinguishes "cool or settled selfishness" that deals with "internal goods," from "passionate or sensual selfishness" that deals with "external goods." The internal good is one's moral well-being; that is self-love. The latter is the desire for self-gratification by enjoying objects; but that may be appropriate rather than sinful, according to Butler, as long as the desire is not inordinate. Genesis 1:28-31 hums in the background.

Passionate selfishness, that is, desires for pleasing objects like "honour, power, the harm or good of another" (p. 21), is not pursuing, that is, being "interested" in one's moral well-being, and thus it is not proper self-love. Yet, that does not mean that the pursuit of pleasing objects is immoral or sinful. If the emotions are inordinately pursuing their object, they can be self-defeating and so untoward, but that is not so by definition.

Self-love, on the other hand, is reflective: it, too, works through emotions but to enable us to live according to God's claim on us. Seeking external goods is only untoward if the desires driving them are "hot" — enough to betray our self-interest. That emotions rush after pleasures is not wrong, but it is not self-love because those emotions do not arise from conscience, "for no one can act but from a desire, or choice, or preference of his own" (p. 21). Interests are not desires: the former are spiritual and directed inward; the latter are material and directed outward. To act from self-interest is to act according to the *imago dei*, which Butler calls the voice of God within.

Faux self-interest is the result of philosophical confusion. True self-love requires properly understanding one's God-given nature. Butler's rehabilitation of self-love aims to clear woolly heads. The three sermons entitled "Upon Human Nature" tell us who we really are and reveal what we truly want for ourselves. He excoriates Stoicism's *ataraxia*, but not its insistence on virtue. Rather, self-love is living according to virtue, though not in spite of the emotions. Indeed, he embraces the emotions and the enjoyment of the material goods they seek.[16]

Self-love can express itself through any emotion. Things get complicated, because "it becomes impossible . . . to determine" whether an action is from self-love or from some "particular passion" (p. 21) that seeks simple enjoyment of things. Confusion sets in when even we ourselves cannot tell how far "cool" self-love is behind our action and how far particular emotions motivate us. Both are influential. Some people do grasp what "interest" is and live accordingly, while others spend their time gratifying particular emotions for the sake of immediate pleasure. This is not bad as long as the emotions are not inordinate, as King David's were in the Batsheva-Uriah narrative.

This is how Butler considers happiness. It is not the product of self-interest, says Butler, but there is no reason why happiness and self-interest should not coexist peacefully. People may love themselves properly, live according to the dictates of conscience, and yet be unhappy with their circumstances. Self-love can help them become happy "by setting them on

16. This could lead to the uncomfortable suggestion that ethics and happiness are completely divorced. That cannot be, however, since self-love is conscience and would judge untoward attempts at happiness to be morally culpable.

work to get rid of the causes of their misery, to gain or make use of those objects which are by nature adapted to afford satisfaction. Happiness or satisfaction consists only in the enjoyment of those objects that are by [their] nature suited to our several particular appetites, passions and affections" (p. 170). "It is not because we love ourselves that we find delight in such and such objects, but because we have particular affections towards them" (p. 22). It is not ourselves (theologically speaking) that we are interested in when we seek good food, drink, or wealth — but the objects. Gratifying desires for external goods brings happiness, but that may or may not be self-love. We are confused if we think that desiring things is self-interest, though some given thing may indeed advance our cause. The confusion is understandable because self-interest — that is, obedience to the voice of God within — works through the same emotions that the desire for specific objects does. Desire for an object (e.g., a certain woman or man) does not pursue a person's self-interest, however, unless it is consonant with conscience — and so is in obedience to the voice of God. Conquering is not pursuing self-interest, for self-interest is one's best interest, not the gratification of desire for an external object. Desiring an object is morally neutral. Desire enables emotions to advance our well-being, but they need to be "settled," not wild. David was not interested in himself when he took Batsheva: it may have made him happy, but it was not an act of self-love since he actually damaged himself.

Emotions are good and "necessary to constitute [both] that interest [and] happiness" (p. 22), but they confuse us if we mistake immediate pleasure (through food or sleep or toys) for self-interest. Having desires and gratifying them is not problematic; those desires are needed to pursue both self-interest and pleasure. That pursuit is not bad — indeed, it produces happiness. The full range of emotions is needed to pursue serious interests; negative emotions such as anger and sadness, when they are used to forward genuine interests, are good. The major step that Butler takes against cynicism is to separate self-love from happiness and to argue that emotions are involved in both. Happiness from sense pleasures is morally neutral, but it is not self-love.

Self-love is obedience to God's command to obey his voice. Self-love is not selfish; rather, it is public-spirited, because when we advance our own best interest we contribute to the well-being of the *polis*. Enjoying things that we desire may or may not bring happiness, but that is a separate question from whether such satisfaction is self-interested. Emotions that are not in the service of self-love but seek a "private good" may be pleasurable and satisfying, and that is all to the good, as long as they are measured (p. 170).

Butler's response to the egoists is to separate happiness from self-interest. The former is pleasure for gratifying appropriate desires for material objects. It consists of emotionally gratifying experiences that come from external pleasures. Self-love is a moral activity and does not aim at happiness (p. 171). Indeed, Butler warns that "inconvenience and disadvantage" may attend immoderate self-love (p. 172). Separating self-love from happiness is perhaps the most bracing move that Butler makes. It is a stunning retort to the Hobbesians, but there is sadness about it as well. To suggest that enjoyment of material pleasures has nothing to do with obedience to God leaves obedience in the ambiguous place that it has always occupied, accompanied only by a plea not to engage in immoderate self-love that would undermine enjoyment of suitable and appropriate pleasure. Given the moral cynicism of his age, however, Butler is to be commended for even seeing the danger of such scrupulosity.

Benevolence

Having construed self-love quite apart from egoism, Butler turns to the larger point of "Upon Human Nature": that is, to demonstrate that self-love is compatible with benevolence. He is responding to the common idea that there is no such thing as benevolence because humans only ever pursue self-interest in the Hobbesian sense of the term. Butler has already provided the terms of his answer: "[S]elf-love and benevolence are not opposed, but are distinct from each other; in the same way as virtue and love of the arts, suppose, are to be distinguished" (p. 23). The idea that benevolence is disinterested, and so morally superior to self-interest, is unwarranted. The moral value of actions is not determined by motivation "but from their being what they are; namely, what becomes such creatures as we are, what the state of the case requires, or the contrary" (p. 23). That is, the moral value of an act is determined by its fittingness to the situation, just as expression of emotion is. It may or may not advance our interest.

"Sermon 11" argues that disregard for the needs of others is quite unrelated to self-love when we understand the latter properly. Benevolence does not oppose self-love, as is generally assumed, because tending to one's well-being in Butler's sense is unaffected by affection for or antipathy toward others. One does not subtract some affection for self and give it to another who needs it. The pleasantness or unpleasantness associated with some forms of benevolence neither enhances nor depletes us, according to Butler. Any inconvenience incurred in the course of pursuing benevolence may interrupt pursuit of desired enjoyments and thus impede happy feelings, but that has nothing to do with self-love (p. 172).

Butler gives examples of the fact that benevolence has nothing to do with the agent's self-interest. He notes that acting benevolently may bring happiness since it brings consciousness of virtue and tranquility of mind, but that still may not touch one's natural interest. Indeed, living benevolently may be the greatest source of happiness, but not be self-interested (p. 175). Enjoyment of one's virtue, if it produces "a general temper, which more or less disposes us for enjoyment of all the common blessings of life," contributes to satisfaction and enjoyment of life just as benevolent activity contributes to the satisfaction and enjoyment of life by the other (p. 176). The sustained virtuous life that garners good reputation and love from others, and the settled satisfaction that comes with it, may be the best happiness that this world can afford. Happiness through benevolence is of the highest order because promoting the good of others is deeply gratifying. Emotions may motivate such gratifying activity, but the happiness that comes from it is not an expression of self-love if it is not motivated by obedience to the voice of God within.

Butler defined self-interest as non-pleasure-seeking behavior. Benevolent activity that brings pleasure to the recipient as well as the agent does not qualify as obedience to conscience (self-interest). Happiness and obedience to divine commands are distinct. Self-love is not pleasurable and happiness is not related to obedience to the voice of God.

This sermon concludes with an appeal to Scripture and to the Creed to the effect that Christians are under particular obligation to live a good life, "as our Saviour has set us a perfect example of goodness in our own nature." Living in obedience to that nature, our very own being as the goodness of God, is to pursue our self-interest: that obedience to God whereby he "might teach us our duty . . . reform mankind, and finally bring us to that *eternal salvation,* of which *he is the Author to all those that obey him.*"[17]

17. Dom Cuthbert Butler, *Benedictine Monachism: Studies in Benedictine Life and Rule* (New York: Barnes and Noble, 1961), p. 183 (italics in original).

Whatever technical philosophical shortcomings there may be in Butler's argument against Hobbes, here we can assess him as a moralist whose starting and ending point is an unusually encouraging moral psychology he developed against the moral cynicism of his day. He works out of the doctrine of creation to argue that God commands us to tend our own little garden, and that means obeying conscience. God is concerned for the well-being of society and has perfectly equipped us to advance it, having placed his own voice within us. Living according to it is self-love because it both obeys God and is faithful to our godly identity.

Butler turned common assumptions on their head. The popular understanding of self-love equates it with external pleasure. That is not self-love, but proper happiness, and here Butler is bucking the whole Western theological tradition. Living according to nature, however, begins when we recognize that our interest in and for ourselves is not to garner happiness. It is good and proper, but it does not forward or retard self-interest/self-love that is heeding the voice of God. Through his moral psychology, Butler beats the cynics at their own game. Self-love is not self-indulgence; rather, it is obedience to God, and as such it is morally uplifting, not shameful.

By making self-love a theological category, Butler detonates not only philosophical moral cynicism but also the common Christian supposition that benevolence requires self-sacrifice. Benevolence does not rob us of something that we need in order to be happy. It does not deplete us, but instead may actually increase our happiness. Butler recognizes that virtuous living garners enjoyment of life. It may be motivated by obedience to conscience, but that only advances our well-being and happiness all the more.

A weakness in Butler's theory emerges at this point. For him, self-interest is living according to our spiritual nature, but he does not think that acting in our own self-interest is pleasing. He does not admit that we need to grow into self-love from the woolly-headedness of self-centeredness, and so he does not explain how self-love is related to happiness. He does not see that happiness is needed for moral growth. Having logically separated happiness from self-interest, he misses the opportunity to say that self-interest can be practiced for increasing happiness. He does not attach happiness to self-love as clearly as he attaches it to gratification of desire.

Love of Neighbor

The second sermon on love of neighbor, "Sermon 12," is also on Romans 13:9 and carries forward the theme of the first sermon: neighbor-love is a Christian requirement. Butler fails to follow through on his retort to Hobbes. He fails to apply the same criteria to benevolence that he did to self-love in order to wrest benevolence that advances the neighbor's happiness from benevolence that advances one's own happiness. One wonders if his separation of self-love from happiness through benevolence is all that clear.

In directly addressing love of neighbor in "Sermon 12," Butler regresses to the conventional view that benevolence is exhibiting kindness, mercy, compassion, and charity toward the other in order to promote her or his happiness, and that in proportion to how we promote our own happiness. The key phrase is the interpretation of "as thyself" in Romans 13:9 (pp. 187-90). We are to seek the happiness of the other to the same degree that we seek our own.

Having been tilting at full strength against moral cynicism, Butler for some reason backs down when it comes to love of neighbor. He has established that "self-love" is obedience to conscience and is not about happiness from gratifying immediate desires. But he fails to apply this distinction to benevolence. That is, he fails to carry his categories forward to argue that benevolence is tending to the other's ability to love herself or himself as one would tend to love one's own ability to do so. Instead, Butler is content to apply the common standard: benevolence consists of promoting the "happiness" of others in terms of sense pleasure, not in terms of their spiritual well-being or their self-love.

Although he focuses on the proportionality demanded by "as thyself," it is the proportion of benevolence that one bestows on oneself and on others, not the proportion of self-love that one demands of self and others (pp. 191-93). He urges proportionality in the degree of one's affection for self and the other, not proportionality of self-interest.

This point establishes a fundamental disequilibrium. Proportionality of affection for self and others is praiseworthy, but it remains at the level of sensual happiness. It does not carry benevolence to the level of moral responsibility on which self-love functions. Butler succumbed to a basic inequality in a person's responsibilities to self and neighbor, retreating into a paternalistic middle-class ethic that provides social services to the less fortunate, even affection and concern for their situation, but fails to hold them to the same moral standard of self-interest to which he holds the agent. His ethic remains condescending because it does not call those for whom we care to self-love. Thus, benevolence remains at the level of social work.

Admittedly, the backbone required to preach something like this is considerable. Few preachers have the stamina for it. Butler wanted to break new ground, and he had been doing so courageously; but he turned back at the final checkpoint. Perhaps he was exhausted from going as far as he did. But benevolence toward neighbors is for their happiness, not for their self-interest. Here he spoke in a different voice, and he lost an opportunity. Still his accomplishment was quite astonishing by any measure.

Benevolence remains at the level of advancing the happiness of others, not their self-interest. Social work hopes to make the beneficiaries' lives more pleasant, at least momentarily, and thus it provides a whiff of happiness. Still, these are external concerns and do not advance other people's self-interest or their ability to pursue their self-interest. That is, compassion, mercy, and charity, if they are the extent of true neighbor-love, never reach the moral height that self-love does. To have affection, compassion, and mercy for the poor is well and good, but it speaks only to their happiness and not to their interest. It remains superficial.

Advancing the neighbor's happiness can be motivated by self-love if one were to derive no pleasure from the pursuit. It can be inconvenient or tiresome, and this is what Christian ethics often calls "self-sacrifice." The calling to increase the happiness of the disadvantaged out of concern for them arises from compassion for their plight. The goal of benevolent action, however, is to improve their circumstance, not advance their self-interest. A more principled teaching on benevolence would be attentive to interest and disinterest, as Butler claims his is. Far from being disinterested (in the sense of being nonmanipulative), benevolence that is truly the antipode of self-love would be quite interested in the self-interest of the neighbor, for that is the only way that public well-being will be promoted. Indeed, on Butler's terms, if we carry the principles to their logical conclusion, self-love and neighbor-love would not conflict at all. Principled neighbor-love would not simply seek the neighbor's happiness, but it might even cause distress by calling the neighbor to attend to her self-interest. Indeed, embracing the neighbor's happiness might mask her call to self-love. There is little wonder that Butler did not go this far. It is a hard message to preach.

Love of God

Of the four sermons on love, the last two, "Sermons 13 and 14," are on love of God. While the sermons on love of neighbor distinguished self-love from happiness in order to argue that benevolence can be genuine, here the argument is that love of God is genuinely enjoyable and constitutes happiness. Love is an emotion, not a rational decision. Loving God is called forth as the place where emotion comes to rest (as Augustine had said so many centuries before). Butler traces the psychological process. We observe divine benevolence toward us, and that instinctively evokes admiration and reverence in us. These feelings intensify when we realize that God's benevolent actions are from our guardian and governor (p. 210). Religious duty demands love of God; yet we instinctively respond to divine goodness affectionately, not because duty demands it.

Butler insists that loving God does not embrace servile fear, only reverence or filial fear. There is no cringing anxiety of the kind that propelled Luther to seek refuge in a gracious God. Butler is assured of the love that Luther craved by the gift of conscience that is his. Here divine love calls forth love in return. Loving is happiness that can be enjoyed over and over again (p. 207). Enjoying God is not hope of such enjoyment; rather, it is being satisfied by that enjoyment and resting in it. It is to be happy.

Enjoying God is analogous to loving a friend: the relationship brings satisfaction and enjoyment, which includes admiration and natural delight in the person's qualities, skills, and strengths (p. 211). Butler's spirituality is never far from the social realm, and he moves easily back and forth between human friendship and friendship with God. We experience God as present with us or as if he were present: he is the object of our affection. "We feel the force of amiable and worthy qualities in our fellow-creatures: and can *we be insensible to the contemplation of perfect goodness?* Pleasure is to turn one's attention to the higher faculties and affections that we do have, that we ascribe to God rather than to the lesser ones that also attend us" (p. 213; italics in original). Loving God thus pulls us up into these higher affections through longing to possess the goodness and wisdom that we admire and by the pure pleasure that they inspire.

Butler, like other eighteenth-century thinkers, was interested in the emotions. Because God gives them, they are good — not desperate, as Hobbes depicted them. After all, love for God is the foundation of the religious life. Butler's second sermon on love of God returns to the theme of happiness now depicted as an affection. It assumes a traditional posture of submission to God that reconciles us to our condition and incorporates us into the divine will (pp. 219-20). That resignation is not dour but delightful. It is happiness in God.

Since people cannot supply their own happiness and they experience themselves as inadequate to it, they reach out for amusements to fill up the time and deceive themselves into thinking that the amusements are happiness. Such diversions are not adequate to the task: they merely pass the time, as Pascal observed. They chiefly suspend our conceptions of and desire for happiness, and they prevent us from seeing our internal poverty. They deceive us. We have a capacity for something that wealth and amusement cannot supply. "Yet surely there is a possibility of somewhat, which may fill up all our capacities of happiness; somewhat in which our souls may find rest" (p. 223). Those "who have got this world so much into their hearts" think that happiness consists in property and possessions, but they are only means to something else" (p. 223). Happiness is enjoying the thing itself. Here Butler is Augustinian: loving God, not diversions, makes us happy.

Assessing Butler's Contribution

Bishop Butler was not constructing a doctrine of happiness but refuting psychological egoism. Happiness came into play as it was set off against his theological doctrine of self-love. His retrieval of theological self-love as obedience to the voice of God within is not happiness that is an emotion, a pleasant feeling that comes from enjoying desired objects, as is still the common understanding. He did not entertain the idea that self-love makes us happy.

However, his doctrine of self-love does pave the way for the view that self-love — that is, a life of obedience to God — does bring happiness, just as enjoying other desired objects does. Here, however, the desired object is one's spiritual well-being. Asherism will go on to say that happiness is simply appropriate pleasure that stems from self-love, just as enjoyment of fine art, music, or literature does. Butler misses the fact that one enjoys being obedient even when one is inconvenienced in the process.

Similarly, benevolent activities provide happiness precisely because they advance our well-being. That is, benevolence may be "selfish" from a certain viewpoint, but it is not paternalistic, as other understandings of benevolence can be. Benevolent activity motivated by self-love does bring the joy of living honestly and according to our nature, as Butler expressed it.

Concluding the Historical Arc

Butler's contribution concludes the historical reconstruction of the zigzag life of the Christian doctrines of happiness. Augustine's doctrine of happiness is primarily theological, eschatological, and conceptual, with room for atheological, temporal, and material happiness — unstable as it may be. Boethius's teaching is theological, temporal, and noetic, not eschatological or material. Aquinas followed Augustine's theological, eschatological, noetic precedent, but he made a small place for theological, temporal, and material happiness.

Fitting Butler into this schema is not easy, because his treatment of happiness is inadvertent as he pursues another project. His understanding of self-love does not recognize happiness as a side effect of obedience to conscience. That remains outside his theological purview, though it is easily incorporated into his doctrine of self-love without damage to his separation of happiness from self-love. Still, we may conclude that his teaching on happiness is material and temporal, and mildly theological to the extent that he recognizes the joy in loving God. He does not ground temporal happiness in obedience to God.

The theological conversation on happiness has staggered across the centuries, with the theologians addressing salient issues of their day. As I have noted at the very outset, this foray into the subject seeks to address two theological concerns: the heavy emphasis on future eschatology at the expense of a temporal, realizing eschatology in the classical tradition, and the academic triumph of theology in the modern university that has obscured the practical task of theology. The first concern, causing an underemphasis on temporal happiness, resulted in the hyper-Augustinian Jansenism of Pascal, which, while it was condemned by the church, has left tracks that make Christians skittish about temporal material happiness, fearing it is untoward from a Christian perspective. The second concern, for the consequence of the scientizing of theology within the theoretical strictures of modern academic convention, has made it difficult for theology to fulfill its proper calling of helping people in their life with God.

The proposal that follows addresses the first concern by suggesting a theological, temporal, realizing eschatology. It addresses the second concern by offering a theological, temporal, and experiential doctrine of happiness in the proposal of asherism.

PART II

Identifying Asherism

CHAPTER 7

Doctrinal Foundation

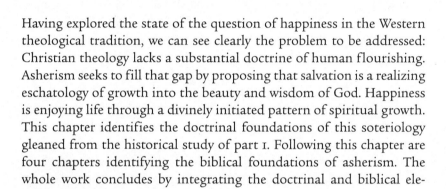

Having explored the state of the question of happiness in the Western theological tradition, we can see clearly the problem to be addressed: Christian theology lacks a substantial doctrine of human flourishing. Asherism seeks to fill that gap by proposing that salvation is a realizing eschatology of growth into the beauty and wisdom of God. Happiness is enjoying life through a divinely initiated pattern of spiritual growth. This chapter identifies the doctrinal foundations of this soteriology gleaned from the historical study of part 1. Following this chapter are four chapters identifying the biblical foundations of asherism. The whole work concludes by integrating the doctrinal and biblical elements of asherism for use by Christian communities.

Theological Precedents

Augustine: Therapeutic Soteriology

Augustine's therapeutic soteriology of ascent is foundational to asherism. His dogmatic examination of the scriptural foundations for the doctrine of God leads to a search for the image of God in us by means of which we discover who we are in God, that is, *who we are*. To know God is to know ourselves, and understanding ourselves theocentrically in terms of Genesis 1:26 is true self-knowledge for true self-love. True self-love is the healing of disordered love (i.e., sin). Although Augustine often names sin as pride, he means simply badly misshapen self-love. This is not evil, but the misoriented good of love for which God created us.

Only the healed person can love well, and loving well is the basis of a flourishing life. The path to that is spiritual penetration of the truth about who God is, what he equips us for, and who he yearns that we become. The equipment is the *imago dei*. Augustine is sure of that. He is also sure that God yearns for us to rest in him. He supplies a spiritual path that crashes through false construals of the *imago dei* that he discards, one after another, like the cups of a Russian nesting doll, penetrating deeper and deeper to find the key to the wisdom, goodness, and beauty of God that will make us whole.

Wholeness here is moral, social, and emotional wellness that is spiritual health. Augustine begins with the assumption that everyone is *capable* of being spiritually well, but is in fact spiritually ill. The illness is caused partly by confusion and partly by willfulness. Willfulness is an expression of deformed love that carries desire in bad directions. God, and only God, can heal love by retargeting and empowering us to love rightly and well. This is the implicit doctrine of happiness beneath the moral psychology of the second half of *De Trinitate*, to which the first half of the work is preliminary.

Augustine's soteriological concern in that work is the theological bedrock from which this proposal is hewn. Augustine tells us that being healed of bad love requires deconstructing bad knowledge, but he does not tell us how to break through bad habits of love that are built on bad knowledge. He tells us where to look to find better knowledge of love — that is, where to find wisdom and goodness — but he does not explain how that actually happens. That is, he explicates the problem beautifully and tells us the answer we are looking for, but he does not fill us in on the details of how we get from the deconstruction to the reconstruction of the "self." Boethius agrees with Augustine that therapy is needed, and he believes that the healing we need is available philosophically, whereas Aquinas and Butler offer more concrete proposals. The latter two are particularly helpful here in the effort to pick up Augustine's therapeutic soteriology of the ascent of the soul to God.

Aquinas: Secondary Agency

Aquinas faces temporal material happiness directly. It requires adequate health, safety, financial security, and social well-being, and it disposes us to perfect happiness in the next life. Although his discussion is both temporal and material, it remains unclear whether it is also genuinely theological, that is, whether divine illumination, necessary for eschatological bliss, is also necessary for temporal happiness. Be that as it may, for our purpose, his notion of secondary agency is helpful for constructing a robust realizing eschatology.

Aquinas introduces the notion of secondary, or instrumental, cause in *Summa Contra Gentiles*.[1] It enables him to explain human creativity while holding to a high doctrine of divine sovereignty.[2] Human skills and abilities are instruments of divine agency and, one might add, for the sake of fulfilling God's intention that creation prosper. Aquinas develops the notion further in his commentary on the fifth-century Neo-Platonic *Book of Causes*.[3] It theorizes three levels of living creatures, depending on how much they partake of divine intelligence. First, God is the original or ultimate cause of everything; the second level ("down") is disembodied intellects (angels and so on); the third is embodied beings. The third level, in turn, has several grades, the highest of which is human. Humans are like angels in that they partake of the divine, but unlike angels in that they are embodied. The distinctive human contribution to creation as embodied is the ability to create something from raw materials, such as in architecture and shipbuilding. Below humans are ambulatory but not creative beings, and below them are living nonambulatory creatures. This ordering of intellects conveys divine intelligence downward. Humans partake of divine intelligence at a high level, which the commentary calls "divine" by virtue of their freedom and creativity.

The hierarchy of intelligences means that, though God is the primary and most powerful cause of everything, the immediate instrument of divine providence is normally a person who plans, envisions,

---

1. Thomas Aquinas, "Summa Contra Gentiles, Book III," in *Basic Writings of Thomas Aquinas*, ed. Anton C. Pegis (New York: Random House, 1945), 3.70 (pp. 129-30).

2. Jill Raitt, "St Thomas Aquinas on Free Will and Predestination," *Duke Divinity School Review* 43 (1978): 188-95.

3. Thomas Aquinas, *Commentary on the Book of Causes*, trans. Vincent A. Guagliardo, Charles R. Hess, and Richard C. Taylor (Washington, DC: Catholic University of America Press, 1996). Thomas wrote this commentary about fifteen years after *SCG*, and it was not related to his doctrine of happiness. *On Causes* is a Neo-Platonist work that Aquinas recognizes as erroneously attributed to Aristotle. It was actually an Arabic compilation of Proclus's *Elements of Theology*, which was translated into Latin in the twelfth century. See Alexander Fidora and Jordi Pardo, "Liber de Causis," *Revista Española de Filosofía Medieval* 8 (2001): 133-52.

and executes action. Providence proceeds through these human agents. Developing the human arts fulfills the niche we occupy in God's scheme of things and advances civilization. Doing so is obedience to our intelligence, which derives from divine intelligence.

The chain of creative intelligences is a sign of divine care for creation, and especially for its most creative element that produces culture and civilizes. Aquinas puts it this way:

> This appears in one way or another in the things of our experience, for nature provides prime matter for all artificial things. Then certain prior arts dispose natural matter to make it suited to the more particular arts. The first cause of all things, however, is compared to the whole of nature as nature is to art. Hence that which first underlies the whole of nature is from the first cause of all things, and the function of second causes is to make it suitable for singular things.[4]

God delegates specific creativity in obedience to human abilities. Creativity honors and expresses human dignity and nobility. Wise and artful use of intelligence is creation's secondary agent: it is being obedient to our true nature. In using ourselves wisely and creatively, we advance creation, and that cannot but please the Creator.

To carry Aquinas's teaching a bit further: since God is goodness itself, and creation exemplifies that goodness, God enjoys his own goodness when we comply with the power delegated to us in this creative way. Using ourselves artfully advances not only creation itself, but also God's enjoyment of us and our enjoyment of ourselves. Godly self-employment both enhances our lives and pleases God, who always enjoys our flourishing. Enacting our identity as instruments of God's intention for creation through wise self-use pleases the agent. Advancing creation's well-being is both enjoyable for its own sake and brings God joy.

There is, of course, the strong possibility that we will misuse our agency, or that we will use it in ways that contravene divine intention. Yet we cannot fail to use what we have in obedience to being instruments of divine intention. Aquinas did not pause over the rapacious potential of human creativity (as Augustine had); he was facing a different opponent.

Of course, neither Augustine nor Aquinas operated in an asherist framework. The Augustinian conviction is that we are too unstable to

---

4. Aquinas, *Commentary on the Book of Causes*, p. 10.

live the beauty of holiness offered by Aquinas's secondary cause. We cannot consistently use ourselves well, not because we are mean-spirited — though some of us may be — but because intelligence is easily confused and distracted from its proper identity as God's creation. We may not even recognize what properly creative activity is, or we may not be able to implement such recognitions when they occur. Aquinas did not pause over these concerns, perhaps because he did not want to allow the slightest opportunity for Manicheanism to creep in. He was intent on teaching people to cultivate the art of being godly agents of civilization.

Thomas's embrace of instrumental cause is central to asherism because it holds that faithfulness to God is faithfulness to one's nature and calling. Enhancing creation's flourishing is obedience to human nature. It is pleasing indirectly because it is obedient, and it is so directly because it is productive. The more we and creation flourish, the more God and we enjoy one another and ourselves.

Butler: Self-Love

Bishop Butler's rehabilitation of self-love as a positive theological category is another plank in the foundation of asherism. It was as remarkable an accomplishment as Aquinas's insistence on imperfect happiness and his celebration of human dignity through secondary agency. What Butler failed to see is that self-love is the happy life because it is the way of obedience, quite apart from simply enjoying objects of desire. It remains to recognize self-love in the theological conversation about happiness.

Butler's self-love resonates with Aquinas's work on secondary agency as obedience: in both cases, living a godly life is obedience to one's nature. The call to spiritual thriving is a priori; we are defined to it, so to speak. God has outfitted us for happiness by being ourselves in the proper theological sense of the term. In Aquinas's case, it is to be an instrument of divine providence in creative activity; in Butler's case, it is pursuing the moral life as self-love. Perhaps we can help Butler here by pointing out that self-love is not only faithfulness to our nature, but it actually enriches us, so that we become happier as we become more adept at being our proper theological selves, that is, as salvation and sanctification realize themselves in us.

Aquinas and Butler rely on a priori conditions that make happiness possible. These conditions mean that all persons are blessed by God to enjoy themselves and their life in him. Believers learn this through the ministrations of the church that orient people toward their proper identity. When believers properly grasp that identity, they should want to become in practice who they are in God by definition. Happiness is a universal possibility for both Aquinas and Butler.

Doctrinal Clarifications

Lest the natural theology of Aquinas and Butler lead to misunderstanding, I should make two dogmatic clarifications. First, the starting point for both Aquinas and Butler is Genesis 1-2: it is "naturalist" in a theological sense. Creation is, of course, a biblical teaching, and, standing at the head of Scripture, is the doctrinal matrix for any Jewish, Christian, and perhaps even Islamic understanding of the relationship between God and humanity. Second, the Western tradition, including Calvin, understands the knowledge of God to arise from reflection on both creation and Scripture — and perhaps other sources as well. Theological convention refers to these two subject areas as "general" and "special" revelation.[5] I will argue here that a rigorous division between these two — as in the supposed division between reason and faith — is unwarranted and that, to the extent that it is used, the conventional order for discussing these two sources of knowledge of God should be reversed. I am suggesting that, rather than moving from "general" to "special" revelation, common experience moves in the opposite direction. One must first be arrested by the biblical narrative, as conveyed by the ministrations of the church, in order to consider the knowledge of God in extrabiblical sources, especially to see the creativity of God at work in one's own body.

Point of Departure

Scripture begins with creation. The first parents betray paradise. The punishments that endure unto this day are not the norm; they are the

---

5. The former term is ambiguous: it can mean philosophy as well as reflection on the natural world or human experience.

abnormal, so to speak. The pain, misery, and shame in the world are badges of dishonor, not signs of our true identity, which assumes obedience to God. Disobedience stands out like a sore thumb, disfiguring but not necessarily redefining human nature. The Fall points out human liability, but moral instability is not the divine intention. In this regard, Aquinas and Butler are more faithful to Scripture's normative intention.

Christian theology, eager to inculcate humility, has at times failed to encourage the natural skills and strengths humans possess for executing their calling as God's emissaries in the world, as Aquinas and Butler do. A shrill cry for humility may discourage trust in our graced nature and thus the freedom and creativity that Thomas highlights in his doctrine of instrumental cause. Trust in these may be construed as lack of complete trust in God, as though God and self are in competition. However, the opposite is true: failing to be confident in the freedom and creativity that become skills for building the world betrays distrust in God. Confidence in forwarding God's purposes for creation advances humility in a robust way, a way that uses the self for the sake of divine enjoyment. Trust in one's obedience to who one is in God is both properly humble and properly proud to be God's faithful and successful servant. This is what Butler means by self-love.

Asherism teaches that happiness is an enjoyable obedient life. As Aquinas and Butler point out, this begins with being ourselves, not in Kant's understanding of autonomy, but in the theological sense of using ourselves through and for the sake of our divinely given nature. Aquinas articulates this in terms of freedom and creativity to build culture and advance civilization through mechanical and liberal arts. Butler articulates it in moral terms that build and protect the social structure of the *polis*. Happiness is an effect of both forms of self-love, which Aquinas and Butler might agree are of a piece in living according to nature.

Sources of the Knowledge of God

Conventional systematic theology holds that reflection on creation and Scripture are two sources of the knowledge of God. In this it follows John Calvin, for whom creation and Scripture are both instructive — albeit with different content. Calvin sees no opposition between the knowledge of God gained by reflecting on the human body and that gained by knowledge of Christ: our own bodies and the incarnate Christ are evidence of God's wisdom, beauty, and power. However, he does find the second more riveting. In the *Institutes* (2.6.1), he argues that, while the knowledge of God the Creator "should be the school in which we were to learn piety" after the first parents' rebellion, it becomes "useless unless faith also followed, setting forth for us God our father in Christ."[6] Thus, the gospel only clarifies the law.

In the preceding subsection I have proposed that Genesis 1-2 is the standard for conceptualizing the God-human relationship. Here I will add that pitting reason against revelation because the former is "natural" while the latter is "supernatural" is theologically confused because "creation" is a theological category. Further, thinking is also a theological category if one recognizes human intelligence as a gracious divine gift that is intended for intelligent stewardship of creation. According to this view, a theologically adept use of intelligence is required for discerning the beauty and wisdom of God implicit in the world and explicit in Scripture.

Empirical science and secular philosophy make it more difficult to read the world through the eyes of faith, but, as Calvin notes, Scripture can also be read atheologically.[7] Whatever the entry point, Calvin notes, the Holy Spirit needs to direct one's attention theologically. In both cases, a certain sensibility must be awakened and developed. As Isaiah 32:15 puts it, "a spirit from on high" must be poured out on us so that we plow our fields fruitfully so that they blossom.

The issue is not whether we construe ourselves rationally or biblically, but whether we construe ourselves theologically. It is a question of whether we think about nature and Scripture inside or outside a theological framework. Reading Kant's moral philosophy atheologically, for example, contributes to the confusion. Part of the difficulty with construing reason theologically in our own day arises from Kant's argument for an "autonomous will" that enables moral self-legislation, as if that were not universal intelligence given by God. If we read this notion atheologically, we will misunderstand it. Kantian autonomy does not entail independence from God, much less the crude notion of "individual

---

6. John Calvin, *Institutes of the Christian Religion*, ed. John T. McNeill, trans. Ford Lewis Battles, 2 vols. (Philadelphia: Westminster, 1960), 2.6.1 (p. 341).

7. Calvin, *Institutes*, 1.7.4 (pp. 78-80).

autonomy." For Kant, such a thing would be a contradiction in terms. His point, like Aquinas's, is that all people are intelligent. Indeed, the universality of intelligence — albeit in varying degrees — implies that it is a divine gift. Regardless of opportunity and education, all people have some access to intelligence by virtue of being human, even if it be limited.

Of course, this idea is quite ancient. Intelligence is the agent of creation in the *Timaeus,* as are the *Logos* of the prologue to John's Gospel, Plotinus's *nous,* and Proclus's "intelligence." Christian theology has read Genesis 1:26 through it. That humans are in the image of God is the theological way of connecting the individual to divine intelligence. For Kant, intelligence yields a single criterion by which all ostensibly moral acts may be judged objectively: obedience to duty. Because it is a universal rational principle on which everyone can act, obedience to duty cannot but have theological overtones. Even if Kant meant to de-theologize it, as we saw with the moral sense philosophers, he cannot — just as they cannot — for according to them God created us with the ability to grasp and act according to duty. This moral sensibility must come from somewhere, for the world cannot be random if all are endowed with moral sensibility. Rationality inheres in the created order, and it must have a source. Kant's hesitance to use theological language does not change the fact. Starkly put, the choice is between order and randomness. Christians have been feisty in holding out for order. Given a forced choice between God and randomness, Kant's Christian roots surely prevailed.

For Christians, a rationally ordered universe is predicated on the *Logos* made flesh as Jesus Christ, rendering a split between "reason" and "revelation" inappropriate. In the incarnation, the principle of universal order became a person — as bizarre as the idea is — lest its divine authority become invisible. Genesis 1 and 2 and the Johannine prologue insist that order, love, and wisdom are more real, or perhaps more true, than randomness, chaos, and chance. Aquinas, Butler, and Kant are all theological rationalists in this sense.

Theological rationalism gave rise to both Protestant scholasticism, a strong form of theism that relies on Scripture for knowledge of God the Redeemer, and later to deism, a weak form of theism that relies on creation for knowledge of God the Creator. Each relies on a different form of knowledge, to the neglect of the other. Calvin, a mediating theologian at every turn, honored both forms of knowledge of God. Anticipating modern secularism, he rails against those who fail to find God in creation, in prose that is too delicious to pass up:

Even today the earth sustains many monstrous spirits who, to destroy God's name, do not hesitate to misdirect all the seed of divinity spread abroad in human nature. How detestable, I ask you, is this madness: that man, finding God in his body and soul a hundred times, on this very pretense of excellence denies that there is a God? They will not say it is by chance that they are distinct from brute creatures. Yet they set God aside, the while using "nature," which for them is the artificer of all things, as a cloak. They see such exquisite workmanship in their individual members, from mouth and eyes even to their very toenails. Here also they substitute nature for God. But such agile motions of the soul, such excellent faculties, such rare gifts, especially bear upon the face of them a divinity that does not allow itself readily to be hidden. . . .[8]

The presupposition here is that Scripture reads the world as created and thus directs us to read it theologically. Calvin is already fighting for the theological readability of the world a good bit before secularism takes off.

For the dubious, Aquinas's secondary causality supports Calvin here by identifying the thought process through which one might interpret the world as itself theological. Theologically construed, intelligence cannot oppose revelation because it participates in divine activity. Being intelligent defines human nobility: partaking of the intelligence that is instantiated in a body from the primary agent. "Now, every effect participates in something of the power of its cause. So it remains that the soul, just as it performs a divine activity insofar as it is from the first cause, so too it performs the activity of an intelligence insofar as it is from [an intelligence] and participating [in] its power."[9] Chickens and trees have "souls" because they are alive, but they lack the moral freedom that higher intelligences possess.[10]

Joseph Butler actually strengthens Aquinas's point and extends it to self-love. That self-love enacts human participation in divine intelligence underlies his insistence that self-love is obedience to God. That is, proper self-love is within the province of revelation because it draws

8. Calvin, *Institutes*, 1.5.4 (pp. 55-56).

9. Aquinas, *Causes*, pp. 23-24.

10. Aquinas assumed this in his *Commentary on the Book of Causes*. Arthur Lovejoy recognizes this classic frame of reference; see Lovejoy, *The Great Chain of Being: A Study of the History of an Idea* (Cambridge, MA: Harvard University Press, 1936).

its strength from the dignity and nobility of intelligence itself. Whether defined in terms of God's election of Israel or of being made in the divine image, the implication is that self-love honors God. To paraphrase Butler, self-love requires fine self-use, and fine self-use is faithful to God.

One cannot reach for self-love: it is not a goal that one sets for oneself, but a reality that one submits to as a result of proper self-knowledge, which is conveyed through Scripture, not through philosophy or science. Enjoying and celebrating the happiness that is coincident with actualizing one's theological identity requires realizing who one is, theologically speaking, and living that identity truly. Happiness is not a matter of manipulating the world to secure our desire, but taking pleasure in being who Scripture teaches we are. Happiness is living with theological integrity. In sum, the knowledge of God, as Aquinas, Calvin, and Butler understand it, comes with a theological worldview. Reading nature, reason, and "self" theologically is a posture, an approach, and an outlook controlled by Scripture.

An objection to self-love as falling under obedience to God, as Butler saw it, or to seeing ourselves as instruments of divine providence, as Aquinas did, or to those who would not read nature theologically, as Calvin did — such an objection may come from those who regard nature atheologically and quite apart from dramatic divine intrusions into the world narrated in Scripture. The words "reason," "nature," and "natural" lost their theological connotations with modernity. Those who trusted in natural law or the laws of nature appeared to have abandoned revelation that focuses on Scripture. The fear is that "the religion of reason" secularizes the understanding of human ingenuity and favors it over the dramatic Scripture narrative. Favoring intelligence begins that slippery slide away from Scripture altogether, as Calvin anticipated. One Christian reaction has been to deny intelligence as a source of the knowledge of God and to focus solely on the biblical narratives.

Eliminating intelligence as an instrument of the knowledge of God makes a fateful decision to set intelligence outside a theological framework. Aquinas, Calvin, and Butler would never have acquiesced. The theological doctrine of intelligence holds reason accountable to divine commands in Scripture in a dynamic way, because reason itself partakes of and is an instrument of divine intelligence. A theological reading of reason and nature locates human ingenuity within a providential framework, lifting it up and ennobling it. Setting reason and nature outside a theological framework permits human ingenuity to regard itself as unaccountable before God. An atheological account of human intelligence sets it free to power its own ship. From a Christian perspective, that is a risky undertaking.

Asherism reads intelligence and nature theologically and thus as called to use itself in the theater of creation in the context of and to the ends for which God created it as a partaker of divine intelligence. Obedience to divine law is the training ground for molding reason to its rightful purpose. In this way it collaborates with God. Personal happiness is a result of making ourselves useful in this partnership.

Scripture concretizes the foregoing asherist understanding of calling via the stories of biblical characters who respond to their call from God. Noah frantically builds an ark while the sun shines. Abram courageously uproots himself and moves to a foreign land. The Israelites daringly walks into the sea. But perhaps the most dramatic event of all is the voluntary execution of a political convict. Watching the last tumultuous week of Jesus' life, seeing him cooperate in his own suffering and death in obedience to the mission he has from God — this gets the reader's attention. The believer's response to a call from God may not be as dramatic as any of the above biblical characters' responses, but the stories will register with thoughtful readers as an invitation to read themselves theologically.

Ordering the Discussion

That the tradition has distinguished general from special revelation supports the previous argument for not restricting revelation to Scripture alone, because "general" revelation is commonly understood to be the province of thought. In this subsection I want to extend the foregoing argument by suggesting that the two traditional forms of revelation — labeled "general" and "special" — should be discussed in reverse order. "Special" revelation presses outward to a broader application and shapes a general ability to seek God outside Scripture, whereas finding evidence for God in creation does not press the mind to seek God in a more specific narrative such as the biblical one. Reading creation theologically requires knowledge of God revealed in the biblical narratives.

A second reason for reversing the order is, of course, that the argument from design, at least in its classic form, does not really work, as David Hume argued so elegantly.[11] Privileging the Bible narratives shapes the reader theologically to be able to see God the Creator at work in the world. At this point, knowledge of God the Creator ceases to be natural theology and becomes an extension of biblical teaching. Intelligence/reason is not left behind; rather, it is used in a theological framework. Gone is the naïve hope that reason is "pure" and can operate outside a worldview, approach, or outlook.

Calvin can help here as well, because he recognized that the particulars of the later biblical narrative are perhaps more arresting than the majestic — but easily taken for granted — beauty of the human body and the order of nature that derive from the creation story. However, in the *Institutes* he treats God the Creator before God the Redeemer. He argues that examining our own bodies should tell us all we need to know of God; sadly, however, we resist, and so God has to take more dramatic action.[12] While one can understand why Calvin proceeded in the order that he did, perhaps it would have been preferable had he reversed the order.

For these reasons, I suggest that special revelation enables general revelation. Pedagogically, the narratives must first become alive before the splendor of divine workmanship in creation can be recognized. What is required is not simply for us to sit down for an hour or so to take it all in; we must stay seated and have our path completely subverted by the narratives so that we come to construe ourselves in their terms. As Paul put it in 2 Corinthians 5:17, "So if anyone is in Christ, there is a new creation: everything old has passed away; see, everything has become new!" If, by the grace of the Holy Spirit, the narratives succeed in getting our attention, then and only then can we construe the world and ourselves in broadly theological terms. In other words, if special revelation rivets attention to divine activity in the world, general revelation carries the fruit of that knowledge into the world and toward knowledge of ourselves as instruments of God's ends.

11. David Hume, *Dialogues Concerning Natural Religion* (Indianapolis: Bobbs Merrill, 1970).

12. Calvin, *Institutes*, 1.5.2-3 (pp. 53-55).

CHAPTER 8

Divine Commands

Having located asherism within the historical arc that has been reconstructed, we now turn to consider divine commands on which an obedient life turns. Biblical commands are of several kinds, two of which are significant here: (1) single-occurrence or rarely occurring punctiliar orders that test obedience, and (2) guidelines that commend an ongoing way of life. Tests, the first type, are *voluntarist* rules that God lays down in particular situations for a specific purpose or around specific events. Voluntarism holds that the divine will defines morality. Even if a command looks arbitrary or even immoral to us, it is good because God commanded it. Divine power defines goodness. The assumption here is that blind obedience is praiseworthy either for its own sake or because it cultivates humility. The second type of command is moral guidelines that cultivate wisdom: they embody broad humanist principles that shape a salutary life for the well-being of both the individual and the community. They are *asherist* commands that are conducive to wise living. While voluntarist commands require blind obedience, asherist commands promote open-eyed obedience because their value for personal and communal well-being is evident. The theological conversation has not distinguished voluntarist from nonvoluntarist commands; yet the first chapters of the Bible illustrate both types.

The pedagogy behind nonvoluntarist, asherist commands is that understandable guidance cultivates wisdom. In this, asherist commands differ from voluntarist commands such as those we meet in Genesis 2:17 and 3:3 (do not eat of the tree of the knowledge of good and evil in the middle of the garden). Voluntarist commands are a test, and their goal is to prompt obedience without understanding in a situation that rubs against inclination. Why is *wanting* to know the difference between good and evil a capital offense?

The asherist command (Gen. 1:28) to be fruitful, multiply, and steward the earth, by contrast, is general and long-term. For our purposes, the difference between God's command in Genesis 1:28 and the command in 2:17 and 3:3 is not that one is positive and the other negative. In Genesis 1, the reward for obedience is distributive reward for individuals and the earth itself. It invites one to look at the long-term effects of one's pattern of living and so to grow in wisdom. The result of obedience is organically related to the command itself: it is designed to safeguard the future well-being of creation, and its pedagogy is to enlist us in that project on an ongoing basis. Human fruitfulness will prosper the creation, assuming a nonrapacious understanding of stewardship of the earth. God commands a way of life that we understand as beneficial and can agree with so that we can put our energy behind it.

Voluntarist Biblical Commands

Although divine commands have been assumed to be voluntarist, those are actually rather few in number. For example, it is not clear that any commandments of the Decalogue are voluntarist, though some might hold that the first three are. But the demand for exclusive worship of this God and the prohibition of idolatry and abuse of the divine name are not tests of obedience for its own sake. They are the framework within which Israel is to become a light to the nations, with its salutary way of life exemplified in the fourth through tenth commandments. The first three commands define God's relationship with Israel. They do not display authority for its humility-inducing power but for the sake of the way of life that opposes idolatry that is morally weaker. I will examine the Decalogue in the next chapter.

The command not to eat of the tree in the center of the garden carries a death threat. When the first parents fail the test, God confronts them; they fail to take responsibility for their actions, trying to lay blame elsewhere. It is a poor showing. It is interesting that they are not immediately struck dead — as one might expect and as happens in later biblical passages — but are afflicted with other punishments. Here is a powerful exposure of human weakness that intends to sober the reader.

It sets up the relationship between God and humanity as a massive power struggle — a battle of wills.

Another voluntarist command is in Genesis 19:17, where God tells the refugees fleeing Sodom not to look back. Lot's wife cannot resist, and she immediately turns into a pillar of salt (Gen. 19:26). A third voluntarist command is God's demand that Abraham sacrifice his son Isaac (Gen. 22): it is a test to show that the divine and human wills are at odds and that the divine will must prevail. It is noteworthy that the command here is not accompanied by the threat of a specific punishment, as was the case in Genesis 2. Without a threat, Abraham passes the test in this instance, and he, too, becomes a model — but now one for humanity to emulate.

These voluntarist commands demand obedience to the divine will, whatever the cost. They do not make sense to us, and they may even be morally repulsive, as in the command that Abraham sacrifice his son. Voluntarism is controversial. Historian of philosophy Jerome Schneewind states the objection succinctly: "Omnipotence is secured, at the cost of making God's commands concerning the moral relationships of human beings to one another an outcome of his arbitrary will. Luther[1] and Calvin[2] did not mind the cost. Voluntarism became an inescapable position for later thinkers because of the decisive place they gave it in their moral theologies."[3] Samuel von Pufendorf, a seventeenth-century natural lawyer, expanded the positions of Luther and Calvin by rejecting the identity of being and goodness. Separating truth from goodness significantly undermined the idea that the moral life flows from understanding. Rather, it flows from obedience to au-

---

1. Martin Luther, "Bondage of the Will 5.5 and 6," in *Divine Command Morality: Historical and Contemporary Readings,* ed. Janine Marie Idziak (New York: Edwin Mellen Press, 1979); see also Luther, "Lectures on Romans: Scholia Chapter 9.6 and 14," in Idziak, *Divine Command Morality.*

2. John Calvin, "Institutes of the Christian Religion 2.8.1, 5; 3.23.1, 2; 4.10.7," in Idziak, *Divine Command Morality,* pp. 98-103.

3. J. B. Schneewind, *The Invention of Autonomy* (Cambridge: Cambridge University Press, 1998), p. 25. Voluntarism is the idea that compliance with divine commands constitutes a moral theory of human action. It appears in the thirteenth century in Duns Scotus and William of Ockham, and was further elaborated in the seventeenth century by von Pufendorf as modern moral theology was aborning (Schneewind, pp. 21-25, 121-22, 139). The separation of truth from goodness effectively demolished the ancient eudaemonist understanding of the moral life as flowing from good character and devotion to certain values by replacing it with obedience to moral absolutes as good in themselves.

thority. People are to obey divine commands because God delivers them, not because they teach a salutary way of life. The assumption is that humility is the key virtue and that it grows from the soil of submission to raw power that is to be unquestioned.

Asherist Biblical Commands

While there are undoubtedly additional *voluntarist* commands in Scripture, many others are *asherist*. These do not define morality as humility before authority, but cultivate moral sensibility in the agent. Here God and humanity work as a team, with God leading and humanity following. Asherist commands regulate the community's moral, social, cultic, and economic life. They are moral exercises through which a person cultivates an asherist spirit by practicing her way into moral and spiritual wisdom for her own well-being and that of the community. Particular to the asherist view of the good life is that the person performs her way into realizing that well-being and obedience are of a piece.

The sweep of the pentateuchal narrative can be read asheristically. Liberation from Egypt is not simply removing Israel from bondage; her character and way of life need to be completely transformed. It requires perhaps two generations of desert living to overcome the experience of slavery and the temptation of idolatry and to be retrained for another way of life. In the desert God consecrates Israel to himself for a new and wise way of life that is to be a model for the nations that are to be blessed by God through Abraham's seed. There is a covenantal arc through Genesis, Exodus, Leviticus, and beyond. In the next chapter I will explore pentateuchal texts that construct an asherist way of life in which God and Israel may enjoy one another and further the flourishing of all the nations as they, too, come to worship Israel's God. The asherist hermeneutic focuses on those commands that outline an obedient, rewarding, and wise life that can be lived now despite grief from sin and life's contingencies.

Theological Treatments of Divine Commands

Despite the prevalence of asherist commands in the Bible, theological voluntarism has been widely considered to represent all divine commands. Voluntarism in Christian moral philosophy was explicitly theorized by two medieval Franciscan philosophers, Duns Scotus[4] and William of Ockham:[5] their idea was that the divine will determines what is good and is to be obeyed for that reason alone. It assumes that obedience to the divine will, arbitrary or vicious though it may be, defines morality. God commands as he pleases.

Current Christian philosophical treatments of divine command morality generally treat only voluntarist commands because they are controversial. This comes from Plato's *Euthyphro* (10a), which poses the voluntarist dilemma: "Is what is holy holy because the gods approve it, or do they approve it because it is holy?" Christian moral philosophers have lately defended theological voluntarism as if it characterized all divine commands.[6] And perhaps, because they treat only voluntarist commands, they leave the impression that all divine commands are voluntarist.

While some moderate the more extreme implications of theological voluntarism, Paul Rooney thinks that all divine commands are fundamentally arbitrary, and he unflinchingly defends the arbitrariness of such commands on the grounds that God is utterly free from constraint, cannot be irrational, and acts with complete control of his will, which is by definition absolutely righteous.[7] Arbitrary commands are not irrational, because they are at God's pleasure: because God is understood to be good, arbitrary commands determine goodness and are to be obeyed.[8]

Asherism argues that a voluntarist interpretation of many biblical commands is inaccurate and so voluntarism fails as a general theory of

---

4. John Duns Scotus, "Paris Commentary on the Sentences 4.46," in Idziak, *Divine Command Morality*, pp. 53-54.

5. William of Ockham, "On the Four Books of the Sentences 2.19," in Idziak, *Divine Command Morality*, pp. 55-57.

6. Robert Merrihew Adams, "Divine Commands and the Social Nature of Obligation," in *Christian Theism and Moral Philosophy;* Adams, "The Concept of a Divine Command," in *Religion and Morality;* Adams, "A Modified Divine Command Theory of Ethical Wrongness," in *Religion and Morality: A Collection of Essays;* Adams, "Divine Command Metaethics Modified Again," *Journal of Religious Ethics* 7 (1979). See also Philip L. Quinn, *Divine Commands and Moral Requirements,* Clarendon Library of Logic and Philosophy (Oxford: Clarendon Press, 1978); Paul Rooney, *Divine Command Morality,* Avebury Series in Philosophy (Brookfield, Vt.: Avebury, 1996); Michael J. Harris, *Divine Command Ethics: Jewish and Christian Perspectives* (London: RoutledgeCurzon, 2003).

7. Rooney, *Divine Command Morality,* p. 111.

8. Rooney, *Divine Command Morality,* pp. 97-114.

divine command. Asherism also objects to the pedagogy of voluntarism because it focuses on humility at the expense of wisdom. Both Augustine and Anselm worried about a divine pedagogy that suggested the arbitrariness of divine actions. The death of Christ looks immoral on the face of it. Why put an innocent man to death when God could redeem us from sin nonviolently? While not in the context of divine commands per se, both Augustine and Anselm responded that the divine pedagogy was after more than bare obedience to authority. Augustine says that "it pleased God to deliver man from the devil's authority by beating him at the justice game, not the power game, so that men too might imitate Christ by seeking to beat the devil at the justice game, not the power game."[9] Anselm took Augustine's point further. He saw in the death of Christ the struggle to uphold both justice and mercy, and he saw that the violence of Christ's death teaches us to be just but also to temper that justice with mercy.[10]

Aquinas on Sin and Obedience

Aquinas was concerned that divine wrath be carefully understood. Punishment for disobedience is not rash retribution, but is used for pedagogical ends. Even harsh punishments can be medicinal. According to him, divine wrath is settled — not hot. Aquinas's treatment of disobedience encompasses six great tractates in his *Summa Theologiae* (1a2ae. qq. 71-114).[11] The first is an extensive, three-tractate account of sin (qq. 71-89), followed by an equally extensive treatment of law (qq. 90-114). In treating sin, he inches his way toward asherism.

Sin

Aquinas roots his doctrine of sin in creation rather than the Fall. The world, including humanity of course, pivots around the divine will, though only humans can sin. Sin is offensive to God and to us because

9. Augustine, *The Trinity,* trans. Edmund Hill, *The Works of Saint Augustine: A Translation for the 21st Century* (Brooklyn, NY: New City Press, 1991), p. 356.

10. Ellen T. Charry, *By the Renewing of Your Minds: The Pastoral Function of Christian Doctrine* (New York: Oxford University Press, 1997), pp. 168-72.

11. Thomas Aquinas, *Summa Theologiae,* 60 vols. (New York: Blackfriars with McGraw-Hill, 1964), 1a. q. 6, a. 4, 12.

it abandons our true and proper theological identity. Sin enacts self-alienation. It is an illness to be cured, not a burden of guilt to be borne. The human ability to obey the divine will is considerably weakened after the Fall, but reparable by grace. Original sin is damaging but not lethal to our ability to comply with divine commands; divinely given identity as the image of God is not demolished. The inclination to virtue that it normally spurs remains, pending divine grace.

Since the inclination to obey the divine will endures, even though weakened, punishment must be reparative. Aquinas casts punishment as rehabilitative rather than retributive. Eileen Sweeney explains Thomas's move thus: "It recasts punishment as imposed from the outside as the loss of the good desired, God, and hence as self-imposed destruction."[12] If punishment is medicinal, eternal punishment is inappropriate because it does not heal. Simple retribution is both unbefitting divine dignity — for it suggests that God enjoys the destruction of his creatures — and unhelpful because, like eternal punishment, it does not rehabilitate. Aquinas sees God punishing through cool anger, not red-hot rage. Rehabilitation is an act of love; retribution proceeds from righteous indignation. Cool punishment advances justice better than hot punishment does because sin reveals a disordered self. It is a disorder of reason. One may benefit from cool punishment, whereas hot punishment, while it may restrain and frighten, does not reorder. Well-disposed punishment will heal the individual and thereby protect the community better than hot punishment will (p. 155).

Aquinas designated degrees of punishment in accordance with the severity of the sin. It is possible that we can learn from our mistakes and correct them. The "will to sin must be countered by a contrary movement back toward the one injured" (p. 156) — in this case, both God and self. Grace is necessary for a willing return that is not under duress. "Grace is that divine call back to community before the sinner is fit to rejoin it; grace makes it possible to ask for the forgiveness the sinner cannot request until he or she can once again be imagined as part of the community" (p. 157). Here the divine pedagogy of wisdom peeks out as an element of punishment apart from obedience to authority for the sake of humility.

---

12. Eileen C. Sweeney, "Vice and Sin (1a2ae. qq. 71-89)," in *Ethics of Aquinas,* ed. Stephen J. Pope (Washington, DC: Georgetown University Press, 2002), p. 154. Hereafter, page references to this work will appear in parentheses in the text.

Aquinas is pastorally concerned for both the community and the individual: "[H]is goal is not just pastoral care of the other but also of self. Medicinal punishment is an invitation to explore and reform one's motives and intentions" (p. 160). Like Butler after him, and asherism here, Thomas holds that disobedience to God is an act of self-betrayal. Sweeney concludes: "Aquinas's account of sin is about how human beings both fall below the possibility of their own natures in sin and fail to rise to their aspirations to the transcendent good" (p. 166). At the same time, Thomas provides for the rehabilitation of our potential for obedience; otherwise chastisement would be to no positive end, and that ill befits God.

Divine Law

Thomas follows his treatment of sin with a symmetrical treatment of law. The first part treats law generally, and the other two treat divine law. Generally, law intends human happiness and the common good.[13] The treatise on divine law is divided into treatments of the "Old Law" (qq. 98-105) and the "Gospel of Grace" (qq. 106-14). This architecture reveals Aquinas's discomfort with Paul's order of law → sin → grace (Rom. 5:20). In Thomas's order, sin and grace are the brackets that enclose the law. The large-scale pattern maintains the fall/sin → redemption/grace dynamic of Paul's Adam/Christ typology (qq. 12-7). Yet, in reversing the order to sin → law → grace, Aquinas has made a significant change. All law drives toward happiness and the common good. At the same time, he maintains the traditional law/grace dualism within his overarching structure. The pattern is sin → Old Law → New Law/grace. Law is encased within the sin → grace dynamic.

Law is enveloped within grace with primordial blessing as the presupposition and Christ as the consummation. Grace works within, not in opposition to law, which is an instrument of grace. The significant difference between the Old and New Law is that the former is external to the self and driven by fear, while the latter is internal — written on

---

13. Aquinas, *Summa Theologiae,* 1a2ae. q. 90, a. 2: "[T]he law must needs regard principally the relationship to happiness. Moreover, since every part is ordained to the whole, as imperfect to perfect; and since one man is a part of the perfect community, the law must needs regard properly the relationship to universal happiness." Hereafter, references to this work will appear in parentheses in the text.

the heart — and justified by the ministration of the Holy Spirit (q. 106, a. 2). The treatises on divine law nuance Pauline thinking to argue that divine law is not the cause of sin; rather, it is an instrument in the rehabilitative process. All divine law is geared toward happiness, that is, both personal happiness and the common good (q. 90, a. 2). The Old Law is not a test to expose human frailty or strength, but is a positive instrument that leads to happiness by limiting and redirecting negative inclinations leading us away from sin.

Fear is to a therapeutic end. In other words, all divine law is a guide that works both negatively and positively. It guides, but the Old Law guides us to self-restraint by fear, while the New Law guides by love (q. 91, a. 4, 5). Aquinas likens the former to being law for a child, while the latter he likens to being law for an adult (q. 91, a. 5). The movement from fear to love — from servile to filial fear — is central in Christian spiritual writings. It comes from Galatians 4:6-7: "And because you are children, God has sent the Spirit of his Son into our hearts, crying, 'Abba! Father!' So you are no longer a slave but a child, and if a child then also an heir, through God."

Aquinas later distinguished two forms of law thus: "If a man turn to *God* and adhere to Him, through fear of punishment, it will be servile fear; but if it be on account of fear of committing a fault, it will be filial fear, for it becomes a child to fear offending its father" (2a2ae. q. 19, a. 2). In the treatise on law, however, he further nuances the contrast, because guidance from the New Law only elaborates what is prefigured in the Old Law (1a2ae. q. 91, a. 5). Although he does not name it, Thomas is inserting the element of wisdom into his theory of command and punishment for transgression.

While Aquinas makes the fundamental asherist move that flows organically from his commitment to the pedagogical function of punishment and law, he does not permit himself the rhetorical luxury of saying so: obeying the written law heals the soul and promotes happiness and social well-being in keeping with punishment's medicinal properties. What he misses is the insight that obedience, even if originally undertaken from servile fear, can become ego-syntonic. It can be naturalized into the personality with practice and become a source of joy and satisfaction rather than remain at the level of external threat. That is, servile fear can be transformed into filial piety. Furthermore, filial piety is proper self-love.

Marcion haunts the treatise on the Old Law, though Aquinas establishes a foundation for another way. Since law is not simply a test by which to trip people up, but the instrument of a happy life and the common good, why should it be obeyed from servile fear and not be embraced with joy and gratitude? Asherist commands are a divine gift; they are not arbitrary but plainly salutary. Obedience to them brings "material and earthly benefit" (q. 91, a. 5). Reward is not apart from but inheres in and arises organically from the activity itself. God variously commands, forbids, permits, and punishes different actions as it is appropriate (q. 92, a. 1-2). This is all for the sake of human well-being, and the assumption is that a good strong deterrent will help it along. Perhaps this is what the execution of Achan (Josh. 7) was intended to signal. Though a harsh punishment indeed, it aims to deter theft of public property and thus is intended toward the proper ordering of the common good. Even if a person avoids theft initially to avert punishment, the goal of respecting public property is to enlist the individual's cooperation in protecting the community. In this way the individual moves into a partnership with God.

Reliance on fear of punishment — even harsh punishment in this case — is different from the fear aroused by voluntarist commands. The point is not that God glorifies himself through displays of power that send people cowering and clamoring for mercy. The moral clarity of the asherist command is rather to encourage people to love themselves as instruments of the divine goal for creation. At least from what we can see in these materials, compliance is not for the sake of instilling fear as valuable in its own right, but to use fear as an attention-getting device to practice how to love oneself in God.

Despite Aquinas's asherist leaning, two objections must be raised here from an explicitly asherist perspective. He recognizes that the Old Law is not monolithic, and he distinguishes three classes of divine command in the Older Testament: moral, religious (ceremonial), and civil (judicial) (q. 99, a. 2-4). He limits moral imperatives to the Decalogue. Ceremonial imperatives pertain to the proper worship of God. Civil law guarantees justice.

The first asherist objection is that Aquinas has conceived the categories too strictly and the moral imperatives too narrowly. The categories that he introduces are artificial, and various statutes overlap the distinctions. He misses the fact that both religious and civic divine imperatives often have moral intentions. Religious imperatives at the individual level, for example, drive the larger biblical concern that Israel worship God alone. Being set apart from the nations is for the sake of Israel's holiness as much as for God's delight, and perhaps these are the same. Similarly, the ordering of sexual and civic affairs in Leviticus 18 and 19 is perhaps the *locus classicus* of civil law's civilizing import. As we will later see, Deuteronomy, Psalms, and Proverbs proceed in a similar vein.

On the other hand, restricting the Decalogue to the sphere of moral law does not work either — scripturally speaking. The commandments to honor parents and to desist from murder, theft, lying, and coveting are civil as much as they are moral. Self-restraint creates stable and healthy communities. Even if initially undertaken out of fear, over time self-restraint may become habitual and a source of satisfaction for individual's long-term wholesomeness. In that case, fear subsides and happiness enters the heart. From the perspective of asherism, by categorizing biblical laws too strictly, Aquinas has truncated asherist imperatives in a way that misrepresents Scripture's understanding of the integrity of a holy life.

Second, asherism must explain how obedience to the Old Law relapses into being exclusively fear-driven even though Aquinas has already set up the mechanism for welcoming at least some of that obedience as rehabilitative, insofar as it enables us to reorient ourselves positively toward the divine will. This case is also complex. Despite Aquinas's presumption that the Old Law is exclusively fear-driven, there can be no doubt that divine imperatives in the Younger Testament are often accompanied by threats of punishment and thus are also fear-driven. Several threaten death. Divine imperatives in the Younger Testament can be even more terrifying than those in the Older because the punishment often extends beyond death to eternal damnation in the fires of hell (Matt. 3:10; 5:29; 7:19; 8:12; 18:8-9; Mark 9:45; John 15:6; Rev. 20:14-15). Here the Marcionite characterization of a vengeful God of wrath in the Older Testament and loving God of salvation in the Younger Testament falls apart. Indeed, some demands for obedience are more extreme, and threats of punishment more dire, in the Younger Testament. Marcion's bifurcation of an angry punishing God and a loving gentle God is biblically untrue; it does not bear up under scrutiny.

In sum, Aquinas recognized a need for asherism and took a decisive dogmatic step toward it by locating obedience to divine law within the scope of grace, even though he could not crawl out from behind Marcion's rhetorical shadow. Aquinas built the scaffolding necessary for repairing the damage to the Christian house left by Marcion, but he did not carry through the repair itself. Marcion's ghost remains at large.

Nevertheless, Aquinas's contribution to asherism reaches beyond Marcion's grasp. The asherism-voluntarism divide is not between commands complied with out of fear and those complied with wholeheartedly. The divide is between commands that are morally opaque and cultivate compliance and those that are morally transparent and cultivate wisdom. Aquinas sympathized with the preference for wisdom-oriented commands because they are pedagogically helpful. He looked beyond the fact of the threat of punishment to their pedagogical and medicinal properties to argue that obedience to divine commands, even under the threat of punishment, is in our best interest, not because we protect ourselves from harm, but because it furthers our own happiness and that of the community. His insistence on the universally constructive power of law and his attention to the medicinal property of punishment are closely linked with his doctrine of secondary agency and the relocation of moral psychology from the fall to creation. Those who understand themselves to be called to a relationship of mutual enjoyment with God, based on Genesis 1:28, and who pursue that calling as the hands and feet of divine providence, read themselves asheristically. They will approach their own creativity within that theological framework. Such well-tempered persons will approach obeying divine commands as opportunities to forward that relationship in service to God's mission for the flourishing of creation that constitutes their own beauty in the enjoyment of God. With this conception of asherism in hand, we turn to Scripture to see how it functions there.

CHAPTER 9

Asherism in the Pentateuch

Asherism proposes that happiness is enjoying life through the way of life to which Israel is called. It begins with the covenant between God and Israel initiated in Exodus 24 and developed throughout Deuteronomy. The argument is that happiness is enjoying God, creation, and self by cultivating the wisdom behind divine commands that enable one to become an instrument of the world's flourishing. Happiness is a discipline that might be called *godly self-enjoyment.*

This chapter examines godly self-enjoyment in the Pentateuch. The following two chapters examine Psalms and Proverbs respectively: each of those books, from its own perspective, expresses the asherist pattern of happiness of the Tanaḥ. The final chapter of this segment argues that the Gospel of John exemplifies the asherist proposal, though it is not of a piece with the witness of the Tanaḥ.

Asherist Commands in the Pentateuch

Covenantal faithfulness is practicing divine legislation. The precepts and statutes cover most areas of life. Those that are socializing teach salutary values for sagacious and artful living. I call them *asherist* commands because they are civilizing. While some are immediately transparent ("do not steal"), others become so upon consideration ("do not seethe a kid in its mother's milk"). Once the underlying value is clear, it can be applied laterally, and the opportunity for expanding the reach of these values takes on a socializing function. That is an application of Aquinas's secondary causality and an instance of Butler's self-love.

The first asherist biblical command ("be fruitful and multiply") is in Genesis 1:28, and it comes in a blessing. Obedience is personally rewarding: enjoying one's offspring and the fruit of one's labor are obvious rewards. Compliance has longer-term consequences: it assures us that human life will continue and will flourish on the earth, while noncompliance would end human life. Contentment is in contributing to the long-term success of God's endeavor. Contributing to society's flourishing is also personally encouraging when our actions succeed, even to a limited extent. The text portrays God as commending behavior that enables creation to flourish. It presupposes partnership between God and humanity.

Civilizing commands continue throughout the Tanaḥ, regulating Israel's social, sexual, religious, and economic life. They are exercises through which one grows in moral and spiritual wisdom for one's own sake, for personal flourishing overlaps with and eventually merges with corporate flourishing. Individuals can lift a society up or bring it down. Particular to the asherist view of the good life is the conviction that personal and corporate well-being are of a piece. Another particularity is that this conviction comes from outside in, as I will explain below.

An Asherist Perspective on the Decalogue

The Decalogue may contain the most obvious asherist commands in the Bible. Commands four through ten are socializing, obviously designed to maintain public order and civility. They fill in the content of the pattern of life that Israel is to model. Still, the negative format in which all but two of them are stated can suggest that obedience to God is defined by what the faithful may not do; but if we state them positively, another perspective emerges.

The first substantive commandment, to remember the Sabbath, is stated positively. It is the longest of the ten; the Pentateuch is strong on rest. Even God needs it. In insisting on rest for people, animals, and land, we not only imitate God, but we learn to respect the limits to which life can be pushed. Sabbath sets limits that we need but may not naturally impose on ourselves, or permit to others. Granting rest to creatures is an act of compassion, for it shows an awareness of their need and a concern for their well-being. It is striking that this group should begin, not with doing things, but with refraining from doing things, that is, with refreshment.

Honoring parents extends the idea of not being valued for productivity alone, which is implied in the previous commandment. Family is the stabilizing unit of society.[1] This commandment is about protecting those most responsible for our very life. It cultivates respect for parents when children are young and compassion for parents when they are old. Some may view this commandment as requiring sacrifice. That may come from an individualist perspective, but not from a communal perspective, for filial piety produces domestic tranquility, from which everyone benefits.

The negatively stated subsequent commandments teach respect through self-restraint: respect for life itself, the sanctity of marriage, property rights, one's integrity, and finally, respect for the neighbor. Delaying gratification is essential for healthy societies, and energy for it is inevitably constructive. It is personally rewarding because it expresses strong character, and that is strengthening. Practicing self-restraint in various contexts develops self-mastery. Scripture does not name or conceptualize it, but it calls for behavior that creates experiences of self-mastery so that one can look back and see the virtue at work. It works from outside in, from practice to life skill.

Some may argue that it is difficult to view the opening framework of the Decalogue asheristically. However, the demand for exclusive worship of this God, the prohibition of idolatry and the abuse of the divine name are the covenantal framework within which Israel is to enact the values that follow. These three define Israel's relationship to God, and in so doing they invest what may be commonsense advice with transcendent power that ennobles the agent more than mere compliance to the arbitrary rules of a jealous and controlling deity could. The seven remaining commands are proper worship of the creator of heaven and earth.[2] In this cosmic framework, energy for self-mastery may be more compelling.

---

1. Christopher J. H. Wright, "The Israelite Household and the Decalogue: The Social Background and Significance of Some Commandments," *Tyndale Bulletin* 30 (1979): 101 (24).

2. Bernhard Lang argues that five of these ten are nonreligious commandments, but that assumes that respect for life and property and sexual fidelity, honesty, and the control of envy are not religious activities. They are not cultic practices, but that does not mean that they are not religious practices. It is highly unlikely that the author of this text would have understood the distinction that comes from a much different cul-

Even this brief sortie toward an asherist reading of the Decalogue suggests that happiness is a corporate activity. Obedience to these commandments makes life satisfying and enjoyable when one defines happiness as promoting the good of the whole.

An Asherist Perspective on the Holiness Code

The Holiness Code (Lev. 17-26) looks like an elaboration of the Decalogue in some respects.[3] It shares with the Decalogue the separation of Israel from idolatry and pagan practices (18:3) and reviews and expands the commands regarding misusing the divine name (18:21, 19:12; 21:6, etc.). It reinforces the corporate orientation to happiness inherent in support for rest and filial piety (19:3). It repeats condemnation of murder (24:17), adultery (20:10), theft (19:11, 13), and false witness (19:12), while it adds other legislation about caring for the poor (19:10; 23:22), the disabled (19:14), and the foreigner (19:33-34). It promotes care for the land by prohibiting its defilement (18:25-28; 19:29) and by protecting it (19:23; 25:3-5, 23-24) and enjoying its fruits (25:18-22). All these commands cultivate respect for social and natural order. These practices of holiness not only encourage self-mastery and the value of compassion, but they encourage proactive efforts to protect natural resources needed for corporate flourishing. These values set Israel apart from the nations as God's own. As in the Decalogue, holiness in Leviticus works from the outside in.

---

ture. Bernhard Lang, "Twelve Commandments — Three Stages: A New Theory on the Formation of the Decalogue," in *Reading from Right to Left*, ed. Cheryl J. Exum and H. G. M. Williamson (London: Sheffield Academic Press, 2003), pp. 290-300.

3. Connections between these two sets of legislation have been drawn by Georg Braulik, "Weitere Beobachtungen zur Beziehung zwischen dem Heiligkeitsgesetz und Deuteronomium 19-25," in *Das Deuteronomium* (Helsinki: Finnische Exegetische Gesellschaft, 1996), pp. 23-55. Braulik recognizes the relationship between the Holiness Code and passages in Deuteronomy, and he concludes that Leviticus is earlier. See also Julian Morgenstern, "The Decalogue of the Holiness Code," *Hebrew Union College Annual* 26 (1955): 1-27. Morgenstern identifies parallels among material in Leviticus 19, the two appearances of the Decalogue, and other texts in Exodus. See also Eckart Otto, "Das Heiligkeitsgesetz Leviticus 17-26 in der Pentateuchredaktion," in *Reventlow Festschrift* (Frankfurt am Main: Peter Lang, 1994), pp. 65-80. In opposition to Braulik, Otto argues that the Holiness Code is a late redaction from the Decalogue, the Book of the Covenant, and Deuteronomy.

Jacob Milgrom points out that the Holiness Code has two major theological strategies — separation and holiness — that "anchor their foundation in the basic themes of creation and life."[4] Separation from idolatrous practices is a precondition for holiness but does not constitute it. Given the rules regulating social life, such as the recognition that sexual behavior grounds the social order, we conclude that the Holiness Code, like the Decalogue, cultivates moral strength.[5] Together they shape Israel's corporate character and locate happiness in a corporate context. Keeping close to Genesis 9:4-6, Leviticus 17:10-13 says that blood symbolizes bare life. Not eating blood cultivates reverence for life, extending that value of the Decalogue. The practice is a constant reminder of the precariousness of life itself, "for the life of the flesh is in the blood" (Lev. 17:11).

The specific manner of slaughtering animals at the altar, proper dietary practices, limits on sexual behavior, regulation of clerical practice, care for the land, the poor, and the handicapped, personal purity laws, and the celebration of festivals and holy days — all these instill the values that are the stuff of holiness. To those already mentioned, I would add the following: specifying slaughtering practices for cultic offerings to God circumscribes those acts and limits them; slaughtering for daily food is a different matter, and Exodus 12:4 suggests that animals should not be slaughtered wastefully. There is no killing for sport; killing animals must be carefully regulated to cultivate reverence for life. Establishing clerical standards (Lev. 21:21-23) elevates ministerial service to a high calling that requires holiness. Care for the land is very important in these chapters; indeed, life itself requires honoring the land. The Holiness Code calls for holiness in the crevices of life. Again, holiness happens by practicing, like playing the violin or playing basketball, until it is ego-syntonic, that is, until it becomes a regular element in one's arsenal of skills and feels "natural." Then one can attend to the music, because one has mastered the technique. Repetition does

---

4. Jacob Milgrom supports an asherist reading of the Holiness Code. *Leviticus 17–22: A New Translation with Introduction and Commentary* (New York: Doubleday, 2000), p. 1371.

5. Patrick D. Miller bemoans the absence of the values of mercy and love in the Decalogue for Christian piety. The lack is repaired by the Holiness Code and Deuteronomy, but these lack the weight of the Decalogue. See Miller, "The Sufficiency and Insufficiency of the Commandments," in *The Way of the Lord: Essays in Old Testament Theology* (Grand Rapids: Eerdmans, 2007), pp. 17-36.

not trivialize these practices, because the skill must be honed to rely on it effortlessly — that it may shine.

A good portion of this legislation is edifying, even when viewed from a twenty-first-century perspective. No doubt, more of it was morally transparent in its own time. One bit of legislation that is no longer morally transparent to us is the exclusion of any form of deformity from the priesthood and the sacrifices, but the intent was to mark out a pure center from which Israel's religious life would flow (Lev. 21). Adjacent to this legislation are rules governing who may eat the food brought by the people to support the nonstipendiary clergy. Here the reason for excluding classes of people, including the laity, is transparent to us, because eating that food would be stealing property that belongs to those without other means of financial support (Lev. 22:10-17). Not eating is thus a benevolent act.

Another stipulation of the Holiness Code that may not sit well with modern sensibilities is the execution of an unnamed man of Israelite-Egyptian parentage who blasphemed (Lev. 24:10-23). The point of the execution, however, is clearly asherist. Blaspheming God's name, a violation of the third commandment of the Decalogue, is as objectionable as murder. The goal of the sentence is to maintain God's leadership. The punishment may be unduly harsh from our point of view, but the reason is clear.

Perplexing Commands

Any number of commands in the Pentateuch are morally perplexing to moderns. Casting them in asherist perspective will not render them less alien, but it may throw light on the asherist perspective. One is a case similar to the execution for blasphemy in Leviticus. It is the execution of Achan ben Carmi and his family for stealing public property (Josh. 7). Many cultures no longer consider blasphemy or theft capital offenses, but that is beside the point. Both actions betray the Decalogue, and the intent of the deterrent is to teach respect for public property. To push that one notch further, it is to wrench thinking of personal flourishing from individualist to communal terms. The individualism implied in Achan's theft is condemned along with him: he could not master his greed for the sake of the well-being of the community.

A command in the Pentateuch that has repeatedly been criticized as irrational is that from which much of the Jewish practice of *kashrut* derives, which Jesus swept away (Matt. 15:11). The command in question appears in Exodus 23:19 and 34:26, as well as Deuteronomy 14:21 (and is hinted at in Lev. 22:28): "You shall not boil a kid in its mother's milk." While the concrete application of the principle as developed by rabbinic Judaism may be morally unappealing to Christians, the command itself is morally transparent. It is wrong to use a substance intended to nourish life to cause the death of the one for whom life was intended. On a practical level, rules for protecting the food source (Lev. 19:23 and Deut. 20:19-20 and 22:6) are far-sighted. Both the moral and the ecologically attuned commands ensure common well-being, and individuals who comply with them enjoy their self-restraint because it advances communal well-being. Foregoing the fruit of the trees is not a sacrifice in this perspective; rather, it is a contribution to communal flourishing that sits well in the heart. The virtue in all three cases is protecting renewable resources for the future.

Another command that deeply perplexes moderns is in the book of Deuteronomy (to which we are about to turn); it is worth considering here because it discloses the dark side of asherism. As Israel is poised to take the land of promise, Moses prepares the people for war on divine orders. Violent conquest is necessary to conquer the land for the reign of God.[6] Sometimes Israel is attacked first and then retaliates; but at other times God orders Israel to strike preemptively and to destroy everything. Violent conquest aims to secure the land in order to eradicate idolatry, not to enrich Israel. Eradicating idolatry itself has two purposes: to protect Israel from profanation and to display divine power so that those on the sidelines will turn to Israel's God. Numbers 25:1-9 illustrates the former, where sex and idolatry are so closely linked. Foreign wives who introduce idolatry into Israel continue to be a central concern as late as the return from exile (Ezra 10:11-44; Neh. 13:23-31). The latter purpose is represented by Balaam in Numbers 22–24.

War-making begins when Israel's army destroys the Canaanites of

---

6. I use the word "reign" advisedly. The phrase "reign or kingdom of God" is from a later time. Divine lordship is not cast in monarchical terms in the Pentateuch. I advert to this work because it captures the sense of the lordship of God over Israel before the clamor for a king of flesh and blood.

Arad in the Negev (Num. 21:1-3) and continues in Transjordan against the Amorites of Heshbon and Bashan (Num. 21:21-35), and in the war against the kings of Midian, east of the Gulf of Aqaba (Num. 31:1-12). Numbers 32 recounts the conquest of Transjordan and Moses' division of it for the tribes of Gad, Reuben, and the half-tribe of Manasseh. Israel is no ragtag band of nomads but a fearsome unified fighting force.

Deuteronomy rehearses this history as Moses prepares the people to move across the Jordan under the generalship of Joshua. In advance, Moses gives the command to "utterly destroy" seven nations in the land, with a special warning not to marry any of the inhabitants of that land (Deut. 7:1-6). Though the text is not as clear as one might wish, the specific order is to destroy the worship places of these nations (7:5). At this point there is no order to commit genocide, and the warning against intermarriage supports the point. The conquest will be slow, but Israel is to persist "until [the Canaanite altars] are destroyed" (7:22-24). Blotting out Canaanite religions is essential to secure the pure worship of God.[7] This point is repeated in Deuteronomy 12:2-3.

Moses' later rules of engagement for the conquest (Deut. 20:10-20) deeply offend modern sensibilities, for he orders genocide.[8] Even noting that these are Moses' orders and not God's is not meliorating, since the rallying cry is that "it is the Lord your God who goes with you, to fight for you against your enemies, to give you victory" (Deut. 20:4). However, the victory is not victory for the sake of establishing an Israelite empire. It is to free the land from idolatry, that the true worship of God may flourish and the people prosper in the beauty of holiness with Israel. Idolatry is God's great enemy, and his means of defeating it is the faithfulness of Israel in moral living, religious practice, and military prowess. Genocide is for the sake of the covenant.

---

7. The text was probably written in hindsight, with Solomon's wives and their religious cults in mind.

8. Israel is to offer terms of peace before attacking a city that is not a part of her inheritance. These terms include having its people serve Israel as forced labor. If the terms are rejected, Israel's army is to besiege the town until it falls. The order to commit genocide is explicit, though it is sometimes partial. In towns outside Israel's geographic inheritance, women and booty were to be spared, but "you shall put all its males to the sword" (Deut. 20:13). For towns that are inside the divine inheritance, however, the command to commit genocide is complete. "You must not let anything that breathes remain alive. You shall annihilate them" (20:16-17). Only food-producing trees are to be spared. The book of Joshua carries this plan through in detail.

The rules of engagement are asherist in the sense that they are in pursuit of Israel's pure worship of God and perhaps the worship of the nations after them, whether from terror or persuasion. It may be repulsive in the abstract, but the twentieth century has exemplified how easy it still is to justify conquest in ethnic, racial, or religious terms. As difficult as it is to swallow, the author(s) and editor(s) of the biblical text present these holy wars as obedience to divine commands that they trust are for the sake of God's plan for the establishment of his holy nation. Perhaps this is a point at which one should confront God, as Abraham did at Sodom, where God did not finally relent (Gen. 18:22-33), and as Moses did at Sinai, where God did relent (Exod. 32:11-14).

Covenantal Holiness

The call to live covenantal holiness is hard won; delivering Israel from Egypt was difficult. Moses became disheartened because the people would not listen to his reports of what God was doing when their situation was deteriorating as Pharaoh was tightening the screws (Exod. 5:10-14). God proposes: "I will take you as my people, and I will be your God" (Exod. 6:7a), but they pay no heed. Only at Sinai, after God's rescue operation has succeeded, can the people hear the covenantal terms. Then they trust God and Moses enough to respond: "All that the Lord has spoken we will do, and we will heed" (Exod. 24:7; my translation).

This bilateral covenant becomes the central organizing principle of Israel's life, and the Tanah regularly points out that covenantal faithfulness is revering the Lord (יִרְאַת יְהוָה).[9] Loving the Lord (e.g., Deut. 6:5, וְאָהַבְתָּ) also designates a proper attitude toward God. Love and fear blend together as reverence that connotes the stance before God that enables devoted and voluntary obedience to the covenant for the well-being of the nation that God enjoys.

The importance of reverence for the Lord of Israel cannot be underestimated. It appears in eighteen books of the Tanah, most heavily in Psalms and Proverbs, which I shall examine below. Perhaps its most ringing verse is "revering the Lord is the beginning of wisdom," a sentiment that resounds in the ears of Scripture readers. It comes from the

---

9. Both to fear and to revere the Lord translate יִרְאַת יְהוָה.

pen of one of Israel's poets (Ps. III:10), from one of the sages (Prov. 1:7; 9:10), and from that great expounder of Israelite wisdom, Jesus ben Sirach (Ecclesiasticus 1:14). All three writers ground revering God in wisdom, and they know that a fine life requires it. Yet practice is required to bring wisdom to full flower.

Asherism argues that that happens when we internalize the values taught by the commands. Asherist commands are compelling because they enact a wise, productive, and happy life. To revere the Lord is to live by these values that are internalized through practices. Deuteronomy, too, holds that reverence for God is commandment-keeping: obedience leads one into the beauty and wisdom of God.

The Witness of Deuteronomy

Revering the Lord appears in Deuteronomy eleven times (4:10; 6:2, 13, 24; 10:12, 20; 13:4; 14:23; 17:19; 31:12, 13). Loving God is commanded five times (6:5; 10:12; 11:1; 13:3; 30:6).[10] As two sides of one proverbial coin of devotion, Deuteronomy 10:12 (echoed by Mic. 6:8) mentions the two together: "So now, O Israel, what does the Lord your God require of you? Only to revere the Lord your God, to walk in all his ways, to love him, to serve the Lord your God with all your heart and with all your soul." This reverence embraces the Deuteronomic precepts because that way those growing into wise and discerning maturity come to know from experience that obedience brings positive results.[11] It is not respect for an authority figure or a bare sense of gratitude for what God has done in the past, but an ongoing set of activities that enact the covenant, grounded as it is in remembering the liberation from

10. William L. Moran identifies the distinctive theme of love for God in Deuteronomy and its relationship to treaty language in the ancient Near East. See Moran, "Ancient Near Eastern Backgrounds of the Love of God in Deuteronomy," *Catholic Biblical Quarterly* 25 (1963): 77-87. However, Moran fails to note that the fear of the Lord is the far more prominent theme in Deuteronomy, or to suggest what the relationship between the two might be.

11. Patrick D. Miller has argued that the call to fear the Lord in Deuteronomy is one of its primary positive manifestations of the first commandment of the Decalogue (Deut. 6:13). It is a positive expression of the commandments not to have other gods (fear him), not to make and worship images (serve/worship him), and not to lift up the name of the Lord in vain (swear by him dishonestly). Miller, "Deuteronomy and Psalms: Evoking a Biblical Conversation," *Journal of Biblical Studies* 118, no. 1 (1999): 15.

Egypt. Obedience along with understanding the goals of covenantal responsibility constitutes God's reign in Israel, that is, on earth. Obedience furthers God's plan to reign over his creatures, beginning with Israel.

In preparing to cross the river, Moses rehearses Israel's history since the Exodus to reinforce the people's covenantal responsibilities. Again, socializing commands teach collaboration (Deut. 17:8-13), domestic and sexual propriety (22:13-30), economic support for the poor and distressed (24:18-22), concern for the disabled (27:18), care of foreigners (10:19), protection of the the public from injury (22:8), and moral business practices (25:13-14).

Moshe Weinfeld notes that Deuteronomy's laws gloss those in Exodus with a more humane outlook. He identifies those that emphasize the value of human life and dignity (21:10-14, 22-23; 22:8; 23:16; 25:1-3), those dealing with interpersonal relations (15:1-11; 21:15-16; 23:25), and those prohibiting cruelty to animals (22:6-7; 25:4).[12] We can add to this list the statutes requiring care of a neighbor's property (22:1-4), levirate marriage that protects widows, honors the dead, and cultivates family loyalty (25:5-10), and — though not humane in the strict sense — protection of natural resources (20:19-20).

Civic standards enact the covenant through standardized employment practices (15:12-15), building codes (22:8), and weights and measures (25:13-14), making employers, artisans, and merchants accountable. Civic commands are religious commands that are all mandated by the covenant (harking back to Exod. 24:3). Fair employment practices are a covenantal responsibility: "Remember that you were a slave in the land of Egypt, and the Lord your God redeemed you; for this reason I lay this command upon you today" (15:15). The whole deuteronomic legislation is under the covenantal rubric of remembering the deliverance from Egypt and agreeing to heed God.

Cultic practices also shape Israel's character. Circumcision is already moralized (10:16; 30:6). Taxation ensures proper worship of God, which requires caring for the clergy (12:17-19; 14:22-29).[13] Reli-

12. Moshe Weinfeld, "Origin of the Humanism in Deuteronomy," *Journal of Biblical Literature* 80, no. 3 (1961): 241.

13. Yochanan Muffs argues that willingness and spontaneity characterize the reciprocal covenantal arrangements between God and Israel. Muffs, *Love and Joy: Law, Language, and Religion in Ancient Israel* (New York and Cambridge, MA: Jewish Theological Seminary of America [distributed by Harvard University Press], 1992), pp. 121-30.

gious festivals are the *cantus firmus* of the covenant, from which the civic and social commandments derive their authority (Deut. 16). Remembering encourages enacting, and enacting the covenant takes the memory out of the past to locate God's ongoing reign in the present. While Moses' leadership began in Egypt, he pushes back to the patriarchs to whom God promised the land (26:5-11). The living covenant is the fruit of God's call to Abram, with its promised blessing of the nations.

Reflection

The covenant grounds the biblical doctrine of happiness. Israel's responsibility is to live the divinely authorized way of life shaped by divine commands that construct and maintain civil society. They structure personal and family life in terms of Israel's corporate well-being, from which all benefit. Reverent obedience to God promotes self-mastery, values, and skills that promote personal well-being and the common good.

Obedience to detailed instruction may not itself be pleasing, but the goal is socialization, and that leads to flourishing, which is pleasing. Israel's faithfulness is remembering God's mercy toward it in order to establish God's reign that it might expand. Outgrowing the habits of slavery and resisting the lure of idolatry, to which Israel seems ever prone, are to a further end. God consecrates Israel to himself at Sinai, and Israel agrees to take up the challenge for a wise and beautiful way of life as a beacon of light to the world, that it, too, may eventually dwell in the divine light of life.

The Decalogue, the Holiness Code, the ensuing Deuteronomic legislation — and even morally perplexing precepts — structure an asherist way of life in which God and Israel enjoy one another, as Israel lives into and rejoices in its covenantal responsibilities. Even military conquest, with its horrific collateral damage, is not for the sake of building an empire, but to extirpate idolatry from God's land and to establish Israel there to be the instrument of divine blessing for itself and the nations.

From these texts it is reasonable to conclude that the Pentateuch understands Israel's thriving as its happiness: happiness is enjoying and celebrating a productive and fulfilling life in obedience to the terms of the covenant with God to which Israel agreed at Sinai. Socializing legislation discloses values and virtues that are to be understood dynamically and applied liberally in analogous situations.

CHAPTER 10

Asherism in the Psalter

Aquinas and Butler based faithful obedience on a graced nature that can function adequately despite sin. The Sinai covenant, on the other hand, grounds Israel's well-being in the context of obedience to God's way of life. The people flourish by practicing the way of life patterned by the edifying legislation offered from Exodus to Deuteronomy. Torah embodies the values and life skills that covenant fidelity expects from Israel.

When we turn to the Psalter, the setting changes dramatically. It backs up from the immediacy of receiving divine guidance to preserving it at a far remove. The Psalter is not only ancient Israel's hymnal, consisting of corporate praise and prayer to God; it is also its teaching, preaching, exhortation, and admonition to the assembly. As Israel's earliest liturgical expression, it proclaims the good news of the covenant that worship transmits down the generations. It presupposes and often summarizes the covenant and sometimes rehearses Israel's history for both present and future (Pss. 78, 105, 106). Even though not frequently mentioned, the covenantal presupposition is in the background undergirding the standards of uprightness that the Psalter highlights.

Theological Background

The psalmists never forget God's promises, and they implore him to restore Israel's well-being promised at election (Deut. 7:12-16; cf. Ps. 105:10-15). On behalf of the people, they praise God profusely when deliverance comes, and they publicly proclaim his fidelity in order to reinvigorate their own. Still, the Psalter gives voice to frustrated individuals — or perhaps individuals speaking for the nation — who complain when deliverance is delayed (Pss. 43, 86), but they do not lose heart. Torah loyalty is their strength. They are perplexed that God seems far away when he is needed on the spot. The pathos of a people trying to maintain its equilibrium between extremes of consolation and desolation is palpable.

Although individuals wax eloquent about both suffering and deliverance, underneath the Psalter sounds the heartbeat of Torah: Israel and God are pledged to mutual fidelity, whatever the case may be. Both benefactor and beneficiary of divine favor have serious responsibilities. Deuteronomy 7:9-16 lays them out:

> Know therefore that the Lord your God is God, the faithful God who maintains covenant loyalty with those who love him and keep his commandments, to a thousand generations, and who repays in their own person those who reject him. He does not delay but repays in their own person those who reject him. Therefore, observe diligently the commandment — the statutes, and the ordinances — that I am commanding you today. If you heed these ordinances, by diligently observing them, the Lord your God will maintain with you the covenant loyalty that he swore to your ancestors; he will love you, bless you, and multiply you; he will bless the fruit of your womb and the fruit of your ground, your grain and your wine and your oil, the increase of your cattle and the issue of your flock, in the land that he swore to your ancestors to give you. You shall be the most blessed of peoples, with neither sterility nor barrenness among you or your livestock. The Lord will turn away from you every illness; all the dread diseases of Egypt that you experienced, he will not inflict on you, but he will lay them on all who hate you. You shall devour all the peoples that the Lord your God is giving over to you, showing them no pity; you shall not serve their gods, for that would be a snare to you.

This passage may sound like quid pro quo bargain, but the central texts we read in the preceding chapter suggest that it is not that straightforward. Keeping the "law," like obeying traffic lights, is bound to have immediate benefits, but, as I noted in the preceding chapter, as the importance of this obedience is assimilated, its benefits spread beyond immediate ends. Traffic laws protect people from immediate harm, but

upon reflection (or perhaps divine illumination), they also edify —
though specifics are rare. They teach that public safety and personal
safety are of a piece. In obeying them, everyone is protecting everyone
else. That is the import of covenantal law (as I have discussed in the
preceding chapter).

While all blessings are from God, the salutary way of life that God's
teaching recommends really is the way to prosper. Idolatry and
syncretism are threatening, not because God is threatened by competitors, but because they weaken the moral fiber of the nation, which
must be God's "light to the nations" (Isa. 42:6). Israel must remain
morally and spiritually vibrant in order both to enjoy and to witness to
the superior way of life that God's way offers.

If the Deuteronomic reform under King Josiah spurred the whole
Deuteronomistic history, with its stories of Israel's tumultuous struggle for covenantal fidelity, this corpus would loom large in Israel's subsequent reflection, particularly in exile. Assuming that Ezra had most
of the Pentateuch, Deuteronomy would have been at the core of the
restoration of the temple and its walls, and it was likely the text that
Ezra read to the people for five or six hours to publicly reestablish
God's way for Israel in Jerusalem, as well as in Babylonia.

Psalms were probably collected in this postexilic period. Some
psalms, along with the Pentateuch, were probably used for worship in
the newly reconstructed temple in Jerusalem. Deuteronomy 7 remains
nearby.

The Psalter expects energetic fidelity to covenantal precepts. Corporate election calls for enthusiastic corporate response. In this, numerous psalms follow the pattern set by the Pentateuchal passages I
have considered above. They testify that Israel's flourishing — or, perhaps better, salvation — lies in learning to live uprightly by carrying out
God's ordinances and applying the values and skills learned from specific practices across life.[1]

---

1. Rabbinic Judaism extended the reach of the law by "drawing a fence around the
torah," which gave rise, e.g., to the rabbinic dietary system from a very few biblical verses.
The Pentateuch's stipulations need not be elaborated by further specification but by
thinking of the specific practice as an edifying example of principle to be extended laterally to other circumstances. The latter is the direction of covenantal obedience that I
take here.

Being "Happy" in the Psalter

Happiness is an important theme in the Psalter, not least because it is linguistically significant. A large group of psalms use celebratory language to describe pious Israel. Among these, several focus on keeping the commandments, celebrating the uprightness that covenantal fidelity shapes, and becoming wise by way of those other two. While these features may, psychologically speaking, suggest stages of spiritual advancement into happiness, the Psalter does not put them together that way, though they often imply one another. It may be psychologically satisfying to think of these features in a funnel shape, but the texts do not.

I will discuss them in that order, however, to point out logical and psychological links among the various features. The argument is that, within the large category of psalms that use the language of delight in election, various psalms unpack this theme from various angles.

The Joy of Election

The first step in discerning happiness in the Psalter is rather straight-forward: its widest parameter includes those psalms that use language indicating Israel's well-being. The signal words here are *ashrey* (אַשְׁרֵי) and *smh* (שָׂמַח).

Being Ashrey (אַשְׁרֵי)

The Psalter presupposes the election of Israel and designates that election status as *ashrey*. It is a slippery word, often translated as "happy," or "blessed," though it does not mean a passing pleasant experience or emotion. *Ashrey* is something else. In the Psalms, it usually appears in a corporate context describing Israel, the upright, or some other group designated by the speaker (1:1; 33:12; 65:4; 146:5, et al.). Far from being a state of subjective feeling, *ashrey* describes something positive about the situation of others, such as being honored or privileged.

Ashrey is a masculine intensive plural noun (it includes women) that functions descriptively. It can never stand alone; it is always connected to another noun. It constructs a relationship with the noun that follows it by describing a positive quality or identity to the second noun. *Ashrey* identifies people who are privileged, fortunate, honored, or blessed:

"*ashrey* [are] those who . . . or the person who. . . ." One declares others to be *ashrey* by virtue of their membership in the people of God. It is not a self-designation, as in "I am happy." Those who accept their blessed status celebrate the privilege of belonging to God.[2] *Ashrey* characterizes the people of God. The word *makarios* functions this way in the Beatitudes.

Being Smḥ (שָׂמַח)

Other words do express happiness as a positive feeling state. Israel rejoices in, is glad about, or celebrates what God has done — and still may do — for her. Various forms of *smḥ* appear frequently in the Psalms.[3] As opposed to the adjectival form of *ashrey*, *smḥ* is a regular Hebrew root that appears in verbs and as the noun "happiness." Psalms using *smḥ* usually assume the covenantal context (including Pss. 19, 33, 64, and 105), but are also associated with delight in family matters (Pss. 127:5; 144:12). They are more often used self-referentially and imply emotional engagement with the situation.

Happiness Psalms

Numerous psalms use either *ashrey* or *smḥ* to indicate Israel's celebration of its covenantal identity and to express the joy of being God's people and of flourishing through its way of life.[4] The two words are complementary. *Ashrey* describes the honor bestowed on Israel by God, and *smḥ* expresses the subjective side of that status. Both are needed and perhaps imply one another. It is provocative to call these "happiness" psalms, since the word may be misleading, but it is a technical term indicating no more than that one of these words appears in the covenantal context. Being comfortable with who we are as members of the people of God and confident in the moral strength that we derive from it are central to the Tanaḥ's way toward a rich and satisfying life, despite our being tormented by cynics and skeptics and our own doubts and temptations.

2. It appears in first-person singular in Gen. 30:13.

3. *Gyl* (גִּיל) and *rnh* (רִנָּה), other words for joy and gladness, appear but are insignificant.

4. Psalms 1, 2, 32, 33, 34, 40, 41, 65, 84, 89, 94, 106, 112, 119, 127, 128, 144, and 146 use *ashrey*, while 5, 16, 30, 32, 34, 35, 43, 86, 90, 92, 97, 105, 113, 122, 126, and 137 use *smḥ*. This list excludes psalms that rejoice over defeat of enemies, although technically they belong to this group (e.g., Ps. 35:15, 26; Ps. 137).

The happiness psalms do not deny that the faithful may suffer (Pss. 40, 86, 119), yet they never fall into despair or cynicism. They expect that the sufferer's moral beauty, the fruit of fidelity to God's way, will stand her in good stead under duress. Perhaps the assumption is that living excellently protects the sufferer from self-despair. Taking refuge in God, a locution for this way, creates spiritual strength that fights psychological defeat and humiliation. Suffering is real and powerful, but spiritual resources march out to do battle with it. The sufferer can stand in the uprightness with which God has trained her. Being mocked and misunderstood may be painful and deeply aggravating, but in the end they do not damage a person. In that place of spiritual strength, we can rejoice in who we are in God and use that strength to fight potentially damaging effects of material deprivation and social degradation, even as David did in Psalm 63. The strength of goodness lights the darkness (Ps. 112:4), and it is more than hope or expectation. It is Paul's "armor of God" (Eph. 6:11, 13) that saves from spiritual death.

Enjoying the Commandments

Enjoying the commandments is the heart of Israel's loyalty to God. In this vein, J. L. Mays identifies Torah psalms, pointing to Psalms 1, 19, and 119.[5] They instruct Israel in God's way "until the matter becomes part of the thinking and willing and doing," that is, until the teaching is internalized.[6] Mays notes similar psalms that teach reverence for God by delighting in the commandments, particularly Psalm 112. He also notes that the didactic and edificatory character of these Torah-psalms brings them into close proximity with wisdom psalms, as we shall see. In pointing out the centrality of the law to Christian readers, he rejects any thought of "self-righteous, single-minded legalism" for Torah-piety. It is rather "devotion to the instruction of the Lord and trust in the reign of the Lord."[7] Torah-piety is reverent covenantal loyalty.

---

5. James Luther Mays, "The Place of the Torah-Psalms in the Psalter," *Journal of Biblical Literature* 106, no. 1 (1987): 3-12.
6. Mays, "Torah-Psalms," p. 9.
7. Mays, "Torah-Psalms," p. 12.

Becoming Upright

The theme of uprightness is ubiquitous throughout the Psalter. It not only flows organically from covenantal fidelity; it is its end. Uprightness, as an orientation toward our lives, is shaped by covenantal practice. It is the way of an excellent life. In the covenantal context, it is not appropriate to think of upright living as general moral standards that do not derive from revelation, as if fine living could be known apart from Torah. This point fuels both Israel's internal and external struggle against idolatry. For the Tanaḥ, there is no excellent living apart from God's way for Israel that is to become the way for all people. Of the many psalms that speak of uprightness, nine are *ashrey* psalms (Pss. 17, 33, 35, 40, 45, 89, 94, 97, 119). The privilege of being Israel is living passionately through God's law (Deut. 6:5). The biblical texts have no thought of formalism. Deuteronomy's passion is for the moral and spiritual energy that the precepts impart, as the discussion of edifying commands has suggested. The same holds true for several psalms.

Becoming Wise

Some psalms speak of growing wise and suggest how to become so. Wisdom is of a piece with keeping covenantal precepts and living uprightly. Several psalms are widely identified as wisdom psalms.[8] While various form critics have different lists of wisdom psalms, several of those commonly listed are happiness psalms (1, 19, 32, 34, 105, 112, 119, and 128). Where covenantal fidelity is not mentioned, it may be presupposed. Practice and growth in uprightness and wisdom, however, may be no more than different ways of speaking about a fine life that lifts everyone.

---

8. Form criticism has debated the identity of "wisdom" psalms within its categorization structure, but it remains fluid. One agreed-on criterion is that the poem be didactic and edifying, though how that is interpreted varies. See Leo G. Perdue, *Wisdom and Cult: A Critical Analysis of the Views of Cult in the Wisdom Literatures of Israel and the Ancient Near East* (Missoula, MT: Scholars Press for the Society of Biblical Literature, 1977), pp. 261-65.

Asherist Psalms

This exercise has been to tease out perspectives on Israel's delight and joy in its calling that may help us find a way to talk about happiness for ourselves. Naming this sensibility is difficult. I have coined the word "asherism" to point to the excellent way of life to which some scriptural texts point. When one includes *smḥ* psalms with *ashrey* psalms, it throws the latter term into dispute. I use asherism, however, to highlight the covenantal grounding of excellent living. While it is possible to construe *ashrey* psalms apart from pleasure, it is impossible to construe *smḥ* psalms apart from the covenantal designation that *ashrey* presupposes. The happiness psalms assume that God's election is the primary cause of flourishing and that Israel's faithful obedience is its secondary or instrumental cause, as Aquinas might put it. I will offer an asherist reading of Psalms 1, 19, 34, and 112. They all are happiness psalms, and they all exhibit or imply at least two of the following three themes of happiness: (a) the importance of Torah faithfulness, (b) uprightness, derived from Torah, and (c) wisdom.

Before proceeding to that exploration, however, I should make one further prefatory comment on flourishing in the Psalter. Waldemar Janzen notes that *ashrey* cannot be applied to God.[9] This is true enough, but two psalms do speak of God's pleasure, though using other words. Psalm 104, a great creation psalm, says that God is pleased with the goodness of his handiwork: "May the glory of the Lord endure forever; may the Lord rejoice in [*smḥ*] his works" (v. 31). The assumption clearly is that the proper functioning of creation itself makes God happy. Taking the idea one step further, we may infer that God's purpose in creating a "very good" world was to enjoy it, and for humans to enjoy it, too. Another psalm of praise exhorting Israel to enjoy God acknowledges that when Israel celebrates God, "the Lord takes pleasure [*rwṣḥ;* רוֹצֶה] in his people; he adorns the humble with victory" (Ps. 149:4). The implication is that God enjoys the fruit of his labor when it all thrives as intended. This will become an asherist theme as we progress (it will suffice simply to note it here).

---

9. Waldemar Janzen, "'Ashrê in the Old Testament," *Harvard Theological Review* 58, no. 2 (1965): 225.

Selected Asherist Psalms

Psalm 1

As the opening word of the Psalter, *ashrey* sets the stage for learning and ingesting God's upright way of life. It is most probable that it was selected for this honor at the head of a collection of psalms. From the asherist perspective, it is perfectly fitting, even expected, that such a piece would frame all that is to follow. Israel is honored by God's teaching: those who want it and constantly chew on it are blessed by their labors (v. 2); they thrive by living artfully and carefully (v. 3).

Yet, in some ways this poem seems an odd choice for the opening word of Israel's earliest "prayer book," because it is actually a threat, speaking more of what not to do than what to do. If this is the Psalter's message, it is short and simple: the upright are blessed and succeed, while the wicked perish and are gone with the wind. If this is the basic message of the Psalter, there can be no doubt about what will follow. Yet the elaboration of that message is worth pursuing, as each psalm applies the message to different circumstances and different people.

As stark as the message is, however, it offers no just-deserts theology. This is not the classic theistic sanction that instills fear by threatening punishment and inspires hope by promising some future reward. The upright prosper by their own hand and the wicked perish by their own hand. Everyone's destiny lies in what they do with the gift of God's teaching. Therefore, just as Aquinas understood human creativity to be ultimately caused by God yet proximately caused by careful use of created resources, so here happiness is ultimately caused by God and proximately by the wisdom and skills of individuals of the nation to use Torah.

This psalm is usually structured as two strophes of three verses each, divided in the middle; but that does not quite work. The first three verses explain who the upright are, since they are the subject of each verse. The first two verses of the second set of three are the antiphon of the first strophe and explain who the wicked are, though the first strophe has lots to say about what the upright are not to do as well. The final verse, however, is not part of the antiphon, but a summary of the two ways, and perhaps an ominous one at that: "For the Lord knows the way of the upright, and the way of the wicked shall perish." Here, as in other psalms, *ashrey* distinguishes the upright in Israel from their disobedient sisters and brothers. There is, as it were, an Israel within Israel, by virtue of whether they accept or reject being *ashrey*. The battle for the hearts and minds of Israel begins with the Psalter's first breath, and it details what each kind of person does using contrasting descriptions, poking under the skin of the hearer. The poem juxtaposes the behavior and virtues of both the wicked and the righteous, but it details the faults and the negative consequences of the former more carefully than the strengths and virtues of the latter.

The first strophe has the upright as the subject. In verse 1, the upright are *ashrey* because they have not gone astray. They refrain from doing what will harm them. The verse offers three things that those who are wise enough to know better do not do: they do not follow bad advice; they do not take the sinner's path; they do not dwell with scoffers who mock the upright — or perhaps the Torah itself. The *ashrey* are distinguished from the wicked first by their skill at self-mastery and then, in verse 2, by their positive behavior. They seek God's teaching and constantly consider it, dwelling in it, for it contains all that they need.

The way of the upright may be difficult, but there is pleasure in it that the wicked who mock God do not know. The riches of God's Torah are not necessarily evident on the surface. We may not simply comply with commandments superficially and be relieved of our covenantal responsibilities. We must plumb the depths of God's law, embedding ourselves in it.

Verses 3 and 4 capture the binary opposition between the two ways. The upright are depicted as saplings planted in a goodly place, near fresh flowing water, whose fruit will mature in due course. Their leaves do not wither. The saplings gently grow into the upright life under divine tutelage; when the "trees" are laden with fruit, they succeed in their purpose. Far from flourishing, the wicked are the detritus of the harvest. To shift the metaphor, when the wheat is winnowed, the wicked are like the chaff driven into oblivion by the breeze. Their way perishes, for they followed a foolish path. The psalmist is interested in defeating the path the wicked have chosen, not in punishing those who have chosen it, for the effects are lasting. Luring the upright with success is preferable to frightening the wicked with destruction.

William Brown catches the import of these images by focusing on the healthy sapling, the central metaphor of the psalm:

> The arboreal image, mapped onto righteous character, connotes various associations such as cultivation, growth, and well-rootedness,

which ethically speaking point to enduring success, maturity, and steadfastness in conduct. As the "leaves" of this tree do not wither, so the individual's integrity remains constant and efficacious.[10]

Verse 5 draws the obvious conclusion from the evidence submitted. The wicked have no place in the court of the just. But no courtroom drama is being played out here: this is no judicial review before an angry God, who is judge and jury. Cynics are simply not among the upright. God need not hunt them down. They have excluded themselves and will lose naturally because their way of life simply leads nowhere. It has no staying power; it is self-defeating. The ways of wisdom and folly in Proverbs make the same point. The foolish way will lose of its own accord because wickedness does not succeed in meeting the goals that God has set for creation — even though it may be powerful. The way of the upright advances those goals.

Patrick Miller sees the evangelistic aim of the psalm: "[I]ts primary aim is to describe the virtues and good outcomes of the way of the upright whose pleasure in the Lord's law eventuates in and has its corollary in the positive emotional response on the part of those who view him or her. The 'way of the righteous' really is a better and more desirable way, and others can perceive and testify to that."[11]

This asherist psalm captures the import of Torah's pattern of a thriving life. Happiness is faithful covenantal living that matures with experience. It is not satisfaction at having ticked off activities on a checklist. Covenantal obedience comes from delighting in the precepts of God's teaching, internalizing the moral standards that they exemplify, and applying them discerningly so that everyone thrives and the way of the wicked shows itself as weightless chaff. Here is the psalmist's vision of happiness.

Psalm 19

Like Psalm 1, this psalm is also a great Torah psalm. Yet it is also a path to wisdom and a plea for uprightness. It is an admonition, an ingenu-

---

10. William P. Brown, *Seeing the Psalms: A Theology of Metaphor* (Louisville: Westminster/John Knox, 2002), p. 58.

11. Patrick D. Miller, *Interpreting the Psalms* (Philadelphia: Fortress, 1986), p. 82.

ous request for acceptance, and probably an artful polemic against worship of the sun, Shamash. The psalmist subordinates the sun to God, its creator and manager who sets its place in the heavens and directs its course (vv. 4b-6).[12]

This psalm has the ring of an erudite and sophisticated sermon to Israel's cultured despisers, hoping to lure them back to covenantal fidelity, for God's teaching is spiritually and practically fructifying. We consider it in its two conventionally recognized parts, each having two subsections with a concluding personal petition. The first strophe, verses 1-6, points to divine control of nature for our physical well-being, while the second and third, verses 7-10 and 11-13, point to our moral and spiritual well-being, wrought by adhering to covenantal precepts. Part 1 (vv. 1-6) builds its case in two steps, beginning with the first verse, which states the thesis of the psalm: God has crafted the heavens. The dependable daily cycle of day and night attests heaven's maker. The stable order on which our life depends wordlessly yet volubly teaches all the earth about God (vv. 2-4a). Anticipating what is to come, no one and no place can ignore the fact that the life-giving cycle of work and rest, coolness and warmth, displays the wisdom of God, whose handiwork enables us to flourish on the earth (v. 7).

The second step of the first part (vv. 4b-6) presses the thesis: day and night proclaim God's authority. This passage is a beautiful and powerful statement that God is the power behind the sun, setting the terms of its strength to warm the earth and feed its people. But God, who provides the sun to serve his creation, does not stop there. He is yet wiser and more penetrating than any runner seeking to sprint across the sky could ever be (v. 5). The poet undermines paganism without even naming it, so clear is God's providential control of the celestial bodies.

Part 2 of the psalm (vv. 7-14) presses the wisdom of God beyond directing celestial cycles. His provision of physical sustenance can only be understood as such from a theological perspective. Any struggle for loyalty between culturally entrenched nature-gods, who run their courses, and the God of Israel can only be cut through by accepting that God is the God of the heavenly bodies. The cosmic theological in-

---

12. For further discussion, see Nahum M. Sarna, *On the Book of Psalms: Exploring the Prayers of Ancient Israel* (New York: Schocken Books, 1993), pp. 70-96; see also Brown, *Seeing the Psalms,* pp. 81-103.

sight is that divine wisdom has put the forces in place precisely to provide sustenance and that God controls their movements.

Sustenance is essential, and God provides it, but it is not sufficient for God's purpose. God aims at the moral and spiritual flourishing of Israel as well. Regulated physical cycles of the cosmos are needed for food, but the purity of Torah is needed to uplift the soul and grow it into wisdom (v. 7), enabling it to be happy and filled with light. Exaltation of the soul is by living the teaching, so that the precepts gladden the heart and the commandments light up the eyes (v. 8) to be alive to the moral truth that God's way of life embodies. The sun's heat may have a purifying effect against the fearsome deeds accomplished by night, but, morally speaking, the Mesopotamian and Egyptian deities are worthless and have been banished by the poet's commanding opening thesis announced in verse 1. That the heavens declare the glory of God is obvious only to those who have knowledge of God the creator. Together, verses 1-6 and 7-10 explain that God provides for both our physical and spiritual welfare through both the light of the sun and the light of Torah, and that reveling in the commandments is the daily path of a fine life, just as the sun runs its mighty course from one end of heaven to the other. Brown puts it this way: "As the sun, cast in the image of an athlete or warrior, exudes energy and strength, so Torah imparts renewed vigor. Through the 'law' one is rejuvenated for the tasks of obedience and empowered to follow the prescribed path of righteousness, which is cosmically forged."[13]

Revering God (v. 9) is living by Torah-righteousness, which is richer than gold and sweeter than honey (v. 10).[14] The ability of divine teaching to inculcate the values and virtues that enable Israel to be morally tall and to embody divine wisdom is carried forward here in the face of cultural challenge. In the desert, Israel innocently embraced divine teaching. Ironically, for all its hardships, the desert proved to be an easier place to worship God than was the promised land, where cultural assimilation threatened Israel's integrity. His job is to recall the people to their high calling: internalizing God's way by chewing (הגה) on it day and night, seeking its wisdom (v. 14; also Ps. 1:2).

The last strophe of this psalm (vv. 11-13) is a candid confession that

13. Brown, *Seeing the Psalms,* p. 93.

14. Sarna provides the pagan background of these metaphors that vivifies their power. Sarna, *On the Book of Psalms,* pp. 89-91.

the author is unable to live up to the standards he has set. It is an anxiety shared by Psalm 119. Although the importance of obedience may be understood intellectually, enacting it is challenging in a powerfully confusing culture, or perhaps in any case. The commandments themselves stand as a warning (v. 11). Like the sun that sheds light on everything (v. 6), God brings to light mistakes that even faithful servants miss. Developing faults is so subtle that one may not even know when it is happening (v. 12). If keeping the commandments implied legalistic scrupulosity, surely the poet would not describe them as "hidden mistakes" (מִנִּסְתָּרוֹת referring to שְׁגִיאוֹת). The idea that one cannot detect one's own errors (not sins) suggests that observing the precepts is not working through a checklist, but pressing on toward wisdom (v. 7b: מַחְכִּימַת פֶּתִי) and illumination (v. 8b: מְאִירַת עֵינָיִם), for the precepts refresh the soul (מְשִׁיבַת נָפֶשׁ). However, it is easy to take divine guidance for granted and come under malicious influence (v. 13). The psalmist, too, is vulnerable and prays for strength. Despite his faults, he longs for innocence, and at the end he supplicates God with words that resound down the generations in the mouths of those who find themselves precisely in his shoes: "May the words of my mouth and the meditation of my heart be acceptable to you, O Lord, my rock and my redeemer" (v. 14).

The asherist dynamic of this psalm carries us from the power of God the creator to the power of God the legislator for the sake of leading us into the power of spiritual enlightenment. The psalmist is anxious that his devotion might not overcome all his weaknesses. His fear is not that God will punish him but that he might miss the wealth and sweetness that God's wisdom promises.

Psalm 34

Psalm 34 is an imperfect acrostic of praise and thanksgiving and is often considered a wisdom psalm. Let us consider it in three parts, verses 1-10, 11-14, and 15-22.

The first ten verses are a sympathetic and encouraging, yet intense, exhortation to those who are troubled, from the mouth of one who speaks in the first person of his wonderful experience with God. He says that he has had troubles, though he details nothing of them, offering only the wisdom he has gleaned from his rescue. Rhetorically, he brings his listeners into the company of the godly, where there are safety and hope. He does not scold. The sermon moves back and forth between him and them. His experience and his faith have cut an encouraging path for them.

The opening salvo is three clipped declarations of what the speaker is doing now: blessing the Lord and praising him continually both orally and silently (vv. 1-2a). He immediately turns to his audience. He has told of his praise aloud to comfort the humble, for on learning of his experience they will be happy (וְיִשְׂמָחוּ). He invites them to join him in exultation. His public praise is to share his joy with them (vv. 2b-3). Verse 4 explains why there is all this praise and adoration of God, turning back to his own experience as an offering of encouragement. He has sought the Lord, who has relieved his terror (מְגוּרוֹתַי).

Again, our speaker looks intently at his hearers, but he speaks in the third person. They, too, turned to God, and thus their faces do not flush with shame (vv. 4-5). Note here that the speaker's problem is terror. However, he does not explain the cause of it, and in turning to his audience, he assures them that their confidence (literally, "radiant faces") will protect them from comparable emotional distress or shame (v. 6). Faces radiant with confidence in God will not flush, for they have nothing to be ashamed of. Alternatively, perhaps the import is that no humiliation that enemies might impose can touch the radiance of those whose moral strength comes from their confidence in God. The speaker is building up their confidence in their ability to withstand trouble by assuring them that they already have the strength they need, for they share the humble, reverent life of their preacher.

Verses 7-9 offer protection for these pious ones (who "fear" the Lord). The scene changes, or rather the scene emerges, for until now there has been no scenery, no images to locate us spatially. With verse 7 we are encamped: we might be in a military theater, or, as verse 10 will suggest, in the jungle — it doesn't matter. We are in a dangerous place. The pious, who have heeded the singer's advice, are protected by an angel (their humility?) and saved, whereupon a peal of rejoicing goes up, in one of the most famous lines in the Psalter. The poet applauds his audience: "O taste and see that the Lord is good; happy (אַשְׁרֵי) is the one who takes refuge in him" (יֶחֱסֶה־בּוֹ) (v. 8). He continues building up his hearers' confidence, reinforcing it by reassuring them that they are God's holy ones, those who revere him and thus lack nothing (v. 9).

Their excellent way of life is all that they need; it is their protection. To reassure them yet once more, the preacher uses a dramatic and unexpected image: he contrasts their satisfaction with their life to the situation of young, hungry lions prowling for food (v. 10). The contrast is to comfort his attentive listeners: they need not worry that they might become prowling lions. The high ground on which they stand is firm, and they are prepared for what may come.

Part 2 of Psalm 34 (vv. 11-14) is markedly different. The speaker is a moral teacher striking the classic instructional pose of Proverbs, the primary reason that this is considered a wisdom psalm. While the first part of the psalm cultivated his hearers' trust by his empathy for and encouragement of his audience, here he takes the holy ones of verse 9 (קְדֹשָׁיו) deeper into their reverence for God and gives their piety concrete form and content. Confidence through taking refuge in God is necessary but not sufficient.

Verse 11 invites the reverent to gather around the teacher to delve into the content of their reverence. Reverence is a strong theme in this poem; it appears in verse 7 and twice in verse 9, where the reverent are protected by God's angel (v. 7) and recognized as holy and thus not lacking anything (v. 9). As in the first half of this psalm, the teacher has avid students. His work will not be difficult because they want his teaching.

When all are gathered, the lesson begins. It is in the form of direct address. The core of the lesson is two straightforward rules for a happy life, which remain unsurpassed (v. 12): the first is to guard the most sinful organ of the body, the mouth (v. 13); its mate is to avoid evil and do good by pursuing peace (v. 14). This is the content of the "fear of the Lord."

Two-thirds of Psalm 34 has been about a beautiful life. In the third part, verses 15-22, God is the subject. Gone are the comforting preacher and the inviting teacher. These last eight verses are impersonal — the voice is in the third person — yet designed to encourage the audience to stay with the way they have chosen because God values it highly. They explain God's attitude toward and actions with the upright and the wicked, but the emphasis is on the righteous. This seems to suggest a classic just-deserts morality and an *ex cathedra* mode of operation. The virtuous flourish and the wicked perish, not in the asherist sense by virtue of their way of life but because God intervenes either to rescue or to punish. God attends to both the upright and the wicked (vv. 15-16):

to save the upright, on one hand, and to erase the memory of the wicked from the face of the earth, on the other.

The final six verses (vv. 17-22) show that God has a soft spot in his heart for the broken-hearted and his afflicted loyalists. In fighting for them, he will protect their bodies and assures them that their enemies will die condemned (v. 21). In the last verse the speaker assures them that God redeems those who cover themselves with him (הַחֹסִים בּוֹ), a reprise of verse 8.

In assessing the asherist bent of this psalm, we see that the first two-thirds of the psalm has a strong asherist "feel," for it emphasizes upright living and seeks to edify its hearers; obedience to the law is assuredly in the background. It encourages and reinforces God's holy ones and takes them into the moral skills necessary for their success. Not only that, but the speaker in both sections is himself practicing what he preaches by using his own wisdom to carry them toward their goal. In exercising fine leadership, he is enhancing the well-being of the nation and his own enjoyment of his calling.[15] He is tending God's vineyard, and that is rewarding. In asherist perspective, he is happy.

The remaining question is whether the last section can also be read asheristically.[16] It may be stretching the point, but it is possible to read these verses existentially.[17] In that reading, God would not be acting ex cathedra or by dint of absolute power, but through the spiritual strengths and weaknesses that the righteous and the wicked have at their disposal by living either well or poorly over the course of their lives; for their character has been shaped, at least in part, by how they live. The first fourteen verses instruct people how to grow into maturity by developing character strengths that God's covenantal way of life intends. The poet, lacking this psychological vocabulary, eloquently

---

15. This is also noted by P. J. Botha, "The Social Setting and Strategy of Psalm 34," *Old Testament Essays* 10 (1997): 187.

16. William P. Brown finds salvation rather than formation predominant here. That may be true for the last six verses, but edification is strong in the rest. To the point here, however, asherism cannot readily distinguish between salvation and formation. Brown, "'Come, O Children . . . I Will Teach You the Fear of the Lord' (Psalm 34:12): Comparing Psalms and Proverbs," in *Seeking Out the Wisdom of the Ancients* (Winona Lake, IN: Eisenbrauns, 2005), p. 92.

17. Botha calls these terms a *state of mind,* noting that Van der Ploeg refers to the "humble," "holy ones," the "righteous," and so on as an *ethical state* (p. 185, italics in original).

condenses it all by saying that the humble, those who cover themselves with God (vv. 8, 22) and revere the Lord (vv. 7, 9, 11) — that is, the upright — have the moral power to flourish while those lacking this strength will perish.

Psalm 112

This psalm is considered the antiphon of its predecessor. They both begin with "Halleluia" and both are short acrostics of about the same length. Psalm 111 is a hymn to the works of God and concludes with the great wisdom verse: "The beginning of wisdom is the fear of the Lord." Psalm 112 is the answer to this exaltation of divine works with righteous human works, implying that "the righteous individual comes to share in YHWH's nature *by virtue of* his or her reverence. Crassly put, 'you become what you revere' ethically and, to a degree, efficaciously."[18] Finally, the last verse of Psalm 111 echoes in the first verse of Psalm 112: "*Ashrey* is the one who fears the Lord." This first verse links three features of an asherist psalm. Those who revere the Lord (i.e., the upright) and desire his commandments are *ashrey*.[19] Like Psalm 1, the fortunate obey and delight in God's law, and this exudes a Deuteronomic outlook.[20] Like Psalms 34 and 1, it is considered a wisdom psalm that emphasizes the integrity and trustworthiness of the wise, who are devoted to God.

The first verse announces the subject of the next eight verses: the character and activities of the reverent and the success that their life produces.[21] Verse 2 begins the recitation by naming both future and present benefits of an upright life. Their descendents will flourish and the present generation will be blessed by their presence (v. 2). Verses 3

18. Brown, "'Come, O Children,'" p. 98.

19. Here, *ashrey* takes on the connotation of emotional pleasure, perhaps warranting "happiness" as a translation.

20. See Patrick D. Miller, "Deuteronomy and Psalms: Evoking a Biblical Conversation," *Journal of Biblical Studies* 118, no. 1 (1999): 16.

21. Marlin Thomas reads Psalm 112 as an elaboration of Psalm 1:3: "They are like trees planted by streams of water, which yield their fruit in their season, and their leaves do not wither. In all that they do, they prosper." Thomas, "Psalms 1 and 112 as a Paradigm for the Comparison of Wisdom Motifs in the Psalms," *Journal of the Evangelical Theological Society* 29, no. 1 (1986): 15-24.

and 5 explain the financial life of the reverent. Wealth that accrues to them is a consequence of their righteous pattern of living, which stands forever; it stands out as a light in the darkness for the upright, who are gracious, merciful, and just (v. 4). The good person lends graciously and his financial life is impeccable (v. 5). The psalmist then pauses to reflect again, as he did in the previous verse, on the moral power the reverent have. They will be remembered forever, for they do not change their ways — that is, they are not corruptible (v. 6).

Verses 4 through 6 depict the way of the reverent in positive circumstances. The next two verses turn to how they hold up in less than optimal circumstances. They do not wilt when hearing bad news but remain strong in their trust in God (v. 7), and they do not flinch when facing opposition (v. 8).

The final verse depicting the character of the just (v. 9) turns back to financial considerations: the just distribute generously to the needy, and their righteousness is honored forever. Because of the mention of wealth in verse 3 and the generosity spoken of here, this is thought to be a psalm for or about the wealthy or those in a position to care for the poor.[22] However, that quite ignores the last line of the poem, which reaches out to the wicked. Be they poor or rich, all can revere God and dwell in his commandments. Perhaps it is better not to assume a two-class theory of the rich and the poor, but rather to suppose that, as in many societies, there are many gradations between the extremes. Perhaps the call is to find a way to share appropriately with the poor whatever our means are.

The final verse is a coda that stands out from the body of the psalm with an apparently new thought. Yet the psalmist is letting the audience in on the evangelistic rationale behind the whole poem: to convert the wicked to righteousness by arousing their anger and jealousy. The wicked have been the intended audience all along. The goodness of the reverent will stand forever. Whatever short-term pleasure the wicked may have from their deeds turns to sand in their mouths. This helps explain a notable rhetorical style of the poet in Psalm 34: it moved back and forth between the speaker's experience and its effect on his audience. Similarly here, the poet moves back and forth between

22. Sherwood concludes that this is not a psalm for everyone. Stephen K. Sherwood, "Psalm 112: A Royal Wisdom Psalm?" *Catholic Biblical Quarterly* 51, no. 1 (1989): 50-64.

the actions of the just and the writer's reflection on their long-term positive effects, especially the honorable legacy they impart (vv. 2, 3, 6, 9). These parenthetical observations contrast sharply with the nonlegacy of the wicked. When they see the moral power of righteousness, they realize that their life will amount to nothing, like the chaff in Psalm 1. The moralist appeals to their vanity; it is never too late to turn around.

The asherist qualities of Psalm 112 are obvious. It is an *ashrey* psalm that celebrates the moral strength of those who revere God by keeping the commandments. They are depicted as the happiest of people. They have a positive effect on the community, and they leave a powerful legacy for the future by modeling the beautiful life that covenantal loyalty is all about. They are acclaimed and emulated, and that cannot but be most satisfying and comforting. In short, the fine life is the most pleasurable life. The psalmist does not suggest that the righteous assume or seek political leadership. Their enjoyment is from their moral leadership, whatever their social status. They lift the moral sights of Israel, which is their delight. Death will take its toll on them, but the truth for which and the power with which they have lived will endure forever. They are content. This is a "happy psalm," but then, all the psalms that believe a righteous life is a happy one are happy psalms.

Conclusion

An asherist reading of these four psalms suggests the following. The specificity of pentateuchal legislation is nowhere in sight. They are summed up as Torah. Divine precepts and ordinances have coalesced into a salutary way of life that is summarized as reverence, keeping the commandments, taking refuge in the Lord, being humble, walking in his way, and so on. Specific practices have been generalized so that revering the Lord is a high-minded life of integrity, justice, generosity, and honesty that encourages others along the same path to a rich and enjoyable life. This is the life for which the law has destined Israel, whose liberation from Egypt was not only for compassionate release from oppression but had international moral leadership as its ultimate goal. Even Israel's difficult and perhaps disturbing military life was for the sake of being a light to the Gentiles. Living reverently is Israel's salvation and greatest pleasure.

A second feature of these psalms is that they recognize Israel's internal struggle to carry out her calling. The prophets are usually called on to make this point, but the psalmists here are doing the same work in another way. Constructing Israel's liturgy and prayerbook is the literary analogue of Ezra's reading of the law and prophetic preaching. The poets are brutally honest with their audience. Israel is divided. The righteous seek to lure the wicked to righteousness by displaying the success and happiness that a fine life yields, even while admitting their own distress at being mocked by those who fail to follow God and their anxiety that they too might be undermined by the short-term benefits that the wicked appear to enjoy. The struggle is to cling to the higher vision, and they believe that it is worth the struggle.

A corollary of this last belief is fixed securely in their hearts: the reverent poets are clear that fidelity to God's way is all that one needs to succeed in life, for success is measured in more than money. Covenantal obedience is the rudder, the compass, the map, and the provision for one's voyage through life. Finally, there is a strong sense in which happiness is a judgment on the quality of one's life as it proceeds and when it is evaluated at its end.

CHAPTER 11

Reverent Obedience: The Witness of Proverbs

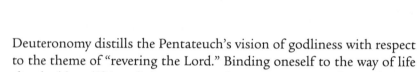

Deuteronomy distills the Pentateuch's vision of godliness with respect to the theme of "revering the Lord." Binding oneself to the way of life sketched by edifying divine commands enacts reverence for God. Deuteronomy poses a clear choice to Israel: the way of life or of death, blessing or curse, loving obedience to or neglect of God's ways (Deut. 30). Psalms elaborates Deuteronomy's vision of godliness as Israel fights apostasy within its ranks. It is honored and celebrates God's calling to covenantal loyalty to Torah, righteousness, and wisdom.

In Proverbs, the challenge to live righteously plays out in another pair of opposing life patterns. The arena shifts from practices and behavior that cultivate fine values and virtues, along with poems that praise those who have them, to direct moral education. Righteousness and wickedness become wisdom and folly, and who wants to be known as a fool? Wisdom is being offered. Being wise or foolish is a decision. Proverbs 9, the concluding chapter of the opening collection, personifies the choice this way: one can enter the homes of two quite different women — Wisdom and Folly — each of whom invites passersby to come and eat at her table.[1] Wisdom offers the food of maturity and insight, while Folly offers those without sense entry into a life of death. The choice is as dramatic and clear as Deuteronomy's plea to choose life (Deut. 30:19, echoed in Ps. 112). Both women are alluring, but one's moral life hangs in the balance. Lady Wisdom enables the godly to live

---

1. For a perceptive discussion of this, see Ellen F. Davis, *Proverbs, Ecclesiastes, and the Song of Songs*, Westminster Bible Companion (Louisville: Westminster/John Knox, 2000), pp. 70-72.

astutely, knowing that the temptation to foolishness and immaturity is always present. The happiness of enjoying an honorable and successful life will follow of its own accord, because a wise life is dignifying and enhances the flourishing of others.

Just as the psalmists understand holiness in their language and setting, so do the proverbial sages. While retaining the rhetoric of reverence and keeping the commandments, they emphasize being wise and discerning — using various words from the Hebrew root *bîn* — showing that these strengths are to adorn Israel as she stands before God and the world (Deut. 4:6). Attributed to King Solomon, to whom God gave the gift of a "wise and discerning mind" as he ascended the throne (1 Kings 3:12), his discerning wisdom is to infuse Israel beginning at the top. Wisdom characterizes the godly, who exhibit moral discipline (מוּסָר), intelligence (שֵׂכֶל), and prudence (מְזִמָּה) (Prov. 1:3).

The wise use themselves well and enhance others, while fools use themselves in ways that invite failure and harm others. As was the case with Moses' speeches in Deuteronomy, the way to a good life seems clear, simple — perhaps even obvious — and commonsensical. All it requires is that revering the Lord, here personified as wisdom, be carefully practiced. Yet Moses' Song (Deut. 32:1-43) already anticipates Israel's future failure, and Proverbs repeats obvious advice, suggesting that wise self-use is quite challenging in practice. While it may be that the young must discover for themselves the benefits of living by some basic rules for life, sometimes through harsh experience, the proverbial sages hope that the wisdom for successful and honorable living that they elucidate is transmissible from one generation to the next: in other words, didactic learning is preferable to the school of hard knocks. In Psalms we moved from specific divine command to general embrace of Torah that enables successful living; in Proverbs the law moves into the background, and wisdom takes center stage.

Proverbial Wisdom

When people refer to the wisdom of the ages, the biblical book of Proverbs is certainly included. The time of its writing and editing overlaps with that of Deuteronomy and Psalms, but, unlike Deuteronomy and many of the psalms, Proverbs is not structured around the story of Israel's life with God, the sacrificial system, or its worship life. It mentions Israel only in the very first verse, which attributes chapters 1–9 to Solomon. It refers positively to the sacrificial system at 3:9 and 14:9, and to the law at 28:4, 7 and 29:18. Proverbs seems to assume that the sacrificial system is operative and the covenant compelling, but these are the backdrop for the teaching at hand. Reverence for the Lord occurs within the web of social relationships: family, business, public responsibilities, and so on. However, the center of gravity remains reverence for the Lord, as it was in Deuteronomy and the Psalms.[2] This motif sounds throughout these texts, and the sages interpret reverence in terms of practical wisdom that cultivates behavior and character traits that build healthy communities.[3]

Some object that the asherist guidance of Proverbs is conventional and boring. It has an "air of somewhat ponderous authority and complacent moralizing," as R. B. Y. Scott puts it, that renders religious obedience dreary.[4] Repetition of a few central theses about the moral life throughout the various collections is monotonous. "The tone of the 'Solomonic' proverbs is didactic, sententious, and moralizing, rather than picturesque, pointed, witty, and sarcastic as so many old proverbs are."[5] Scott may envision a group of restless pubescent males trapped in a hot Middle Eastern classroom being scolded by a crotchety old martinet snapping injunctions such as "don't chase after women," "obey your parents," "don't hang around with scoundrels," and "watch your mouth," all the while fearful that the teacher will rap their knuckles — or worse — at any sign of fidgeting. Perhaps compared to the au-

---

2. This point is effectively made by Jamie Grant, following Raymond C. Van Leeuwen. Grant, "Wisdom and Covenant: Revisiting Zimmerli," *European Journal of Theology* 12, no. 2 (2003): 109-10; Van Leeuwen, *Book of Proverbs: Introduction, Commentary, and Reflections,* vol. 5, New Interpreter's Bible Commentary (Nashville: Abingdon, 1997), p. 33.

3. R. E. Clements has argued that biblical wisdom literature provides a different framework for understanding time and space than sacrificial worship does. It is a broader, secular, and universal portrayal of life with God suited to life in the Diaspora and away from the promised land. The Zion-centered cultic orientation simply could not work outside the land of Israel. R. E. Clements, *Wisdom in Theology* (Grand Rapids: Eerdmans, 1992). Bruce K. Waltke notes, however, that "the fear of the Lord" brings Proverbs into the orbit "of Israel's covenant faith." Waltke, *The Book of Proverbs,* New International Commentary on the Old Testament (Grand Rapids: Eerdmans, 2004), pp. 50-55.

4. R. B. Y. Scott, *Proverbs, Ecclesiastes,* vol. 18, Anchor Bible Commentary (Garden City, NY: Doubleday, 1965), p. 8.

5. Waltke, *The Book of Proverbs,* p. 20.

dacious exploits of some biblical characters, the predictable advice of Proverbs is for the most part lackluster. How much more riveting to be taught about the dangers and consequences of adultery by being told the story of Joseph resisting Potiphar's wife (Gen. 39), or the story of royal disaster beginning with Nathan the prophet dramatically rebuking King David (2 Sam. 12), or Amnon's rape of his half-sister Tamar (2 Sam. 13) following fast on the disclosure of his father's crimes! On the other hand, Proverbs contains its own striking images, such as the figure of the seductive adulteress ensnaring the vulnerable (Prov. 7) and, in her own quite dignified and elegant way, that of the inviting Lady Wisdom promising power, riches, and prosperity to an entirely different end (Prov. 8).

Despite these heady passages, it cannot be denied that the didactic tone of much proverbial wisdom can be like reading a moral telephone book.[6] Still, the stuffy classroom setting need not be the only — or even the primary — way that such instruction was originally transmitted.[7] Parents and teachers cannot but take advantage of teachable moments to warn their children and students of threats and dangers, pointing them out as precarious situations arise. Those who have been burned by experience, or who can learn from negative examples, want to prevent others from repeating costly mistakes, if they can. There is no reason not to take the literary intentionality of the text seriously and to see it not as the portrait of a dreary scene, but as the literary distillation of fidelity to divine teaching written down for posterity because it promotes the common good through personal maturity, stable long-term relationships, and the binding social institutions of marriage, family, and work. Cautious living may be pedestrian, but it is essential for civil concord, social stability, and personal flourishing. Indeed, the text regularly repeats the main point of our inquiry: "Fortunate (אַשְׁרֵי) are those who find wisdom and those who get understanding" (Prov. 3:13). Perhaps the point is that a happy life is not sensational, for living on the daring edge would court disaster. It may be more difficult for those

---

6. To appreciate the significance of the mundane nature of Proverbs, see Ellen F. Davis, "Wise Ignorance," in *Getting Involved with God: Rediscovering the Old Testament*, ed. Ellen F. Davis (Boston: Cowley, 2001), pp. 91-103.

7. Scholars debate whether individual proverbs circulated orally prior to writing, whether the various collections are intentional literary compositions, and whether they originated at court or in a folk setting. For a recent summary of the discussion, see Waltke, *The Book of Proverbs*, pp. 58-62.

who tend to be more foolhardy to choose Lady Wisdom over "the loose woman" (2:16; 5:3; 7:5; 22:14) because they mistake excitement for happiness. The happiness of reverence must be learned.

A clear picture of happiness in Proverbs emerges when we consider the character of the reverent and the agility with which they handle themselves. Like the poet of Psalm 34, the sages believe that reverent obedience is the basis of the successful life.[8] Those who trust in the Lord (16:20), keep God's law (29:18), and follow Lady Wisdom's ways welcome guidance and correction, guard their tongues (Ps. 34:13), and are self-disciplined and discreet in all things. Becoming wise by revering God is a program of self-development as well as support for others, though our text does not exactly put it that way (Prov. 15:33). It may be appropriate to call it maturity-as-modesty. The godly seek wisdom, and the wise are godly. In addition to being prudent, discreet, and open to reproof, the wise are industrious, diligently fair, and honest while acting boldly and with integrity (4:27; 31:8-9). This is the ideal person that we met in Psalm 112.

As with the psalms, the opposite of this strength of character is always clearly in view as the sages use the contrast to exhort their readers to wisdom. Virtue opposes folly. When they act or speak brashly, impulsively, and imprudently, the foolish scoff at wisdom's ways and therefore at God. Foolishness harms self, family, and community. In a word, as surely as the opposite of honor is humiliation, the opposite of maturity is the sabotage of self and others.

Our texts know that, whether one is the king or a farmer, everyone's business quickly becomes known. One's degree of maturity and immaturity is public knowledge. The sages consider various settings in which wisdom and folly play out. In short, Proverbs sees a happy life as patterns of wise self-use. It examines these in terms of how they enhance the web of relationships within which family, neighborhood, and public life occur, and the social skills and habits Proverbs hopes to impart are enduringly pertinent. To mine the ore uncovered here, we focus on the character and the patterns of behavior that Proverbs commends.

---

8. Reverence for the Lord appears in about half of the chapters of Proverbs, in some cases multiple times. The phrase is more concentrated here than anywhere else in the Tanah.

Wisdom and Folly

For these sages, the happy life echoes its analogue in the Psalms, which we explored earlier. The connection between fine character and success is clear.

> Trust in the LORD with all your heart, and do not rely on your own insight. In all your ways acknowledge him, and he will make straight your paths. Do not be wise in your own eyes; fear the LORD, and turn away from evil [cf. Ps. 34:14]. It will be a healing for your flesh and a refreshment for your body. Honor the LORD with your substance and with the first fruits of all your produce; then your barns will be filled with plenty, and your vats will be bursting with wine. My child, do not despise the LORD's discipline or be weary of his reproof, for the LORD reproves the one he loves, as a father the son in whom he delights. Happy are those who find wisdom, and those who get understanding, for her income is better than silver, and her revenue better than gold. She is more precious than jewels, and nothing you desire can compare with her [cf. Ps. 19:10]. Long life is in her right hand; in her left hand are riches and honor [cf. Ps. 112:3]. Her ways are ways of pleasantness, and all her paths are peace. She is a tree of life to those who lay hold of her; those who hold her fast are called happy [cf. Ps. 1:3]. (Prov. 3:5-18, NRSV)

The key to happiness here is recognizing that we need divine guidance in order to discern what mature and honorable self-use is, and that God has commended civilizing precepts, practices, and patterns of thought and behavior to accomplish that. We flourish by dining at Lady Wisdom's table (9:1-5), and Proverbs gives us the menu for that feast. The table is laden with tasty morsels, with heaping plates of modesty, openness to correction, self-restraint, and respect for others. These and other virtues are clearly presented, not as worldly wisdom, but as the wisdom of God, for she is eternal (8:22).

Spiritual Strength

Like Socrates, Israel's sages declare that the wise are so because they know that they are not wise. "Do not rely on your own insight; do not be wise in your own eyes." The wise are modest, assuming that they do not have all that they need to "do life" well, and that others do not have it either. We are neither born mature, nor can we wrest maturity from others in an adversarial procedure. Maturity cannot be bought, but all can have it: "The fear of the LORD is the beginning of wisdom" (9:10).

Another crucial aspect of maturity is being "helpable." By my count, fully twenty-seven verses in Proverbs (equal to about a whole chapter) commend openness to guidance, advice, reproof, and correction (including 1:8; 10:17; 11:14; 12:1; 13:1; 19:25; 21:11). The "unhelpable" fool, by contrast, becomes defensive and rebuffs correction because he experiences it as a threat. "Whoever corrects a scoffer wins abuse; whoever rebukes the wicked gets hurt. A scoffer who is rebuked will only hate you; the wise, when rebuked, will love you" (9:7-8). Defensiveness, the sages would say, is foolish, for it closes one off from growth and companionship that the wisdom of God intends one to enjoy. It is reclusive and, in a way, morbid.

Proverbs counsels self-restraint in many areas of life, and the book places heavy weight on the sword of the tongue, elaborating the advice of Psalm 34:13: "Keep your tongue from evil, and your lips from speaking deceit." About two chapters worth of verses commend prudent speech or castigate rash speech, lying, gossiping, flattery, slander, and loquaciousness. Scorn is particularly offensive, as the first verse of the Psalter makes plain (also Ps. 22:7). About a dozen proverbs condemn contempt (including 1:22, 26; 3:34; 9:12; 13:1; 14:6, 9); it is considered the epitome of folly. Mocking the reverent ridicules Lady Wisdom, and — since wisdom is God's — jeering the poor or the reverent mocks God (17:5). After all, God has provided this pattern of life for us in the commandments and the admonitions of Israel's prophets, poets, and sages.

Scoffing at the godly or the poor is both foolish and immodest — not to mention rude! — for the wise are those who are mature enough to recognize that they need direction and to seek it. Those who deride the wise may irritate them but cannot hurt them, for they stand above such foolishness. Scorners hold others in contempt and by so doing seal themselves off from the very wisdom they need to be brought to their senses. Their tragic flaw is that they cannot learn, and the wise will be smart enough not to try to teach them, for "[a] wise child loves discipline, but a scoffer does not listen to rebuke" (13:1). Finally, the sage adds, with a dollop of frustration: "Crush a fool in a mortar with a pestle along with crushed grain, but the folly will not be driven out" (27:22).

Among the spiritual weaknesses, anger is a special danger. Eight proverbs commend slowness to anger or condemn the foolish danger of losing one's temper too quickly (12:16; 14:29; 16:32; 19:11, 19; 29:11, 22; 30:33). "Fools show their anger at once, but the prudent ignore an insult" (12:16). Still, there is a lot more work for self-control, not least sexual restraint. We meet this a bit further on.

In summary, immaturity is an unsightly expression of self-possession from which the mature will turn away. Fools often first make themselves known verbally by scoffing at the reverent (14:9), attracting attention to themselves (9:13), slandering others (the shame is brought on themselves, however, as 10:18 notes), showing anger precipitously (12:16 and 14:17), being opinionated (18:2), or speaking inanely (14:3 and 15:2). They disclose their immaturity by making trouble at home (11:29; 14:1), thinking they are right, exalting themselves, failing to take advice (12:15; 26:12; 28:26; 30:32), and being generally quarrelsome (20:3). Fools are quite tiresome, and it is better to avoid them. These spiritual strengths and weaknesses are the canvas on which we paint our life. Now we look at the colors applied to different parts of that canvas.

Sustaining Family

Proverbs dwells on the character traits that sustain the social institutions of successful societies. Family is the most important unit of society for our sages, and with good reason. Since the sages speak to life's novices, filial piety comes in for special consideration. Each of the first seven chapters of Proverbs opens with a call from a parent or teacher to heed the wisdom for a good life that is about to be set forth.[9] Proverbs may be read as a peroration on the fifth commandment of the Decalogue: "Honor your father and your mother" (Exod. 20:12; Deut. 5:16). Nothing is more important for sustaining civilization than the transmission of values from parent to child, and nothing is more painful and embarrassing than godly parents whose children mock them by engaging in foolish and destructive behavior (15:25; 17:25; 19:13a). Proverbs expresses the longing of every parental heart. Over and over, the

---

9. J. Kenneth Kuntz, "The Canonical Wisdom Psalms of Ancient Israel: Their Rhetorical, Thematic and Formal Dimensions," in *Rhetorical Criticism* (Pittsburgh: Pickwick Press, 1974), pp. 194-95.

teacher implores his students to heed parental advice. It is an ageless tale, for every parent yearns to spare his or her child the pain of bad living by providing guidance for a successful, often noble, life.

The counterpoint to filial piety is, of course, parental devotion to children. Here Proverbs is out of sync with contemporary attitudes when it insists on discipline that is not balanced by encouragement and protection. Of the eight references to parental discipline, five counsel corporal punishment (13:24; 19:18; 22:15; 23:13-14; 29:15).[10] What is missing here is the reciprocal call to parents to love and nurture their children in the fear and love of the Lord and in the habits of wisdom that are identified, for example, in Ephesians 6:4.

Respect for children as separate individuals and the cultivation of their gifts for their own sake is a product of modern individualism, which was unknown to our sages. Proverbs sees the child as a member of the household unit: his or her training and discipline for a righteous life are essential to the welfare of the family.[11] Discipline, even corporal punishment if necessary, intends to stamp out folly (22:6, 15; 23:13-14, 24; 29:17; 30:17). However, when it is used injudiciously or too frequently, it misses its mark and becomes counterproductive. It expresses tough parental love for the sake of the moral formation of the child, the welfare of the family, and the success of the larger community. One need not flounder to reinvent the wheel of wise living. Wise parents and teachers help those already wise enough to accept being led.[12]

While filial piety comes to the fore in Proverbs, the sages equally emphasize the foundational nature of the marital bond for social well-being. They take the condemnation of adultery most seriously. Singleness and monastic solitude are unknown to them. Monogamous heterosexual marriage is the normal adult estate, and extramarital sex —

---

10. Ellen Davis nuances this stern advice considerably: "The sages' advocacy of physical punishment of young children may be challenged in light of modern insights. But two cautions should be observed before a saying such as [23:13-14] is wholly dismissed. First, the key word here is 'discipline' (v. 13), which for the sages denotes primarily an internal disposition, not an application of force. They are wisely insistent that it is the parent's responsibility to help the child acquire discipline early in life." Davis, *Proverbs, Ecclesiastes, and the Song of Songs*, p. 126.

11. William P. Brown, "To Discipline without Destruction: The Multifaceted Profile of the Child in Proverbs," in *The Child in the Bible*, ed. Marcia J. Bunge (Grand Rapids: Eerdmans, 2008), pp. 63-81.

12. Brown, "To Discipline without Destruction," pp. 63-81.

especially adultery — comes in for the same harsh sanction it receives in Deuteronomy, because it portends household and community destruction. Our text speaks to men with roving eyes, showing the author's respect for wives and children. While Proverbs harshly condemns adultery, it extols the beauty of sustained monogamous love. The erotic pulse of the Song of Songs is at hand in Proverbs 5:15-19:

> Drink water from your own cistern, flowing water from your own well. Should your springs be scattered abroad, streams of water in the streets? Let them be for yourself alone, and not for sharing with strangers. Let your fountain be blessed, and rejoice in the wife of your youth, a lovely deer, a graceful doe. May her breasts satisfy you at all times; may you be intoxicated always by her love.

Proverbs 5 counsels sexual self-discipline, as does a long section of chapter 6 (vv. 20-35). The latter passage inveighs against sex with loose women, and it ties sexual responsibility back to the commandments. Responsibility for sociosexual health lies squarely with men. Women are recognized as — but not castigated for — appealing to vulnerable men for money or even for adulterous adventuring (Prov. 7), but this passage speaks to men. They are responsible for the well-being of the community via sexual loyalty to their wives. Sexual self-discipline is the foundation of healthy community. Adultery courts disaster (7:26-27), as the experienced sage sadly bemoans (5:13-14). The condemnation of adultery, of course, elaborates the Decalogue's seventh commandment (Exod. 20:14; Deut. 5:18). Adultery damages spouse, children, parents, neighbors, and the wider community because it betrays all these relationships and brings the threat of reprisal from the offended parties. The text does not mention paternity questions or the possibility of financial ruin, but these are just beneath the surface. Marital fidelity may not always be exciting, but it is better for everyone. Sexual propriety protects others from our worst selves and echoes Leviticus 19:18b, that we love our neighbors as ourselves.

Similarly, Proverbs — speaking in an androcentric mode — recognizes women's part in promoting stable, happy marriages. The contentious wife is the object of frequent complaint (19:13b; 21:9, 19; 25:24), whereas an excellent wife is a priceless gift from God. She is perhaps the most important stabilizing and unifying force in family and community life (19:14; 31:10-31). An overwhelmingly positive image of upstanding women emerges. A woman portrays the wisdom of God (9:1-12), sexual enjoyment nourishes good marriages (5:15-20), and a diligent wife sustains the entire community (Prov. 31).

One other great virtue that the sages single out for attention, both within the family and beyond, is industriousness. Its nemesis is laziness. A passel of proverbs extols the virtues of manual — primarily agricultural — labor (12:11; 20:4; 24:30-34; 28:19, etc.) and faithfulness in one's appointed task (10:26; 15:19; 18:9), while they condemn laziness and worthless pursuits, which can result in poverty (10:4; 12:27; 14:23; 20:13; 23:21; 28:19). On the other hand, Proverbs exhorts the wealthy and powerful to care for the poor, and castigates the powerful should they ignore them (14:21, 31; 19:17; 21:13; 22:9-23; 28:3, 8; 29:14; 30:9; 31:20). The sages are sympathetic to the plight of the poor (16:19; 17:5; 18:23; 19:1-7; 22:7; 28:11-15, 27; 29:7; 30:14; 31:9), and they know that poverty is ruinous (10:15; 13:23; 14:20).[13] Working the land is noble engagement with the earth: it honors the land, one's body, and one's family. Both women and men are adjured to work hard and honorably, thereby earning the respect of others and supporting a household. As I have noted above, the industrious wife garners the highest praise: an encomium to her concludes the whole collection (31:10-31).

Beyond the Family

That sexual behavior is a public matter points to the importance of cultivating and sustaining good relationships and a good reputation outside the family. Both nonfamilial personal relationships and public relationships are important. Strong relationships with wise friends and

---

13. The issue of wealth and poverty is more prominent in Proverbs than in any other book of the Tanaḥ. Some concern has been raised about the elitist tone that castigates the poor as slothful. See Timothy J. Sandoval, *The Discourse of Wealth and Poverty in the Book of Proverbs* (Leiden: Brill, 2006), p. 32. R. N. Whybray opines that the sages seem "detached" from rather than concerned for the plight of the poor, and he suggests a rural-middle class origin for the sayings before social stratification set in. R. N. Whybray, *Wealth and Poverty in the Book of Proverbs* (Sheffield, UK: JSOT Press, 1990), p. 31. Harold C. Washington suggests a subsistence-level agricultural setting. Washington, *Wealth and Poverty in the Instruction of Amenemope and the Hebrew Proverbs* (Atlanta, GA: Scholars Press, 1994), p. 185. More recently, Sandoval argues that the material is the product of a scribal elite, a kind of intelligentsia distinct from both rich and poor. See Sandoval, *The Discourse of Wealth and Poverty*, p. 39.

with neighbors are important to cultivate (17:9, 17), yet not easy to maintain (18:24; 24:28). The sages realize the instability of human nature and the delicacy of most relationships (22:24-25; 29:5). Loyalty is needed, but is not easy to come by (20:6; 27:10). Perhaps for this reason, friends and neighbors are not to be taken for granted or taken advantage of; we will need them in times of trouble (17:17; 25:17). One's personality and skills are disclosed in civic and judicial proceedings, business transactions, treatment of the poor, and moral leadership, as Psalm 112 emphasizes. Godly maturity is the key to success, and that entails honesty. The commandment that prohibits bearing false witness against one's neighbor (Exod. 20:16; Deut. 5:20) echoes plainly in Proverbs (6:19; 12:17; 19:5, 9; 21:28; 25:18), as does the condemnation of lying in general (6:17; 10:18; 12:19, 22; 21:6; 26:28; 30:8). Greed also comes in for censure, with special concern for honesty in business transactions (1:19; 11:1; 16:11; 20:10, 23).

An important test of honesty is how one deals with the poor, for they are too weak to fend for themselves, and the greedy are tempted to take advantage of them. Treating the poor unjustly is self-defeating (13:23; 22:16, 22), while generosity toward them — and toward those who are not poor — is self-enhancing and honors God (14:21, 31; 19:17; 21:13; 22:9; 29:7). The last chapter of Proverbs sums up these matters well: "Speak out for those who cannot speak, for the rights of all the destitute. Speak out, judge righteously, defend the rights of the poor and needy" (31:8-9). Using oneself wisely on behalf of the vulnerable is itself deeply satisfying, as the sage notes: "Happy are those who are kind to the poor" (14:21b). Enhancing the well-being of others is self-enhancing, not self-promoting.

Everyone has opportunities for wise self-use, but it is especially salient for those in positions of familial or public leadership. The sages are attuned to the opportunity and responsibility that public leaders have to use themselves well and enhance the well-being of others. As an added benefit, this strengthens a leader's authority. Our text assumes a monarchial form of governance: the king, modeled on the Solomonic ideal, is assumed to be godly and wise. He is the just and righteous protector of his people, and is to be trusted (8:15-16; 20:8, 26; 29:14). At the same time, a successful reign requires the honesty and loyalty of the people (25:2-7; 28:2). Good leaders need the support of the led. Just as the sages realize how difficult friendship and neighborliness can be, they also understand — from experience — how corrupting the exercise of power can be (16:12; 17:7; 28:3, 15-16; 29:2-4, 12). They are acutely aware of the Israelite monarchy's instability. All the virtues that the sages commend for a successful and happy life apply even more stringently to a nation's leaders, who have superior power and influence.

Reflection

As I have observed above, the adventuresome might object that Proverbs is dull and pedestrian. It is a quiet homegrown pattern for a satisfying and stable life that eschews the fast lane, urging the values, strengths, and behavior that peaceful societies require. Proverbial wisdom has antecedents and strong parallels in ancient Egyptian, African, and Mesopotamian texts now brought under the auspices of the Creator of heaven and earth.[14] Objecting to wisdom ethics because it is boring or simplistic misses the point that constructing and maintaining healthy societies is not simply a political art. Civilizations only flourish as the spiritual strengths that the sages cherish capture the imagination of the people. For Scripture, enjoying advancing in this strength is the happy life.

The skeptical might object that the promise of a happy life held out by the wisdom ethic of Proverbs is simply naïve. Happiness is a fragile gossamer fabric, as Job and Ecclesiastes know. Yet the skeptics are a breath of fresh air in a room of unrelenting trust in goodness. No matter how prudent, careful, and wise one may be, illness, injury, war, and natural disaster can strike anywhere and at any time. Life is not fair, and the just can seem abandoned. Tragedy does not avoid the mature, so the lament goes. Proverbs hopes that life is fair and just, and that the world is morally ordered. The question for the skeptic is whether, in the dark night of the soul, happiness as Scripture understands it can be eradicated or whether the comfort and enjoyment of a reverent life is a tool for fighting tragedy and rebounding from it.

---

14. See Claus Westermann, *Roots of Wisdom: The Oldest Proverbs of Israel and Other Peoples* (Louisville: Westminster/John Knox, 1995), p. 140; Waltke, *The Book of Proverbs*, pp. 28-31.

Conclusion: Happiness in
Deuteronomy, Psalms, and Proverbs

In concluding this asherist discussion of happiness in the Tanaḥ, I should note that, though these texts articulate happiness differently, all embrace the beauty of holiness that accrues to those who revere the Lord and take refuge in his wisdom. It is tempting to see a spiritual trajectory here. Formation for happiness begins with concrete practices, advances into a broader understanding of fine covenant fidelity, and matures as the spiritual power for fine citizenship in God's reign.

Enthusiastically embracing the precepts delivered to Moses, exemplifying that way of life to the resistant within Israel, and perfecting habits and patterns of social and sexual behavior that promote family and community well-being finally call the Gentiles to the mountain of the Lord that Isaiah 2 so forcefully envisions. Curiously, the progression seems to be at both the literary and the spiritual levels. The canonical order — Pentateuch, Psalms, and Proverbs — is matched by spiritual progress along the same lines. The asherist construal of happiness should now be evident. It is enjoyment of ourselves, others, and the earth itself in obedience to God's call, and it is the celebration of that call by donating ourselves to the flourishing of creation.

Having argued for an asherist reading of these Older Testament texts, I will now turn to the Younger Testament to see whether an asherist construal of happiness is sustained there.

CHAPTER 12

Eternal Life: The Witness of the Gospel of John

In turning to the Younger Testament, we shift mood and setting yet again. The atmosphere is tense. The air is charged with conflict, anger, passion, and confusion. Israel is being torn apart from within before our eyes in a volcanic explosion whose molten lava has never cooled. Israel's identity as the people of God is denied by some Jews, who are creating a new vision of the people of God. The question for us is whether the new definition of the people of God sustains the picture of the beautiful life with God that we saw in the Tanaḥ.[1]

I will argue that the asherist vision of happiness is sustained in the Gospel of John. Here the tensions that were aflame in first-century Judaism have reached the boiling point. Israel is ablaze. We enter the story *in medias res*: characters are in turmoil, either implacably opposed to Jesus or courageously supporting him. There is no middle ground; positions have hardened and a dogfight is in progress. Some characters are torn between what they know to be God's path for Israel and sympathies with the new way of belonging to God that Jesus has announced.[2] The confusion expressed by characters in the story — for ex-

---

1. To find the Younger Testament's teaching on a happy life in asherist perspective, many will turn to the Sermon on the Mount in Matthew, where Jesus lays down rules for his followers as the new Moses speaking atop a mountain. As central as that text is for the Younger Testament, it is not the only location for discerning a distinctively Christian and biblical treatment of our topic. I treated the Sermon on the Mount in *By the Renewing of Your Minds: The Pastoral Function of Christian Doctrine* (New York: Oxford University Press, 1997), pp. 61-83.

2. This is a more contextually sensitive interpretation of characters such as Nicodemus, who have been described by some as failing in trying circumstances. See, for

ample, Nicodemus, Peter, Joseph of Arimathea, Thomas, and the disciples as a group — indicate the passions aroused by the ecclesiological and soteriological issues at hand.[3] Israel is being rent asunder by the rude and shocking charge by Johannine Jews that they alone are children of Abraham because Jesus has condemned their fellow Jews as children of the devil (John 8:44).

Vituperative and condemnatory denunciations are also found in the Dead Sea Scrolls from about the same period. But despite the common use of "children of light" and "children of darkness" language in both John's Gospel and the war scroll, the texts are not comparable. The Gospel is a dramatic presentation of actual events. It is the Bible's reality television. With the exception of the prologue, the dogfight takes place in numerous spontaneous confrontations among people who are striving together. There is no hint of cool reflection to prepare for staged warfare, as the Dead Sea Scrolls do. The Scrolls are written for the "children of light." They do not purport to be reportage as most of John's Gospel does. The Gospel's narrator is like the stage manager in *Our Town*. His job is to draw the audience into the events taking place in Grover's Corners. Conversely, the Scrolls are internal documents, a pep rally of sorts to enthuse the troops. Immediate theological engagement is not in evidence. The community's opponents have become that great faceless "they." Scroll texts are more like Moses' speeches at the end of Deuteronomy than the words of a hot-tempered Jesus that we find in John's Gospel.[4]

---

example, Schnackenburg, Brown, Meeks, Loisy, and de Jonge as cited by David K. Rensberger, *Johannine Faith and Liberating Community* (Philadelphia: Westminster, 1988), p. 40. Such an interpretation thinks in christological terms developed later that were not available to the actors in the story or to the author.

3. Since the work of Louis Martyn, it has become generally accepted that an important motivation in the Gospel of John's composition was that Johannine Jews were threatened with being barred from synagogues (John 9:22; 12:42; 16:2). See J. Louis Martyn, *History and Theology in the Fourth Gospel*, 2d ed. (Nashville: Abingdon, 1979). While there may be truth to this claim, one needs to appreciate the theological issues behind drawing such a line in the sand.

4. 1QS II, 4b-18 is an extended curse against "the lot of Belial" and another against community members who "stray from following God." The war scroll is about preparing for war between "the sons of darkness," "the army of Belial," and "the sons of light." 1QM I, 4b-13; II, 9; IX, 5b-7a are war preparation instructions with orders to destroy the enemy. Florentino García Martínez, *The Dead Sea Scrolls Translated: The Qumran Texts in English*, 2nd ed. (Leiden: Brill, 1996), pp. 4-5, 95, 96, 101-2.

The Ecclesiological Struggle

The ecclesiological struggle is about whether the people of God is constituted by God's election or by accepting Jesus.[5] Within that struggle is the issue of the criteria for judging whether Jesus is who he claims to be. In John's Gospel, Jesus is authenticated by John the Baptist's report that he saw a dove-like heavenly spirit resting on Jesus (John 1:32-34). The language of the report is ambiguous: it is not clear who is speaking to John about Jesus in verse 33, nor are the words "this is the Son of God" (v. 34) reported as direct speech. In this Gospel, apart from what Jesus says about himself, his identity is authorized by the *report* of an event that only John witnessed, and it is ambiguously stated. The ambiguity invites the intense conflict between those who do and do not accept Jesus, since most of the testimony for Jesus' identity comes from Jesus himself.

Indeed, many points of discontinuity arise because the Pharisaic and the Johannine communities work from radically different presuppositions. The debate turns on what counts as evidence for belief in Jesus' claims; but the text does not present it that way. From the first, we have the inkling of the notion of the blindness and stubbornness of the Jews who cannot make the leap based on the evidence offered.

One discontinuity is that the Tanaḥ assumes that Israel has immediate access to God, whereas the Johannine literature assumes that access to God is now channeled through Jesus (John 1:17-18). Another is that, for the Tanaḥ, corporate Israel is chosen by God for a global purpose, while Johannine Jews join the new community one by one. A third discontinuity is that in the Tanaḥ generally — and Psalms specifically — laments and songs of thanksgiving usually refer to rescue from opponents, whereas in the Johannine literature salvation requires accepting that Jesus has been sent by God. Despite these discontinuities, there are important asherist continuities between the Tanaḥ and Johannine theology.

The discontinuities I have mentioned clarify the scene. From a Pharisaic perspective, Jesus' followers are rebellious secessionists; from the Johannine perspective, Pharisaic Jews are stubborn and disobedient because they fail to embrace the new truth of God that Jesus proclaims

---

5. Stanley B. Marrow articulates the christological basis of Johannine ecclesiology well in "Johannine Ecclesiology," *Chicago Studies* 37, no. 1 (1998): 27-36.

about himself. Pharisaic and Johannine Jews operate from such different assumptions that they can only shout past one another. But the fierceness of this struggle masks deeper discontinuities between what are rapidly becoming two communities.[6]

For the Tanaḥ, God's covenant with Israel is an act of sheer grace. Israel has done nothing to warrant her election and mission — indeed, at times has tried to flee from it. However, the paradigm shifts when Jesus enters. The disbanding and reconstructing of Israel is announced at the beginning of John's Gospel: "He came to his own home, and his own people received him not. But to all who received him, who believed in his name, he gave power to become children of God; who were born, not of blood nor of the will of the flesh nor of the will of man, but of God" (John 1:11-13). The die has been cast. The election and mission of Israel that is difficult to hear and more difficult to enact has settled on a remnant of Israel that carries out Israel's calling, albeit in unrecognizably novel form, under the leadership of Jesus. According to the Jesus followers, the Jewish people are no longer the Israel of God (Deut. 7:7-8). The Jesus community is now the Israel of God (John 8:39-44).

This contentious state of affairs raises the question of "salvation." Amidst the ecclesial struggle to define the people of God, the question of what is at stake in that controversy comes to the fore for Johannine Jews. The central soteriological category in this Gospel is "eternal life."[7] The phrase appears in the Tanaḥ only in Psalm 133:3. Its analogue in rabbinic literature is "life of the world to come," but that is rare and

---

6. For a discussion of the influence of the biblical wisdom tradition on the Gospel of John, see Raymond E. Brown and Francis J. Moloney, *An Introduction to the Gospel of John,* Anchor Bible Reference Library (New York: Doubleday, 2003), pp. 259-65; Cornelius Bennema, *Saving Power of Wisdom: An Investigation of Spirit and Wisdom in Relation to the Soteriology of the Fourth Gospel,* ed. Joerg Frey et al. (Tübingen: Mohr Siebeck, 2002). For an extensive treatment of the use of the Psalms in John, see Margaret Daly-Denton, *David in the Fourth Gospel: The Johannine Reception of the Psalms,* Arbeiten zur Geschichte des Antiken Judentums und des Urchristentums 47 (Leiden: Brill, 2000). On the special attention to John's use of "'royal lament psalms' to portray Jesus as the king who was maltreated, pursued, or deserted by his contemporaries," see Marianne Meye Thompson, "'They Bear Witness to Me': The Psalms in the Passion Narrative of the Gospel of John," in *The Word Leaps the Gap: Essays on Scripture and Theology in Honor of Richard B. Hays,* ed. J. Ross Wagner et al. (Grand Rapids: Eerdmans, 2008), quoting p. 269.

7. His task is to bring "eternal life" (John 3:15-16, 36; 4:14, 36; 5:24, 39; 6:27, 40, 47, 54, 68; 10:28; 12:25, 50; 17:2-3).

not quite on point. Jesus is hailed as savior only in John 4:42, his messianic identity is obscure, and there is no linking of these two notions. He proclaims himself to be a messenger from his father, and his message is about eternal life; but the content of the message remains elusive. This chapter examines eternal life as being born of God, being illumined by God, and becoming intimate with God; and it highlights love and obedience to Jesus' commandments as the way to — or, perhaps better, the content of — eternal life.

An Invitation into Life with God

Johannine Jews were so excited about Jesus that they needed many images to express who he was and what believing him did for them. There is openness about the content of the gift that Jesus claims to bring.[8] This may suggest different writers, as Paul Meyer has suggested, but perhaps no single image could capture the excitement aroused by the new and intense way of life through Jesus, and in their scrambling it remains nebulous.[9] Jesus offered a way of life organized around love, which Paul later proposed as the greatest virtue (1 Cor. 13:13). The Johannine Jews invite people into this life through a cluster of striking images to capture their experience of life lived to the fullest.

This Gospel speaks in unprecedented ways of individual knowledge and experience with respect to God. The language of birth or rebirth, becoming children of God/light, being illumined, having eternal life, abundant life, or simply life, abiding in Jesus, having fellowship with or being one with the Father and the Son, and, tellingly, keeping the commandments that the Son gives — all of this sings of the wonderful life that Jesus passionately and urgently proclaims is to be had through him. Like Roman candles spraying sparks of color into the

8. Rudolf Bultmann famously held "that Jesus as the Revealer of God reveals nothing but that he is the Revealer. . . . John, that is, in his Gospel presents only the fact of the Revelation without describing its content." But the Gospel uses many terms trying to capture the content, among them rebirth/birth, eternal life/life, illumination/light/light of life. Bultmann, *Theology of the New Testament* (New York: Charles Scribner's Sons, 1955), 2:66.

9. Paul W. Meyer, "'The Father': The Presentation of God in the Fourth Gospel," in *Exploring the Gospel of John,* ed. R. Alan Culpepper and C. Clifton Black (Louisville: Westminster/John Knox, 1996), p. 262.

night sky, the exploding images form a massive shimmering light — for all sparks are instances of a life driven by the love for and awe of God.

Much scriptural imagery for the divine presence is deeply place-centered.[10] God dwells on a mountain, in a house, in a tent, or simply in a place (e.g., Ps. 15:1; 23:6; 26:8; 74:2; Isa. 2:2; Joel 3.17; Zech. 2:10; 8:3). Without naming a town, Deuteronomy insists that God will choose a place for his name to dwell or for him to dwell that will be the center of Israel's worship once they take possession of the land (Deut. 12, 14-18, 26, and 31). Other texts identify this place as Jerusalem (Isa. 27:13; Jer. 3:17) or Shiloh (Jer. 7:12). Perhaps more to our purpose, God also dwells with people (Isa. 57:15), but especially in corporate Israel (Exod. 25:8; 29:45-46; Num. 5:3; 35:34; 1 Kings 6:13; Jer. 7:3, 7; Zech. 2:11-12).

While the image of God's house does not drop out entirely (John 14:2), the Johannine vision of eternal life transforms the biblical assumption that God dwells in a place. It is not the tabernacle, a city, house, mountain, or even with Israel — but an individual! Not only the places, but the commandments, the wisdom psalms, and the proverbs all collapse into Jesus, who embodies them all.[11]

If this be accepted, we are ready to consider how the evangelist invites people into the intense life, the eternal life to which Jesus beckons. The articulations of eternal life appear like facets of a diamond, each flashing different colors. The whole glistens like the pavement of sapphire-like stones on which God stood in the presence of Moses and other leaders of Israel (Exod. 24:9-11), like the beaming face of Moses when he descended Mount Sinai (Exod. 34:29-35), and like the luminescent face and clothing of Jesus at the Transfiguration (Mark 9:2-8; cf. Matt. 17:2-8; Luke 9:28-36). The eternal life that Jesus offers captures the drama of the several flashes of divine glory. The images draw us in.

---

10. The theme is missing in Proverbs since it was most likely oriented toward Diaspora Jews.

11. While Johannine soteriology reads like a realized eschatology, the promise of dwelling in the father's house has often been read as future eschatology, as has the hope of resurrection promised in 6:54, so it is better to think of Johannine soteriology as a realizing eschatology. See Dorothy Lee, "'The Darkness Did Not Overcome It': Theodicy and Eschatology in the Gospel of John," in *Theodicy and Eschatology*, ed. Bruce Barber and David Neville (Adelaide: ATF Press, 2005), pp. 57-61.

Being Born of God

Being born of God (John 1:13), becoming children of God (1:12; 11:52), and being reborn from above or of the Spirit (3:3-8) constitute an important — if threatening — slant on Israel's way of life. Nicodemus's frustrating conversation with Jesus about being part of the reign of God reinforces the provocative claim of the prologue to John's Gospel (1:12-13): Jews are not children of God, but must become so by receiving Jesus. The nighttime conversation with Nicodemus maintains that point, but it suggests that baptism is also needed to become part of the reign of God that Jesus brings.

Nicodemus's bewilderment illustrates how perplexing the requirement of "being born from above" was. Nicodemus may not be quite as dense as John 3:4 suggests. Both John 1:12-13 and 3:1-10 would deny that Nicodemus, along with all other Jews, are children of God as they know they are, but must become so by accepting Jesus. He is telling native citizens that their citizenship has been revoked because the government passed a new law and now they must apply for citizenship in their own country! Equally confusing, but less provocative, is the issue of how one does this, whether by decision, as the prologue suggests (John 1:12), or whether it must be "by water and the spirit" (John 3:5) through a rite performed on one, as suggested by the questioning of John the Baptist in John 1:25-33.[12] The phrase "by water and the spirit" brings further questions because John 1:25-33 separates John's water baptism from his spirit baptism, which seems somewhat arbitrary (John 3:8). It is possible that water and spirit baptism are two separate events and that both are needed. It is implied that baptism by water and the spirit (John 3:5) — and the acceptance of Jesus according to the prologue — enable one to re-become a child of God and to participate in the reign of God through Jesus.

Being Illumined

A metaphor for becoming a child of God is being illuminated or moving from darkness into light (1:5; 3:19-21; 8:12; 9:5; 11:9-10; 12:35-36, 46). The

---

12. Although in this Gospel Jesus calls only one disciple with "follow me" (1:43), he insists that his followers have not chosen him but he them (15:16).

light-darkness contrast is another inflammatory jibe. The first twelve chapters of John's Gospel refer to Jesus as light that sheds light but also sheds heat. Apart from Jesus, one is in darkness — the darkness of spiritual death. With dripping irony, the prologue anticipates Jesus' rejection by his blood kin who are still in darkness (1:11). In contrast to his people, Jesus claims to be the light of the world (8:12; 9:5). Following him banishes the darkness of evil (3:18-21). He sustains the theme as he goes to Bethany in Judea, against advice that it is dangerous for him there (11:7-8). Yet he presses on, determined that while he is alive there is a chance that some might be brought into his light (11:9-10).[13] The same urgency prevails in 12:35-36, 46, where Jesus hints that death is pursuing him and people should take advantage of his light while it is still available. The author of the Gospel hopes the Jews, like heliotropic plants, will be drawn to Jesus' light. The urgency increases as his death approaches.

In this Gospel, being illumined is to be "in" him, and those who are, are "in" one another. Spiritual bonding comes with accepting Jesus' claims about himself and rejecting being a child of God by birth. Yet the Johannine language of fellowship (κοινωνία) with God and other believers is not quite as jarring as it might at first seem. In a sense, the myriad images in both the Tanaḥ and John's Gospel express an intimacy with God that comes with his presence. In the Tanaḥ, God freely dwells in Israel for the sake of its global mission. His presence is with the corporate body, and he hopes that they will follow the way of life and worship that he has set for them. Here God's presence is through Jesus.

The fantastic claim that God is a person means that he indwells individuals. Personal indwelling brings a sharply more intimate vision of life with God than the Tanaḥ imagines. The Johannine vision radicalizes, personalizes, and intensifies the heritage by individualizing salvation. This Gospel rushes around trying to convey the idea that those who believe that Jesus really is who he claims to be have eternal life (3:15-16, 36; 4:14; 5:24; 6:40, 47; 10:28; 17:2). Knowing him is to have eternal life (17:3). Those in whom he dwells and who dwell in him (15:4) have it by having him.

---

13. Although a common interpretation of Nicodemus is that coming under the cover of darkness was an admission of cowardice, such a contemptuous interpretation of the character is not necessary. The night cover may just as well signify that Nicodemus was trying to negotiate a way out of the polarized standoff. Quite aside from this, coming to Jesus at night, Nicodemus personifies the theme of illumination that is important in this text.

Graphic metaphors and images bubble over trying to convey this soteriology. Eternal life is drinking the water that he gives (4:14; cf. Isa. 55:1; 58:11), and eating his body that endures even unto resurrection (John 6:27, 54). At the same time, eternal life is in his words (5:24; 6:68) and in obeying his commandments (12:25). It is to obey God through Christ's intervention (17:3). Desire for eternal life lures those who crave intimacy with God by telling them that they can taste God now. Johannine talk of eternal life may be nebulous, but it points toward a realizing eschatology rooted in individual decision. One can experience life in eternal perspective.

Perhaps the most graphic imagery for the way Jesus brings eternal life is the visceral language found in John 6, where Jesus himself is the food of, for, or unto (εἰς) eternal life (6:27).[14] His death is for life in the world (6:51), and "eating" him symbolizes the eternal life that he secures for his friends. Such "eating" links eaters to Jesus' resurrection from death (6:54). This raw image smacks Jesus' point home: his becoming human enables followers to "eat" his teaching that they may dwell in it and it in them. This psychological unity with the Son is eternal life: according to Paul, "Let the same mind be in you that was in Christ Jesus" (Phil. 2:5). Those who resist it "have no life in [them]" (6:53). At stake is the difference between spiritual life and spiritual death. Those who follow Jesus into this life are in God because the Father and the Son indwell one another (14:6-7, 9-11). When believers "eat" Jesus, the Father comes to dwell in them. Disciples make this move from darkness to light, from being children of Israel to being "children of God," on the new theological assumption that the former are no longer tautologically the latter.

The traumatic transition requires abandoning family and friends. Believers are locked together, as it were, in a tiny boat crossing a vast uncharted ocean in order to taste life more intensely.[15] It is not enough to leave home; one must embrace fellow believers as one's new family.

---

14. Leon Morris attributes this sacramental interpretation to the majority of modern commentators on John 6. Morris, *The Gospel According to John,* rev. ed., New International Commentary on the New Testament (Grand Rapids: Eerdmans, 1995), p. 311. However, that is not universally accepted. For a list of detractors, ancient and modern, see Raymond E. Brown, *The Gospel According to John* (Garden City: Doubleday, 1966), p. 272.

15. Matthew 6:19, 25-32 makes this plain. Luke 9:59-62 and 12:49-53, e.g., point out the emotional pain that this transition can produce.

One does not have eternal life simply by agreeing that Jesus is the true revelation of God and by worshiping with an outcropping of the synagogue. Following Christ packs a moral punch, as John's Gospel has already hinted (13:14). The corporate soteriology of the Tanaḥ is lost, but communal solidarity is strengthened. Loyalty to the group becomes foundational for abundant life with God. Bringing eternal life is Jesus' mission, but its content is elusive.

Becoming Intimate with God

John's Gospel is bursting with enthusiasm for the intense love of God. Jesus concretizes the craving for intimacy by pointing out how love builds and flows between God and the faithful. The process begins when one accepts that Jesus is who he claims to be; this confession is rebirth. Next, one must prove oneself faithful under risky circumstances. One must keep Jesus' commandments and abide in his love (15:10) amidst the raging ecclesiological war. Those steadfast in their faith must fight for it.

While loyalty is central, the meaning of steadfastness modulates in the course of this Gospel, blossoming kaleidoscopically into a panoply of intensifying images.[16] At one level, abiding in Jesus and being a member of the new company require that followers reestablish their identity in Jesus' claims about his identity and mission and keep his word and commandments. At another level, abiding in Jesus and in his word is eternal life (17:2-3). Its content is loving intimacy with him and his Father so that they ground one's life in community in love (5:38; 15:7). Keeping Jesus' commandments and loving are one and the same.

The eating metaphor of John 6 is supplemented by viticultural imagery in John 15, the metaphor of Jesus as a grapevine from which the blood of the grape flows; the disciples are branches that bear fruit.

> Abide in me as I abide in you. Just as the branch cannot bear fruit by itself unless it abides in the vine, neither can you unless you abide in me. I am the vine, you are the branches. Those who abide in me and I

16. The modulation and intensification of this loving intimacy are not offered in graduated steps in the text, as I am suggesting here. Noting shifts of intimacy is just a tidy way of highlighting the fluidity of expression about the intimate love that binds the characters together.

239

in them bear much fruit, because apart from me you can do nothing. Whoever does not abide in me is thrown away like a branch and withers; such branches are gathered, thrown into the fire, and burned. If you abide in me, and my words abide in you, ask for whatever you wish, and it will be done for you. My Father is glorified by this, that you bear much fruit and become my disciples. As the Father has loved me, so I have loved you; abide in my love. If you keep my commandments, you will abide in my love, just as I have kept my Father's commandments and abide in his love. (15:4-10)

As the last verse of this pericope says, abiding is more than cognitive assent to the truth of Jesus' message. To internalize him and obey his commands is not to obey him because of his authority, but to embrace him genuinely and his teaching personally, just as Israel's poets and sages embrace the law, covenant, and way of life they receive. Here loving establishes us in Jesus. Those who abide in Jesus partake of the intimacy between Father and Son by extension, which is to have an abundant eternal life. In the Scripture that Johannine Jews honored, God claimed Israel passionately, and Israel promised to reciprocate (Exod. 19:8; 24:3, 7). Yet the Psalter and the Deuteronomistic history tell of Israel's struggle to forsake all others and cling passionately to the one who created her, rescued her from Egypt, and brought her to the land of promise. Knowledge of that history is in the background when the Johannine author threatens those who fall away with destruction (15:6).

Asherist Continuities

The strife we are in here reflects the struggle to redefine Judaism after the destruction of the Temple. Despite glaring discontinuities between the Older and Younger Testament texts that we have considered, this text transforms what obedience to divine command looks like. It sustains the asherist conviction that a fine life with God is a happy and fulfilling one.

The Fourth Gospel's talk of becoming a child of God, being born or reborn of God, being illumined or living as a child of light, having eternal life, and being one with God by keeping the commandments of Christ are analogues of the Tanah's references to keeping the commandments, taking refuge in the Lord, living in God's house, and revering the Lord. Here, in John, we love God by loving Jesus, and we abide in his teaching, which is participation in Jesus' unity with the Father. These images recall and intensify the asherist vision of reverence in the Older Testament materials we have examined, but with an excitement missing in the older settled texts. John 6's insistence that those who eat the flesh and drink the blood of the Son of man live forever may sound as bizarre now as it did to those who first heard it, but the graphic language most dramatically drives home the visceral longing that many have for salvation.

Jesus' small, impassioned band of followers radically commited itself to his own mission from his Father. Aquinas put it more gently — and not christologically — but the dynamic is comparable. Each person is called to advance God's intention for creation's flourishing. Obeying divine commands, whether those articulated in Deuteronomy, those restated as the wisdom of Proverbs, or those summarized by Jesus himself, as John tells us, expresses a common asherist vision. Abiding by divine commands is the wisdom of God for the Tanah; in John's Gospel it becomes loving intimacy with God. Eternal life with God is to abide in Jesus' wise guidance. By submitting to it, we experience the wisdom that strengthens, empowers, and liberates the soul for a happy life. To grow to our full spiritual height is to have abundant life (10:10).

John 15 speaks of intimacy between God and the believer from the perspective of God as the one who rewards disciples' tenacity by indwelling them (vv. 4, 5, 7) and by granting whatever they ask (vv. 7, 16) — so that their "joy may be complete" (v. 11). Love between God and disciples is mutually engaging and rewarding. They claim one another passionately. I have noted that Scripture is filled with images of God dwelling on his mountain, in his house, in Jerusalem, amidst Israel, and in other metaphorical locations. In the Johannine literature the Father, the Son, and the disciples are "in" one another as long as the disciples remain steadfast in the teaching that Jesus has brought — about who he is and the eternal life that he offers — nebulous though it may be. God's dwelling in Israel's space, previously envisioned as both stationary and ambulatory, is here personalized in each believer. The transformation of received biblical ecclesiology is clear. In the Tanah, God dwells in corporate Israel by gracious election; Johannine Jews claim that God dwells in Jesus and in them through bonds of love.

God as Agent of Love and Glory

Jesus and his Father share the bond of love that unifies them with those who have received Jesus. Disciples form a triumvirate with the Father and Son. Sometimes the initiative comes from the disciples, but at other times it comes from Jesus and his Father. The relationships are as follows: the Father and the Son abide in one another (John 10:38; 14:10-11, 20; 17:21, 23); the Son and the disciples abide in one another also (6:56; 14:20; 15:4-7; 17:23); the Father dwells in disciples who embrace Jesus (14:23). Jesus exemplifies how this comes about: he abides in his Father's love and commands his followers to abide in his love for them (15:10) and to obey him (14:15; John 21). By extension, the Father dwells in the disciples. Jesus comes to ferry people to his Father, and he can do this because he presents God in person.

With the lure of his claim that he is God's emissary, Jesus invites his hearers to receive him as the doorway into life with him and the Father. Both first- and second-generation Johannine Jews must remain steadfast in their conviction; those who do will sustain the bond of love that comes from the Father. Those who enter this bond are subject to Jesus' "new" command to embrace all faithful disciples in a community of divine and human love. Love spreads from the Father to Jesus, binds Jesus and the disciples to one another, and finally binds the disciples together. The final image is of Father, Son, and faithful community unified in mutually reinforcing love that embraces an expansive vision of life in community.[17]

The author of John's Gospel celebrates this fellowship as sharing in one another's glory and mutually glorifying one another. Glorification as an activity is often associated with Jesus' death (e.g., 17:5). How-

---

17. This discussion is indebted to the work of Fernando Segovia (*The Farewell of the Word: The Johannine Call to Abide* [Minneapolis: Fortress Press, 1991]), but offers a slightly different image for understanding abiding in John's Gospel. Segovia imagines the intimacy among Father, Son, and disciples as a hierarchically ordered descending and expanding chain of love from the Father to the Son to the individual disciple, and finally to other disciples (pp. 148-63). I prefer to imagine the relationships Trinitarianly, specifically perichoretically, because some verses indicate that the flow of love is effective in multiple directions (John 15:4-5, 7, 9, 16). Some maintain that Jesus and his Father reciprocate the love that disciples have for them by dwelling in or loving them (vv. 4-5, 9) or by agreeing to give them whatever they ask (vv. 7, 16). Segovia, of course, considers these verses but does not take them into account when using the image of a chain.

ever, glory is shared among Father, Son, and disciples before his death as well. The glory of the Lord is, of course, central in Exodus (Exod. 16:7, 10; 24:16-17; 29:43; 33:18, 22; 40:34-35). In John's Gospel the glory of God is imparted to believers and seen through the Son (1:14; 8:54; 13:32), who shows it to the disciples (1:14; 7:18; 8:40; 17:22). The result of this impartation is that God, Jesus, and the disciples are united (17:22). The disciples are themselves glorified, and they in turn glorify the Father (15:8) and the Son (17:10).

The Commandments

Commandment-keeping is foundational to eternal life with God in Johannine theology. In the Gospel, the theme is concentrated in chapters 12-15. Commandment-keeping is modeled by Jesus, who portrays himself as following his Father's commandments (10:18; 12:49-50). The disciples are to do as he does and keep his commandments.

Imitating Jesus

Commandment-keeping begins by seeing Jesus model it. He is obedient to the mission to do something in and through Israel in the world. Since the things he says and does are so strange and often insulting, he repeatedly restates who he is, where he has come from, what his mission is, and — more pungently — that he knows God while his opponents do not (5:30; 7:28-29; 8:14, 28, 42, 55). He repeats these exhortations often to persuade the unpersuaded of his authenticity. They cannot accept either that they do not know God or that they should obey one who claims that they do not know God. The point of these numerous and frustrated interactions and repetitions is for Jesus to address the charge that he is demon-possessed (7:20; 8:48, 52; 10:20) by insisting that he says and does only what he has been told to say and do by his Father (12:49-50; 14:24, 31). "I have not spoken on my own, but the Father who sent me has himself given me a commandment about what to say and what to speak. And I know that his commandment is eternal life. What I speak, therefore, I speak just as the Father has told me" (12:49-50; see also 14:24, 31). However, claiming this authority may only have made the situation worse, as would the insistence that "the Father" loves — perhaps only? — those who accept who Jesus claims to be (16:27), because the idea that God could or would have human off-spring is preposterous to many in his audience. That Jesus was de-ranged (demon-possessed) was more sensible.

Next, Jesus presents himself as taking up this mission out of love for his Father, making it an act of his own free will, even unto death. Je-sus explains: "I lay down my life in order to take it up again. No one takes it from me, but I lay it down of my own accord. I have power to lay it down, and I have power to take it up again. I have received this com-mand from my Father" (10:17-18). That Jesus is sent to bring eternal life is well established by this time in the narrative.

Chapter 10 attempts another metaphorical explanation of what eternal life looks like. The Son is a "gate" through which "his sheep" can enter the "sheepfold," where they will be safe (10:7). It is a difficult metaphor, and Jesus shifts it a bit, calling himself the shepherd of the sheep (v. 11). These shepherding metaphors symbolize eternal life, but this becomes clear only in 10:28, where we see that the "gate" — Jesus — will die for the sheep (v. 15). This is the devastating price of carrying out his Father's mission, which appeared to many to be rabble-rousing (v. 18). The expediency argument attributed to Caiaphas (18:14) rings true. Such turmoil could not but irritate Rome, which never hesitated to quell revolts in the empire. Troops were at the ready. Jesus has come to shepherd his sheep into the sheepfold, being himself the door to their eternal life, and he will die to save the lives of his sheep! Although he did not think up this mission, he has pursued it vigorously. He now sees the writing on the wall and says that dying will be his choice (10:18).[18]

John the Baptizer says that Jesus is the lamb of God who takes away the sin of the world (1:29). The lamb image symbolizes atonement, but that idea does not recur in this Gospel. Yet, the fact that Jesus takes away sin fits perfectly with the idea that "sin" here is not embracing Je-

---

18. There is debate on the significance of Jesus's death in John's Gospel. Rudolf Bultmann rejects the idea that Jesus' death atones for sin in the Pauline sense. See Bultmann, *Theology of the New Testament* (New York: Charles Scribner's Sons, 1955), 2:52-53. Leon Morris counters by pointing out how central Jesus' death is in this Gospel. Leon Morris, "The Atonement in John's Gospel," *Criswell Theological Review* 3, no. 1 (1988): 49-64. However, pointing to the importance of Jesus' death in this Gospel does not address Bultmann's claim. Morris may be thinking in much later soteriological cat-egories that took Pauline soteriology in a certain direction with Anselm of Canterbury.

sus or obeying his commands, a theme that dominates John's Gospel. Death is a horrible price to pay for bringing eternal life to the world, but it is not clear that the death itself atones for all sins, and there is no indication that it atones for not accepting Jesus.

There is strong support for the view that receiving Jesus in his incarnate mission and obeying his commandments takes away sin, but that is not in the framework of atonement. Jesus's great battle with those who do not accept him would be largely evacuated of value if belief in his identity and the power of his commandments were ancillary to the atoning power of his death, for how would that address the suspicions of his hearers? Further, Jesus never tells them that his death, instead of the sacrificial system, will atone for their sins. Rather, the struggle between Pharisaic and Johannine Jews is a life-and-death battle for a saving way of life in community that Jesus teaches. Readers must work through the struggle to see what is at stake for them.

Jesus's death (variously described as his "hour," his "lifting up," his "work," his "glorification," etc.) is adumbrated as both necessary and beneficial (3:14-16; 8:27-28; 12:23-32; 16:7-9), and the anticipation of it dominates the second half of this Gospel. His death is the climax of the drama, as it concludes his earthly mission; but that does not mean that it atones in a metaphysical, ontological, or juridical sense — as later theology thought. None of these passages mentions or even hints at atonement. One of them (8:27-28) explains precisely what this death accomplishes: "They did not understand that he was speaking to them about the Father. So Jesus said, 'When you have lifted up the Son of Man, then you will realize that I am he,' and that I do nothing on my own, but I speak these things as the Father instructed me." His death clears away the confusion that powers the struggle in this Gospel, but it is not Pauline atonement soteriology as later construed by Latin theology.

Of the three remaining passages, John 3:14-16 says that those who believe in Jesus have eternal life. This is a dominant motif in this Gospel, and the point is not connected to atonement, but it, too, fits perfectly with the teaching that the acceptance of Jesus' identity and commandments constitutes eternal life. The next passage (12:23-32) suggests that Jesus' death is necessary in order for his teaching to spread abroad; but again, it concurs with 8:27-28 and is not connected to atonement. In 16:7-9, Jesus comforts those already grieving by saying that after his death he will send them an advocate that they may hold to their faith in the face of what would surely be stiff opposition from those who read Jesus' death as demonstrating the falsity of his claims. Again, it has nothing to do with atonement as forgiveness of sins that in and of itself constitutes salvation. In summary, Jesus' death is very important in John's Gospel, but there is no atonement soteriology of the second-millennium, Western kind.

Obedience unto death shows how deep Jesus' loyalty to his Father is. Similarly, he loves the disciples and they should love him as staunchly. They may not have to give their lives, but John 15:12-13 implies that it could be necessary: "This is my commandment, that you love one another as I have loved you. No one has greater love than this, to lay down one's life for one's friends." He is, of course, referring to his own death, but they know that they are at risk as well. By their love for Jesus — and perhaps for one another — they participate in the love of the Father and the Son for one another: "As the Father has loved me, so I have loved you; abide in my love. If you keep my commandments, you will abide in my love, just as I have kept my Father's commandments and abide in his love. I have said these things to you so that my joy may be in you and that your joy may be complete" (15:9-11).

Loving Jesus means keeping his word and commandments just as he keeps those of his Father (14:15, 21, 23-24). This is the way to eternal life. Proclaiming the word of eternal life is Jesus' act of obedience. He is living the obedience that he requires of his followers. He both proclaims and exemplifies what is required so that his followers can see it and do likewise. By pointing to his own obedience, he prepares those who accept his identity and authority to follow his example, even unto death.

Keeping Jesus' Commandments

Having set the example of love as obedience to the mission his Father had given him, Jesus urges his hearers to imitate him by keeping the new commandments that he will give them (13:34-35; 14:15, 21-23). Since Jesus delivers only what he has received, he is inviting his hearers to obey the Father both with and through him. The Son obeys the Father directly, while the disciples obey the Father indirectly — by obeying the Son. This does not mean not keeping the other commandments. There is no polemic against the law here (nor is there in the synoptic Gospels in general, for that matter), only a focus on the two new ones that Jesus adapts to his own purpose. Jesus' two commandments to love God and neighbor appear in various forms.

Loving God

John urges people to "love the Father" (14:31) and Jesus (8:42; 14:15, 21-24). The phrases reformulate the Deuteronomic command to "love the Lord your God" (Deut. 6:5; 11:1; 13:3; 30:6), now mediated through Christ's words spoken at the instruction of the Father. Yet what is the content of that love? In the Tanah, loving God is the reverent way of life specified by commands, patterns of behavior, and cultivation of character strengths. Here the activities of love are imprecise because the various elements of eternal life imply and often collapse into one another.

John 14 charts Jesus' leading into eternal life as follows: (1) "Believe in God" (14:1). (2) Accept Jesus' claims about himself at face value: "Believe also in me," or simply "believe me" (4:21; 5:46; 8:45-46; 10:37-38; 11:25; 14:1-11; 16:9; 17:20). That is, believe that I am sent to you by my Father, and "believe me that I am in the Father and the Father is in me" (14:11). (3) Abide in Jesus' word of loving intimacy, that is, hold tight to the first two points. (4) Imitate Jesus: "The one who believes in me will also do the works that I do" (14:12). (5) Love Jesus by obeying him: "If you love me, you will keep my commandments" (14:15, 21, 23, 24; 15:10). (6) The process is to carry believers to the Father (14:2-3, 6-7).

The result of or reward for this believing and for keeping Jesus' commandments is participating in the love that binds Father and Son: "They who have my commandments and keep them are those who love me; and those who love me will be loved by my Father, and I will love them and reveal myself to them" (14:21). Receiving Jesus is not an end in itself, just as Israel's liberation from Egypt is not an end in itself. Both are means to greater ends. There, it is a means to embody the social arrangements that make for flourishing societies; here, it is a new way to be the people of God, in which all may have eternal life.

There is circularity in the fifth step. Those who love Jesus will obey him, but his primary command is to love him. Which comes first? How does one enter the circle? Ultimately, it does not matter, for loving and obeying Jesus are one activity, just as in the Tanah loving and revering God, taking refuge in him, and keeping his commandments are of a piece. It is natural for one who loves Jesus to believe what he claims about himself, to follow him by living as he directs. The initial requirement of believing (in) Jesus and in his intimate relationship with "the Father" is important in John's Gospel as the necessary step into the Johannine community.

The Tanaḥ does not need to establish such an entry point because the authorization of the way of life commended by God is uncontested. The ecclesiological and soteriological crisis in John makes this christological confession necessary. Yet, at the same time, the stunning christological claim precipitates the ecclesiological and soteriological crisis. Believing in, loving, and doing the works that Christ does and commands — that is, imitating his obedience to the Father — now constitute a new pattern of the reverent life of commandment-keeping. The result is a dramatically more intimate and riveting vision than the Tanaḥ imagined. Psalm 15:1-2 longingly considers the question of who will dwell in the house of the Lord. "O Lord, who may abide in your tent? Who may dwell on your holy hill? Those who walk blamelessly, and do what is right, and speak the truth from their heart."

That same desire defines Jesus' image of a mansion with many dwelling places (John 14:2). Chapter 14 begins with Jesus preparing a place for the disciples in his Father's house; but he reverses that dramatically to say that God — Father and Son — will make their home in those who believe in, love, and keep Jesus' commandments. "Those who love me will keep my word, and my Father will love them, and we will come to them and make our home with them" (14:23). It is a show-stopping moment. While the psalmist's longing is to "dwell in the house of the Lord all the days of [his] life" (Ps. 23:6), the Johannine author has God dwelling in Jesus' followers. John 15 points to the fruit of eternal life into which believers have entered:

> My Father is glorified by this, that you bear much fruit and become my disciples. As the Father has loved me, so I have loved you; abide in my love. If you keep my commandments, you will abide in my love, just as I have kept my Father's commandments and abide in his love. I have said these things to you so that my joy may be in you and that your joy may be complete. (John 15:8-11)

The Tanaḥ proclaims that a happy life is loving God, obeying his commandments, and dwelling in the house of the Lord. John's Gospel proclaims that a happy life is loving and obeying Jesus to be indwelt by God.

Loving One Another

Jesus' second commandment presses love beyond the happy triumvirate to create community solidarity. The command to love one another appears as the "new" commandment (13:34-35; 15:12, 17). Although presented as "new," the Johannine exhortation to horizontal love clearly echoes Leviticus 19:18. However, the Levitical command is interpreted afresh in the Johannine context. Horizontal love creates the church. It is not a common meeting space for those who love Jesus, but a society of those bonded together in love, sharing the eternal life of God.

As previously noted, the greatest discontinuity between the Older and Younger Testaments on loving God and keeping his commandments is that obedience is mediated through Christ in the Younger Testament. Perhaps this harks back to John's Gospel's insistence that Jesus himself is the obedient model on which we pattern our obedience. The suggestion seems to be that, in the first century, some Jews had lost sight of the excellent life that Judaism offered. Perhaps time and hardship had dulled the people's imagination, and they needed a concrete model to reinvigorate it. If so, God sent Jesus to bring eternal life.

Eternal Life in the Fourth Gospel

Eternal life occupies the place of *ashrey, smh,* and reverence for the Lord that is dominant in the texts from the Older Testament that we have previously examined. Admittedly, the Psalms and Proverbs detail and celebrate the rewards and delight of the happy life, but the Younger Testament was written in a situation of turmoil that allowed little room for reflection or encouragement of that kind. The evangelist wrote in the middle of strife, a time when every encounter was a skirmish in a greater conflict.

It is sadly ironic that John's message — that eternal life is love — that binds the Father, Jesus, and disciples together into one body, was formed in the crucible of rancor and malice. Despite the vituperation and anger in this Gospel, the eternal life that Jesus was sent to deliver is the love of God, the knowledge that love locates God in us, us in God, and us in one another as members of Christ's body. Love is the dynamic power that reaches down in Jesus and carries us into the love he shares with his Father, out into the community that is formed by this love, and back up into the beauty of the Father, who is responsible for this saving happiness. The wisdom of divine love is eternal life. It is living from, for, and through that wisdom. Although this text does not ring with celebratory songs, the message is triumphant for those who "taste and see that the Lord is good; happy are those who take refuge in him" (Ps. 34:8).

Biblical Asherism

Across epochs, locations, languages, circumstances, cultures, and discourses, texts in both Testaments of Scripture agree that the maker of heaven and earth seeks creation's flourishing. All the texts we have considered argue that reverent devotion to the creator and redeemer of the world is the happy life, for it crafts one into an instrument of divine wisdom, love, and goodness.

The various patterns of life that Scripture intends to draw the reader into drive toward one goal: organizing ourselves around life in God that we may enjoy ourselves as we are buoyed by the love, beauty, goodness, and wisdom of God, which hoist us aloft. That the visions they paint frame the issue differently is a great strength rather than a conundrum, for here specificity would be stultifying, since the ways in which God is to be enjoyed are inexhaustible. The Pentateuch, Psalms, and Proverbs suggest that living into salvation is incremental. John's Gospel, by contrast, talks of achieving eternal life as a dramatic commitment to leave one's trusted way of life and embrace Jesus. It is far more nebulous — but perhaps even more passionate — in its call. Through struggle, confusion, internal dissension, resistance, and neglect, all call their readers into a beautiful and fulfilling life as the people of God. Perhaps John 15:11 summarizes the asherist ethic most elegantly: "I have said these things to you so that my joy may be in you, and that your joy may be complete."

CHAPTER 13

God and the Art of Happiness

We have arrived at the last turn in this road. The biblical materials I have examined in the preceding four chapters go a considerable way toward filling in the gap between Augustine's therapeutic soteriology, based on the recognition that sin is the result of disordered love, and how that spiritual healing is actualized. This is especially important for those who experience themselves as suffering from the sins of others.

I should make one comment before proceeding further. Augustine believes that all humans are broken by disordered love and that their spiritual search is for healing. The tradition has not generally taken account of the harm done to those being sinned against, but more of the damage to the sinner. However, some people experience themselves as psychologically broken in a particularly dramatic way as a result of being sinned against, particularly if that experience has extended over time, such as in severe domestic or political dysfunction. While the sinned against suffer from such experiences, the image of God in them is not necessarily damaged beyond the proper kind of brokenness that is the fallen nature that everyone bears. That is, although they may be emotionally hurt, they are not theologically damaged. Indeed, the sinner damages himself, not his victim, as Boethius points out.[1]

There are two important exceptions to this. One is when the victim has so absorbed dysfunctional behavior toward her that she becomes what she fears and hates the most, and perpetuates the sin by repeating

---

1. See also John Chrysostom, "Treatise to Prove That No One Can Harm the Man Who Does Not Injure Himself," in *Nicene and Post-Nicene Fathers of the Christian Church,* ed. Philip Schaff (Edinburgh: T. & T. Clark, 1889).

it. Resisting doing to others what has been done to her is spiritual health because, apart from that, sin damages the sinner but not the victim. The sinner succeeds when the victim becomes another himself, but short of the victim's becoming another perpetrator, the devil is locked out of the victim's soul. The other exception is when the pain takes up so much space in the person's life that it crowds out other important things and spawns pathological patterns on its own terms — from jealousy and resentment to the desire to harm oneself or others. In these cases there may be theological damage; but, in Augustine's terms, because the image — though broken — is still present, no external harm can destroy it.

Short of becoming people who cause hurt in response to being hurt, those who suffer exceptional hurt are not theologically damaged. Their task is that of everyone else. Those who have not suffered exceptionally are still in need of the therapeutic soteriology that characterizes Augustine's search for the image of God in us, which is our primary source of strength and power. At this point Boethius's counterintuitive argument that the wicked are weak even if they appear powerful, and that the good are powerful even when they are in tight straits, comes back into view. Clinging to the part of us that cannot be damaged by others because they have no access to it is the theological ground on which the healing of love can occur. This is the place in us that can rest in God, and it is a refuge in times of trouble.

We return now to the scriptural material. Taken as a whole, the Older Testament texts that I have examined here, interpreted in their canonical setting, suggest that insight and clarity follow from, rather than motivate, habits formed by practice. Teaching virtues and values is essential to naming the goal and shaping self-understanding, but they remain abstractions if they do not hit the ground — as covenantal obedience does. Healing is learned by enacting healing behavior, not first by talking and thinking about healing as an outcome.

This is the apprenticeship model and also the way children acquire language. To put the matter in contemporary parlance, psychodynamic and cognitive-behavioral therapies are complementary, but the canonical ordering seems to argue for the cognitive-behavioral approach as the first step. Behavioral skills enable personal dynamics to assume a different place in our arsenal of skills. Theologically put, obeying divine commands enables us to experience the reverent life as pleasing and rewarding. We do better by practicing than by being talked into it.

Experiencing godly living or covenantal faithfulness, whether as Deuteronomy or as Proverbs understands it, heals love.

Practicing our way into healing offers a special challenge to those who experience exceptional suffering from the sins of others, but Augustine may still be of help. If sin is the product of warped love, perhaps the best way to heal the image in ourselves is to heal the perpetrator, whose distorted love is not only pathological (as everyone's is) but exceptionally pathological. To work toward the healing of the victimizer gives the victim back the power that was taken away or denied by the victimization. Facile forgiveness does not heal. Our healing of others heals ourselves and contributes to the healing of community, for damaged spirits fan out like the ripples from a stone thrown into a lake. Like wickedness, healing is not personal or private but public and social. Some believe that condemnation is more powerful and hence more socially useful than commendation; others champion the importance of encouragement and empowerment of the ability to heal and thus to be healed. Claiming one's power to heal distorted love in others *is* love of enemies. Like win-win resolutions, it is a heal-heal situation in which not only the principals are healed but also the body politic. The personal is public, for it builds strength for further healing, just as personal harm builds malice for further damage.

While the Gospel of John neither offers the specificity of Older Testament commands nor identifies their character-forming and healing power, it points to what is perhaps the unspoken goal of covenantal training: the simple view that love for the God who loves and love for the neighbor, who is similarly loved, is eternal, abundant life. Perhaps the command to love Jesus — a challenge in the Johannine environment — functions like the Older Testament commandments that practice Israel into spiritual health and growth. John, distracted by conflict, teaches simply that loving Jesus is abundant life (which is what later theologians were to call "salvation" and "sanctification"); but in his environment, commanding love was not simple. Perhaps it never is. Still, like Augustine's work, John's Gospel does not specify what that looks like. Love remains vague, vulnerable to becoming a cipher until we fill it in.

John taught that loving Jesus is eternal life: if that is truly to be loved of God — and John certainly must have thought it was — it must be healed love. It is not immediately clear how that — or even *if* that — relates to Augustine's teaching that happiness is possible only when love is healed. But I am arguing here that the Christology of John's Gospel can be read through the Augustinian filter. Later readers read Johannine eternal life outside the stressful situation in which it was forged. Loving Jesus, being taken into the divine life by that love, and being bound to the community through it, cannot help but be healing in something close to the soteriological sense that Augustine seeks. The power for abundant life in loving Jesus, who carries his lovers to his Father, has to be both relocatable and relocated into other contexts. What John established for those who would later be mostly Gentile followers of Jesus is that loving (Jesus) is eternal life, which heals the distorted love under which all suffer.

At this point we read John in Augustinian terms and consider how he accomplishes his construal of happiness — the eternal abundant life of undistorted love with which he lures his readers — christologically at the micro level. John's Gospel makes a desperate plea for everyone to enter eternal life with Jesus, but that call must be readable outside his context. Later Christians read his exhortation through the Nicene Creed, and we follow that lead. The second half of the second article of the Nicene Creed telescopes salvation into a few phrases. It reviews moments in Jesus' biography that are "for us and for our salvation," but it does not define the goal. Its clipped phrases note his coming from heaven, becoming human, dying and being buried, rising from the dead, and returning to the Father. There is no definition of salvation here, only the assurance that all of this was "for our salvation" and "for our sake."

No single event or moment in that narrative constitutes salvation. All the events listed are for our spiritual health. If we read "for our sake" through Augustine's therapeutic soteriology, the whole Younger Testament narrative summarized in a few phrases of the creed is intended to carry those who profess this creed into John's eternal life. Jesus' story is for our salvation, and by practicing ourselves into it, we reap its benefits and grow into salvation as Augustine articulated the painstaking process. The process is like a double helix: the sides of the helix, understanding and acting, continuously nourish the DNA molecules connecting them as the helix turns, expands, and contracts. Realizing that one is called to salvation may happen in a startling moment, but becoming spiritually well is a journey enabled by Christ's biography that is recalled by the creed. Happiness is a realizing eschatology: it is the intensification of spiritual maturity in which happiness expands and deepens as people become spiritually stronger and better able to contribute to their own and the world's well-being. The creedal narrative is a road map to healing.

Christ the Healer

Christ's offer of eternal life was obscure to his compatriots. Perhaps a metaphor for what was being pointed to was Jesus' healing of a blind man in Mark 8:22-25. Jesus had to lay his hands on the man twice before the latter could see everything clearly. When he first began to see, things were blurry to him. Salvation is seeing the world afresh, and it takes time to adjust. Eternal life in John is also vague, as we have seen. Following the Nicene Creed can clarify the recovery of sight, but Christ's death is the riveting event of the creed's biographical sketch. The dangerously provocative healing ministry of Jesus of Nazareth in Galilee went exactly where he knew it would: he disrupted life in Israel to make a point. The attentive reader is pinned to the decisive moment like a butterfly on linen.

A person needs to be pinned silent for a time, jarred from comforting but distorted responses and defensive reactions rutted in bad love by the love gushing forth from Christ on the cross along with his blood and water. Being interrupted by Christ's willingness to go to the cross is becoming vulnerable by opening ourselves to self-critical examination of patterns of thought and behavior built on interactions from which Jesus has been absent. Confessing Jesus means allowing him to stand in the middle of every interaction in which we engage. Receiving him means never being alone again. He accompanies the broken, both to encourage and to stay their hand or — perhaps more frequently — their tongue.

Christ is the invisible shield given in baptism. The baptized die into his death and rise into his resurrection and become participants in the Trinitarian drama of redemption. Baptism makes one an instrument of God's redeeming agency. Like the blind man in Mark 8, living in that light takes getting used to. The spiritual power of God the Holy Spirit given in baptism screens both what comes in and what flows out of the baptized in every interaction.

This is a sacramental way of reading Augustine's quest for the repair of the image of God in us. I will return to it shortly, but suffice it to say here that just as Aquinas insisted that the ability to see and know God depends on the gift of divine grace that makes that sight and knowledge possible, here the church's sacramental agency offers Christians an abiding in the Holy Trinity and the power of Christ and the Holy Spirit to heal and be healed.

Historically, Jesus' demise looks like a voluntary death that was meant to prevent Rome from forcibly repressing the unrest he had aroused. He allowed himself to be executed to save others from being massacred. He apparently agreed with Caiaphas that it was best for one person to die in order to save many (John 11:50). In a calculated exchange, he died in place of the people — including those who followed him at first but later demanded his execution, and those disciples who abandoned him at the last. From this perspective, Christ was in control of his death: it was a great gift of love. In Butler's terms, it was an extraordinary act of self-love.

At the same time, Matthew and Mark report that Jesus quotes from Psalm 22:1 on the cross: "My God, my God, why have you forsaken me?" Perhaps he thought that he would be able to take the heat when the time came. Yet, when his closest friends fell asleep, leaving him alone, he was afraid; but it was too late to escape. He did not flee, but allowed himself to be kissed and taken. On the face of it, Jesus seems to have been utterly defeated by political power. His revolutionary movement collapsed as he was publicly humiliated, mocked, and tortured to set an example. Lest any others should try to disrupt the delicate détente between Rome and Judea, the authorities showed him to be a failed revolutionary.

This way of reading the story offers bad news. Well-meant revolutions and social movements fail because passion is not enough. Errors in judgment, tactical missteps, and negative reactions from those threatened, as well as unpredictable responses from those on whose behalf risks are being taken, may derail the most well-intentioned reform movements, which in their verve may be naïve. Jesus' failure fits into some of those categories.

Christians believe that more is going on in these events than debacle. They read the story as good news. The wisdom of divine love is active at every step of the riveting drama, reversing the world's values and conventional understandings of power. Paul identifies this as the great reversal of wisdom and power wrought by the cross (1 Cor. 1:19-25). To grasp this is to begin the Christian journey into God.

In hindsight, Jesus knowingly courted danger by going from town to town, indiscriminately healing and feeding people. Reports of the last days and moments of his life and beyond that time affirm his power to heal, though in a different key. One such moment is his final speech to his disciples, in which he comforts them in anticipation of his impending death (John 14); he tells them why he must leave them. It is not that he has accomplished his mission on earth, but that in order to do so he must return to his Father to prepare a place for his devoted followers with him (John 14:2-3), that they might dwell with him and his Father forever, as later theology explained it. This reassures his friends that his leaving them is not abandonment but is for their sake. Furthermore, he will send, or ask his Father to send, another in his place to advocate for, comfort, and lead them into all truth in the meantime (John 14:16, 26; 15:26; 16:7). He would leave them, only to return and be vindicated as the instrument of eternal life. Those who had been given the grace of the Holy Spirit to grasp the triumph of God's wisdom in the cross were beginning to see as their love was healed.

As Augustine's deconstruction of our false construals in relationship to God shows, we too, like Jesus, court danger. Like him, we move on, seeming to leave those we love, or those we try to love, sometimes in the face of their having betrayed and abandoned us, as Jesus' most trusted friends eventually did. When he needed them, they protected themselves instead. Jesus continued to comfort people even as he was dying. In his last moments, he was able to look beyond his suffocating pain and see others. Luke recounts that he prayed for his accusers and executioners: "Father, forgive them, for they know not what they do" (Luke 23:34). This plea is on behalf of his fickle followers, Caiaphas and his associates, and the Romans. Jesus is teaching those who love him to become healers, for that straightens their loving unto salvation.

In John's account, even at the end, Jesus sees his mother grieving and asks his beloved disciple to care for her as he would his own mother (John 19:26-27). Preparing for her life without him is extraordinary. Who among us can think and see beyond our pain in general, let alone in such pain and anguish? It is difficult not to fixate on one's physical pain and indignity in general, let alone in the case of one who is suffering an untimely, violent, and seemingly unjust death on imperial orders. Seeing beyond one's own dying as it is happening, in order to meet the future needs of others, is another of God's great gifts to us through Christ. It is again the wisdom of love (John 19:26-27). At the very end, Jesus is happy in his great self-donation: his death for the sake of life that repairs the world in the reign of God.

Through these incidents, eternal life becomes clearer. In dying to protect those who abandon him, comforting them in advance, and caring for them beyond the grave, Jesus teaches those who watch his self-love straighten others' ability to love themselves well that the *imago dei* may be reconstructed. Both perpetrators and victims of damaged love may drink at this well. Jesus heals his beloved disciple by instructing him in what it means now to love Jesus. It is not to weep and wail but to pour his grief into care for Jesus' mother, so that they might grieve and comfort one another together. Jesus may die, but the love that he teaches will thrive, for he discloses how self-love elicits God's enjoyment of us as we heal.

According to the synoptic Gospels, people mocked Jesus as he was crucified, addressing him with the satire against idolatry from Isaiah: "A deluded mind has led him astray, and he cannot save himself" (Isa. 44:20). "He saved others; he cannot save himself" (Matt. 27:42; Mark 15:31; Luke 23:35). The taunt reveals their inability to grasp what they were seeing. Jesus had not failed to save himself; he died to save others, and no amount of physical pain can halt that even for a moment. Because Jesus obeyed his Father, even to the point of his death, asherism affirms that Jesus was sanguine in his death because it was a piece of a larger pilgrimage that concludes with his return to his Father and session at the latter's right hand, as the creed puts it. His death may be the triumph of his life and is often pointed to as epitomizing divine love, but the triumph of his ministry is drawing people into the perfect loving that he teaches.

The celebrated miracle is that Jesus rose from the dead, but perhaps it truly is that he returns to take care of those who harmed him. The account of the ways in which Jesus saves his followers extends beyond the biblical narrative in the Apostles' Creed, which is oddly missing in the Nicene Creed. After his death, the latter creed says that Jesus was in hell, where, according to tradition, he released the biblical patriarchs and other righteous people who had died before his coming from that prison. He could not stop healing, indeed, sought every opportunity to do so, even under the most trying circumstances. Even among the dead and those suffering hell's torments, Jesus was there, healing, releasing others, extending to the dead the eternal life that he wrought among the living.[2]

Those gifted with spiritual vision see the wisdom emanating from

2. Hans Urs von Balthasar, *Mysterium Paschale: The Mystery of Easter* (Grand Rapids: Eerdmans, 1990), pp. 148-88.

Jesus. The template for eternal life is being colored in with love that is not an empty set but is populated by tiny acts of love perfectly targeted to the needs of those he seeks out. In this, Jesus is not continuing his self-sacrifice: his target love is not at his expense, and its effectiveness is not tied to self-emptying. It is not disinterested love, but deeply interested in what he can give that others need. The giving is no loss. On the contrary, by his power he undertakes the giving of a love that empowers, releases, cares for, and heals others, and it displays the power of love. He is strengthened, not weakened, by these specific acts of love.

The resurrection appearances further fill in the template. All the Gospels report that Jesus returns to comfort friends who had abandoned him and fled in fear three days before. At this point he explains to them that his death is not tragic but purposeful. At the end of John's Gospel, Jesus continues to feed his disciples by bringing in a massive catch of fish, at which point they recognize him (John 21:4-13). Jesus is a consummate and adept lover. He loves by providing for both innocent and guilty, on this occasion by feeding those who had abandoned him. Imagine being fed by the one you abandoned just a few days before. It is the quintessential teachable moment; the gift is priceless.

The postresurrection visitations persuade the foundering disciples that the mission to which they have committed themselves in following Jesus has not collapsed, but that they — fumbling fools who fell asleep at the calamitous moment — are charged with building the church under the guidance of their advocate, who now comes as Jesus has previously promised (John 14:16).[3] John 20 says that, immediately after rising from death, Jesus sets out to redirect the lives of his disconsolate followers, who have understandably locked themselves away from public scrutiny for fear of reprisals. This is not an act of cowardice. Their association with Jesus is known, and now it is a liability. What good would they be to Jesus dead? When he shows up among them, they are thrilled. He does not scold them for their fickleness or for anything else; rather, he charges them to move ahead. Those who cower in fear are to go out in danger, encouraged by the Holy Spirit in their midst with the authority to remit sin at their discretion. The disciples may have thought that Jesus' movement was dead, but their task now is to revive it and thus be healed of their shame at having abandoned Jesus.

3. The synoptic Gospels have similar scenes (Matt. 28:18-20; Mark 16:17-18; Luke 24:47).

The most striking example of turning grief and fear into action for healing is the rehabilitation and commissioning of Simon/Peter (John 21:15-17). Having thrice denied even knowing Jesus, his heart must have been heavy indeed. Jesus confronts Peter, but instead of chastising him as Peter must have expected, Jesus restores him. He knows that Peter's denials came from fear for his safety, not from doubt about Jesus. Jesus matches each of Peter's denials with equal opportunities to profess his love and vindicate himself. Do you love me? Do you love me? Do you love me? Peter knows that Jesus knows that he loves him. The persistence of the question must have been a bit trying. The triplicity of the interrogation is essential, however, for the resounding echo of Peter's "yes, I love you" itself enacts his forgiveness and healing. Jesus is not angry but determined. He allows Peter's love for him to overcome his chagrin and actually heal him. Three times Jesus tells him the path to recovery: "Feed my sheep. Feed my sheep. Feed my sheep." Peter's sin is not healed by a declaration of forgiveness that Peter could rest in, but by Jesus' simple command: "Follow me," and again, "follow me" (John 21:19, 22). Peter's salvation is his obedience to Jesus' call to start again. Of all the disciples, the denier alone is privileged to have this opportunity, perhaps because his betrayal was so blatant. According to Matthew, Jesus had given Simon the epithet Peter (rock) early on to designate him as the leader of the church (Matt. 16:18). The rock shatters under pressure, yet according to the Fourth Gospel, Jesus heals him.

It is little wonder that people began to suspect that Jesus really was the one he claimed to be in John's Gospel. Jesus enacts love of enemies more than he preaches it. The medium is the message. Peter, the one he has empowered, rejects his call, and Jesus rejects the rejection. By rehabilitating Peter, Jesus teaches him to lead, for the leader is the consummate lover called to empower the sinner unto repaired love. We can be thankful that John wrote this down for us and for our salvation.

In these events, Jesus is enacting the wisdom of divine love that is eternal life. Peter must not fret over his sin, for he has been given the work that Jesus was about. His trust in Jesus was truer than his betrayal. Just as Jesus' death could not be allowed to impede the spreading of eternal life, Jesus will not permit Peter's broken love to have the last word. Jesus heals that love may triumph. Here Jesus reaches the height of his earthly power and freely gives it away to Peter and those watching them century after century. To love is to heal, to heal is to love.

The template is forged. Eternal life in God, made possible by Jesus, is the movement from darkness into light that John 1:4-5 articulates. Those who can see the wisdom of divine love unfurled here are truly blessed, and they grasp proper self-love. In the face of corrupting and paralyzing forces of spiritual darkness that threaten everywhere, Jesus forges another way. Redemption from evil, sin, and death shines here, where anger, self-despair, and cynicism fade away. Perhaps this is the import of Psalm 30:11-12: "You have turned my mourning into dancing; you have taken off my sackcloth and clothed me with joy, so that my soul may praise you and not be silent. O Lord my God, I will give thanks to you forever."

In summary, for the spiritually sighted, the biographical sketch of Jesus in the creeds reveals the wisdom of eternal life redemptively working itself out in him for them. The healing power of divine love pours out as Christ lives beyond his own physical and emotional limits, addressing grief, shame, fear, and failure. His care for his mother, those suffering unjustly, and his errant followers demonstrates that God does not permit hurt or failure to overwhelm the capacity to love, for love transforms and thereby heals unto eternal life. Christ's life, death, resurrection, and ascension testify to the great reversal of worldly wisdom that Paul articulates so eloquently (1 Cor. 1:18-25).

Watching Jesus heal others in his death as in his life (the woman taken in adultery being a stellar example) is not only beautiful but healing for onlookers, for Jesus is instructing them as he enacts the eternal life of healed love for which he was sent. Like all apprentices, the novice learns by watching the master practicing the craft, and then practices it herself — haltingly at first. Late readers of these texts are Jesus' apprentices, just as the disciples turned apostles were.

Learning the Wisdom of Divine Love

Those being saved can now say with the centurion, according to Matthew and Mark, "Truly this was God's Son" (Matt. 27:54; Mark 15:39). Others may say, with the Lukan account of the centurion, "Certainly this man was innocent" (Luke 23:47), but Christianity preferred the stronger claim that God became a Jewish artisan and traveled around Galilee making trouble in order to make love, as John's Gospel argues so dramatically. Jesus' love-making is the revelation of God to those who know that the image of God that they are is broken, perhaps tortured, into powerlessness and fear. Jesus' actions in his life, death, and afterlife reveal God as the consummate lover who takes the broken shards, like the dry bones in Ezekiel's valley, and brings them bone upon bone into wholeness with sinews, flesh, skin, and breath.

The tradition read Christ through John 1:1: this man was the "Word" of God; he was not only originally with God but *was* God." Through him God imparts eternal life to those who follow, love, and obey him. In him, humanity participates in the drama of the redemption of the world. The incarnation is a gift of hope that says that God came graciously to us quite apart from anything that we do or any cry of distress that we may utter. In his wisdom, God has become us that he may be in us and we in him. The wisdom of divine love behind the incarnation is the eternal life that Jesus gives. This doctrine and the doctrine of the Trinity that we can infer from it reinforce this claim that Paul makes explicit in 1 Corinthians 1:24: "Christ [is] the power of God and the wisdom of God," even — or perhaps especially — at the cross. In Jesus, the spiritually able meet the power of love working in his life, death, descent to the dead, resurrection, and ascension. By the wisdom of this love, sin is slowly healed by strategies of love that begin new life. Salvation is a slow, therapeutic process because learning to love perfectly is a healing of, not a deliverance from, our nature. It takes time to solidify.

Learning to live from divine wisdom is an artful undertaking. Christ embeds us in it that it may become us. At that point, we begin to work out our salvation with fear and trembling (Phil. 2:12), that is, to absorb the wisdom of love in order that it might become truly ours so that we cannot be separated from the redemption being accomplished by its power. Having been co-opted into that drama at baptism, the believer is dressed in the vestments of salvation, the armor of God.

Assimilating salvation into our personalities requires developing a new outlook on things and strategies for accomplishing them. Just as Paul says that novice Christians are fed with milk and not solid food (1 Cor. 3:2), it is wise to begin with baby steps in practicing divine wisdom. Being renewed by God through the template for enacting love, perhaps timidly at first, mandates new attitudes and behavioral styles. While these attempts may be fitful and only partially successful at first, the joy of mastering them is encouraging, and the styles and patterns of interaction that are being replaced grow stale because they do not bring that joy. Loving effectively is delightfully reinforcing. The power of Christ's love, being absorbed into the spiritual bloodstream, as it were, can eat away at ingrained temperamental and dysfunctional character traits that retard flourishing until maladroit behaviors wear thin and functional behaviors and attitudes replace them.

We enjoy ourselves as others benefit from our agility at using salvation. Happiness is mastering foolishness and becoming powerfully wise and spiritually strong in the knack of loving well, in order that we may heal those who have harmed us emotionally, that we may be strengthened and they healed of illness. There may not be face-to-face reconciliation. The victim of extraordinary suffering may simply need space in which to practice loving better apart from that relationship. Or that relationship may not be reachable or reparable. That does not mean that the sufferer must bear the pain; but giving it over to love requires deep and abiding faith in Christ that becoming a healer is the way to be healed. Faith in Jesus here is faith that his way forward crushes pain and brings comfort and rest by healing the disordered love that brutalization has exacerbated in its ugly path.

Perhaps the second article of the creed is like a film to be watched many times in slow motion, filling in the gaps with still shots taken from the Gospel narratives, so that one might get the knack of healing loving. Aquinas's idea that one is an instrument of divine providence rings true. By embracing that instrumentality joyfully, we enjoy ourselves in God. This is the happiness of abundant life. Those co-opted into the drama of redemption have no choice but to embrace their providential responsibility energetically, for they have become servants of the world's flourishing and of God's enjoyment of creation. Their happiness is in enjoying God and the world as servants. Enjoying eternal life is doing this excellently and energetically.

Admittedly, loving well is an art. Misguided, superficial, or inadequate love can harm both ourselves and the object of our care. Jesus saw the needs of others accurately. From the stories we have, he decisively discerned their need and knew how to address it. This is difficult for us if we see another's suffering through our own needs or experience. Offering parallel experience and false encouragement may harm another person if they come from a desire to soothe in the absence of knowing how to help. The saved in turn save. The lost cannot be trusted, as Israel's poets and sages know, and as Jesus demonstrates.

Jesus healed by setting people at tasks that would empower them in new ways, training them away from dysfunctional emotions and patterns of behavior and toward salutary ones. The spurs to action he gave to his beloved disciple as he died, his breathing the Holy Spirit on the disciples, his sending them as he was sent, and the restoration of Peter after the resurrection are examples. Those being saved will be healed by learning to heal and to take up their new life in Christ.

Sacramental Consecration

The church equips those who wish to be healed unto eternal life through public initiatory rites.[4] Christian initiation imposes an identity not of one's choosing. Like being *ashrey,* we must grow into this identity, since, as Paul put it, Christians have the Holy Spirit in them. They are not their own but God's (1 Cor. 6:19). The long process of formal enrollment in the catechumenate, prayer, study and instruction, formally renouncing another way if appropriate, and formal initiatory rites outfit the Christian for eternal life now.

The retrieval of catechesis is essential in the current climate, which is as heterogeneous as was that of the early church. One cannot walk a path that one does not understand. Every new Christian needs guidance. In the liturgically renewed rites of the *Book of Common Prayer 1979,* those presenting someone to be baptized promise that they will "by their prayers and witness help this [person] grow into the full stature of Christ," which we saw earlier in this chapter.

The baptism itself is entry into Christ's death and resurrection. As Paul puts it:

> For if we have been united with him in a death like his, we will certainly be united with him in a resurrection like his. We know that our old self was crucified with him so that the body of sin might be destroyed, and we might no longer be enslaved to sin. For whoever has died is freed from sin. But if we have died with Christ, we believe that we will also live with him. We know that Christ, being raised from the dead, will never die again; death no longer has dominion over him. The death he died, he died to sin, once for all; but the life

4. This section follows the rites of the Episcopal Church, *Book of Common Prayer* (New York: Seabury Press, 1979). Hereafter, references to the *Book of Common Prayer* (*BCP*) will appear in parentheses in the text.

he lives, he lives to God. So, you also must consider yourselves dead to sin and alive to God in Christ Jesus. (Rom. 6:5-11).

Entry into Christ's death and resurrection is followed by a further step into the divine mission: the giving of the Holy Spirit in chrismation. The chrismated are anointed with oil, "sealed by the Holy Spirit in Baptism and marked as Christ's own forever" (*BCP*, p. 308, following Eph. 1:13). This sealing and marking make up a spiritual tattoo, as it were. The baptized are inserted into Christ's death and resurrection and sealed with and for God's holiness. It is a spiritual shield. Divine power surrounds us both to protect us from others and to protect others from ourselves. We must pass through this shield when interacting with others, and others must pass through it when interacting with us, the baptized.

The way forward is lit by the light of Christ, which is now at work in the new Christian, which is symbolized by a burning candle given to the newly baptized. He or she is formally welcomed into the body of believers, who pledge their support for this new member, saying: "We receive you into the household of God. Confess the faith of Christ crucified, proclaim his resurrection, and share with us in his eternal priesthood" (*BCP*, p. 309). It is preferable that baptisms be celebrated in the public assembly of the gathered community that reaffirms their baptismal vows along with those being baptized, so they experience being bonded with the congregation that is confessing the same faith and traversing the same path. No one is alone. The newly baptized are then informally greeted by the congregation and led to feast with them at the Lord's table, to "feed on [Christ] in [their] heart by faith with thanksgiving" (*BCP*, p. 365). All is ready. The path to eternal life beckons.

Initiation is an awesome undertaking, for through it one is consecrated to God's way. The nonreligious can own their identity. However, Jews, Christians, and Muslims renounce the freedom to define themselves apart from God. They have renounced autonomy as inadequate to the task of bringing them into the happy life. Initiates embark on life in the beauty of holiness in the company of compatriots, who regularly remind one another that they are God's temple and that God's Spirit dwells in them (1 Cor. 3:16). Paul presses the point: "Your body is a temple of the Holy Spirit within you, which you have from God . . . you are not your own. For you were bought with a price; therefore glorify God in your body" (1 Cor. 6:19-20). The gift of the Spirit makes this possible and empowers the faithful to grow one another into eternal life.

As a parent or teacher gently guides the hand of a small child learning to hold a pencil and draw letters, Christ carries his members into the beauty of holiness. Perhaps this is the meaning of Colossians 3:1: "So if you have been raised with Christ, seek the things that are above, where Christ is, seated at the right hand of God." Those who are strengthening their ability to love well are becoming the wisdom of love that they cannot but celebrate. John 14:23 puts it this way: "Those who love me will keep my word, and my Father will love them, and we will come to them and make our home with them."

Paul's remark that the Holy Spirit dwells in the bodies of the baptized and that they are no longer their own is central to appreciating the weight of baptism. They are inserted into the drama of salvation, that is, into the joint mission of the Father, the Son, and the Holy Spirit for healing the broken Trinitarian image of God that they are, as Augustine put it. Initiatory rites are therapeutic because through them God equips people with spiritual power tools to become the "new creation," which they have been made by the Trinitarian work of creation, healing, and empowerment, not by their own strength.

When a person enters an unfamiliar city or country, she does not know her way around. Catechesis is like the guidebook that she would read in advance of the journey, but arriving would be an entirely different experience. In the ancient church, catechesis could take up to three years, and it could be tailored to individual need. Further, the first week after baptism consisted of continued study and instruction to help novice Christians move from preparation into the nitty-gritty of quotidian Christian living.

The foregoing description comes out of a liturgical perspective; nonliturgical churches will form their members in other ways. In either case, practicing the Christian life requires discerning reflection and practice. With the widespread adoption of the practice of infant baptism, the catechumenate declined and the church needed to catechize the baptized or those seeking entry into the community. Mentoring new Christians has not been a recent practice, but mentoring by wise, seasoned Christians who eat "solid food" (Heb. 5:11-14) may be warranted. These people are appropriate for pastoral leadership, as 1 Peter 5 spells out. In asherist terms, these people are healing through incorporation into Christ's life, death, resurrection, and ascension, which I have explored above.

If the triune God has taken on the task of curing souls that Augustine lays out in *De Trinitate,* the ongoing care of those yearning to experience that healing personally is the task of Christian ministry. Preaching teaches the baptized how to read the story of God in Christ in this theological framework. John Calvin made this point when, on July 21, 1555, he preached on 2 Tim. 3:16-17: "All Scripture is divinely inspired and is profitable for teaching, for reproof, for correction, for the training which is in righteousness; that the man of God may be whole, furnished to every good work."[5] Like many Christian thinkers before him, Calvin also undertook this task in his Scripture commentaries. Preaching and guided Scripture study are the discourse of Christian living. They teach what is to be looked for in worship and Scripture reading by unpacking the meaning and purpose of the second article of the Nicene Creed.

Still, the slower among us will want personal help on how not only to understand that discourse but also to "speak" it day by day. Of late, this task has fallen to ordained pastors, professional pastoral counselors, parish nurses, and the like, as people seek to learn how God heals them that they may become healers. These roles and offices assume the medical model's orientation toward pathology — in many cases, self-identified pathology. Augustine, on the other hand, teaches that everyone labors under the illness of disordered love. One should not need to single oneself out or be singled out for special attention.

To discuss a topic such as happiness in a theological framework is to claim fresh language for talking about the realizing eschatology that is the core of Augustine's therapeutic soteriology. Christian ministry aims to abet that task. It will be helpful, as we refresh Christian talk of salvation, to speak not only about the academic dimension of salvation, as I have here, but also about its practical aspect to render the theology limped. Here are some programmatic suggestions.

The care of souls is a delicate matter because it involves not only encouragement but also occasionally a call to accountability by offering alternative perspectives and behavior. Some people present themselves for care while others do not. A way to involve more people in the spiritual care of their own lives would be to offer church members the opportunity for an annual spiritual self-assessment. All Christians are ministers, but some lack the language to articulate their ministry. An annual spiritual review of one's life might both give that language and

5. T. H. L. Parker, *Calvin's Preaching* (Louisville: Westminster/John Knox, 1992), p. 8.

encourage the faithful toward a self-reflective frame of mind through which they can assess how their Christian life is going. An appropriate time for this of course is Lent, and appropriate places for it are in the home or other places of business to emphasize that Christian ministry happens in the world. A cadre of seasoned Christians could be trained for this task, as Stephen Ministries does for people in crisis.[6] Here the purpose is annual or at least regular self-assessment rather than adapting in time of crisis. The Religious Society of Friends, having dispensed with ordained leadership, developed the practice of clearness committees to help people make life decisions, including joining the Society, marriage, divorce, and so on.[7] However a community chooses to address this, involvement in one another's lives is necessary.

Practicing the Happy Life

Asherism's realizing eschatology functions in two directions, suggesting that healing is healing: that is, being healed by Christ strengthens one's ability to heal others. At the same time, healing others is therapeutic, because it is empowering and it is empowered by and for the beauty of holiness that is obedience to God. It is an ever-widening circle. Being healed enables healing, and healing heals. This is God's primary business. Being led by the disclosure of God in Christ and empowered by the spiritual gifts given in initiation offer the healing of the broken image in us that Augustine worked so hard to draw us into, for healing and empowering love water the soul. Isaiah put these words in God's mouth: "For as rain and snow fall from the heavens and return not again, but water the earth, bringing forth life and giving growth, seed for sowing and bread for eating, so is my word that goes forth from my mouth; it will not return to me empty; but it will accomplish that which I have purposed, and prosper in that for which it is sent" (as translated in *BCP*, p. 87). Repair of the broken image is the straightening of love toward an undivided self.

In concluding this proposal, I here offer three vignettes of asher-

6. Stephen Ministry is a program of training for laypeople to provide personal Christian care to those in crisis. See www.stephenministries.org

7. Patricia Loring, "Spiritual Discernment: The Context and Goal of Clearness Committees," in *Pendle Hill Pamphlet* (Wallingford, PA: Pendle Hill Publications, 1992).

ism: one with strangers, one within the family, and one the story of a prison inmate.

Eva

The first is an incident among strangers who had never met before and will probably never meet again. The story is rather trivial, but perhaps that illustrates the point well, since asherist happiness is modest. Modest incidents add up, however, just as trivial incidents in a child's interaction with adults create patterns of expectation, attitudes, and behavior. This incident exemplifies obedience to Deuteronomy 22:1: "You shall not watch your neighbor's ox or sheep straying away and ignore them; you shall take them back to their owner." And perhaps it echoes Leviticus 19:18: "You shall love your neighbor as yourself."

Eva, a young math teacher whose attention Christ's power has grasped, was driving on a city street during rush hour. As she approached an intersection, an obviously lost dog was wandering in the street amid the cars hurrying on their way. Eva pulled over and approached the dog. He had a collar on but no identification tag. Unsure of what to do, she called her husband for advice, and he suggested calling the animal rescue squad. She was not satisfied with that; she sensed that the dog lived nearby and was simply confused. Grabbing his collar, she started walking the dog around the neighborhood. Eventually, the dog began heading in a single direction on his own and went directly to his house. When the family opened the door, they were overjoyed, crying "Where have you been!" and so on. At that point the dog turned to Eva, happily jumping up on her and licking her in thanksgiving.

This little story illustrates obedience to a command that requires interrupting one's activity and being somewhat inconvenienced. In that sense, it is an application of the story of the Good Samaritan (Luke 10). However, that does not mean that the inconvenience was self-sacrificial. The Samaritan was no doubt pleased to have the opportunity to minister to the man who had been attacked by thieves.

On a basic level, of course, Eva rejoiced that the dog had returned home, was pleased to have enabled it to do so, and was perhaps even more pleased that God's claim on her life had pressed her to stop and do so. This is genuine self-enjoyment that is enjoying God. Yet, there is more. Eva enacted self-love. She benefits in a tiny incremental way from the incident, for her success encourages her to trust the commandment (Deut. 22:1), perhaps to trust others by association, and to expect herself to act similarly at the next opportunity. It pulls her deeper into obedience. At first she was timid and called for help, but the advice was not quite right and she proceeded on her own. She landed on the right procedure and successfully accomplished her mission. That encouraged her. Next time she may be quicker to trust herself and to enact self-love.

The incident was rewarding and strengthened Eva's confidence in serving God well. She was slightly inconvenienced by the dog, but that mattered little in the face of her success. She was pleased and could count it as overall gain. She experienced momentary pleasure, and because the incident increased her self-confidence and went into the store of experiences that constitutes her personal strength, the momentary pleasure joined with a deeper theological happiness. In being obedient to God, she was being the person God calls her to be. Being obedient to God is being obedient to herself. It is self-love.

Eva accomplished more than obeying God graciously. Heeding her Christian vocation advanced her self-confidence. That is, it gave the bent-over love in her an experience of standing up straight. It was a deeply personal pleasure. As she accumulates more experiences like this while watching Jesus crushed and triumphant, she becomes better at being a healer and becomes happier as she enacts self-love more effectively. The image of God that she is, is not only healing, but beginning to shine, and that heals her more — or perhaps better.

Such experiences have several effects. One is that, by experiencing covenantal faithfulness as pleasurable, Eva will seek out future experiences like this. Success encourages. She will better experience her baptism into Christ. Another effect is that virtuous behavior patterns "naturalize," as do daffodils, crocuses, irises, and tulips. Neighbor-love spreads beyond where it was originally planted to other parts of one's garden and causes flowers to bloom. Increasing artfulness in one setting encourages one to transfer the skills acquired there into other venues. Becoming strong by enacting the well-being of others actualizes the call to holiness, so that it may be touched and tasted.

This little incident contributes to the realizing eschatology of Eva's Christian journey into God. She is not simply pleased by what she did, for as a theologically aware Christian she can see the power of the Holy Spirit guiding her, and she can be thankful with quiet joy. Nonreligious people perform acts of kindness like this, of course, but they do not experience them theologically. They miss the awe, gratitude, and uplift that give one's life a larger and more powerful arena in which to glow.

Amanda

The second case illustrates one woman's struggle to find the image of God that she is, but that she has lost touch with because of abuse. Amanda is the older of two children in the Annette and Arthur Anscombe family. She was born in the second year of her parents' marriage, when they were thirty years old. It was her mother's second marriage; the first was to a man who abused her. Arthur was on the scene and intervened to rescue Annette from the abusive situation, so he is her hero and she is profoundly grateful to him.

Arthur is a successful systems and software analyst for a major U. S. corporation. He travels a good deal, and he is generous with the bounty he has received. A highly skilled professional, Arthur is of an intellectual bent. He is a staunch cultural relativist, and he struggles with anger. Amanda recalls that when she was six or seven, in response to something she had done wrong, her father pinned her to the wall with one hand around her throat demanding that she answer to him about the misbehavior. She could not breathe, understand what he was saying to her, or even speak. Mother vanished from the scene. Eventually her father let her go, but the incident has not let go of her.

Arthur's outbursts of mocking anger toward Annette and the children have persisted. Annette is afraid of her second husband and has emotionally shut down. She was unable to succor and support her children, so much so that she did not permit them to have birthday parties as children and does not speak to them on the phone as adults. Arthur treats her badly, but, out of gratitude for what he did for her, she does not resist him. The marriage is weak; there is little affection between them. Annette wants to leave, but she is financially dependent on her husband and afraid of his wrath. She is isolated and feels helpless.

Growing up, Amanda thought that her family's dynamics were normal. Her friends suffered worse physical and verbal abuse from their parents, she thought. Compared to them, she was much better off. Her father carefully planned for her to follow his footsteps into engineering and arranged for scholarships for her and a job with his firm when she would graduate. But Amanda ran the other way — toward a college known for conservative evangelicalism. Her father, though disappointed and dismayed, paid for her whole college education nonetheless. His disappointment with his marriage and with Amanda's turn from him has left him beaten. He loves his daughter and struggles to let her have her own life. She feels sexual urges from him toward her from time to time; and though he has restrained himself, these frighten her and drive her further from him.

This family suffers from sour love, because self-love is absent and self-hatred has free reign. Like many victims, Amanda has begun to harm other people as she was harmed. Fortunately, a friend has confronted her. Being a victim does not entitle one to become a perpetrator, a situation in which self-hatred becomes an art. In flying to Christ, Amanda found a wounded God who understood and embraced her woundedness. With Jesus, she was not trapped alone in her fear; she did not have to dissociate from her pain, nor suffer silently, alone and abandoned.

Jesus provides compassionate companionship and, beyond that, carries broken ones from the cross to Easter. The three-day journey is arduous, for even when we see that we are the image of God, the craving to be restored is obscured. Being befriended by the dying Jesus may be *necessary*, but it is not *sufficient* to repair the broken image to enable strong self-love. One must not only be accepted as broken but also be embedded in the wisdom that offers hope by seeing those who are being healed empowered by the Holy Spirit of Christ. One must be able to take a rightful place in the community of love and health fed by the body and blood of Christ, where one takes pleasure in God and grows in self-love that is obedience to God.

By taking refuge in the body and blood of Christ's wounds, we can see our own wounds scar over and our love straighten. One may need to rest there a long time before venturing out into the world. To escape from becoming a perpetrator is to distinguish self-hatred from self-love; unlearning and relearning that love is the wisdom of God disclosed in the drama of God in Christ as he mortifies the weakness that slays in incident after incident and vivifies the strength that builds up. Scars are the constant reminder that one has been made new. All this is of the Spirit, who embeds one into the death and resurrection of Christ — destroying destruction — and implants one in the body of the wounded that becomes a "new creation," in which "everything old has passed away; see, everything has become new" (2 Cor. 5:17). With the death of destruction, the new creature is healed in the divine image to become an accomplice to its healing in others.

Nancy, Donald, and Barbara

The third example is the story of a prison inmate. God called Nancy and her husband, Bob, to care for a floundering and abused inner-city child, Donald, when he was six years old. But Bob died only five years later, and despite their extensive care, including taking him into their own home, Donald fell apart. He ended up murdering Nancy when he was sixteen in the course of taking money from her that he thought belonged to him. He is now serving a life sentence in a state prison for first-degree aggravated felony murder, eligible for parole after thirty-five years.

After the murder, Barbara, who had known Donald since he was eleven, read Matthew 25:36: "I was naked and you gave me clothing, I was sick and you took care of me, I was in prison and you visited me," and she felt the call to complete Nancy's unfinished work of rescuing one child. The work has been, by turns, discouraging and rewarding over the past twenty years. Remarkably, during his years of incarceration — given administrative corruption and the negative influences of prison life — Donald has been inching toward the repair of the shattered image of God that he is. He is slowly separating himself from the destructive yet emotionally satisfying patterns of lethal behavior that both his original and current circumstances keep before him. It is terribly trying for him; yet, though society has let him go, God has not.

Finding an identity apart from the epithet "murderer" has not been easy. At times Donald has rejected God, but to no avail. He is created in the divine image that God has been slowly healing as he has experienced love and has been able to give it to others. Barbara's standing by him all the time testifies to this painfully incremental process. She is an instrument of divine providence in Aquinas's sense. This stabilizes and centers them both, testifying that Nancy and Bob's ministry may not have been in vain.

Donald is being healed by experiencing trust and love simply in the tenacity of someone from the outside being a stable presence in his life. He is now Barbara's son, and she is his mother. He struggles with being dependent on her. Like all children, he wants to be an adult, but prison

273

is a deeply infantilizing experience. The two-decade period that he has had to reflect on his youthful mistakes and crimes has enabled him to see that he lacked the tools and experience to make discerning judgments and control raw emotion and behavior. He has grown cautious in relying on his own judgment, to the point of seeking Barbara's guidance on matters that he must answer for himself. Sending him back to himself with God sometimes feels like rejection to him, but so it must be. His emotional neediness is reinforced by his financial dependence on his "mother." When he is able to find a prison job, he earns $2 a day, and a can of tuna fish at the prison store costs $1.50.

Barbara's support has been costly. It took years to gain Donald's trust. He told her half-truths (partly because he could not speak freely on the phone), wangled money to pay illegal prison debts, was cited for various infractions of prison rules, got into fights with inmates and officers, and repeatedly failed to act on his own behalf. Yet, over time, the joy and pleasure from the relationship have outweighed the frustration, for it has honed Barbara's ability to love more effectively.

There have been flashes of momentary elation when Donald and Barbara together celebrate his moral growth. Barbara's happiness comes from seeing love heal, and she is healed of other attempts at love that soured. Finally, the divine image is being healed in both Donald and Barbara through their relationship. They have learned just how tender love is and how costly distorted love is. They have learned that Christ's wounds are his power to heal others. Donald began serving his prison sentence not realizing how broken he was or the extent to which he had damaged creation. Time and the suffering of prison life had to break him yet further, into undeceived self-knowledge, so that the shards of the broken image in him might come together one piece at a time, like the dry bones in Ezekiel's valley, to resurrect him, straighten his crippled spirit, and give sight to his blind, violent anger. Barbara, too, had to be brought to healing, had to work past her exalted "messiah complex." She had to learn that healing was not from her "do-gooding" but from the strength of the relationship itself. That is, it was not until the differential power dynamics lost their power and love was purged of self-congratulation that she became the midwife of Christ's healing power to destroy savagery and bring life from death.

Being Happy

The vision of happiness proposed here is theologically qualified. Under normal circumstances, delighting in felicitous experiences and advancing creation's well-being is multidimensional. Such moments are pleasurable in themselves and joyful in the longer term both because they both enhance God's happiness in creation's flourishing under human stewardship and because they enhance our happiness at being agents of that flourishing. Happiness is celebrating our own spiritual growth and well-being and God's enjoyment of these. God enjoys our happiness and we enjoy God's happiness.[8]

Happiness in this particular sense of living in the beauty of holiness is fed by successful self-love in Butler's sense. Just as human life would cease if sex were not pleasurable, living in the beauty of holiness would be undermined if it were not pleasurable. Christians must delight in the pleasure of holiness lest they become less able to thrive in it, causing creation to suffer. Covenantal faithfulness requires tending to one's own needs, that God may enjoy his beloved creation the more. Self-love, as Butler says, is incumbent on us — that God may be happy in our happiness.

Not living within normal circumstances — such as in war, random violence, and the deprivation of normal agency — will, of course, interrupt the ability to live beautifully. Circumstances that cause people to become mean and vicious for a time in order to preserve their own lives and safety are proper self-love as part of the give and take of finding equilibrium in the changes and chances of life. However, when such deprivation is prolonged to such an extent that one loses an identity outside the abuse, and one's agency is permanently — not just temporarily — damaged, the possibility of happiness in the sense discussed here may be severely limited.

In normal circumstances, growth in the art of happiness requires stewarding one's talents and strengths adeptly, growing into what Butler would call a "cool" or "settled" citizenship in the reign of God. The skills of loving well bring increasing control over one's life, as well

---

8. Discussion of God's happiness is almost nonexistent. A singular exception is Terence E. Fretheim's "The Pursuit of Happiness: God and Creation," which he prepared for the Bible and the Pursuit of Happiness project, Center for the Study of Law and Religion, Emory University, Atlanta, GA, Dec. 11-13, 2009.

as unashamed use of one's talent and treasure in God's service. Eternal life demands no choice between material well-being and godliness. Moderate material thriving abets eternal life, for it frees the mind to attend to the quality of one's loving more artfully.[9] Struggling for daily survival can hinder the ability to enjoy God through reverent faithfulness.

The word from asherism is that healing creation by having one's love strengthened and healed is enhancing, not depleting, as long as rest and adequate self-care are strong. Caring for children and family, co-workers and strangers, and "this fragile earth, our island home" requires donations of time, talent, and treasure (*BCP*, p. 370). As long as caregivers are properly nourished and cared for, that is not necessarily self-sacrifice but self-enrichment. Enjoying oneself in God no doubt pleases him: "For the Lord takes pleasure in his people; he adorns the humble with victory" (Ps. 149:4). Indeed, many Older Testament verses depict God as delighting in, rejoicing in, enjoying, and taking pleasure in — or shining his face upon — Israel, his people, the righteous, Jerusalem, and so on.[10]

Although actualizing ourselves in God and advancing creation for his enjoyment of its flourishing is our perfect end in this life, the tragic character of human life means that such growth can never be more than fitful. Expectations of what we hope to accomplish remain out of reach. We cannot serve God and creation as we wish. Adversities set us back like breakthrough bleeding.

However, such self-disappointment is a trap. The point is not how much we accomplish, but enjoying what God accomplishes with us. Nevertheless, those outfitted for eternal life, those being healed by Christ and sacramentally empowered by the Holy Spirit, will be buoyed by seeing the fruit of their labors flourish. Excellent love is an antacid that protects against loss so that one can rebound from defeat and cling to the flashes of eternal light of divine love that comfort, encourage, and strengthen. Enjoying God in the beauty of holiness is possible in this life, but it cannot be complete. Happiness can only be perfected when we are no longer able to fall short of loving as we would. There-

---

9. John Wesley is noted for advocating this position in his famous sermon on "The Use of Money," in which he preaches: "Gain all you can, save all you can, give all you can." Albert Outler, ed., *John Wesley* (New York: Oxford University Press, 1964), pp. 238-50.

10. Michael Chan has compiled a list of perhaps one hundred such texts in unpublished research findings.

fore, sanctification now is toward glorification, when love is perfected and none shall make us afraid.

The scope of this vision of happiness has not been containable in carefully delineated vocabulary. Diverse language and images have poured in from many biblical texts all of the theologians examined here. The terms these sources use are not synonyms for one another, nor are they analogues, although perhaps some function this way. Rather, all their ways of articulating God's purpose for and interaction with creation are entry points into the complexity and subtlety of God's labors for his garden's flourishing. Scripture offers guidance as long as the virtues, values, and patterns of behavior that it forwards are internalized in order to bloom in various parts of our garden. In this way, each garden will yield pleasure, and God will partake of that beauty and pleasure. What we have are the seeds, bulbs, saplings, shrubs, and bushes to plant, the tilled and fertilized soil to plant them in, the spade, trowel, rake, and hose to plant them with, and the know-how to water, weed, and feed them tenderly.

People become lighter as they become stronger. As great artists perform with seeming effortlessness and can enjoy the beauty of their own artistry, people become happier as they love more supplely, enskilled by divine wisdom. This joy is the pinnacle of human happiness, theologically speaking. It may not be linear or steady progress, yet it cannot be nullified, even by adversity. Knowing that God delights as we grow from strength to strength encourages those in the light to stay the course, enjoying their participation in God's enjoyment of his cherished creation. "May the glory of the Lord endure forever; may the Lord rejoice in his works" (Ps. 104:31).

Works Cited

Albee, Ernest. *A History of English Utilitarianism.* London: Macmillan, 1902.

Allen, Daniel. "Building on Positive Relationships." *Mental Health Practice* 12, no. 7 (2009): 6-7.

Althaus, Paul. *The Theology of Martin Luther.* Philadelphia: Fortress Press, 1963.

Annas, Julia. *The Morality of Happiness.* Oxford: Oxford University Press, 1993.

Aquinas, Thomas. *Commentary on the Book of Causes.* Translated by Vincent A. Guagliardo, Charles R. Hess, and Richard C. Taylor. Thomas Aquinas in Translation. Washington, DC: Catholic University of America Press, 1996.

————. *Knowing and Naming God.* Translated by Herbert McCabe, OP. Edited by Thomas Gilby. Vol. 3, *Summa Theologiae.* London: Blackfriars, 1964.

————. *Purpose and Happiness.* Translated by Thomas Gilby. Edited by Thomas Gilby. Vol. 16, *Summa Theologiae.* Cambridge: Blackfriars, 1969.

————. "Selections from Thomas' 'Commentary on the Sentences of Peter Lombard.'" In *Saint Thomas Aquinas,* edited by Hugh McDonald: http://www.hyoomik.com.

————. *Summa Contra Gentiles.* Translated by Roberto Busa, SJ. Corpus Thomisticum. Pampilonae: Fundación Tomás de Aquino, 1961.

————. *Summa Contra Gentiles.* Romae: Apud Sedem Commissionis Leoninae, 1934.

————. "Summa Contra Gentiles, Book III." In *Basic Writings of Thomas Aquinas,* edited by Anton C. Pegis, pp. 3-1224. New York: Random House, 1945.

————. *Summa Theologiae.* 60 vols. New York: Blackfriars, 1964.

————. "Supplement, qq. 1-99." In *Summa Theologica,* pp. 2573-3013. New York: Benziger Brothers, 1948.

————. *Treatise on Happiness.* Englewood Cliffs, NJ: Prentice Hall, 1964.

Aristotle. *Nicomachean Ethics.* Translated by Christopher Rowe. Edited by Sarah Broadie. New York: Oxford University Press, 2002.

Augustine. *Against the Academicians; the Teacher.* Indianapolis: Hackett, 1995.

————. *The Augustine Catechism: The Enchiridion on Faith, Hope, and Love.* Translated by Bruce Harbert. Edited by John E. Rotelle. The Augustine Series. *The Works of*

Saint Augustine: A Translation for the 21st Century. Hyde Park, NY: New City Press, 1999.

———. *The Catholic Way of Life.* Translated by Donald Arthur Gallagher and Idella J. Gallagher. Fathers of the Church. Washington, DC: Catholic University of America Press, 1966.

———. *City of God.* Translated by Henry Bettenson. Harmondsworth, UK: Penguin Books, 1984.

———. *Confessions.* Translated by Henry Chadwick. Oxford: Oxford University Press, 1991.

———. "Corpus Augustinianum Gissense," edited by Cornelius Mayer: Makrolog GmbH, 2000.

———. "The Happy Life." In *Augustine of Hippo: Selected Writings,* edited by Mary T. Clark, pp. 165-93. New York: Paulist Press, 1984.

———. "Homilies on the First Epistle of John." In *Augustine: Homilies on the Gospel of John, Homilies on the First Epistle of John, Soliloquies,* edited by Joseph H. Meyers, pp. 459-529. Peabody, MA: Hendrickson, 1994.

———. *Letters: 100-155.* Translated by S. J. Roland Teske. The Works of Saint Augustine: A Translation for the 21st Century. Hyde Park, NY: New City Press, 2003.

———. *Letters 156-210.* Edited by Boniface Ramsey. Vol. II.3, *Works of Saint Augustine.* Hyde Park, NY: New City Press, 2004.

———. "Letter 147: On Seeing God." In *Letters 100-55,* edited by Boniface Ramsey, pp. 317-49. Hyde Park, NY: New City Press, Augustinian Heritage Institute, 2003.

———. *On Christian Teaching.* World's Classics. Oxford: Oxford University Press, 1997.

———. "On Free Will." In *Augustine: The Earlier Writings,* pp. 102-217. Philadelphia: Westminster Press, 1958.

———. *The Retractations,* Vol. 60 of The Fathers of the Church. Washington, DC: Catholic University of America Press, 1968.

———. "Sermon 23." In *Sermons II (20-50) on the Old Testament,* edited by John E. Rotelle, OSA, pp. 51-56. Brooklyn, NY: New City Press, 1990.

———. "Sermon 368: Whoever Loves His Soul Will Lose It." In *Sermons 341-400,* edited by John E. Rotelle, pp. 229-303. Hyde Park, NY: New City Press, 1995.

———. "Soliloquies." In *Augustine: The Earlier Writings,* 23-63. Philadelphia: Westminster Press, 1958.

———. *Teaching Christianity.* Translated by Edmund Hill, OP. Edited by John E. Rotelle. Pt. 1, vol. 11, The Works of St. Augustine. Hyde Park, NY: New City Press, 1996.

———. *The Trinity.* Translated by Edmund Hill. The Works of Saint Augustine: A Translation for the 21st Century. Brooklyn, NY: New City Press, 1991.

Balthasar, Hans Urs von. *Mysterium Paschale: The Mystery of Easter.* Edinburgh: T. & T. Clark, 1990.

Bennema, Cornelius. *Saving Power of Wisdom: An Investigation of Spirit and Wisdom in*

Relation to the Soteriology of the Fourth Gospel. Edited by Joerg Frey et al. Tübingen: Mohr Siebeck, 2002.

Boethius. *Consolation of Philosophy.* Translated by P. G. Walsh. Oxford: Clarendon Press, 1999.

————. *The Theological Tractates and the Consolation of Philosophy.* Translated by E. K. Rand, H. F. Stewart, and S. J. Tester. Cambridge, MA: Harvard University Press, 1973.

Botha, P. J. "The Social Setting and Strategy of Psalm 34." *Old Testament Essays* 10 (1997): 178(96).

Boyle, Leonard, OP. "The Setting of the *Summa Theologiae* of St. Thomas — Revisited." In *Ethics of Aquinas,* edited by Stephen J. Pope, pp. 1-16. Washington, DC: Georgetown University Press, 2002.

Bradley, Denis J. M. *Aquinas on the Twofold Human Good: Reason and Human Happiness in Aquinas's Moral Science.* Washington, DC: Catholic University of America Press, 1997.

Braulik, Georg. "Weitere Beobachtungen zur Beziehung zwischen dem Heiligkeitsgesetz und Deuteronomium 19–25." In *Das Deuteronomium,* pp. 23-55. Helsinki: Finnische Exegetische Gesellschaft, 1996.

Brown, Oscar James Patrick. "St. Thomas, the Philosophers and Felicity." *Laval Théologique et Philosophique* 37 (1981): 69-82.

Brown, Raymond Edward. *The Gospel According to John.* Garden City, NY: Doubleday, 1966.

Brown, Raymond Edward, and Francis J. Moloney. *An Introduction to the Gospel of John.* Anchor Bible Reference Library. New York: Doubleday, 2003.

Brown, William P. "'Come, O Children . . . I Will Teach You the Fear of the Lord' (Psalm 34:12): Comparing Psalms and Proverbs." In *Seeking Out the Wisdom of the Ancients,* pp. 85-102. Winona Lake, IN: Eisenbrauns, 2005.

————. *Seeing the Psalms: A Theology of Metaphor.* Louisville: Westminster/John Knox Press, 2002.

————. "To Discipline without Destruction: The Multifaceted Profile of the Child in Proverbs." In *The Child in the Bible,* edited by Marcia J. Bunge, pp. 63-81. Grand Rapids: Eerdmans, 2008.

Bultmann, Rudolf. *Theology of the New Testament.* 2 vols. New York: Charles Scribner's Sons, 1955.

Butler, Dom Cuthbert. *Benedictine Monachism: Studies in Benedictine Life and Rule.* New York: Barnes and Noble, 1961.

Butler, Joseph. *Fifteen Sermons Preached at the Rolls Chapel and a Dissertation upon the Nature of Virtue.* London: Bell, 1949.

Calvin, John. *Institutes of the Christian Religion.* Translated by Ford Lewis Battles. Edited by John T. McNeill. 2 vols. Philadelphia: Westminster Press, 1960.

Chadwick, Henry. *Boethius: The Consolations of Music, Logic, Theology, and Philosophy.* Oxford: Clarendon Press, 1981.

Charry, Ellen T. *By the Renewing of Your Minds: The Pastoral Function of Christian Doctrine.* New York: Oxford University Press, 1997.

Chrysostom, John. "Letter to a Young Widow." In *Chrysostom,* edited by Philip Schaff, pp. 121-28. Peabody, MA: Hendrickson, 1994.

———. "Letters to Theodore after His Fall." In *Chrysostom,* edited by Philip Schaff, pp. 91-116. Peabody, MA: Hendrickson, 1994.

———. "Treatise to Prove That No One Can Harm the Man Who Does Not Injure Himself." In *Nicene and Post-Nicene Fathers of the Christian Church,* edited by Philip Schaff, pp. 269-84. Edinburgh: T. & T. Clark, 1889.

Cicero, Marcus Tullius. *The Nature of the Gods.* Translated by P. G. Walsh. Oxford: Clarendon Press, 1997.

———. *On Moral Ends.* Translated by Raphael Woolf. Edited by Julia Annas. Cambridge: Cambridge University Press, 2001.

———. *Tusculan Disputations.* Translated by J. E. King. Cambridge, MA: Harvard University Press, 1950.

———. *Tusculan Disputations II and V: With a Summary of III and IV.* Edited by A. E. Douglas. Classical Texts. Warminster: Aris & Phillips, 1990.

Clements, R. E. *Wisdom in Theology.* Grand Rapids: Eerdmans, 1992.

Cole, Graham. "Theological Utilitarianism and the Eclipse of the Theistic Sanction." *Tyndale Bulletin* 42, no. 2 (1991): 26-44.

Colish, Marcia L. *Peter Lombard.* 2 vols. Medieval Theologians. Oxford: Blackwell Publishers, 2001.

———. *Stoicism in Christian Latin Thought through the Sixth Century.* Vol. 2, *The Stoic Tradition from Antiquity to the Early Middle Ages.* New York: E. J. Brill, 1990.

Conybeare, Catherine. *The Irrational Augustine.* Oxford Early Christian Studies. Oxford: Oxford University Press, 2006.

Cooper, John M. "Greek Philosophers on Euthanasia and Suicide." In *Reason and Emotion: Essays on Ancient Moral Psychology and Ethical Theory,* edited by John M. Cooper, pp. 515-41. Princeton: Princeton University Press, 1999.

Crabbe, Anna. "Literary Design in the *De Consolatione Philosophiae.*" In *Boethius,* edited by Margaret Gibson, pp. 237-74. Oxford: Basil Blackwell, 1981.

Culverwell, Nathaniel. "Light of Reason Is Calm and Peaceable." In *Cambridge Platonist Spirituality,* edited by Charles Taliaferro and Alison J. Teply, pp. 137-49. New York: Paulist Press, 2004.

Dalrymple, Theodore. "Discovering La Rochefoucauld." *New Criterion* 19, no. 8 (2001): 28(4).

Daly-Denton, Margaret. *David in the Fourth Gospel: The Johannine Reception of the Psalms.* Arbeiten zur Geschichte des Antiken Judentums und des Urchristentums. Vol. 47. Leiden: Brill, 2000.

Davis, Ellen F. *Imagination Shaped: Old Testament Preaching in the Anglican Tradition.* Valley Forge, PA: Trinity Press International, 1995.

———. *Proverbs, Ecclesiastes, and the Song of Songs.* Westminster Bible Companion. Louisville, KY: Westminster/John Knox, 2000.

———. "Wise Ignorance." In *Getting Involved with God: Rediscovering the Old Testament,* edited by Ellen F. Davis, pp. 91-103. Boston: Cowley, 2001.

Dougherty, M. V. "The Problem of 'Humana Natura' in the *Consolatio Philosophiae* of

Boethius." *American Catholic Philosophical Quarterly: Journal of the American Catholic Philosophical Association* 78, no. 2 (2004): 273-92.

Downey, James. *The Eighteenth Century Pulpit. A Study of the Sermons of Butler, Berkeley, Secker, Sterne, Whitefield and Wesley.* Oxford: Clarendon Press, 1969.

Eardley, P. S. "Conceptions of Happiness and Human Destiny in the Late Thirteenth Century." *Vivarium* 44, no. 2/3 (2006): 276-304.

Elders, Leo. *The Ethics of St. Thomas Aquinas: Happiness, Natural Law and the Virtues.* New York: Peter Lang, 2005.

Episcopal Church. *Book of Common Prayer.* New York: Seabury Press, 1979.

Epstein, Joseph. "La Rochefoucauld: Maximum Maximist." *New Criterion* 14, no. 10 (1996): 14-23.

Fedler, Kyle. "Calvin's Burning Heart: Calvin and the Stoics on the Emotions." *Journal of the Society of Christian Ethics* 22 (2002): 133-62.

Fidora, Alexander, and Jordi Pardo. "Liber de Causis." *Revista Española de Filosofía Medieval* 8 (2001): 133-52.

Finnis, John. *Aquinas: Moral, Political, and Legal Theory.* Founders of Modern Political and Social Thought. Oxford: Oxford University Press, 1998.

Fortin, John R. "The Nature of Consolation in 'The Consolation of Philosophy.'" *American Catholic Philosophical Quarterly: Journal of the American Catholic Philosophical Association* 78, no. 2 (2004): 293-307.

García Martínez, Florentino. *The Dead Sea Scrolls Translated: The Qumran Texts in English.* 2nd ed. Leiden: Brill, 1996.

Gatti, Maria Luisa. "Plotinus: The Platonic Tradition and the Foundation of Neoplatonism." In *The Cambridge Companion to Plotinus,* edited by Lloyd P. Gerson, pp. 10-37. Cambridge: Cambridge University Press, 1999.

Gert, Bernard. "Hobbes's Psychology." In *The Cambridge Companion to Hobbes,* edited by Tom Sorell, pp. 157-74. Cambridge: Cambridge University Press, 1996.

Gilson, Etienne. *The Christian Philosophy of Saint Augustine.* The Random House Lifetime Library. New York: Random House, 1960.

Grant, Jamie. "Wisdom and Covenant: Revisiting Zimmerli." *European Journal of Theology* 12, no. 2 (2003): 103-11.

Grislis, Egil. "Seneca and Cicero as Possible Sources of John Calvin's View of Double Predestination: An Inquiry in the History of Ideas." In *In Honor of John Calvin, 1509-64,* pp. 28-63. Montreal: McGill University Press, 1987.

Hadot, Pierre. *Philosophy as a Way of Life.* Translated by Michael Case. Oxford: Blackwell Publishers, 1995.

———. *Plotinus, or, the Simplicity of Vision.* Chicago: University of Chicago Press, 1993.

Hamain, L. "'Beatitudo Imperfecta' et Théologie des Réalités Terrestres." *Ephemerides Theologicae Lovanienses* 36 (1960): 685-93.

Hare, Robert D. "Psychopaths: New Trends in Research." *Harvard Mental Health Letter* 12, no. 3 (1995): 4.

Harrison, Carol. *Augustine: Christian Truth and Fractured Humanity,* Christian Theology in Context. Oxford: Oxford University Press, 2000.

Henry, Paul. "The Place of Plotinus in the History of Thought." In *Plotinus: The Enneads,* pp. xxxv-lxx. London: Faber & Faber, 1962.

Hobbes, Thomas. *Leviathan.* Edited by Richard Tuck. Cambridge Texts in the History of Political Thought. Cambridge: Cambridge University Press, 1996.

Houser, Rollen E. "The *De Virtutibus Cardinalibus* and Aquinas' Doctrine of Happiness." In *Atti del IX Congresso Tomistico Internazionale,* 3:250-59: Vatican City: Libreria Editrice Vaticana, 1991.

Hume, David. *Dialogues Concerning Natural Religion.* Indianapolis: Bobbs Merrill, 1970.

Hundert, E. J. *The Enlightenment's Fable: Bernard Mandeville and the Discovery of Society.* Ideas in Context. Cambridge: Cambridge University Press, 1994.

Hutcheson, Francis. *An Essay on the Nature and Conduct of the Passions and Affections: With Illustrations on the Moral Sense.* Edited by Aaron Garrett. Indianapolis, IN: Liberty Fund, 2002.

———. *An Inquiry into the Origin of Our Ideas of Beauty and Virtue: In Two Treatises.* Edited by Wolfgang Leidhold. Indianapolis, IN: Liberty Fund, 2004.

Irwin, Terence H. "Augustine's Criticisms of the Stoic Theory of Passions." *Faith and Philosophy* 20, no. 4 (2003): 430-47.

———. "Socratic Paradox and Stoic Theory." In *Companions to Ancient Thought.* Vol. 4: *Ethics,* edited by Stephen Everson, pp. 151-92. New York: Cambridge University Press, 1998.

Jack, Malcolm. *The Social and Political Thought of Bernard Mandeville.* Political Theory and Political Philosophy. New York: Garland Publishers, 1987.

Janzen, Waldemar. "'Ashrê in the Old Testament." *Harvard Theological Review* 58, no. 2 (1965): 215.

Jones, John D. "Natural Happiness: Perfect Because Self-Sufficient?" *Gregorianum* 83, no. 3 (2002): 529-44.

Julian of Norwich. *Showings.* Translated by Edmund Colledge and James Walsh. The Classics of Western Spirituality. New York: Paulist Press, 1978.

Kerr, Fergus. "Thomas Aquinas." In *Medieval Theologians,* pp. 201-20. Oxford: Blackwell Publishers, 2001.

Kirby, W. J. Torrance. "Stoic and Epicurean? Calvin's Dialectical Account of Providence in the Institutes." *International Journal of Systematic Theology* 5, no. 3 (2003): 309-22.

Kirk, Kenneth E. *The Vision of God: The Christian Doctrine of the Summum Bonum.* 2nd ed. Bampton Lectures. London: Longmans, 1932.

Kuntz, J. Kenneth. "The Canonical Wisdom Psalms of Ancient Israel: Their Rhetorical, Thematic and Formal Dimensions." In *Rhetorical Criticism,* pp. 186-222. Pittsburgh, PA: Pickwick Press, 1974.

La Rochefoucauld, François. *Maxims.* Translated by Stuart D. Warner and Stéphane Douard. South Bend, IN: St. Augustine's Press, 2001.

Lactantius. *Divine Institutes.* Translated by Anthony Bowen and Peter Garnsey. Liverpool: Liverpool University Press, 2003.

————. "A Treatise on the Anger of God." In *Fathers of the Third and Fourth Centuries*, edited by A. Cleveland Coxe, pp. 259-80. Peabody, MA: Hendrickson, 1994.

Lang, Bernhard. "Twelve Commandments — Three Stages : A New Theory on the Formation of the Decalogue." In *Reading from Right to Left*, edited by Cheryl J. Exum and H. G. M. Williamson, pp. 290-300. London: Sheffield Academic Press, 2003.

Lee, Dorothy. "'The Darkness Did Not Overcome It': Theodicy and Eschatology in the Gospel of John." In *Theodicy and Eschatology*, edited by Bruce Barber and David Neville, pp. 43-65. Adelaide: ATF Press, 2005.

Leithart, Peter J. "Stoic Elements in Calvin's Doctrine of the Christian Life." *Westminster Theological Journal* 56, no. 1 (1994): 59-85.

Lerer, Seth. *Boethius and Dialogue: Literary Method in the Consolation of Philosophy*. Princeton: Princeton University Press, 1985.

Long, A. A., and D. N. Sedley. *The Hellenistic Philosophers*. Cambridge: Cambridge University Press, 1987.

Loring, Patricia. "Spiritual Discernment: The Context and Goal of Clearness Committees." In *Pendle Hill Pamphlet*. Wallingford, PA: Pendle Hill Publications, 1992.

Lovejoy, Arthur O. *The Great Chain of Being: A Study of the History of an Idea*. Cambridge, MA: Harvard University Press, 1936.

Mandeville, Bernard. *The Fable of the Bees or Private Vices, Publick Benefits*. Edited by F. B. Kaye. 2 vols. Indianapolis: Liberty Classics, 1988.

Marenbon, John. *Boethius*. Great Medieval Thinkers. Oxford: Oxford University Press, 2003.

Marrow, Stanley B. "Johannine Ecclesiology." *Chicago Studies* 37, no. 1 (1998): 27-36.

Martyn, J. Louis. *History and Theology in the Fourth Gospel*. 2nd ed. Nashville: Abingdon, 1979.

Mays, James Luther. "The Place of the Torah-Psalms in the Psalter." *Journal of Biblical Literature* 106, no. 1 (1987): 3-12.

McMahon, Darrin M. *Happiness: A History*. New York: Atlantic Monthly Press, 2006.

Mercken, Paul. "Transformations of the Ethics of Aristotle in the Moral Philosophy of Thomas Aquinas." In *Agire Morale*, pp. 151-62. Naples: Edizioni Domenicane Italiane, 1977.

Meyer, Paul W. "'The Father': The Presentation of God in the Fourth Gospel." In *Exploring the Gospel of John*, edited by R. Alan Culpepper and C. Clifton Black, pp. 255-73. Louisville: Westminster/John Knox, 1996.

Milgrom, Jacob. *Leviticus 17–22: A New Translation with Introduction and Commentary*. New York: Doubleday, 2000.

Miller, Patrick D. "Deuteronomy and Psalms: Evoking a Biblical Conversation." *Journal of Biblical Studies* 118, no. 1 (1999): 3-18.

————. *Interpreting the Psalms*. Philadelphia, PA: Fortress Press, 1986.

————. "The Sufficiency and Insufficiency of the Commandments." In *The Way of the Lord: Essays in Old Testament Theology*, pp. 17-36. Grand Rapids: Eerdmans, 2007.

Monck, W. H. S. "Butler's Ethical System." *Mind* 3, no. 11 (1878): 358-69.

Moore, Will Grayburn. *La Rochefoucauld: His Mind and Art.* Oxford: Clarendon Press, 1969.

Moran, William L. "Ancient Near Eastern Background of the Love of God in Deuteronomy." *Catholic Biblical Quarterly* 25 (1963): 77-87.

Morgenstern, Julian. "The Decalogue of the Holiness Code." *Hebrew Union College Annual* 26 (1955): 1-27.

Morris, Leon. "The Atonement in John's Gospel." *Criswell Theological Review* 3, no. 1 (1988): 49-64.

————. *The Gospel According to John.* Rev. ed. New International Commentary on the New Testament. Grand Rapids: Eerdmans, 1995.

Muffs, Yochanan. *Love and Joy: Law, Language, and Religion in Ancient Israel.* New York and Cambridge, MA: Jewish Theological Seminary of America (distributed by Harvard University Press), 1992.

O'Daly, Gerard J. P. *The Poetry of Boethius.* Chapel Hill, NC: University of North Carolina Press, 1991.

O'Donovan, Oliver. *The Problem of Self-Love in St. Augustine.* New Haven: Yale University Press, 1980.

————. "Usus and Fruitio in Augustine, De Doctrina Christiana I." *Journal of Theological Studies,* 33 (1982): 361-97.

Oakes, Edward T. "Pascal: The First Modern Christian." In *The Second One Thousand Years,* edited by Richard John Neuhaus, pp. 76-91. Grand Rapids: Eerdmans, 2001.

Oberman, Heiko A. "The Pursuit of Happiness: Calvin between Humanism and Reformation." In *Humanity and Divinity in Renaissance and Reformation,* pp. 251-83. Leiden: Brill, 1993.

Olmsted, Wendy Raudenbush. "Philosophical Inquiry and Religious Transformation in Boethius's the Consolation of Philosophy and Augustine's Confessions." *Journal of Religion* 69, no. 1 (1989): 14-35.

Otto, Eckart. "Das Heiligkeitsgesetz Leviticus 17-26 in der Pentateuchredaktion." In *Reventlow Festschrift,* pp. 65-80. Frankfurt am Main: Peter Lang, 1994.

Outler, Albert, ed. *John Wesley.* New York: Oxford University Press, 1964.

Parker, T. H. L. *Calvin's Preaching.* Louisville: Westminster/John Knox, 1992.

Pascal, Blaise. *Pensées.* Translated by William Finlayson Trotter. London: Dent, 1954.

————. *Pensées: The Provincial Letters.* Translated by William Finlayson Trotter and Thomas McCrie. The Modern Library. New York: Random House, 1941.

Pegis, Anton C. *Introduction to Saint Thomas Aquinas.* New York: Random House, 1948.

Perdue, Leo G. *Wisdom and Cult: A Critical Analysis of the Views of Cult in the Wisdom Literatures of Israel and the Ancient Near East.* Missoula, MT: Scholars Press (for the Society of Biblical Literature), 1977.

Pinckaers, Servais. "La Voie Spirituelle du Bonheur selon Saint Thomas." In *Ordo Sapientiae et Amoris,* pp. 267-84. Fribourg, Switzerland: Universitätsverlag Freiburg Schweiz, 1993.

Plato. "Meno." In *The Dialogues of Plato*, pp. 193-229. New York: Bantam Books, 1986.

Plotinus. *The Enneads*. Translated by A. H. Armstrong. Edited by Paul Henry and Hans-Rudolf Schwyzer. Loeb Classical Library. Cambridge, MA: Harvard University Press, 1966.

Polanyi, Michael. *Personal Knowledge: Towards a Post-Critical Philosophy*. New York: Harper and Row, 1958.

Porter, Jean. "Right Reason and the Love of God: The Parameters of Aquinas' Moral Theology." In *The Theology of Thomas Aquinas*, pp. 167-91. Notre Dame, IN: University of Notre Dame Press, 2005.

Post, Stephen Garrard. *Christian Love and Self-Denial: An Historical and Normative Study of Jonathan Edwards, Samuel Hopkins, and American Theological Ethics*. Lanham, MD: University Press of America, 1987.

Raitt, Jill. "St. Thomas Aquinas on Free Will and Predestination." *Duke Divinity School Review* 43 (1978): 188-95.

Reardon, Patrick Henry. "Calvin on Providence: The Development of an Insight." *Scottish Journal of Theology* 28, no. 6 (1975): 517-33.

Reiss, Edmund. *Boethius*. Twayne's World Authors Series. Boston: Twayne Publishers, 1982.

Relihan, Joel C. *Ancient Menippean Satire*. Baltimore: Johns Hopkins University Press, 1993.

Relihan, Joel C., and William Earnshaw Heise. *The Prisoner's Philosophy: Life and Death in Boethius's Consolation*. Notre Dame, IN: University of Notre Dame Press, 2007.

Rensberger, David K. *Johannine Faith and Liberating Community*. Philadelphia: Westminster Press, 1988.

Roizen, Ron. "God and the English Utilitarians." http://www.roizen.com/ron/bentham.htm.

Sandoval, Timothy J. *The Discourse of Wealth and Poverty in the Book of Proverbs*. Leiden: Brill, 2006.

Sarna, Nahum M. *On the Book of Psalms: Exploring the Prayers of Ancient Israel*. 1st paperback ed. New York: Schocken Books, 1993.

Schneewind, J. B. *The Invention of Autonomy*. Cambridge: Cambridge University Press, 1998.

Scott, R. B. Y. *Proverbs. Ecclesiastes*. Vol. 18, Anchor Bible Commentary. Garden City, NY: Doubleday, 1965.

Segovia, Fernando F. *The Farewell of the Word: The Johannine Call to Abide*. Minneapolis: Fortress Press, 1991.

Seneca, Lucius Annaeus. "De Consolatione ad Helviam Matrem." In *Seneca: Moral Essays II*, edited by John William Basore, pp. 416-89. London: William Heinemann, 1932.

———. "De Consolatione ad Marciam." In *Seneca: Moral Essays II*, edited by John William Basore, pp. 2-97. London: William Heinemann, 1932.

———. "De Consolatione ad Polybium." In *Seneca: Moral Essays II*, edited by John William Basore, pp. 356-415. London: William Heinemann, 1932.

————. "On the Happy Life." In *Moral Essays,* edited by T. E. Page, pp. 98-179. Cambridge, MA: Harvard University Press, 1958.

Shaftesbury, Anthony Ashley Cooper, Earl of. *Characteristics of Men, Manners, Opinions, Times.* Edited by Lawrence E. Klein. Cambridge Texts in the History of Philosophy. Cambridge: Cambridge University Press, 1999.

Sherwood, Stephen K. "Psalm 112: A Royal Wisdom Psalm?" *Catholic Biblical Quarterly* 51, no. 1 (1989): 50-64.

Staley, Kevin M. "Happiness: The Natural End of Man?" *Thomist* 53 (1989): 215-34.

Stump, Eleonore. "Augustine on Free Will." In *The Cambridge Companion to Augustine,* edited by Eleonore Stump and Norman Kretzmann, pp. 124-47. Cambridge: Cambridge University Press, 2001.

Teresa of Avila. *The Autobiography of Teresa of Jesus,* edited and translated by E. Allison Peers. Garden City, NY: Image Books, 1960.

Theron, Stephen. "Happiness and Transcendent Happiness." *Religious Studies* 21 (1985): 349-67.

Thomas, Marlin E. "Psalms 1 and 112 as a Paradigm for the Comparison of Wisdom Motifs in the Psalms." *Journal of the Evangelical Theological Society* 29, no. 1 (1986): 15-24.

Thompson, Marianne Meye. "'They Bear Witness to Me': The Psalms in the Passion Narrative of the Gospel of John." In *The Word Leaps the Gap: Essays on Scripture and Theology in Honor of Richard B. Hays,* edited by J. Ross Wagner et al., pp. 267-83. Grand Rapids: Eerdmans, 2008.

Van Leeuwen, Raymond C. *Book of Proverbs: Introduction, Commentary, and Reflections.* Vol. 5, New Interpreter's Bible Commentary. Nashville: Abingdon, 1997.

Walker, D. P. *The Decline of Hell; Seventeenth-Century Discussions of Eternal Torment.* London: Routledge & Kegan Paul, 1964.

Walsh, P. G. "Introduction." In *Boethius: The Consolation of Philosophy,* edited by P. G. Walsh, pp. xi-l. Oxford: Clarendon Press, 1999.

Waltke, Bruce K. *The Book of Proverbs.* New International Commentary on the Old Testament. Grand Rapids: Eerdmans, 2004.

Washington, Harold C. *Wealth and Poverty in the Instruction of Amenemope and the Hebrew Proverbs.* Atlanta: Scholars Press, 1994.

Wéber, Edouard-Henri. "Le Bonheur dès Présent, Fondement de L'Éthique selon Thomas d'Aquin." *Revue des sciences philosophiques et théologiques* 78 (1994): 389-413.

Weinfeld, Moshe. "Origin of the Humanism in Deuteronomy." *Journal of Biblical Literature* 80, no. 3 (1961): 241-47.

Westermann, Claus. *Roots of Wisdom: The Oldest Proverbs of Israel and Other Peoples.* Louisville: Westminster/John Knox, 1995.

White, Nicholas. *A Brief History of Happiness.* Oxford: Blackwell Publishing, 2006.

Whybray, R. N. *Wealth and Poverty in the Book of Proverbs.* Sheffield, UK: JSOT Press, 1990.

Wieland, Georg. "Happiness: The Perfection of Man." In *The Cambridge History of*

Later Medieval Philosophy, edited by Norman Kretzmann et al., pp. 673-86. Cambridge: Cambridge University Press, 1982.

Williams, A. N. "Mystical Theology Redux: The Pattern of Aquinas' Summa Theologia." *Modern Theology* 13 (1997): 53-74.

Wippel, John F. "Thomas Aquinas and Participation." In *Studies in Medieval Philosophy,* edited by John F. Wippel, pp. 117-58. Washington, DC: Catholic University of America Press, 1987.

Wright, Christopher J. H. "The Israelite Household and the Decalogue: The Social Background and Significance of Some Commandments." *Tyndale Bulletin* 30 (1979): 101-24.

Index

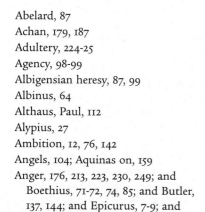